NF

UNINTENDED EFFECTS OF GOVERNMENT POLICIES

ECONOMISTS OF THE TWENTIETH CENTURY

General Editors: Mark Perlman, *University Professor of Economics, University of Pittsburgh* and Mark Blaug, *Professor Emeritus, University of London, Professor Emeritus, University of Buckingham and Visiting Professor, University of Exeter*

This innovative series comprises specially invited collections of articles and papers by economists whose work has made an important contribution to economics in the late twentieth century.

The proliferation of new journals and the ever-increasing number of new articles make it difficult for even the most assiduous economist to keep track of all the important recent advances. By focusing on those economists whose work is generally recognized to be at the forefront of the discipline, the series will be an essential reference point for the different specialisms included.

A list of published and future titles in this series is printed at the end of this volume.

Unintended Effects of Government Policies

Theory and Measurement for Economic Policy
Volume III

Herbert G. Grubel

Professor of Economics
Simon Fraser University
British Columbia

Edward Elgar

Published by
Edward Elgar Publishing Limited
Gower House
Croft Road
Aldershot
Hants GU11 3HR
England

Edward Elgar Publishing Company
Old Post Road
Brookfield
Vermont 05036
USA

338.973
G88t
v. 3

British Library Cataloguing in Publication Data
Grubel, Herbert G.
  Theory and Measurement for Economic
  Policy. – Vol. 3: Unintended Effects of
  Government Policies. – (Economists of the
  Twentieth Century Series)
  I. Title II. Series
  337

ab

Printed in Great Britain at the University Press, Cambridge

ISBN 1 85278 905 0 (Volume I)
     1 85278 906 9 (Volume II)
     1 85278 907 7 (Volume III)
     1 85278 787 2 (3 volume set)

Contents

Acknowledgements   vii

Introduction   ix

1 'Risk, Uncertainty and Moral Hazard', *Journal of Risk and Insurance*, **XXXVIII**(1) (March 1971), 99–106.   1

2 'Real and Insurance-Induced Unemployment in Canada' with Dennis Maki and Shelley Sax, *Canadian Journal of Economics*, **VIII**(2) (May 1975), 174–91.   9

3 'The Effects of Unemployment Benefits on U.S. Unemployment Rates' with Dennis R. Maki, *Weltwirtschaftliches Archiv*, **CXII**(2) (1976), 274–97.   27

4 'A Note on the Effects of Unemployment Insurance, Minimum Wage Legislation and Trade Union Growth on Reported Unemployment Rates in Canada, 1950–75' with Dennis R. Maki, *Relations Industrielles*, **36**(4) (1981), 922–7.   51

5 'The Costs of Canada's Social Insurance Programs' in G. Lermer (ed.), *Probing Leviathan: An Investigation of Government in the Economy* (Vancouver: The Fraser Institute, 1984), 59–85.   57

6 'Government Deposit Insurance, Moral Hazard and the International Debt Crisis' in Herbert Giersch (ed.), *The International Debt Problem: Lessons for the Future* (Tübingen: J C B Mohr, 1986), 172–86.   84

7 'The Taxation of Windfall Gains on Stocks of Natural Resources' with Sam Sydneysmith, *Canadian Public Policy*, **1**(1) (Winter 1975), 13–29.   99

8 'Towards a Theory of Free Economic Zones', *Weltwirtschaftliches Archiv*, **118**(1) (1982), 39–60.   116

9 'Singapore's Record of Price Stability, 1966–84' in Kernial Singh Sandhu and Paul Wheatley (eds), *Management of Success: The Moulding of Modern Singapore* (Singapore: Institute of Southeast Asian Studies, 1989), 373–98.   138

10 'Capitalism Needs Risk-, not Profit-Sharing', *Kyklos*, **40**(2) (1987), 163–74.   164

11 'Reflections on a Canadian Bill of Economic Rights', *Canadian Public Policy*, **VIII**(1) (Winter 1982), 57–68.   176

12 'Constitutional Limits on Government Spending Deficits and Levels in Canada' in Herbert G. Grubel, Douglas D. Purvis, and William M. Scarth (eds), *Limits to Government: Controlling Deficits and Debt in Canada* (Toronto: C.D. Howe Institute, 1992), 1–43.   188

13 'Canadian Economists' Citation and Publication Records',
    Canadian Journal of Higher Education, **XI**(1) (1981), 27–43.   231
14 'Citation Counts for Leading Economists', *Economic Notes*, **8**(2)
    (1979), 134–44.   248
15 'Citation Counts for Economists Specializing in International
    Economics: A Tribute to the Memory of Harry G. Johnson',
    Malayan Economic Review, **XXV**(1) (April 1980), 1–18.   259
16 'On the Efficient Use of Mathematics in Economics: Some
    Theory, Facts and Results of an Opinion Survey' with Lawrence
    A. Boland, *Kyklos*, **39**(3) (1986), 419–41.   277
17 'The Making of Canadian Economists – Results of a Survey of
    Graduate Students', *Canadian Journal of Higher Education*,
    XXI(3) (1991), 1–23.   300

Name Index   323

Acknowledgements

The publishers wish to thank the following who have kindly given permission for the use of copyright material.

American Risk and Insurance Association, Inc for article: Herbert G. Grubel (1971), 'Risk, Uncertainty and Moral Hazard', *Journal of Risk and Insurance*, **XXXVIII**(1), March, 99–106.

Canadian Journal of Economics for article: Herbert G. Grubel, Dennis Maki and Shelley Sax (1975), 'Real and Insurance-Induced Unemployment in Canada', *Canadian Journal of Economics*, **VIII**(2), May, 174–91.

Canadian Journal of Higher Education, Canadian Society for the Study of Higher Education for articles: Herbert G. Grubel (1981), 'Canadian Economists' Citation and Publication Records', *Canadian Journal of Higher Education*, **XI**(1), 27–43; Herbert G. Grubel (1991), 'The Making of Canadian Economists – Results of a Survey of Graduate Students', *Canadian Journal of Higher Education*, **XXI**(3), 1–23.

Canadian Public Policy for articles: Herbert G. Grubel and Sam Sydneysmith (1975), 'The Taxation of Windfall Gains on Stocks of Natural Resources', *Canadian Public Policy*, **1**(1), Winter, 13–29; Herbert G. Grubel (1982), 'Reflections on a Canadian Bill of Economic Rights', *Canadian Public Policy*, **VIII**(1), Winter, 57–68.

Fraser Institute for article: Herbert Grubel (1984), 'The Costs of Canada's Social Insurance Programs', Chapter 3 in G. Lermer (ed.), *Probing Leviathan: An Investigation of Government in the Economy*, 59–85.

Helbing & Lichtenhahn Verlag, AG Basle for articles: Herbert G. Grubel (1987), 'Capitalism Needs Risk-, not Profit-Sharing', *Kyklos*, **40**(2), 163–74; Herbert G. Grubel and Lawrence A. Boland (1986), 'On the Efficient Use of Mathematics in Economics: Some Theory, Facts and Results of an Opinion Survey', *Kyklos*, **39**(3), 419–41.

C.D. Howe Institute for article: Herbert G. Grubel (1992), 'Constitutional Limits on Government Spending Deficits and Levels in Canada' in Herbert G. Grubel, Douglas D. Purvis and William M. Scarth (eds), *Limits to Government: Controlling Deficits and Debt in Canada*, 1–43.

Institute of Southeast Asian Studies for article: Herbert G. Grubel (1989), 'Singapore's Record of Price Stability, 1966–84', Chapter 17 in Kernial Singh Sandhu and Paul Wheatley (eds), *Management of Success: The Moulding of Modern Singapore*, 373–98.

Laval University Press for article: Herbert G. Grubel and Dennis R. Maki (1981), 'A Note on the Effects of Unemployment Insurance, Minimum Wage Legislation and Trade Union Growth on Reported Unemployment Rates in Canada, 1950–75', *Relations Industrielles*, **36**(4), 922–7.

J C B Mohr (Paul Siebeck) Tübingen for articles: Herbert G. Grubel and Dennis R. Maki (1976), 'The Effects of Unemployment Benefits on U.S. Unemployment Rates', *Weltwirtschaftliches Archiv*, **CXII**(2), 274–97; Herbert G. Grubel (1986), 'Government Deposit Insurance, Moral Hazard and the International Debt Crisis' in Herbert Giersch (ed.), *The International Debt Problem: Lessons for the Future*, 172–86; Herbert G. Grubel (1982), 'Towards a Theory of Free Economic Zones', *Weltwirtschaftliches Archiv*, **118**(1), 39–60.

Monte dei Paschi di Siena for article: H.G. Grubel (1979), 'Citation Counts for Leading Economists', *Economic Notes*, **8**(2), 134–44.

Singapore Economic Review, Economic Society of Singapore for article: Herbert G. Grubel (1980), 'Citation Counts for Economists Specializing in International Economics: A Tribute to the Memory of Harry G. Johnson', *Malayan Economic Review*, **XXV**(1), April, 1–18.

Introduction

The purpose of this Introduction is to put the articles in this volume into the intellectual, institutional and policy context within which they originated. It also affords me the opportunity to reflect on the professional attention received by the selection, to indicate where I have changed my views and to acknowledge debts of gratitude to sponsors, co-authors and collaborators.

1.   In 1969 the Dean of Wharton School at the University of Pennsylvania had me act as his representative during a PhD examination in the insurance department of that school. The discussions during the examination stoked my interest in the phenomenon of moral hazard and induced me to write the paper reproduced as Chapter 1 in this volume.

This study has influenced much of my subsequent professional research. It also made a contribution to the history of thought which is summarized by a rejection letter from one of the editors of the *Journal of Political Economy*: 'The paper does not quite do to Knight's concepts of risk and uncertainty what Friedman's paper did to Marshall's concept of demand. Reject'.

The central point of the paper is that an insurance contract or the provision of social insurance protection by the government lowers the cost of being afflicted by the insured hazard. As a result, insured individuals rationally change their behaviour and consequently are afflicted by the hazard more often than they would have been in the absence of the insurance. A popular notion illustrates the point well: insured restaurants burn down more often than those which are not insured. Important for the assessment of major government spending programmes is the implication that persons covered by medical and unemployment insurance fell victim to these hazards more than they would otherwise.

The extent of behaviour modification is different for each hazard and depends on a variety of factors, the most important of which are (1) the ability of insurers to prevent individual changes in behaviour, (2) the degree of co-insurance, and (3) the development of institutions and moral codes of conduct. According to this model, profit insurance is not sold because of the impossibility of controlling moral hazard behaviour and the resultant need to charge such high premiums that no-one would buy the coverage. The absence of such insurance has nothing to do with the existence of what Knight called 'uncertainty' for which no distribution of incidence of the hazard is known. Profit insurance is not sold because moral hazard cannot be controlled; the resultant costs of the insurance make it non-economic to sell and buy.

2.–6.   Chapters 3 through 6 apply the concept of moral hazard to the analysis and empirical measurement of the effects of government insurance programmes on public behaviour and the costs resulting from it. The papers are co-authored with Dennis Maki and, in the case of Chapter 2, with a graduate student, Shelley Sax.

All of these econometric papers introduce into equations the ratio of unemployment insurance benefits to wages as the key variable to reflect the strength of the incentives created by the programme. This variable is statistically very significant and explains much of the growth in unemployment rates in Canada and the US during the post-war years – after proper inclusion of the normal variables to account for cyclical and labour force supply influences. In one study the level of unionization was found to be an additional influence on the rates of unemployment.

The quantitative importance of the moral hazard effect may be seen from the implication of the econometric estimates for Canada. The liberalization of the unemployment insurance programme during the early 1970s was found to have been responsible for about 1.5 to 2 percentage points of the unemployment rate of about 7 per cent prevailing at the time.

When these papers were first circulated and published, they encountered extreme hostility from other economists and intellectuals from other disciplines in particular. Today, the ideas have almost become conventional wisdom. They have undoubtedly contributed to the lack of public uproar over unemployment rates during economic booms, the height of which in earlier decades would have evoked demands for massive government intervention. I have been told by Simon Reisman, then Canada's Deputy Minister of Finance, that during the late 1970s the paper was decisive in persuading members of Trudeau's cabinet in Canada that expansionary monetary and fiscal policy should not be used to lower the unemployment rate which had been increased by the more liberal insurance provisions introduced a few years before.

The moral hazard concept explains why the cost of social insurance programmes like medical care, support for single mothers, work-related disability and general welfare is always much above that projected on the basis of data from periods when no such insurance existed. In Chapter 16 it is used to explain the origins of the International Debt Crisis of the 1980s. Unfortunately, this line of argument and empirical evidence on the magnitude of the moral hazard effect remain ideologically tinted. As a result, the ever-increasing costs of social and other government insurance programmes in most industrial countries are addressed by policies which do not deal with the heart of the matter, but which instead result in a continuous erosion of freedom and a threat to democracy.[1]

7.   After the formation of OPEC and the resultant increase in world energy prices, the Canadian government under the leadership of Prime Minister Trudeau introduced the National Energy Policy. This policy was designed to tax away the windfall gains of the owners of energy resources, most of which are located in Alberta.

Chapter 7, co-authored with Sam Sydneysmith, addresses the longer-run economic implications of this policy. We argued that the legislation destroyed the sanctity of contracts between the government and private agents. This contract had stipulated

---

[1] In Britain the quantitative evidence on the moral hazard effect has evidently been found to be small, with a concensus emerging on this subject. The empirical evidence is reviewed in A.J. Oswald (ed.), *Surveys in Economics, Volume I* (Oxford: Blackwell, 1991), p.166.

that the successful bidder for an oil-drilling lease would pay a certain royalty and tax on earnings from the resource. The size of the bid for the drilling rights was based on a distribution of expected future returns, which included possible large losses as well as gains. The National Energy Policy in effect signalled to future bidders for such contracts that if conditions produced a very favourable outcome, the government would insist on a new contract. If the outcome was unfavourable, the government would still insist on its validity and force the private partners to accept the consequences of their legal commitment.

The National Energy Policy was equivalent to a law which expropriates all large winnings from government-sponsored lotteries on the grounds that such winnings create an unfair income distribution. Everyone can readily see that the introduction of such a policy will drastically reduce the sale of lottery tickets. We argued that the National Energy Policy would drastically lower the government's return from the auctioning of oil leases in the future. The lower returns would offset much, if not all, of the short-run gains from the tax. The central proposition of our article is the subject of at least one university-level Canadian textbook in natural resource economics.

8.   Since the middle 1970s the world has been swept by a wave of deregulation brought on by the realization that most regulation did not serve the public interest, but rather that of the government in power and the special interests it benefited. During this period the special interest groups benefiting from regulation were able to resist much of this reform policy.

In Chapter 8 I consider the merit of using free economic zones to overcome this resistance to deregulation. Such zones are set aside as special territories within which business is able to operate with a minimum of regulation. Special interests like workers and firms benefiting from the zone represent a powerful counterweight to the defenders of regulation. The commercial success of the zones would invite imitation and produce more general deregulation. The paper also discusses the problems associated with such zones, the most important of which is the diversion of economic activity away from other efficient locations. Free economic zones have become important elements in the development plans of many low-income countries of the world; some, like Jack Kemp, former US Secretary of Housing, also see them as a way of restoring prosperity to inner cities.

9.   After Singapore gained its political independence, its real economic growth rate averaged 10 per cent, unemployment was low and prices were stable. In 1985 I served as the Distinguished Fellow in International Banking and Finance at the Institute of Southeast Asian Studies in Singapore. It was an exciting period since, for the first time in 15 years, the country's unemployment rate had risen and the growth rate had become negative.

In Chapter 9 I examine the economic policies which resulted in both the country's outstanding success and its current problems. I concluded that the success was due to the use of policies which encouraged growth and stability by employing proper microeconomic incentives and the depoliticization of macroeconomic stabilization policies. I also identified as the cause of the then current problems the deliberate policy of raising labour costs by over 50 per cent in a short period. This exceptional policy had been based on the theory that high wages would force employers to substitute capital for labour and thus produce accelerated economic growth.

The reversal of this wage policy and the introduction of a system ensuring more flexibility in the wage-setting process promptly eliminated unemployment and restored economic growth. The government of Singapore, with its trust in microeconomic principles, had smartly resisted the advice of some prominent US economists to attack the problem by the lowering of interest rates and government deficits to stimulate aggregate demand.

10. The early 1980s brought to prominence old ideas about the usefulness of profit-sharing as an institution which would make capitalism more humane, reduce industrial conflict, raise productivity and increase real wage flexibility. The ideas, propagated mainly by some economists and ideologues from the left, never created much interest from labour or management.

Chapter 10 identifies as the reason for this distrust of profit-sharing the failure of the proposals to take proper account of the role of profits in a market economy. Profits are the returns to entrepreneurial risk-taking. Most workers and entrepreneurs do not want to assume or share the risks from this activity. Nor is such sharing in the interest of a dynamically efficient economy.

On the other hand, real wage flexibility and incentives for productivity would be increased and industrial conflict decreased if labour and management accepted contracts which shared the risks of developments that affect the performance of firms and which are totally external to the actions of workers or managers. Examples of such influences are the world prices of inputs like energy and the world prices of output. Under such proposed contractual arrangements, labour would be paid periodic bonuses on top of normal pay at a lower scale. The size of the bonuses would be determined by the aim of achieving an equitable and efficient sharing of the consequences of such exogenous influences on the economic performance of firms.

11.–12. All democratic legislatures have constitutional limits on their ability to use simple majority voting for laws which restrict personal freedoms. These constitutional limits have much popular support and are based on widely accepted views about the nature of man. The preservation of the freedom of speech and the right to trial are principles which are too easy to violate by a simple majority in quest of short-run political or economic goals seen to be in the public interest. Yet, cumulatively through time, such laws destroy personal freedoms and ultimately democratic systems as well.

In Chapters 11 and 12 I argue that the justification for the need to protect personal freedoms from simple legislative majorities is also valid for the protection of economic rights. One of these rights is for future generations to inherit a system free from excessive government debt which results in undue claims on their taxation capacity. The unrestrained ability of legislatures to tax and incur deficits threatens not only traditional rights of people to enjoy the returns from their labour, savings and risk-taking, but also the very existence of the democratic system. The growth of debt and spending can ultimately destroy incentives to a degree where economic growth stops, popular unrest develops and the public becomes receptive to the ideas of extremist demagogues of the left or right.

Chapters 11 and 12 may be exaggerating the danger facing democratic industrial countries. The proposed constitutional changes may not be needed because democratic systems are resilient and flexible. Only the future will tell, but constitutional limits on spending levels and imbalances appear to be insurance taken out at a low cost.

13.-15.   The regular publication of the *Social Science Citation Index* has created a large and valuable data base permitting interesting studies of the productivity and sociology of the economics profession. Chapters 13 through 15 present the results of my study of the citation and publication records of economists before the late 1970s: economists teaching in Canada, those in the world specializing in international economics and those who have been honoured by their associations and through the Nobel prize.

The results of my analysis were of particular interest to the then current generation of economists. However, they also revealed some basic facts of lasting value for the assessment of the work of individuals, university departments and scientific activity in general. Thus, they confirmed what had been known from other professions: the top 10 per cent of individuals produce 50 per cent of all output and citations while the bottom 50 per cent produce nothing. Citations to the work of outstanding scientists are a good predictor of their selection to office in the American Economics Association and the award of the Nobel prize. In his discussion of the Nobel prize selection process, Assar Lindbeck referred to this finding. On the other hand, the existence of citation cartels and different propensities to cite techniques, invalid findings and ideas that have become quasi public domain limit the usefulness of such measures.

16.-17.   In my view, the economics profession in North America and in parts of Europe has gone too far in its use of mathematics and formalism in research and training. As a result, it is losing influence on the education of students, economic policies and the formation of public opinion. These personal views were confirmed by a study committee formed by the American Economics Association and chaired by Ann Krueger.

Chapter 16 is co-authored with Larry Boland and presents some evidence on the growth of mathematics in professional economic journals. It also contains the results of a survey of economists which permitted them to express their views on the merit of the increasing use of mathematics (1) in teaching and research and (2) in the value-system of the profession responsible for promotions and the allocation of government support for research. A majority of respondents to the survey thought that the use of mathematics in economics, especially in research, has gone too far. Chapter 17 replicates with Canadian graduate students in economics a survey by Arjo Klamer and David Colander of US graduate students.

In both surveys the central and disturbing result was that the students believed that, for professional success, it was more important to be able to build logically rigorous models than to know about the working of real economies, institutions and history. Given the budget constraint on time for training, such students obviously chose to devote much more effort to the former than the latter category of lecture courses and research projects. Having acquired a vested interest in the exercise of modelling skills, they used their influence to promote and reward similar work in their universities and research outlets.

The result has been what someone has called the education of a generation of *idiots savants* teaching and researching economic problems. We attribute this development to the support of mathematical economics by government in the wake of Sputnik and the post-war belief that all social problems of the world can be solved through rigorous science. The small elite of economists who used these tools during the 1960s was encouraged to expand the training and strengthen the reward system for this type of work. The emerging interest group, largely without contact with the ultimate market for the services of economists, created and used their own value system to funnel increasing resources from non-profit institutions to their own creed.

There are no obvious methods available for any institution to change the value-system of the economics profession. Perhaps the AEA committee findings and the public response to our own and similar studies indicate the beginning of an endogenous reversal of trends. It cannot come too early. Only time will tell what economic programmes will be initiated by future generations of politicians who learned economic principles from sociologists and political scientists and who missed learning about the power of the invisible hand, its limitations and the role of history and institutions in the development of the industrial world.

[1] [1971] USA

G22

I18

I11

RISK, UNCERTAINTY AND MORAL HAZARD

HERBERT G. GRUBEL

ABSTRACT

This paper gives precision to the meaning of the term "moral hazard." It then analyses the implications which the phenomenon of moral hazard has on the welfare effects of public insurance schemes and the present shortage of medical doctors and hospitals in the United States. It concludes that the existence of moral hazard does not necessarily invalidate the case for welfare increasing public provision of insurance as Pauly has claimed in his criticism of Arrow. Finally, the analysis explores the implications the phenomenon of moral hazard has for Knight's famous distinction between risk and uncertainty.

The analysis of the conditions under which compulsory government insurance schemes raise public welfare is of considerable theoretical and practical significance. One aspect of Arrow's important contributions to this issue[1] has recently been challenged by Pauly,[2] who argued that Arrow's formal demonstration of the welfare raising effects of compulsory insurance is invalidated by the proper consideration of an empirical phenomenon

Grateful acknowledgment is made for the helpful comments Herbert S. Denenberg and Mark V. Pauly made on an earlier draft of this paper. However, since all of their advice was not followed, remaining errors and ambiguities are solely the responsibility of the author.

Herbert G. Grubel, Ph.D., is Associate Professor of Finance in the University of Pennsylvania. In 1969, Dr. Grubel was Visiting Fellow, Australian National University, Institute of Advanced Studies. His previous teaching includes service at Yale, Stanford, and the University of Chicago.

This paper was submitted in April, 1970.

[1] K. J. Arrow, *Aspects of the Theory of Risk-Bearing*, Helsinki, 1965; "Uncertainty and the Welfare Economics of Medical Care," *American Economic Review*, December 1963, 53, 941-73; "The Economics of Moral Hazard: Further Comments," *American Economic Review*, June 1968, 58, 537-39.

[2] M. V. Pauly, "The Economics of Moral Hazard: Comment," *American Economic Review*, June 1968, 58, 531-37.

known in the literature of insurance economics as "moral hazard."

The paper is designed to give greater precision to the concept of moral hazard than has hitherto been available and to analyze its cause in some detail, in the process shedding light on the Arrow-Pauly controversy. The concept is shown to have very important implications for current and future decision-making about public insurance schemes and the alleged present shortage of medical doctors and hospital space in the United States.

The second part of the paper develops a criterion allowing the judgment to be made whether or not a given compulsory public insurance scheme improves welfare even when moral hazard exists. In the last part, it is shown that the concept of moral hazard and the previously developed decision-making criteria add to an understanding of Frank H. Knight's famous distinction between risk and uncertainty.

Concept of Moral Hazard

The literature dealing with the economics of insurance defines "moral hazard" as "the intangible loss-producing pro-

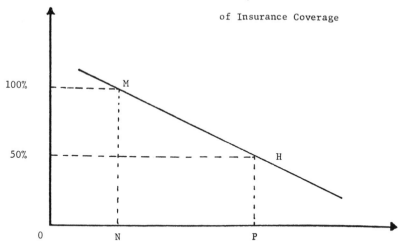

Figure 1

Demand for Hospital Beds as a Function

of Insurance Coverage

Marginal Cost of
Hospital Confinement

Number of Hospital bed days required
per 100,000 persons/year

pensities of the individual assured."[3] Moral hazard thus refers to the generally well known empirical phenomenon that a group of persons which is insured against a certain risk tends to become victimized by the risk more often or more severely than a comparable group not insured.

The concept of moral hazard can be made more precise with the help of Figure 1, where the horizontal axis measures the statistical frequency with which persons in a group of 100,000 individuals, randomly selected from the population, fall victim to a particular risk during a specified period of time.

For example, consider the risk of falling ill resulting in the number of hospital bed occupation days ON required each year by the randomly selected group of 100,000 persons. The vertical axis measures the proportion of the marginal cost

[3] E. J. Faulkner, *Health Insurance*, New York, 1960.

of hospital confinement, including the out-of-pocket cost of the care, the psychic cost and the opportunity cost of the person's time, which is borne by the person in the hospital. At 100 percent of the marginal cost borne by the individual the number of hospital bed days is ON, at 50 percent it is OP. A category of risk which exhibits a perfectly vertical line MH is said to be free of moral hazard. The more elastic the line MH the greater the moral hazard.

The functional relationship shown assumed the existence of the specific form of coinsurance known as the percentage deductible. An analogus functional relationship exists when the insurance provides for a fixed-sum deductible, except that it is more difficult to show diagrammatically. However, it is worth noting that percentage deductible coinsurance is universal if one considers properly all costs associated with the occurrence of any insured damage, for there are no known insurance schemes which compensate the insured for all losses, including those of a psychic nature and the foregone income.

From the economist's point of view, one of the most interesting aspects of the moral hazard phenomenon is its ultimate cause. Textbooks in insurance tend to stress the lack of "morality" on the part of the insureds, which leads them to exaggerate the size of their losses and to contribute actively to the occurrence of the loss. It is a well-known fact that insured bankrupt retail stores and restaurants tend to go up in flames more often than do financially sound establishments of this type.

However, the moral hazard phenomenon, probably most often and quantitatively most significantly, is due to behavior which only in a very special sense can be considered to be against society's moral norms. Medical doctors in the United States have given the following account of their decision-making processes resulting in claims on hospital insurance: Faced with a patient who shows the symptoms of an illness which is difficult to diagnose in the office, a doctor often recommends hospital confinement for a thorough analysis of the person's functions, or exploratory surgery because of the possibly serious consequences of a wrong or late diagnosis of the true illness.

Doctors readily admit that for any given set of undiagnosed symptoms their decision to admit a person to the hospital depends on their judgment as to the individual's ability to bear the cost, i.e., whether he has hospital insurance or not. Similarly, the length of hospital stay demanded and accepted by a patient or recommended by a doctor in connection with a given illness is increased in attempts to reduce the probability of relapse. In general, the level of relapse probability chosen is lower and therefore hospital confinement longer the lower the individual's marginal cost of hospital stay.

In the case of other insurance forms such as automobile, fire, theft and life insurance the moral hazard phenomenon arises from the willingness of the insured to take greater risks on an uncertain outcome. The electric wiring in a house always represents some fire danger. If persons are willing to forego repairs to the housewiring when they have insurance, which they would undertake in the absence of insurance, "moral hazard" as defined above exists.

Even in the case of life insurance there is likely to exist positive moral hazard in this sense. Consider a person who is at the margin concerning the decision to take a job involving much hazardous travel or a job in an office. If this person is induced to take the more hazardous job through the availability of life insurance and the knowledge that his family is financially secure in case of his death, then logically death rates for that person's age group are greater when life insurance is available than when it is not. It is clear that in the case of death, accident, and fire insurance the element of coinsurance tends to be extremely high so that moral hazard tends to be small.

Unfortunately, at present there appear to exist no systematic measures of moral hazard even though multiple regression techniques lend themselves readily to the measurement of the phenomenon from data available to insurance companies. However, in the absence of careful statistical inquiries, it may be worth quoting the statistics presented privately to the author by an officer of the American Medical Association. This medical doctor made the empirical judgment that the U.S. demand for hospital beds would decrease by at least 40 percent if coinsurance on hospitalization were 100 percent, i.e., if there were no hospital insurance and individuals were required to bear the full marginal social cost of hospital confinement. This is not the place to discuss the validity of the specific estimate quoted. However, it is clear that if moral hazard in connection with health insurance is anywhere near this figure, recent public discussions about the shortage of hospital facilities and medical personnel staffing them, may well have been based on false premises.

The preceding description of the motivation underlying the actions which give rise to moral hazard support strongly Pauly's argument that the phenomenon is wrongly called a "moral" hazard.[4] For the most part, these actions are expected, economically rational behavior of persons confronted by the lowered price for a service. Arrow, on the other hand, while agreeing with the general validity of this proposition nevertheless expresses the hope that the public can be persuaded to set its demands for medical services in "accordance with some commonly accepted norms,"[5] presumably in light of true social marginal rather than only private marginal cost. He believes that such a persuasion could be successful since the public attitudes to be developed are much like the ones which result in "the relations of trust and confidence between principal and agent . . . so that the agent will not cheat even though it may be 'rational' economic behavior to do so."[6]

Whether it is possible to develop such public attitudes is an extremely important question for governments which are contemplating the institution of compulsory insurance schemes in the future, because if they cannot be developed the case for such schemes will be weakened considerably. Therefore, it is worth analysing this problem of the development of public norms of behavior in some detail. In this context it is useful to consider the

question whether butchers do not cheat with their weight because they act according to some accepted norm of behavior or because they are afraid of being found out and losing customers? Do people obey traffic signals because of commonly accepted norms or because they are afraid of accidents and of being caught by the police?

Some reflection on the nature of these behavioral patterns, their relation to commonly accepted norms and self-interest reveals the following principles. In cases where common norms of behavior serve public welfare, but there are private incentives to break the norms, society passes laws which through a system of punishments for violators change private incentives in favour of norms' obeyance. In general, such laws are passed only if their enforcement is technically feasible and does not require excessive resource expenditures. Most butchers have sufficient private incentives to use honest weights; easily enforceable laws strengthen incentives to conform to the public norm. Most motorists obey traffic laws because it is in their private interest to do so, but the existence of a ready law enforcement machinery has added incentive effects for those tempted to break the norm when it would otherwise not suit their self-interest.

Arrow's formal demonstration that compulsory public insurance increases welfare if moral hazard is absent provides a rationale for setting out a norm which states that hospital space paid for by the insurance should be demanded only under conditions which would also have led to the demand for it in the absence of the insurance. Obedience of this norm is in individuals' self-interest since it makes the government insurance feasible and a rational government would introduce it, raising overall welfare. But, as was argued above, the demonstration that obedience of a norm is in one's own interest is in-

[4] Pauly, *op. cit.*, p. 534.

[5] Arrow, *American Economic Review*, June 1968, p. 538.

[6] *Ibid.*, p. 538.

sufficient for its universal acceptance whenever private incentives to break the norm are strong.

In the case of the norm under discussion, private incentives to break it are strong because of the peculiarity of the service and as the estimate of the magnitude of moral hazard referred to above indicates. Laws designed to create a better balance of incentives have not been and probably never will be passed because their enforcement is impossible with the present state of technology. This is so because presently no-one can prove in any court of law that a given patient who stayed in the hospital five days with the cost paid by his insurance, would have stayed fewer days, had he been forced to pay the costs out of his own pocket, anymore than it is possible to prove that my consumption of beer would be smaller if the price were doubled.

There is no harm done by the publication of the issues, private and social costs and the specification of a public norm of behavior in countries which already have widespread public health-insurance schemes. However, it is highly unlikely that, for the reasons just discussed, such publication will reduce the extent of moral hazard in the long run and by a significant degree.

An interesting fact bearing on this question is that in the United Kingdom the elasticity of moral hazard regarding drugs was found to be so large when the degree of coinsurance approached zero, that the labor government of Prime Minister Wilson was forced to reintroduce a greater percentage of coinsurance through a charge on prescriptions, even though this step was ideologically against the principles of the labor party.

Moral Hazard and Social Insurance

As Arrow admits, the existence of moral hazard invalidates his formal proof that

welfare is raised by the compulsory government provision of insurance to cover a previously uninsurable hazard.[7] However, it is possible to show that under certain circumstances compulsory insurance raises public welfare even when moral hazard exists.

Consider Figure 1 and assume that the line MH represents the U.S. demand for visits to dentists at various levels of coinsurance. Pick one level of coinsurance, say 50 percent, where the average U.S. public demand for dentist visits is OP per year. At a cost of D dollars per visit the total cost of these visits is OP x D dollars. Assuming the cost of administering the scheme to be K and the total U.S. population to be Q, then the average premium required to cover the cost of the scheme is $C = ((OP \times D) + K)/Q$ dollars per year. Theoretically, the government institution of the dentist insurance scheme not now available from private industry is equivalent to the introduction of a service in the market, i.e., protection against 50 percent of the cost of dental care expenses, at the price C per year.

It is now possible to pose tests for social acceptance or rejection of the scheme. Consider first the possibility that all people voluntarily would purchase the protection at cost C. Clearly, under these circumstances total welfare would be increased by the introduction of the scheme. However, the nagging question arises why under these conditions the private insurance industry does not provide such a service in the market.

While there may be institutional restrictions and market imperfections, there are only two important economic reasons why a competitive insurance industry does not provide the service. First, the actual magnitude of moral hazard is unknown and experimentation to discover it is too risky and costly for a single entrepreneur to

---

[7] Arrow, *ibid.*, p. 538.

undertake. It could be said that the knowledge has large externalities associated with it. If this is the case, then the government should make the investment in the assembly of the knowledge, which it has to do whether the service is ultimately provided privately or not. It should then make this knowledge available to the public free of charge. Under competition, entrepreneurs will utilize it to sell the public dental insurance at premium C.

Second, the actual cost of operating the scheme is smaller under government than under private auspices, possibly because of economies of scale in administration or because of lower selling (information distribution) costs under government sponsorship. However, it should be noted that the difference in these costs must be substantial in order to lead to the result that at the government premium C_G the entire public would purchase it voluntarily while at the private industry premium C_f no-one would purchase it. While it is hard to know ex ante what the cost differences are, it is worth noting that the government also has selling costs if the condition is to be met that the insurance is bought voluntarily by all.

Turn now to the more realistic case where offering to the public a 50 percent coinsurance for dental care at an annual premium C results in the situation where some people do and some do not wish to purchase it at this price. Under these circumstances, the government institution of the scheme can be made to break even only if it is made compulsory for everyone to purchase at price C. This compulsion lowers the welfare of those who do not consider the service worth purchasing at price C, and raises the welfare of those who previously had to do without it but would have been willing to purchase it. Whether the introduction of the scheme raises or lowers overall welfare can be decided scientifically only if the gainors bribe the losers into its voluntary acceptance of the scheme and the gainors are still better off after the compensation. Governments willing to make value judgments can justify the institution of a compulsory insurance scheme if they decide that welfare would be raised if compensation were undertaken.

Again the question arises why private industry does not supply insurance to the segment of the population willing to purchase it at price C. As in the preceding case, the reasons for not doing so are uncertainty or higher costs and premiums. It may be worth noting one important source of higher costs encountered by private but not by compulsory insurance. Whenever a private insurance scheme is offered for sale, the seller is faced with the problem of adverse selection, which means that at the given premium proportionately more loss-producing individuals are induced to sign up than there are in the population as a whole. Private insurers take account of this phenomenon by setting up risk classes with different premiums, to which they assign individuals according to the best estimates of their loss-producing propensities. The administration of these risk classes and the investigation of individuals result in costs not experienced under compulsory schemes and contribute to the existence of types of hazard for which private insurance is not available because it cannot be sold at a profit, but which some people are willing to purchase at the government encountered cost.

Finally it is necessary to introduce into the analysis the possibility that external effects or socially desirable income redistribution effects are associated with the universal introduction of an insurance scheme. In connection with health insurance it is often argued that such effects are positive and large. These effects can be incorporated into the analysis by subtracting an estimate of their social values (E) from the costs and recomputing a premium necessary to cover the net social cost of the scheme, i.e., $C_e = (OP \times D) - E + K)/Q$.

This premium estimate then has to be presented to the public and the same decision-making calculus as before has to be applied. It is clear that if external and income redistribution effects and the government administrative savings are large enough, it is much more likely that at the resultant C_e the entire public would purchase it voluntarily while at the private C it would be totally unsalable.[8]

The preceding analysis has been presented for the case where a 50 percent coinsurance was offered at the appropriate breakeven costs C and C_e. Logically it is possible to engage in analogous experiments using all other levels of coinsurance and corresponding cost estimates. For any given insurance scheme the following outcomes may result:

First, at no level of coinsurance different from 100 percent the service is purchased voluntarily by all or net welfare benefits are positive. Under these conditions the hazard is genuinely non-insurable.

Second, at several levels of coinsurance all people wish to purchase it and at no levels is there lack of unanimity. The problem is here to choose among levels of coinsurance all of which are desired universally. There are no economic criteria for choosing among the alternatives and a plebiscite or value judgment is necessary for the choice of an optimum level of coinsurance.

Third, at several levels of coinsurance it is decided that the welfare losses of the coerced are smaller than the gains of the remaining population and at no level the scheme is accepted voluntarily by all.

In this case optimisation requires choice of the level of coinsurance with the highest level of total welfare, which requires no more interpersonal comparisons of utility than already have been undertaken in the initial estimates of overall net gains.

Lastly, at some levels of coinsurance there is voluntary unanimity and at some other levels welfare gains outweigh losses from coercion. Under these circumstances no economic criteria of choice are available and value judgments have to be brought into the decision.

In sum, the analysis of this section has shown that differences in private and public administrative and selling costs, and the existence of external and income redistribution effects, can lead to the situation where total welfare is raised by the introduction of a government sponsored compulsory insurance scheme against a form of risk for which no private insurance is available, even though moral hazard exists. This result is not too surprising if it is realized that private insurance is available for many forms of risk for which moral hazard exists.

Risk and Uncertainty

The preceding analysis can be used to give greater precision to F. H. Knight's famous distinction between risk and uncertainty, where the former is an insurable and the later an uninsurable hazard. The alleged economic cause for the observed distinction in risk-classes is that for the first there exist objective experience rates, on the basis of which profitable premiums can be set by insurance companies, while for the second no such objective data exist.[9]

---

[8] It goes beyond the scope of this paper to analyse the argument whether, even under these circumstances, it would not be more efficient to attain the desired income redistribution effects through direct transfer payments and to subsidize private industry to the extent of the externalities.

[9] "The practical difference between the two categories, risk and uncertainty, is that in the former the distribution of the outcome in a group of instances is known (either through calculation a priori or from statistics of past experience), while in the case of uncertainty this is not true . . ." F. H. Knight, *Risk, and Uncertainty and Profit*, Houghton Mifflin, Boston and New York, 1921.

The best known of non-insurable risks discussed by Knight is, of course, profits. The preceding analysis suggests that the essential difference between business and fire losses is not the unavailability of statistics on their frequency, for certainly it is possible to estimate what proportion of businesses will make losses in the future or fail to attain a given return on their capital just as it is possible to estimate the proportion of houses consumed by fire and flood in the future. While the standard error of the forecasts may be different and while there may be a greater interdependence of the risk of business losses, the two classes of risk can be estimated identically by consideration of the past experience amounting to millions of observations spanning a long period of time.

However, what is available for fire losses and not for business losses are objective data on the degree of moral hazard, that is how much losses would increase at the different marginal private cost of each loss to the insured between zero and 100 percent. But still these data are attainable in principle. Historically many forms of risk, which at one time were considered uninsurable because of the unavailability of measures of moral hazard, have become insurable as some entrepreneurs or governments attained experience and were able to produce estimates of the degree of moral hazard. Thus, even on this basis, the risk of fire loss is not essentially different from the risk of business loss. After all, there now exists a form of coinsurance for business loss through U.S. government-tax laws and many governments have provided insurance against losses from foreign trade. In both of these cases moral hazard is measurable for the degree of coinsurance employed and experience has shown that it is not particularly large.

Thus, what remains of Knight's distinction between risk and uncertainty? The preceding discussion suggests that, theoretically, a socially uninsurable risk is one for which at all degrees of coinsurance the premiums required to cover the cost of losses and administration are so large that the group to be insured is unwilling to pay the premium in order to obtain the coverage. There are no a priori reasons for believing that business losses are uninsurable at all levels of coinsurance, but if they are it may be worth while to retain the distinction between risk and uncertainty.

[2]

Real and insurance-induced unemployment in Canada

HERBERT G. GRUBEL, DENNIS MAKI,
SHELLEY SAX / Simon Fraser University

Real and insurance-induced unemployment in Canada. Changes in unemployment insurance programs, either changes in the level of benefits relative to wages or in the nature and enforcement of eligibility rules, can affect reported unemployment rates by altering workers' work/leisure tradeoff and job-search behaviour. It is essentially an empirical question whether the net change in the unemployment rate is positive or negative. This paper presents empirical evidence, in the form of an econometric model estimated using annual time series data for Canada covering the period 1953–72, suggesting that changes in the unemployment insurance scheme have substantially increased the unemployment rate in recent years.

Le chômage réel et le chômage induit par l'assurance-chômage, au Canada. Les changements des régimes d'assurance-chômage (en ce qui concerne le rapport des prestations aux salaires, ou la nature et l'application des règles d'éligibilité) peuvent affecter les taux de chômage mesurés par la modification de l'arbitrage travail-loisir des travailleurs et de leur comportement de recherche d'un emploi. D'après des raisonnements théoriques simples sur les prix élaborés dans l'article, l'effet d'un accroissement des prestations relativement aux salaires, qui n'est pas compensé par un resserrement des conditions d'éligibilité, devrait conduire à une augmentation du chômage. Il y aurait alors substitution au revenu du bien devenu relativement moins cher (le loisir). Par ailleurs, des prestations de chômage plus élevées permettent aux travailleurs d'allonger la durée de recherche de nouveaux emplois. Cela peut avoir pour résultat un meilleur mariage entre les caractéristiques des travailleurs et celles des emplois, et par suite des taux de roulement et de chômage moins élevés. De plus, dans la mesure où le rapport des prestations aux salaires et l'application des conditions d'éligibilité suivent une évolution discontinue, la question de l'effet net (positif ou négatif) sur le taux de chômage au Canada des changements du régime d'assurance-chômage, est essentiellement une question empirique. Les auteurs contribuent ici à son étude en présentant un modèle économétrique dont l'estimation a été faite à l'aide de séries chronologiques pour la période 1953–72. Il semble que le taux de chômage canadien de 1972 aurait été inférieur de plus d'un point de pourcentage si le régime d'assurance-chômage était resté le même que celui en vigueur en 1955–6, pour cer-

We acknowledge helpful comments made on earlier drafts of this paper by R. Rogow, J. Moroney, R. Holmes, S. Ostry, C. Archibald, and anonymous referees.

Canadian Journal of Economics/Revue canadienne d'Economique, VIII, no. 2 May/mai 1975. Printed in Canada/Imprimé au Canada.

taines dispositions importantes. Les auteurs présentent une courte discussion des implications de politique de ce résultat.

After the second world war, Canadian aggregate monetary and fiscal policies successfully reduced the amplitude of fluctuations in the unemployment rate below that experienced before the war. However, there remained the welfare costs of high *average* rates of unemployment during the period. These costs were attacked in two ways. First, a social concensus gradually evolved that a 4 to 4.5 per cent target of 'full employment' should be pursued by the government in spite of expected accompanying costs in the form of rates of price increases of about 2 per cent per year. Second, unemployment benefit programs were designed to reduce directly the welfare cost confronting persons out of work and to lower the average unemployment rate through increased labour market efficiency. The latter result was expected to follow from the fact that unemployment benefits permitted workers to search longer for new jobs, which therefore were likely to involve a better match between the characteristics of the workers and jobs and result in a lower job turnover rate.

However, simple price-theoretic considerations to be developed in part I below suggest that unemployment benefit payments also may have the effect of altering workers' work/leisure tradeoff and therefore may induce unemployment not present in the absence of the benefit payments. It is essentially an empirical question whether the Canadian unemployment benefit program has on balance reduced or increased unemployment. In part II of this paper, we present an econometric model and in part III interpret the evidence suggesting that leisure substitution has outweighed increasing efficiency by a substantial margin. The paper closes with an analysis of the implications of our findings for existing targets of full employment and the level of unemployment benefit payments.

The present paper is related to the literature on the microeconomics of the labour market (see Phelps et al., 1970) and the literature dealing with the effects of welfare programs on work incentives.[1] However, to the best of our knowledge this paper is the first dealing with the effect of unemployment benefits on unemployment rates at the aggregate level through the use of regression analysis for the measurement of elasticities.[2]

This study appears to be timely since in Canada in 1972 the unemploy-

---

1 Several papers on the topic are in Cain and Watts (1973)
2 The papers by Felstein (1972) and Green (1973) approached the problem through the use of non-parametric estimates, though it should be noted that Green's result is very close to our own. We have made a study paralleling the present one for the United States (Grubel and Maki, 1974). Chapin (1971) has estimated the effect of unemployment benefits on the average duration of unemployment in the United States. There has been some reference to insurance-induced unemployment in Canada by the OECD (1972, 4, 32) and the argument has been presented in the context of an explanation of world inflation by Arndt (1973).

ment benefit program was liberalized by making eligible persons who had worked eight weeks during the preceding year, as compared with thirty weeks during the two preceding years under the old regulation, and by making eligible persons who had quit their jobs under certain, non-stringent conditions rather than requiring that recipients be laid off by their employers. Furthermore, the new law extended coverage to include virtually all persons for whom an employer-employee relationship exists. Very importantly, the law raised maximum weekly benefits to two-thirds of average weekly insurable earnings, though the benefits were made taxable at the normal income tax rate of the recipient. Maximum benefits in 1972 were $100 per week and were subject to an escalation clause for future years based on trends in average weekly wages and salaries. As a result of these changes, average weekly benefit payments in 1972 represented 41 per cent of average weekly wages and salaries, compared with an average of 29 per cent during the period 1953–72.[3]

The coexistence of efforts to reduce unemployment to the 4 to 4.5 per cent targets and inducements that increase non-work time through higher transfer payments to the unemployed must theoretically lead to added inflationary pressures not anticipated when these full employment targets were set. In the light of the rapid rates of inflation in Canada and the United States since 1972 this study of the level of induced unemployment in Canada takes on special significance as pointing to a fundamental cause of these price increases transcending the many industry-specific and other ad hoc explanations of the inflation that have been advanced.

I / THE THEORETICAL MODEL

The argument that unemployment benefits induce unemployment can be made simply by the following analysis.[4] Consider an 'average' worker earning K dollars per week. In the absence of unemployment benefits the cost of leisure is K dollars per week, abstracting from taxes, work expenses, etc. In the presence of unemployment benefits of B dollars a week, yielding a benefit income ratio $R = B/K$, the cost of leisure for this worker is $(1 - R)K$ or, more simply, $K - B$ dollars per week. Clearly, the cost of leisure is a decreasing function of B and R. However, the incentives to consume the cheapened good, leisure, depend crucially not only on the size of B and R but also on the following three costs every worker has to incur if he wishes to receive unemployment benefits: the cost of finding a new job at the end of the period, the cost of not receiving any income between the commencement of unemployment and the initial receipt of benefits, and

3 For details of the act, see Statistics Canada (71–201, 1972, 71–5).
4 We have developed a geometric representation of the following arguments in Grubel and Maki (1974).

the cost of documenting to the authorities that search has yielded no suitable job. We will now discuss the nature of these costs in detail.

Cost of job search

Since unemployment benefits are of limited duration, the enjoyment of leisure is necessarily accompanied by the need to search for a new job at the end of the period. The disutility of this job-search activity must be subtracted from the utility of the leisure to arrive at the net gain from drawing unemployment benefits. This disutility is an increasing function of the length and intensity of the search required to find employment with certainty before benefits are exhausted. Generally, the time spent in search depends on over-all labour market conditions and the individual's skill requirements and tastes.[5] At one extreme, when expected job-search days equal maximum benefit coverage and search activity has the same disutility as work, then incentives to consume the good, leisure, created by the unemployment scheme, are zero. On the other extreme, if job-search costs are zero, the entire period under unemployment coverage can be enjoyed as leisure. If the difficulty of matching job requirements and applicant characteristics is an increasing function of skill levels, our model implies that incentives for the substitution of 'not working' for 'working' created by the benefit scheme are a decreasing function of skill levels. If it is true that the utility of leisure relative to income tends to be higher for young workers without family obligations than for older, married heads of families, then our analysis implies that the incentives created by the benefits tend to induce more unemployment among teenagers than older persons.

The preceding analysis implies that the unemployment benefit program does not create a changed work/leisure opportunity locus in the conventional sense but that the tradeoff is between work, on the one hand, and leisure, net of job-search cost, on the other. However, if workers are induced to enjoy leisure in this manner, the entire period spent in job search plus leisure is recorded as unemployment in official statistics.

Up to this point, we have considered only the effects on work incentives of persons who are employed and who therefore have to quit or get themselves fired in order to be able to consume more of the cheapened good, leisure. As we shall analyse in the following section, the need to have oneself fired is likely to lead to added costs. We now turn to the incentives to consume leisure operating on persons who are laid off involuntarily. These workers' tastes are such that the lowered cost of leisure net of search cost is insufficient to induce them into increased consumption. However, once such workers have been forced into the expense of job search, the marginal

---

5 It should be possible to extend and enrich our model by the incorporation of a job-search model in the recent tradition of literature (see Phelps et al., 1970). We did not do so here since it would distract from the main points of our analysis.

178 / Herbert G. Grubel, Dennis Maki, and Shelley Sax

cost of leisure is equal to the forgone income minus the benefits received. Therefore, workers may be induced to consume leisure at this low marginal cost and thus increase the average length of regular cyclical, seasonal, or structural unemployment.

Finally, unemployment benefits create incentives for persons to enter the labour force temporarily. In the absence of unemployment benefits some persons who could earn a certain wage do not find it worthwhile to work. Instead, they enjoy leisure or, as in the case of housewives, use their time to produce valuable goods and services for their families. The availability of unemployment benefits enables such persons to work for a certain length of time, at least as long as necessary to establish eligibility for unemployment compensation, and then draw benefits, which in effect raise their hourly wage rate during actual work. This higher rate of pay creates incentives to join the labour force, though the implicit gross pay has to be lowered for the cost of job search both upon entering the labour force and subsequently if the cycle of work and unemployment is to continue. However, it is important to note that persons induced to enter the labour force by this opportunity to increase their hourly rate of pay may be counted as being officially unemployed just like those out of work for cyclical, seasonal, or structural reasons, since in order to protect their eligibility to receive benefits they have every incentive to answer survey enumerators that they are looking for work.

To summarize: the main point of the preceding analysis has been that availability of unemployment benefits creates incentives to increase the consumption of leisure by persons employed and unemployed involuntarily and it creates incentives to join the labour force with the intention of working only temporarily. These incentives are a decreasing function of the cost of finding a job, though for the involuntarily unemployed the marginal cost of leisure does not have to be adjusted in this manner. Whether and how much induced unemployment has been created by these incentives is an empirical question, which we shall attempt to answer in parts II and III of this paper.

Waiting time

The net cost of leisure which a worker can enjoy by drawing unemployment benefits is increased further by the existence of a waiting period between the commencement of unemployment and receipt of the benefits. Historically in Canada, this interval has been nominal for workers laid off involuntarily, but it has been substantial for workers who quit voluntarily or were laid off with cause, such as tardiness or substandard work. In practice, both employers and the administrators of the Canadian unemployment benefit program have some discretion in their documentation and interpretation of evidence in the course of a person's unemployment. There have been periodic crackdowns on 'cheaters' through stricter interpretation of eligibility rules, mostly following public outcries over abuse of the system. The 1972 change in the Canadian laws for the first time made immediately eligible workers who quit voluntarily because 'conditions were intolerable.' This wording gives even more discretionary power to the administrators of the scheme than they had before.

For the purposes of our analysis the most important facts are that the hiatus between the commencement of unemployment and the receipt of benefits increases the cost of leisure and therefore reduces the incentives for induced unemployment created otherwise by the benefit payments, and that this cost is an increasing function of administrators' strictness in the application of eligibility rules under the law. In the empirical parts of our study we have attempted to measure this cost of documentation by the percentage of applicants ruled ineligible for unemployment benefits.

Cost of documentation
Under the Canadian unemployment compensation program, recipients of benefits must periodically produce evidence that they have been searching for work and have been unable to find suitable positions. If such evidence is not forthcoming, a worker becomes ineligible for further benefit payments.

The need for this sort of documentation imposes an added cost on the unemployed worker and further increases the net cost of leisure a person has to incur to take advantage of the opportunities created by the unemployment benefit scheme. This cost is different from and in addition to the genuine cost of job search discussed above.

In principle, the requirement to produce job-search evidence provides the government with the tools to eliminate all opportunities to abuse the unemployment system through the consumption of leisure. By the application of proper standards, workers can be made to behave *as if* they received no benefits. If they do not behave accordingly, they can be made ineligible and the distorting incentives discussed above disappear. However, in practice these objectives probably can never be achieved because of the fundamental problem of cost of information and the inability to know a person's true preferences if he is unwilling to reveal them. To be able to know whether a person has searched for a job with the proper intensity or has turned down a suitable job he would have taken in the absence of the benefits requires that administrators be given operational criteria of 'proper intensity' and 'suitable job' for every individual. While it is possible to make expensive lists of objective indicators of job search and characteristics of occupational suitability, a worker can never be forced to reveal what job he would take and when he would take it in the absence of unemployment benefits. This is the 'free-rider' problem familiar from public finance.

180 / Herbert G. Grubel, Dennis Maki, and Shelley Sax

Setting of criteria that are not too expensive to enforce will do injustice to some workers who are forced into genuinely unsuitable jobs and may increase rather than decrease the labour market inefficiencies the program of benefits was originally designed to relieve. Furthermore, being ordered regularly and frequently into the acceptance of certain jobs by bureaucrats is a practice that the Canadian public would probably consider to be an intolerable interference with their personal freedom.

Because of these costs and difficulties associated with the construction and enforcement of criteria for the evaluation of proper job search, it is highly likely that workers will always find ways to enjoy the leisure opportunities brought about by the availability of unemployment benefits. However, few workers tend to 'cheat' outright in the sense of spending long periods fishing or skiing. The majority of workers tend to consider it to be their right, not a privilege, as taxpayers and as contributors of unemployment insurance premiums to behave in the way the benefits permit them to. As individuals, they have no incentives to behave as if they did not receive these benefits. Consequently, we find that the availability of unemployment compensation induces workers to quit jobs more readily and set higher standards of acceptability on a new job, to search with less intensity, and to decrease their willingness to incur the cost and troubles of retraining for new skills while at all times producing adequate evidence of job-search activity to the administrators of the unemployment benefit scheme. Administrators of the unemployment scheme also have considerable discretion in enforcement of the rules of job-search documentation. In the empirical part of our study we assume that the rate at which applicants are ruled ineligible for benefits reflects discretionary changes in the application of these rules and therefore the costs of job-search documentation.

Conclusion

The preceding analysis leads to the important conclusion that the introduction of an unemployment benefit scheme alters the relative cost of work and leisure net of the costs of job search, waiting period, and documentation of search for Canadian workers. The benefits thus create incentives for the average worker to increase his consumption of leisure, not as a matter of cheating but as a rational response to the lowered price of a good available to him. How much unemployment has been induced in Canada by the compensation plan is an empirical question to be considered in the next part of this paper. Our theoretical considerations suggest that induced unemployment is an increasing function of the ratio of benefits to income from work (R) and a decreasing function of the costs of job search, waiting period, and documentation of search, where the latter two influences are measured by the rate at which applicants for benefits are ruled ineligible.

II / THE SPECIFICATION OF THE MODEL

As a result of our theoretical analysis, we hypothesize that the traditional classification of unemployment into structural (SU), cyclical (CU), and seasonal (TU)[6] should be amended to read

$$U = f(\text{SU, CU, TU, IU}), \tag{1}$$

where IU is induced unemployment in the sense defined in part I and arises from increased unemployment in all three traditional forms.

The basic assumptions underlying our econometric model are that, through time, structural unemployment is a constant that changes only slowly, cyclical unemployment is functionally related to an index of economic instability such as the growth rate of GNP, seasonal unemployment is zero because of the use of annual data,[7] and induced unemployment is an increasing function of the ratio of unemployment benefits to income R in our analysis in part I and a decreasing function of the cost of waiting and job-search documentation.

In our econometric estimation we used data covering the period 1953–72. The year 1953 was the first normal one after the economic upheavals following the second world war and the Korean war, and some time series for variables used in the study were unavailable on a consistent basis for preceding years. At the time of writing, 1973 data were not available.

Table 1 shows the ratio of unemployment compensation benefits to average weekly wages ($R = \text{UCB/AWW}$) for the years considered here. As can be seen, there has been a slight downward trend in the ratio in the period 1953–71. The mean was 0.29 for the period as a whole, and the jump from a value of 0.29 in 1971 to 0.41 in 1972 is noteworthy.

6 While there is sufficient concensus regarding concepts among the various writers on the subject to justify using the term 'traditional theory,' there is certainly no concensus on terminology. Our category 'structural' corresponds to Peitchinis's categories 'structural, frictional and technological' or to what Ostry and Zaidi term 'non-demand deficient' unemployment; see Peitchinis (1970, 249–59) and Ostry and Zaidi (1972, 129–32).

7 We have used annual data in order to avoid the need to deal with seasonal influences on unemployment. Proper consideration of seasonal factors would have necessitated specification of a larger econometric model with many complications which would have tended to distract from the main points of this paper. Theoretically, differences in the strength of seasonal influences from year to year should influence average annual rates of unemployment. This effect is probably negligibly small, and in our analysis we have, in effect, assumed it to be zero. Another point related to seasonal unemployment is that the availability of benefits indirectly permits marginal seasonal employers to stay in business because they can pay a wage rate lower than that necessary if seasonal employment represented the only source of income for the workers. Consequently, unemployment compensation for seasonally employed labour contributes to structural unemployment in a way not reflected in our model. We owe this last point to Sylvia Ostry.

182 / Herbert G. Grubel, Dennis Maki, and Shelley Sax

TABLE 1

Annual ratios of unemployment compensation benefits
to average weekly wages in Canada

Year	UCB/AWW	Year	UCB/AWW	Year	UCB/AWW
1953	0.31	1960	0.29	1967	0.25
1954	0.31	1961	0.30	1968	0.24
1955	0.30	1962	0.30	1969	0.27
1956	0.29	1963	0.29	1970	0.28
1957	0.31	1964	0.28	1971	0.29
1958	0.30	1965	0.27	1972	0.41
1959	0.29	1966	0.25		

See Table 2.

A four-equation model was employed. It was estimated using two-stage least squares to deal with overidentification and simultaneous equation bias.[8]

In Table 2 we provide detailed information on the sources and derivation of the data used in the study and present the best results of a set of experiments with different specifications of the model, in the sense of significance of the *t*-values and correctness of the theoretically predicted signs of coefficients. The multiple correlation coefficients and Durbin-Watson statistics are reported, but the reader is cautioned that they are of ambiguous interpretation when calculated from a two-stage regression.

Specification of the equations
In equation (1) of Table 2 we show that the unemployment rate, as measured by the *Monthly Labour Force Survey*, in logarithmic form (to be explained below) is an increasing function of the ratio UCB/AWW, as hypothesized, and a decreasing function of the percentage change in current-dollar gross national product (PCGNP) and the same variable lagged one period (PCGNP-1). The changes in GNP are designed to capture the changes in unemployment due to cyclical factors. Since some cyclical unemployment may be of very long duration, the lagged change in GNP variable was included along with the current one. The coefficients have the correct sign since we expect cyclical unemployment to be a decreasing function of the rate of growth in GNP during the current and preceding period.

Into equation (1) we added male and female labour-force participation rates (MLFPR and FLFPR respectively) to account for the influence on unem-

8 The technique is standard and described in Wonnacott and Wonnacott (1970, chap. 19). It involves the first stage regression of each endogenous variable on all exogenous variables. Then, the calculated magnitudes of the dependent variables in the equation were used as instruments for the respective endogenous variables whenever the latter appeared on the right-hand side of the structural equations reported in Table 2.

TABLE 2

The model

$$\ln U = -15.15 + 2.35 \frac{\text{UCB}}{\text{AWW}} - 0.03\,\text{PCGNP} - 0.05\,\text{PCGNP}{-}1 + 0.12\,\text{FLFPR}$$
$$\quad (2.71)\ (2.96) \qquad (4.32) \qquad\qquad (7.07) \qquad\qquad\quad (3.85)$$
$$+ 0.17\,\text{MLFPR} - 0.02\,\text{INEL.}\quad\text{(I)}$$
$$(2.76) \qquad\quad (4.26)$$
$$R^2 = 0.90,\ \text{DW} = 2.14$$

$$\frac{\text{UCB}}{\text{AWW}} = 0.39 - 0.001\,U - 0.002\,O/\text{MH} + 0.003\,\text{MAXBEN.}\qquad\qquad\text{(II)}$$
$$(16.16)\ (0.40) \qquad (7.92) \qquad\quad (8.59)$$
$$R^2 = 0.84,\ \text{DW} = 2.36$$

$$\text{FLFPR} = -25.22 - 0.41\,U + 0.22\,\text{AWW}{-}1 + 2.27\,(\text{F40-9}).\qquad\text{(III)}$$
$$(5.29)\ (4.15) \quad (36.36) \qquad\quad (8.54)$$
$$R^2 = 0.99,\ \text{DW} = 1.18$$

$$\text{MLFPR} = 21.93 - 0.40\,U + 0.03\,\text{AWW}{-}1 + 1.45(\text{M25-44}).\qquad\text{(IV)}$$
$$(3.20)\ (4.22) \quad (2.20) \qquad\quad (9.42)$$
$$R^2 = 0.98,\ \text{DW} = 1.20$$

$$\ln U = -8.09 + 2.54 \frac{\text{UCB}}{\text{AWW}} - 0.04\,\text{PCGNP} - 0.05\,\text{PCGNP}{-}1 + 0.08\,\text{FLFPR}$$
$$(1.88)\ (3.89) \qquad (5.01) \qquad\qquad (7.40) \qquad\qquad\quad (3.37)$$
$$+ 0.09\,\text{MLFPR} - 0.02\,\text{INEL.}\quad\text{(Ia)}$$
$$(1.96) \qquad\quad (4.65)$$
$$R^2 = 0.92,\ \text{DW} = 2.29$$

NOTE: t-values in parentheses.
SOURCES: All data are from Statistics Canada publications, noted here by catalogue number and page; see list of references for full citation. U – (11-505), 48, for 1953-71, and (11-003), 42, for 1972; GNP – (11-505), 14, for 1952-68, and (11-003), 14, for 1969-72; UCB – amount of benefit paid divided by number of weeks compensated, from (11-505), 50, for 1953-71 and (11-003), 48, for 1972; AWW – (11-505), 58, for 1953-71, and (11-003), 52, for 1972. AWW reported values for 1953-6 were multiplied by 1.0004 to adjust for differences between data based on the 1948 and 1960 Standard Industrial Classifications. FLFPR and MLFPR – (71-201), 158; INEL – computed as noted in text from (73-001), various issues; O/MH – for Commercial Industries, (14-201), 15, for 1953-60, the values for 1961-1972 being computed by taking the ratio of the output index from (61-005), 9 and 17, to the index of man-hours from (11-001), 3; MAXBEN – calculated from information in (73-201), various issues, as discussed in text (see Table 4 for values used); (F40-9) and (M25-44) – calculated from (91-512), 42-60, for 1953-71 and (91-202), 2, for 1972.

ployment of changes in these variables. Theoretically, the unemployment rate should be an increasing function of these labour-force participation rates on the ground that entries into the labour force increase supply and, ceteris paribus, therefore unemployment. The signs of the coefficients are positive, as hypothesized. Furthermore, the two variables capture the effect of the secular decline and rise in male and female labour-force participation rates respectively. The variables thus reflect a structural shift in labour supply during the period. Below, in connection with equation (III) and (IV) we will discuss arguments that unemployment itself influences participation rates.

The final variable in equation (I) is INEL, which is designed to capture

184 / Herbert G. Grubel, Dennis Maki, and Shelley Sax

TABLE 3

Percentage of new and renewal claims for
unemployment insurance benefits which
were ruled ineligible

Year	Percentage	Year	Percentage
1953	27.6	1963	20.2
1954	25.3	1964	21.5
1955	31.6	1965	25.1
1956	32.5	1966	26.9
1957	17.1	1967	25.6
1958	15.4	1968	25.6
1959	17.4	1969	23.1
1960	16.6	1970	22.9
1961	18.0	1971	27.2
1962	19.8	1972	33.6

SOURCE: see Table 2.

the effect on the rate of unemployment of the enforcement of unemployment benefit eligibility rules. The variable was introduced for the theoretical reasons concerning the cost of waiting and job-search documentation discussed above. It is equal to the percentage of new and renewal claims for unemployment benefits which are ruled ineligible during the period, adjusted for cyclical variation. The raw data, unadjusted for cyclical variations, are shown in Table 3.

As can be seen, the variable is cyclically unstable, showing the highest rejection rates during boom years and the lowest during cyclical troughs. For this reason, inclusion of the variable in its original form causes serious problems of multicollinearity with the cyclical variables PCGNP and PCGNP-1. We therefore regressed the data in Table 3 on these two cyclical variables and derived the variable INEL as the residuals from that regression. Therefore, the variable INEL as used in equation (I) is orthogonal to PCGNP and PCGNP-1. It represents discretionary changes in the enforcement of eligibility rules net of those that have taken place cyclically over the period under consideration.

Our theoretical considerations suggest that when the authorities tighten eligibility rules and increase the rate of rejection of applicants, the cost of leisure increases, and therefore, ceteris paribus, the rate of unemployment declines. This negative functional relationship between unemployment and the variable INEL is found in equation (I).

The use of the logarithmic form of the dependent variable U in equation (I) requires the following comment. This specification implies that the different classes of unemployment outlined in equation (1) in the text are related to each other not in additive form, but as follows:

$$U = e^{SU} \cdot e^{CU} \cdot e^{IU}. \tag{2}$$

In the preceding paragraphs we have justified the variables used in the estimation of equation (2); moreover, one of the determinants of IU is UCB/AWW. Consequently, the relevant part of equation (2) can be written as

$$\ln U = B(\text{UCB}/\text{AWW}) + ... \tag{3}$$

so that

$$\partial U/\partial(\text{UCB}/\text{AWW}) = BU. \tag{4}$$

We can see from this equation that the semi-log specification of the basic equation implies that the change of the unemployment rate with respect to the benefit-wage variable is a function of the unemployment rate, which itself consists of structural and cyclical unemployment. This implication is consistent with our theoretical analysis, which suggests that induced unemployment is drawn from the changed behaviour of workers who are structurally and cyclically unemployed and that unemployment itself, through its effect on the cost of job search, influences the net incentives for the consumption of leisure created by the benefits alone.

Turning now to equation (II) in Table 2, we note that it was included in the model in order to take account of the fact that UCB/AWW may itself be an increasing function of the rate of unemployment U for the following reasons. First, the average skill level and past earnings of the unemployed increases with the level of unemployment, since workers with low skills and seniority are laid off first. Consequently, average benefits based on past earnings should be an increasing function of unemployment. Second, the difficulty of finding part-time work increases with the unemployment level. Since part-time earnings decrease average weekly benefits received by the unemployed, the average should rise with the reduced availability of part-time work. The coefficient of U in equation (II) turns out, however, to be insignificant.

The second variable in equation (II) is output per man-hour (O/MH). It was included in order to capture the well known price-theoretic properties that wage levels are directly related to labour productivity for which output per man-hour is a proxy. Since benefit levels are related to the preceding period's wages, when output per man-hour is rising, current average wages increase and the ratio UCB/AWW is lowered. For this reason, the coefficient associated with O/MH has the expected negative sign.

The third variable in equation (II) is the maximum level of benefits an unemployed worker can receive under the current provisions of the law (MAXBEN), and it is, furthermore, a proxy for the entire benefit structure in existence. We considered it useful to include this variable since in Canada there always are a number of unemployed persons whose wages would have entitled them to higher absolute benefits than the law permitted, given that benefits are a certain, stipulated percentage of past earnings. Consequently, whenever the absolute maximum benefits increase, average compensation

186 / Herbert G. Grubel, Dennis Maki, and Shelley Sax

TABLE 4

Values of MAXBEN (dollars per week)

Year	MAXBEN	Year	MAXBEN
1953	24.00	1963	36.00
1954	24.00	1964	36.00
1955	25.50	1965	36.00
1956	30.00	1966	36.00
1957	30.00	1967	36.00
1958	30.00	1968	45.92
1959	32.00	1969	53.00
1960	36.00	1970	53.00
1961	36.00	1971	76.50
1962	36.00	1972	100.00

SOURCE: see Table 2.

rises and the ratio UCB/AWW goes up. Therefore, the sign of the coefficient associated with MAXBEN should be positive, as is shown in equation (II) of Table 2. Since MAXBEN was estimated by linear interpolation for those years when statutory benefits changed during the year, the actual values used in regression are shown in Table 4.

In equations (III) and (IV) in Table 2 we intended to capture the well known fact that unemployment tends to discourage labour force participation, while higher wages with some lag tend to encourage it.[9] These propositions are supported by the negative sign of the unemployment coefficients and the positive sign of the lagged wage coefficients in both equations. In equation (III) we included as a variable the proportion of females aged fourteen and over who are in the age group forty to forty-nine years (F40–9), since women in this age group tend to have a high participation rate, increasing markedly in the period of analysis. The positive sign and high *t*-value of the coefficient justifies this proxy for structural changes on the supply side of the female labour market. Analogous reasoning applies to the inclusion of the variable representing the proportion of the male population aged fourteen and over which is in the age group twenty-five to forty-four years (M25–44), which also has a positive coefficient in equation (IV).[10]

As can be seen from Table 2, all regression coefficients are different from zero at the 5 per cent level of significance, except for the coefficient of *U* in

9 The available evidence on the relationship between unemployment and labour-force participation of women is contradictory. See Officer and Andersen (1969), Proulx (1969), and Swidinsky (1970). Our results imply that during the period under consideration in Canada, participation was a decreasing function of unemployment for both males and females.
10 Attempts to include the benefit wage ratio, UCB/AWW, in equations III and IV as an additional explanatory variable did not produce statistically significant coefficients and created multicollinearity problems.

equation (II). At the bottom of Table 2 we give equation (Ia), which has been estimated by ordinary least squares. As can be seen, the signs and *t*-values of the independent variables closely resemble those found in equation (I). The coefficient of the most important variable UCB/AWW is slightly larger (2.54) in equation (Ia) than in equation (I), (2.35). This similarity of the results suggests that simultaneous equation bias in the one-equation model is in fact not serious. However, this fact could be established only by the approach used here, and because the coefficients are different we will use the results from the more sophisticated model in the following section.

We re-estimated equations I to IV and Ia, dropping the 1972 observation to check for stability of coefficient estimates. The same patterns of significance shown in Table 2 were obtained for the shorter period. The coefficient of UCB/AWW increased from 2.34 to 3.86, but the coefficient from each equation is easily within the 95 per cent confidence interval for the coefficient estimated from the other. Applying the statistical test for a structural shift suggested by Johnston (1972, 207) to equation (Ia) yields an $F = 2.10$, so the hypothesis of stability cannot be refuted at the 0.05 level. Finally, predicting the unemployment rate for 1972 using the coefficients estimated on the period 1953–71 and actual 1972 values for all variables yields 8.8 per cent. The model in Table 2 predicts 6.7 per cent, also an overestimate of the actual 6.3 per cent.

III / INTERPRETATION OF THE EMPIRICAL RESULTS

In the light of the theoretical and policy problems raised in part I, the most important empirical results are that the elasticity of the unemployment rate with respect to the ratio of benefits to wages, measured at the point of means, is 0.69. This implies that if in 1972 the UCB/AWW and INEL variables had both been at their mean values over the period 1953–70, ceteris paribus, the unemployment rate would have been 5.5 per cent instead of the 6.3 per cent actually observed in 1972.[11] Thus, our point estimate of the effect of the new unemployment insurance legislation that took effect in mid-1971 is that it has raised the reported rate of unemployment by 0.8 percentage points.

This is, of course, not a measure of the magnitude of induced unemployment but merely of a change in that magnitude. Since our data do not go back to a period when UCB was zero, it is very hazardous to use the model to forecast what would have happened if it were zero, so we adopt a more conservative approach. The Economic Council of Canada (1970, 18–19) calculated potential gross national product on the basis of an unemployment rate of 3.8 per cent, performance which is approximated by the average of

---

11 The ceteris paribus assumption as used here includes the assumption that any change in PCGNP caused by the hypothetical change in unemployment insurance benefit level was offset by other exogenous factors.

188 / Herbert G. Grubel, Dennis Maki, and Shelley Sax

the years 1955 and 1956. Hence we calculate our estimate of induced unemployment in 1972 by taking the difference between the actual rate and the rate which our model predicts would have occurred if UCB/AWW and INEL had been at their 1955–6 average values. The resulting difference is 1.4 percentage points, i.e. in 1972 we estimate induced unemployment to be 22 per cent of total unemployment by this method.

In general, we consider the econometric model and results presented here to be exploratory rather than definitive. There are many ways in which the model can be refined and extended. In the process, many different estimates of the crucial elasticities will be generated. However, as is well known from experience with other econometric models, it will probably be extremely difficult to reach convergence of results on one unique figure and to reach concensus among economists about the best estimate. Yet, our theoretical and empirical work have convinced us that the results presented here are of sufficient robustness and reliability to warrant the general policy conclusions to be discussed next.

IV / POLICY IMPLICATIONS

Our policy conclusions are as follows. First, and foremost, it appears to us that the appropriateness of the full-employment target of 4 to 4.5 per cent unemployment needs to be re-evaluated. This target was set at a time when unemployment benefits were much lower and the welfare costs of unemployment to individuals out of work were higher than they are today. It seems to us that in the quest for the minimization of the welfare costs associated with business cycles in capitalist societies, low unemployment and high insurance benefits are substitutes, not complements as is widely believed. It is also worth noting that the value of such a re-evaluation of full employment targets is independent of any judgment about the validity of the Phillips-curve concept in either the long or short run. Even if the critics of the concept should be correct and there is no inflation employment tradeoff, there is still value in knowing the functional relationship between the natural rate of unemployment[12] and unemployment benefit levels.

Second, our considerations lead us to believe that there must be a socially optimum level of unemployment benefits relative to the wages available from work. Higher benefits increase the welfare of the insured but cause losses in society's aggregate output of market goods because of the induced unemployment. Consequently, there must be a level of benefits at which equality of the gains and losses at the margin assures optimality. The choices of optimum benefits and of a full employment target are interdependent. Value judgments are necessary to decide upon the proper level of benefits, but the

12 For a discussion of the controversy over the Phillips curve and the natural rate of unemployment, see Friedman (1968).

quality of these judgments should be improved by the availability of the kind of information presented here. Our theoretical and empirical analysis suggests the need for a renewal of public discussion of socially optimal full employment targets and of the ratio of unemployment benefits to wages.

Third, because of the existence of maximum unemployment benefits, the ratio of benefits to earnings from work tends to be higher for low-paying than for well-paying occupations. Therefore, ceteris paribus, incentives for induced unemployment are higher in low-wage than in high-wage occupations. This fact is consistent with the more frequent coexistence of unemployment and job vacancies in low-paid than in high-paid occupations. To solve this problem, government programs for retraining and relocation of workers and for increasing the efficiency of labour markets have been initiated. Because such programs decrease the availability of low-skilled labor, the market will react by forcing up the prices of the goods and services requiring such labour. Our analysis suggests that the upgrading of skills and jobs will have the desired effect of reducing induced unemployment only if unemployment insurance benefits are not raised simultaneously, as has been the case traditionally to adjust benefits to over-all standards of living. Thus, the levels of optimum public expenditures on labour force retraining and the perfection of labour markets are seen to be interdependent with the choices of full employment targets and the optimum level of insurance benefits relative to wages.

Fourth, one way of looking at the cause of the induced unemployment is to consider that under the current system the marginal tax rates on work are extremely high in the sense that, when switching from unemployment benefits to work, employment is rewarded by only the small amount of extra income which represents the difference between the unemployment insurance benefits and wages. This phenomenon has been noted widely in connection with other welfare programs and has led to the proposals for minimum guaranteed incomes and the negative income tax. Our analysis implies that such programs would also have beneficial effects on induced unemployment.

The analysis of this paper has some interesting implications for a number of problems and phenomena in today's world that we can only sketch briefly here. First, periodic crackdowns on unemployment insurance 'cheaters,' characterize such insurance schemes and tend to occur whenever public outrage over the unexpected high cost of the program reaches a peak, normally around crucial points in the budgetary process. Our analysis implies that we are not dealing with cheaters but with individuals who are acting rationally in response to the lowered price of leisure. Therefore, it will always be expensive both administratively and in terms of labour market efficiency and individual freedom of choice, to attempt to use bureaucratic means to make people behave as if the price of the good they are consuming were different from what it is. The cause of these problems is that people cannot be

190 / Herbert G. Grubel, Dennis Maki, and Shelley Sax

made to reveal their true preferences, and the enforcement of excessively detailed eligibility rules will lead to many arbitrary decisions, will be resisted by the public, and will tend to cost more than it saves in expenditures. However, there is also clearly an optimum level of enforcement of eligibility rules, which may or may not have been reached on the average in Canada in recent years. Work on the theoretical definition and empirical specification of such an optimum level of enforcement seems to be required urgently.

Finally, it might be interesting to use the analytical framework of the present paper to explain the observed and puzzling differences in average unemployment rates among different industrial countries at a moment in time through history and among different regions within the same countries. Related to this question of international differences in average unemployment rates is the prevalence of foreign workers in many countries of western Europe with low unemployment rates. We might hypothesize that foreign workers are not induced to accept unemployment by high insurance benefits because of the threat of depatriation if they do not hold a job, while native workers are induced by unemployment benefits to be unemployed rather than work for low pay. This fact has led to the peculiar and other wise puzzling situation that with the stock of foreign workers representing about 30 per cent of the total, the British inflow of foreign workers continues, while at the same time unemployment among native workers is at a relatively high level (United Kingdom, Department of Employment and Productivity, 1972).

REFERENCES

Arndt, H.W. (1973) 'Inflation: new policy prescriptions.' *Australian Economic Review* 3, 41–8
Cain, G. and H. Watts (1973) *Income Maintenance and Labor Supply.* Institute for Research on Poverty Monograph Series (Chicago: Markham/Rand McNally)
Chapin, G. (1971) 'Unemployment insurance, job search, and the demand for leisure.' *Western Economic Journal* 9, 102–7
Economic Council of Canada (1970) *Performance and Potential: Mid-1950s to Mid-1970s* (Ottawa)
Feldstein, M.S. (1972) 'Lowering the permanent rate of unemployment.' Harvard Institute of Economic Research, Discussion Paper 259
Friedman, M. (1968) 'The role of monetary policy.' *American Economic Review* 58, 1–17
Green, C. (1973) 'The impact of unemployment insurance on the unemployment rate.' (mimeo, McGill University)
Grubel, H. and D. Maki (1974) 'The effect of unemployment benefits on us unemployment rates.' Simon Fraser University Discussion Paper 74-2-1
Johnston, J. (1972) *Econometric Methods* 2d ed. (Toronto: McGraw-Hill)
OECD (1972) *Canada.* Economic Surveys, December
Officer, L.H. and P.R. Andersen (1969) 'Labour force participation in Canada.' This JOURNAL 2, 278–87

Ostry, S. and M. Zaidi (1972) *Labour Economics in Canada* (Toronto: Macmillan)

Peitchinis, S. (1970) *Canadian Labour Economics* (Toronto: McGraw-Hill)

Phelps, E. *et al* (1970) *Microeconomic Foundations of Employment and Inflation Theory* (New York: Norton)

Proulx, P.-P. (1969) 'La variabilité cyclique des taux de participation à la main-d'œuvre au Canada.' This JOURNAL 2, 268–77

Statistics Canada (73–201) *Benefit Periods Established and Terminated Under the Unemployment Insurance Act* (Ottawa) various issues

Statistics Canada [Dominion Bureau of Statistics] (14–201, 1970) *Aggregate Productivity Trends, 1946–1968* (Ottawa)

Statistics Canada (11-505, 1972) *Canadian Statistical Review: Historial Summary 1970* (Ottawa)

Statistics Canada (11-003, 1973) *Canadian Statistical Review* August (Ottawa)

Statistics Canada (11-001, 1973) *Daily* June 8 (Ottawa)

Statistics Canada (91-202, 1973) *Estimated Population by Sex and Age Group, for Canada and Provinces, June 1, 1972* (Ottawa)

Statistics Canada (61-005, 1973) *Indexes of Real Domestic Product by Industry.* 1973 Supplement (Ottawa)

Statistics Canada (91-512, 1973) *Population 1921–1971* (Ottawa)

Statistics Canada (71-201, 1973) *Seasonally Adjusted Labour Force Statistics: January 1953–December 1972* (Ottawa)

Statistics Canada [Dominion Bureau of Statistics] (73–001) *Statistical Report on the Operation of the Unemployment Insurance Act* (Ottawa) various issues

Swidinsky, R. (1970) 'A note on labour-force participation and unemployment.' This JOURNAL 3, 146–51

United Kingdom, Department of Employment and Productivity (1972) *Employment and Productivity Gazette* (London)

Wonnacott, P. and R. Wonnacott (1970) *Econometrics* (New York: Wiley)

[3]

The Effects of Unemployment Benefits
on U.S. Unemployment Rates

By

Herbert G. Grubel and Dennis R. Maki

Contents: Introduction. — I. The Theoretical Model: 1. Voluntary Unemployment, Job Search, Evidence and Eligibility; 2. Involuntary Unemployment and Leisure; 3. Summary and Conclusions of the Models; 4. Some Real World Phenomena and the Model. — II. Econometric Estimates: 1. Time-Series Analysis; 2. Cross-Section Analysis. — III. Conclusions and Policy Implications.

Introduction

In this paper we present a theoretical model and empirical evidence concerning changes in reported aggregate U.S. unemployment induced by unemployment insurance benefits[1]. The theoretical model analyzes the manner in which unemployment benefits alter the income-leisure opportunity locus of an "average" worker. The simplest version of the

---

Remark: We acknowledge helpful comments on an earlier draft of this paper made by A. Rees, H. C. Lewis, F. Brechling, A. Zellner, and participants at seminars at the University of British Columbia, Vancouver, B. C., Northwestern University, Evanston, Ill., and the University of Chicago.

[1] There is some literature on this subject, though the theoretical and empirical approach developed here has not been used before. See Gene Chapin, "Unemployment Insurance, Job Search, and the Demand for Leisure", *Western Economic Journal*, Vol. 9, Salt Lake City, 1971, pp. 102sqq. — Martin S. Feldstein, *Lowering the Permanent Rate of Unemployment*, Harvard Institute of Economic Research, Discussion Paper, 259, Cambridge, Mass., 1972. — C. Green, *The Impact of Unemployment Insurance on the Unemployment Rate*, McGill University, Montreal, P. Q., 1973, mimeo. — Damodar Gujarti, "The Behavior of Unemployment and Unfilled Vacancies", *The Economic Journal*, Vol. 82, London, 1972, pp. 195sqq. — *Idem*, "A Reply to Mr. Taylor", *ibid.*, pp. 1365sqq. — Arlene Holen and Stanley Horowitz, "Partial Unemployment Insurance Benefits and the Extent of Partial Unemployment", *The Journal of Human Resources*, Vol. 9, Madison, Wisc., 1974, pp. 420sqq. — *Idem*, "The Effect of Unemployment Insurance and Eligibility Enforcement on Unemployment", *The Journal of Law and Economics*, Vol. 17, Chicago, Ill., 1974, pp. 403sqq. — J. B. Komisar, *Unemployment Compensation and the Rate of Unemployment*, Columbia University, New York, 1968, unpubl. diss. — C. A. Lininger, *Unemployment Benefits and Duration*, University of Chicago, 1962, unpubl. diss. — D. I. MacKay and G. L. Reid, "Redundancy, Unemployment and Manpower Policy", *The Economic Journal*, Vol. 82, 1972, pp. 1256sqq. — Raymond Munts, "Partial Benefit Schedules in Unemployment Insurance: Their Effect on Work Incentive", *The Journal of Human Resources*, Vol. 5, 1970, pp. 160sqq. — R. M. Schmidt, *The Theory of Search and Duration of Unemployment*, The Graduate School of

model assumes job search costs to be zero and the absence of involuntary unemployment. We then extend the model to include job-search costs and genuine structural or cyclical unemployment. The theoretical analysis accomplishes two important tasks. First, it shows how institutional safeguards in the unemployment insurance programs of the United States in principle can prevent workers from consuming added amounts of leisure, the price of which is lowered by the program itself, but that in practice the cost of preventing all increased consumption of leisure through institutional safeguards is very high and not practicable. Second, the theoretical model suggests what variables should be included in the empirical analysis of the determinants of the unemployment rate, what form the variables should take and what signs the regression coefficients of these variables can be expected to have.

In the empirical parts of this paper we present first a number of well-known empirical phenomena which are consistent with our theoretical model. The main empirical analysis consists of measurements of the elasticity of the reported U.S. unemployment rate with respect to changes in the ratio of unemployment benefit payments to average weekly wages, first in a time-series analysis covering the period 1951—1972 and second, in a cross-section study of the 48 contiguous U.S. states in the year 1971. The paper closes with a discussion of the implications our findings have for the determination of the U.S. target level of unemployment, the future level of insurance benefits and the measurement of the output gap. Finally we discuss some areas for future research which have been suggested by our findings.

I. The Theoretical Model

Our basic model of how the introduction of unemployment insurance influences the choice between work and leisure of an average worker in the sense of the mean characteristics of the total labor force is summarized in Figure 1. The number of days per period are measured along the horizontal axis and income per period along the vertical. The traditional leisure-income trade-off is XY, the slope of which is determined by the individual's wage rate. Our average worker is assumed to have a potential

Management, University of Rochester, Working Paper Series, No. 7317, 1973. — Jim Taylor, "The Behaviour of Unemployment and Unfilled Vacancies: Great Britain, 1958—71, An Alternative View", *The Economic Journal*, Vol. 82, 1972, pp. 1352sqq. — The basic model presented in this paper has also been applied to Canada by Herbert G. Grubel, Dennis Maki, and Shelley Sax, "Real and Insurance-Induced Unemployment in Canada", *The Canadian Journal of Economics*, Vol. 8, Toronto, 1975, pp. 174sqq.; and to Great Britain by Z. A. Spindler and Dennis Maki, "The Effect of Unemployment Compensation on the Rate of Unemployment in Great Britain", *Oxford Economic Papers*, N.S., Vol. 27, 1975, pp. 440sqq.

income of OY if he takes no leisure at all during the period. In the context
of our analysis it is convenient to choose the number of days in the period
according to the sum of the minimum working periods required to establish
rights for unemployment compensation benefits plus the maximum duration of the benefit payments under the specific regulations of the state in
which the worker resides plus the number of paid holidays and weekends
normally found in this period. His preferences reflected by the indifference
map I_0—I_2 makes him choose OY_0 income and OX_0 days of leisure in
initial equilibrium before the availability of unemployment insurance.
The days of leisure OX_0 are assumed to be the number of weekend, legal
and paid holidays the individual spends in non-income earning activities.

Let us now consider that the government introduces an unemployment
compensation plan which is financed out of a general government budget
surplus so that the XY locus is not shifted by increased personal taxation.
For expositional ease we introduce the following three important assumptions to be dropped below. First, the worker can obtain benefits immediately upon being out of work and whether he quits voluntarily, has himself
dismissed through misconduct or is involuntarily unemployed. Second,
the worker does not have to engage in and document job-search activities
to receive benefits. Third, job-search costs are zero and the worker can
obtain employment at his previous wage the instant he wants it. Under
these assumptions, the introduction of the unemployment benefit scheme
changes his leisure-income opportunity locus from the original XY to
YE_0ACX in Figure 1.

Figure 1 — *Unemployment Insurance and the Work-Leisure Frontier*

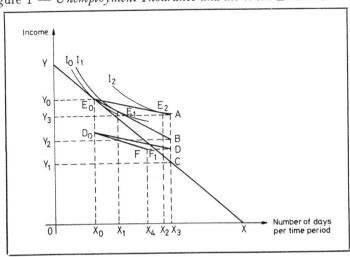

Two analytically important features of the unemployment compensation plan are reflected in the shape of the frontier as follows. First, the slope of the line E_0A relative to that of XY measures the ratio of compensation benefits to income from employment per time period. Thus, without the benefit plan X_0X_3 leisure costs Y_0Y_1 income. With the plan it costs only Y_0Y_3. The ratio important for our empirical studies below is equal to $Y_3Y_1/Y_0Y_1 = R$, the ratio of unemployment benefits to earnings from work. Second, the maximum length over which unemployment benefits are available is reflected in the horizontal length of the line E_0A. In Figure 1 the maximum is X_0X_3.

From the preceding analysis it follows that, ceteris paribus, a ratio of benefits to income from work lower than Y_3Y_1/Y_0Y_1, say such as Y_2Y_1/Y_0Y_1 in Figure 1, results in the leisure income trade-off locus YE_0BCX.

In this simple version of our model it follows that if leisure is a normal good, the introduction of the unemployment compensation scheme induces the average worker to consume added amounts of leisure per time period. The quantity consumed is an increasing function of the ratio of benefits to income from employment. All this can readily be seen from Figure 1 where the equilibrium relationships are: at E_0, $R_0 = 0$; at E_1, $R_1 = Y_2 Y_1/Y_0 Y_1$; $X_1 = OX_1$ and at E_2, $R_2 = Y_3 Y_1/Y_0 Y_1$; $X_2 = OX_2$, where $R_0 < R_1 < R_2$ and $OX_0 < OX_1 < OX_2$. In the context of the present model we shall call "induced unemployment" the increased amounts of leisure consumed by workers as a result of the introduction of an unemployment benefit plan. This definition of induced unemployment seems appropriate since the workers must register as unemployed to receive the assistance and since they are likely to report to survey enumerators that they are unemployed and seeking work in order to protect their eligibility.

The model of Figure 1 can also be used to show how the introduction of the unemployment insurance program may induce persons to join the labor force and then become unemployed. For this purpose consider a worker, whose opportunity locus is described by the line YX in Figure 1, in analogy with the preceding model. But in contrast with the worker analyzed before the present one is assumed to be in equilibrium at point X, or at zero days of work and income. We do not show the indifference curve representing this situation to keep Figure 1 simple. In the real world, such a case may describe a housewife, teenager or retired person, where tastes and wage rate are such as to make leisure preferable to working.

Now consider that the government introduces an unemployment insurance scheme which requires a minimum of $X_3 X$ days of work to establish eligibility for the receipt of $X_0 X_3$ days of benefits at the rate

Herbert G. Grubel and Dennis R. Maki

given by the slope of the curve E_0 A relative to that of YX in Figure 1. Consequently, the person's opportunity locus becomes YE_0 ACX and it is possible that an indifference curve higher than the one going through X goes through point A. Under these conditions the person originally not in the labor force is induced to join the labor force, to work X_3 X days, draw $X_0 X_3$ days of benefits and in consequence enjoys a rate of pay per day worked equal to the slope of the line connecting points XA (not shown in Figure 1), higher than the daily wage rate available in the absence of an unemployment insurance program. Important for our purposes of analysis is the fact that the insurance program may induce workers to join the labor force and to become voluntarily unemployed because the program raises the effective wage rate for days worked.

The preceding example can readily be modified to explain how unemployment insurance programs lead to the subsidization of seasonal industries and increased seasonal unemployment. For this purpose consider that a worker, say a fisherman in New England, would be at point X in Figure 1 in the absence of unemployment benefits. This position indicates that at the rate of pay offered him he would not be willing to work as a fisherman, but would be idle, or, in an extension of the model, work in another industry or migrate. However, given the length of the fishing season X_3 X and the availability of subsequent unemployment benefits as in the preceding case, his opportunity locus becomes YE_0 ACX and he is induced to stay in the fishing industry by moving to point A in Figure 1. He may not accept non-seasonal employment, even if it pays a higher wage rate than fishing because including the unemployment benefits the wage rate *per hour worked* in fishing may be higher than the wage rate from working in the next best job without unemployment compensation. Employers face reduced incentives to make their industry less seasonal. In effect under these conditions, the unemployment benefit payments amount to a subsidy from other industries to fishing[1]. For our purposes of analysis again the most important result of this analysis is that the unemployment benefits available to workers in industries with seasonal fluctuations in employment raise the recorded average unemployment rate during the year above what it would be without the benefits.

1. Voluntary Unemployment, Job Search, Evidence and Eligibility

Under most U.S. state unemployment schemes persons who quit a job voluntarily or are dismissed for cause, such as misconduct or tardiness, can receive unemployment benefits only after a certain waiting period,

---

[1] We owe this point to S. Ostry.

say Z days. The existence of such a rule effectively transforms the leisure-income locus to $YE_0 D_0 DCX$ in Figure 1, where $D_0 D$ is parallel to $E_0 A$ and implies a benefit-income ratio of $Y_3 Y_1/Y_0 Y_1$ and the distance $E_0 D_0 = AD$ represents an income equal to Z times the worker's daily wage.

A second modification of our model involves the fact that a necessary condition for the receipt of unemployment benefits in many U.S. states is evidence of job-search activity. Let us assume that on average it takes a fraction of a working day to produce and present evidence of unsuccessful job search. This activity diminishes leisure and results in a new leisure-income locus $YE_0 D_0 FF_1 X$ where the distance FD represents the number of days spent in job-search evidence and presentation if the full maximum unemployment coverage is exhausted, and $X_4 X_3/X_0 X_3$ is the fraction of each day required for these activities. For days of unemployment short of the maximum, the leisure-income segment of the locus is $D_0 F$, which is equi-proportionately below and to the left of $D_0 D$.

We will not engage in a tedious geometric demonstration that in this version of the model the quantity of induced unemployment, ceteris paribus, is a decreasing function of the waiting period between the layoff and the receipt of benefits and of the fraction of time required for job search and documentation, jointly or separately. These results can be derived in a straightforward way and are intuitively obvious. However, as the empirical work of Holen and Horowitz[1] has shown and as will be indicated by our empirical results, the strength of enforcement of eligibility rules and the associated costs for workers have a powerful negative effect on induced unemployment.

Job-Search Costs

Let us now drop the assumption that the worker can find a new job with equal pay and other characteristics immediately after he decides he wants it. To facilitate exposition we return to the assumptions of no waiting period between unemployment and the receipt of benefits and of no need for job-search documentation.

Consider that the average worker faces known functional relationships between the number of days spent in job search (horizontal axis) and the probability of success (vertical axis), as shown in Figure 2. When general cyclical economic conditions are favorable (α), OP days are required to find a job of given characteristics with a probability of one; when general

---

[1] Holen and Horowitz, "The Effect of Unemployment Insurance", *op. cit.*

Figure 2 — *A Simple Job-Search Model*

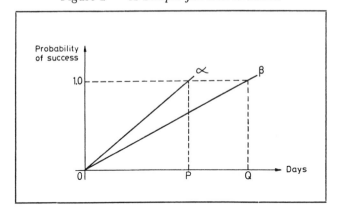

economic conditions are less favorable (β), OQ days are required[1]. We now consider the case where the average worker requires OP days to find a new job with characteristics identical to the one he held before.

In Figure 3 we reproduce the leisure-income opportunity locus of our average worker in the presence of a given ratio of benefits to income represented by the relative slopes of the lines $E_0 A$ and YX. Under the assumption that OP days of job search are considered equal in disutility to OP days of work, the leisure-income locus becomes $Y E_0 G_1 A_1 C_1 X$, where the distance $G_0 E_0 = X_1 X_0$ represents OP days spent in leisure reducing job search and the distance $E_0 G_1$ is the reduction in income incurred by drawing unemployment benefits during the job search. The latter proposition follows directly from the fact that the line $G_0 A_1$ is parallel to $E_0 A$. It is obvious that the opportunities available in the presence of job-search costs are inferior to those in the absence of such costs.

Let us now assume that the worker's preferences induce him to choose point E_1 in the leisure-income space. He reaches a higher level of welfare than he had in the absence of the benefit plan, $I_0 < I_1$. He earns $X_2 E_1$ income, is unemployed $X_1 X_2$ days, $X_1 X_0$ of which are spent in job search and $X_0 X_2$ in leisure. In this model we must broaden our definition of induced unemployment from that used in the preceding version of the model to include both the periods spent in job search and in leisure, i. e. the entire distance $X_1 X_2$.

---

[1] This model can readily be extended to include the possibility of search for jobs with different characteristics, which themselves may or may not be a function of time spent in job search. Such extensions, however, would lead us too far away from the main purpose of the present paper.

Figure 3 — *Model with Job-Search Costs*

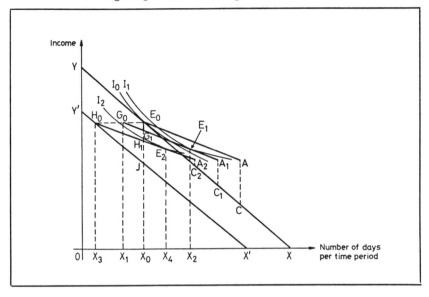

It is easy to work out and we do not show in Figure 3 that the magnitude of the downward shift of the E_0 A segment of the leisure-income opportunity locus is an increasing function of the number of days required to find a job and that therefore the amount of induced unemployment and leisure are decreasing functions of the cost of finding a job. In the extreme, if economic conditions make it very difficult to find a new job, the availability of unemployment benefits may not induce any unemployment by the average worker, as for example in the case where the search cost adjusted locus is $YE_0 H_1 A_2 C_2 X$ and E_2 involves a lower level of welfare (I_2) than the original E_0 and I_0.

2. Involuntary Unemployment and Leisure

In the preceding analysis we have dealt with the changes in the leisure-income opportunity locus of an average worker brought about by the introduction of unemployment benefit schemes under the assumption that the worker was fully employed and all unemployment was induced either by quitting voluntarily or by bringing about dismissal through deliberate misconduct[1]. Now we turn to the derivation of a leisure-income

---

[1] Much of the immorality implied by this postulated behavior could be removed in versions of the model where workers are assumed to have the opportunity to search for "better" jobs, which is a socially acceptable reason for quitting and which therefore is likely

opportunity locus of a worker who during the given period is laid off as a result of cyclical, seasonal or structural changes in the demand for labor, and who requires OQ days of search to find an equivalent new job.

In Figure 3 we show the worker's opportunity locus $X'Y'$ as it would be in the absence of unemployment benefit programs. The OQ days of job search reduce his annual income by $E_0 J$ for reasons discussed above. Which point along this frontier he chooses depends on the worker's income elasticity of demand for leisure and for our purposes of analysis is irrelevant.

Let us now consider the leisure-income locus in the presence of unemployment benefits at the rate specified above and of $OQ = X_3 X_0$ days of job search. For reasons discussed in the preceding section, the opportunity locus is $YE_0 H_1 A_2 C_2 X$. The highest level of welfare is attained at E_2.

As already mentioned above, this point E_2 yields a lower welfare than point E_0 and therefore the assumed conditions would not have induced the worker to choose voluntary unemployment. However, having been laid off work involuntarily, the point E_2 yields a higher welfare than he would have had to accept in the absence of unemployment benefits and the need to be somewhere along the $X'Y'$ locus. This fact is, of course, the very objective of all unemployment benefit programs.

Most important for our purposes of analysis is the implication of Figure 3 that our involuntarily unemployed worker spends $X_3 X_0$ days in job search, but he is also induced to consume $X_0 X_4$ days of leisure. While therefore $X_3 X_0$ is the usual unemployment for which the benefit scheme has been created, our analysis implies that the scheme lowers the marginal cost of leisure and induces an additional amount of unemployment, which in practice is indistinguishable from the "genuine" unemployment. As a result of many discussions with economists we have come to the conclusion, which unfortunately we cannot document objectively, that quantitatively the most important source of induced unemployment is likely to stem from workers who have been laid off involuntarily and for whom the *marginal* cost of leisure is lowered by the availability of benefits, while induced unemployment through voluntary layoffs is relatively less important.

In concluding this theoretical analysis we should note that a certain proportion of induced unemployment in the sense defined in this paper is not used in the enjoyment of leisure, but in the socially productive search for better jobs, which should increase labor market efficiency and decrease average unemployment. However, it is clear that this activity is being

---

to be used by workers to rationalize their behavior to themselves and to interviewers from social welfare agencies.

subsidized by public funds and does represent an addition to recorded unemployment. To the extent that the activity increases labor market efficiency and reduces unemployment, the empirical estimates of the elasticity of unemployment with respect to variables measuring the benefits and other aspects of insurance programs give the net of the induced unemployment and efficiency effects. It is an empirical question which of the two effects dominates.

3. Summary and Conclusions of the Models

The main conclusions of our models are that the introduction of unemployment benefit payments tends to induce workers holding jobs and those being laid off involuntarily to consume additional periods of leisure, which show up statistically as unemployment and which in practice are indistinguishable from periods spent in genuine job search. The quantity of induced unemployment (IU) is an increasing function of the benefit-income ratio paid under the unemployment benefit plan (R) and a decreasing function of the time cost of job search and documentation (C) and of the waiting period between the onset of unemployment and of the receipt of payments. Disregarding the latter factor, our main hypothesis to be analyzed empirically is

$$IU = f (R, C) \tag{1}$$

$$R' > 0; C' < 0$$

We should note in general defense of our empirical approach using aggregate data that the collection of unemployment statistics and the establishment of compensation benefits are in practice separate in the United States. However, the systems provide workers with incentives to hide their true preferences and tell every unemployment benefit administrator, survey enumerator and social worker that they have been laid off, are searching for work with the greatest possible intensity and are adhering to reasonable requirements for an acceptable job. They have nothing to gain and face the loss of benefits by revealing their true motives. Moreover, the unemployment compensation programs provide workers with new sets of opportunities and relative prices to which they are reacting rationally. The new conditions permit them to be more selective in jobs, to quit more readily, take more time in job search, search less intensively per time period and perhaps even take some days to loaf, fish or ski. By paying unemployment insurance premiums they consider it their moral right to behave in this manner. For all of these reasons induced unemployment cannot be discovered by interviews or other direct analysis of motives.

It can only be measured by the direct analysis of revealed preference along the lines presented in Part II below. Before we turn to our attempts to specify the function of equation (1) and derive elasticity estimates econometrically, we will discuss briefly some well-known phenomena consistent with our model.

4. Some Real World Phenomena and the Model

A widely held popular view is that unemployment benefit schemes induce "cheating" and many people can relate episodes where they had encountered evidence that workers had themselves fired, engaged in only apparent job search and engaged in outright or thinly disguised leisure activities while receiving unemployment benefits. Our model explains how workers are induced to behave in this manner and suggests that the resultant behavior can be considered "cheating" only by the application of standards of morality divorced from economic incentives. Our model implies that the workers react rationally to a set of new opportunities and relative prices created by the government. For this reason workers are reluctant to admit that they are "cheating" and tend to rationalize low intensive job search interspersed with leisure as being justified by their right to find and accept only a job of particular characteristics. Having exhausted job interview possibilities within a certain geographical range, they tend to decline acceptance of interviews at greater distance; they refuse to be interviewed for or accept jobs of low pay or high disutility relative to their previously held jobs. All of this behavior leads to the consumption of more leisure during unemployment than would have been the case without the availability of benefits.

It is also a popularly held view that persons in highly paid managerial and professional positions are less prone to become recipients of unemployment benefits and of induced leisure than are workers at the lower ends of the skill and pay spectrum. This phenomenon is consistent with our model once we introduce the facts that maximum benefit levels are fixed and produce a low benefit-income ratio for the highly skilled. Furthermore, the skill requirements of managerial and professional jobs together with the mix of abilities of individuals tend to be such as to result in high job-search costs. Consequently, the bulge in the leisure-income opportunity locus produced by unemployment benefit plans tends to be much smaller for the highly skilled than for less skilled workers, and the former are induced less to increase their consumption of leisure than are the latter. According to the argument in the preceding paragraph, this different behavior is not explained by differences in standards of morality but differences in economic opportunities.

Another popularly held view is that teenagers and young workers more generally show a greater propensity to be induced into the consumption of leisure and unemployment than older workers. This phenomenon can be explained within the framework of our model by considering that younger workers tend to be unmarried and without financial or family obligation. Therefore, their marginal rate of substitution of income for leisure tends to be lower than that for older workers. In Figure 1 the indifference map over the relevant range is steeper and more leisure is induced for a given opportunity locus. Again, this behavior does not reveal anything about lower moral standards of the young. Instead, they are acting rationally given their leisure-income preferences, and these are likely to change as they grow older and incur family and financial obligations.

II. Econometric Estimates

The theoretical considerations of Part I suggest the extension of the traditional model of the cause of unemployment

$$UR = SU + CU + TU \qquad (2)$$

where UR is the officially reported unemployment rate, SU is the structural or frictional, CU the cyclical and TU is the seasonal unemployment rate, to the following:

$$UR = f \, (SU, CU, TU, IU) \qquad (3)$$

where IU is induced unemployment of the nature explained above. IU is due to the increased consumption of leisure both by workers who otherwise would have been employed and by workers laid off due to cyclical, seasonal and structural or frictional unemployment, hence (3) theoretically is not of linear additive form.

The empirical estimation of the hypothesized functional relationship between the total unemployment rate and its various components is undertaken first, using annual time-series data for the period 1951—1972 for U.S. aggregates and second, using a cross-section of the 48 contiguous U.S. states in 1971. We now present the results of our empirical estimates and explain the use of proxies, sources and specific functional forms.

1. Time-Series Analysis

The model presented in Table 1 consists of two equations estimated simultaneously using the two stage least squares technique. In equation (4) the dependent variable is the unemployment rate among workers

Table 1 — *Time-Series Estimate of Induced Unemployment, 1951—1972*

$$
\text{(4)}\quad \text{Ln } UR_I = -1.271 + 17.622\ UCB/AWWCE - .039\ INEL - .035\ PCGNP
$$
$$
(1.67)\qquad (9.92)*\qquad\qquad (4.21)*\qquad (5.26)*
$$
$$
- .027\ PCGNP\text{-}1 - .052\ PCOV
$$
$$
(4.04)\qquad\qquad (4.27)
$$

$$
\text{(5)}\quad UCB/AWWCE = .302 + .0054\ UR_I + .0017\ TIME
$$
$$
(60.63)\quad (5.06)*\qquad (9.49)*
$$

Notes: Figures in parentheses give t values. Asterisks indicate coefficients statistically significantly different from zero at the 5 percent level, one-tailed test.

DW = 1.74 R^2 = .93 for equation (4)
DW = 1.66 R^2 = .84 for equation (5)

though it should be noted that in models estimated by two stage least squares, these statistics do not have the usual interpretation. See R. L. Basmann, "Letter to the Editor", *Econometrica*, Vol. 30, New Haven, Conn., 1962, pp. 824sqq.

Source: UR_I — *Economic Report of the President*, Transmitted to the Congress, January 1973, Washington, D.C., Appendix C, p. 225.

UCB — *Ibid.*

AWWCE — U.S. Department of Labor, Manpower Administration, Washington, D.C.: *Handbook of Unemployment Insurance, Financial Data, 1938 to 1970*, p. 145; *Unemployment Insurance Program Letters* (cited *Letter*, No. ..), Nos. 1238, May 31, 1973; 1251, November 14, 1973.

PCGNP, PCGNP-1 — *Economic Report of the President*, p. 193.

PCOV — Calculated by dividing Average Weekly Insured Unemployment (from *ibid.*, p. 225) by UR_I and then dividing this in turn by the Civilian Labor Force (from *ibid.*, p. 220).

AG/TOT — U.S. Department of Labor, Manpower Administration, *Manpower Report of the President*, Washington, D.C., March 1973, Stat. Appendix, p. 144.

MFG/TOT — *Ibid.*, p. 188.

INEL — Calculated as the residual from an equation in DENIALS is the dependent and PCGNP and PCGNP-1 are the independent variables.

DENIALS — U.S. Department of Labor, Bureau of Employment Security, Washington, D.C.: *Employment Security Review*, Vol. 27, 1960; *The Labor Market and Employment Security*, Statistical Supplement, various issues. — U.S. Department of Labor, Manpower Administration, *Unemployment Insurance Statistics*, Washington, D.C., various issues.

TIME — A Series of consecutive integers.

insured against unemployment (UR_I). The semi-log form of equation (4) is justified on the grounds that induced unemployment is itself a function of the level of unemployment. This proposition follows from the theoretical analysis which implies that insurance benefits lower the marginal cost of leisure for persons unemployed for cyclical or structural reasons. Consequently, the higher these forms of cyclical and structural unemployment, the greater is induced unemployment created by the available benefits. That their relationships are implicit in the semi-log specification may be seen from the fact that if $Ln\ U = \alpha + \beta\ UCB/AWWCE$, then $\partial U/\partial UCB/AWWCE = \beta U$, where UCB is the average unemployment compensation benefit payment per week received by unemployed workers and AWWCE is the average weekly wages of workers in covered employment, all in dollar values average for the year.

The key independent variable in our analysis is UCB/AWWCE, which according to our theoretical model is expected to determine induced unemployment and therefore show a positive functional relationship with the overall rate of unemployment. In Table 2 we show the raw data for this variable used in the time-series and cross-section study in panels A and B respectively. As can be seen, the time series has a mean of .342 with a low of .321 in 1955 and a high of .367 in 1972 with an intermediate peak of .354 in 1961, while the cross-section data have a mean of .352 with a low of .220 in West Virginia and a high of .430 in Rhode Island.

The second independent variable in equation (4) is ineligibility for benefits, INEL, a proxy for the strength of enforcement of eligibility rules, which according to our theoretical analysis results in costs of engaging in and documenting job-search activity. This cost, ceteris paribus, reduces the incentives to induced unemployment created by benefits and therefore is expected theoretically to be negatively related to the dependent variable, the overall unemployment rate. The variable INEL was constructed from a published series "Denials per 1,000 Claimant Contacts." In Table 3 we show the raw data for this variable in the time series for the aggregate United States and for individual states in panels A and B, respectively. As can be seen from the table, denials have a mean of 21.6 and a range of 14.0 in 1958 to 27.2 in 1966. The mean for the states in 1971 is 25.6 with a low of 7.8 in Tennessee and a high of 67.4 in Colorado.

The time series for denials is strongly cyclical. It is high during periods of low unemployment and low when jobs are less readily available. Such a cyclical behavior of the time series would be expected from an efficient and equitable application of the principle that unemployment benefits should not be available to persons who have "failed to accept suitable employment," even if the operational definition of failure to accept suitable employment and therefore the rate of denials varies through time as a result of changes in administrative directives. These directives in turn are influenced by public opinion, such as the well-known periodic revelations about "cheating" in the press, by the person-

Table 2 — *Benefit-Income Ratios, United States*

A. *Benefit-Income Ratios, U.S. Aggregate 1951—1972*							
Year	UCB/ AWWCE	Year	UCB/ AWWCE	Year	UCB/ AWWCE	Year	UCB/ AWWCE
1951	.322	1957	.335	1963	.346	1969	.344
1952	.330	1958	.353	1964	.337	1970	.357
1953	.323	1959	.335	1965	.338	1971	.363
1954	.335	1960	.352	1966	.347	1972	.367
1955	.321	1961	.354	1967	.347		
1956	.333	1962	.349	1968	.343		

Mean: 0.342

B. *Benefit-Income Ratios by State 1971*					
State	UCB/ AWWCE	State	UCB/ AWWCE	State	UCB/ AWWCE
Alabama .	.336	Maine	.388	Ohio	.313
Arizona .	.314	Maryland . . .	.404	Oklahoma . .	.305
Arkansas .	.365	Massachusetts .	.391	Oregon	.317
California .	.337	Michigan . . .	.337	Pennsylvania .	.361
Colorado .	.414	Minnesota . .	.345	Rhode Island .	.430
Connecticut	.408	Mississippi . .	.311	South Carolina	.357
Delaware .	.327	Missouri . . .	.334	South Dakota .	.361
Florida . .	.295	Montana . . .	.314	Tennessee . .	.332
Georgia .	.336	Nebraska . . .	.345	Texas	.298
Idaho . .	.398	Nevada . . .	.333	Utah	.370
Illinois . .	.316	New Hampshire	.374	Vermont . . .	.409
Indiana .	.277	New Jersey . .	.397	Virginia . . .	.361
Iowa . . .	.395	New Mexico .	.365	Washington . .	.397
Kansas . .	.388	New York . .	.350	West Virginia .	.220
Kentucky	.349	North Carolina	.329	Wisconsin . .	.397
Louisiana .	.335	North Dakota .	.384	Wyoming . . .	.389

Mean: 0.352

Source: See Table 1.

ality and attitudes of top-level bureaucrats and by the state of the budget of the unemployment insurance programs. We did not test this hypothesis directly, but instead estimated a regression with the denials ratio as the dependent variable and the current and lagged percentage changes in GNP as independent variables. The residuals from this equation are defined as our variable INEL and are assumed to reflect the cyclically unrelated changes in the strength with which eligibility rules for benefit

Table 3 — *Denials of Applications for Unemployment Benefits, United States*

A. *Denials per 1,000 Claimant Contacts, U.S. Aggregate 1951—1972*							
Year	DENIALS	Year	DENIALS	Year	DENIALS	Year	DENIALS
1951	19.3	1957	18,5	1963	22.7	1969	26.7
1952	19.0	1958	14.0	1964	23.5	1970	23.2
1953	21.1	1959	18.0	1965	25.7	1971	23.9
1954	16.1	1960	18.5	1966	27.2	1972	27.0
1955	20.2	1961	17.5	1967	26.4		
1956	19.5	1962	21.1	1968	26.6		

Mean: 21.6

B. *Denials per 1,000 Claimant Contacts by State 1971*

State	DENIALS	State	DENIALS	State	DENIALS
Alabama .	23.5	Maine	20.8	Ohio	26.0
Arizona .	41.4	Maryland . . .	25.8	Oklahoma . .	38.0
Arkansas .	18.7	Massachusetts .	12.2	Oregon	29.8
California .	31.4	Michigan . . .	34.5	Pennsylvania .	18.6
Colorado .	67.4	Minnesota . .	37.5	Rhode Island .	15.8
Connecticut	11.8	Mississippi . .	25.2	South Carolina	31.4
Delaware .	20.2	Missouri . . .	22.1	South Dakota .	16.3
Florida . .	21.9	Montana . . .	22.7	Tennessee . .	7.8
Georgia .	36.8	Nebraska . . .	66.0	Texas	38.5
Idaho . .	22.9	Nevada . . .	25.2	Utah	25.3
Illinois . .	22.9	New Hampshire	22.5	Vermont . . .	13.6
Indiana .	21.5	New Jersey . .	23.8	Virginia . . .	44.5
Iowa . . .	26.4	New Mexico .	18.7	Washington . .	11.8
Kansas . .	19.9	New York . .	23.6	West Virginia .	38.2
Kentucky	15.7	North Carolina	17.5	Wisconsin . .	14.8
Lousiana .	14.7	North Dakota .	15.5	Wyoming . . .	29.8

Mean: 25.6

Source: See Table 1.

recipients are enforced by the administrators of the insurance programs[1]. The tougher the level of enforcement, the smaller are the incentives for induced unemployment from benefit payments, ceteris paribus.

---

[1] Equation (4) estimated with the variable DENIALS remains largely unchanged from the one shown, with the difference that the known correlation between DENIALS and the cyclical variables makes the regression coefficient of PCGNP statistically insignificant with a t value of 1.41.

Herbert G. Grubel and Dennis R. Maki

The third and fourth variables in equation (4) are the current percentage change in GNP (PCGNP) and lagged one year (PCGNP—1). These variables are assumed to reflect cyclical variations in demand which affect the overall unemployment rate negatively. The lagged term was included under the assumption that some unemployment may be two years.

The last variable in equation (4) is PCOV, the percentage of the civilian labor force covered by unemployment insurance. We include this variable because during the period under consideration the percentage of the labor force covered by state unemployment insurance programs increased through legislative increases in occupations covered[1] and through structural shifts in employment pattern. This fact is revealed by equation (6), where MFG/TOT and AG/TOT are the percentage of total employment in manufacturing and agriculture, respectively[2]. We hypothesize that the

$$\text{PCOV} = 51.23 + .68 \text{ MFG/TOT} - 1.71 \text{ AG/TOT} \qquad R^2 = .75 \qquad (6)$$
$$(5.19) \quad (1.61) \qquad\qquad (3.88) \qquad\qquad DW = 1.06$$

workers newly covered through legislation and changes in the occupational mix were less prone to unemployment than those covered earlier and the overall average work force, so that through time the unemployment rate among the insured relative to that of the overall unemployment rate showed a downward trend. This fact is revealed by equation (7):

$$\text{UR}_I = .017 + .988 \text{ UR} - .08 \text{ TIME} \qquad R^2 = .96 \qquad (7)$$
$$(.67) \quad (20.18) \qquad (9.71) \qquad\qquad DW = 1.85$$

where UR is the overall unemployment rate and TIME is a series of consecutive integers. The preceding considerations lead us to predict that the sign of the coefficient of the variable PCOV should be negative.

The relationship between the general theoretical arguments underlying equation (3) and the econometric specification of equation (4) is that cyclical unemployment is proxied by the changes in GNP, current and lagged, induced unemployment is proxied by the benefit-income ratio and

---

[1] *The Employment Service Review*, Vol. 7, Washington, D.C., 1970, notes: "Especially since 1954, much of the increase in the number of workers covered has resulted from legislative extension of the program to groups of workers formerly not covered" (p. 7), and "One group of workers whose coverage has increased considerably in recent years is the employees of State governments" (p. 8). State government employees may reasonably be assumed to enjoy greater than average employment stability, contributing to the phenomenon described in the text.

[2] Sources of the data in equations (6) and (7) in the text are given at the bottom of Table 1.

the denials rate, structural unemployment is assumed to be constant or changing only slightly during the period under study and therefore is reflected in the intercept of the equation, and seasonal unemployment is assumed to be constant during the annual periods under consideration[1].

Equation (5) in Table 1 is included in the model to eliminate simultaneous equation bias resulting from the fact that the benefit-income ratio is itself a function of the unemployment rate because both wage rates and benefits tend to change pro- and contra-cyclically, respectively, around a trend. The counter cyclical behavior of benefits arises from the fact that during periods of high unemployment the skill mix of the unemployed rises and as a result earnings related average benefits increase. Furthermore, during periods of high unemployment there are fewer benefit payments covering less than a full week than during periods of low unemployment. Part-of-the-week benefits lower overall average weekly averages.

Inspection of the regression results in Table 1 shows that all coefficients have the expected sign and are significantly different from zero at the 5 percent level of confidence, using a one-tailed test. The elasticity of the unemployment rate with respect to the benefit income ratio is 6.0. Since our observations do not include periods without unemployment insurance programs in operation it is not reasonable to estimate what the unemployment rate would have been if the benefits had been zero. Instead, we consider what the unemployment rate among the insured workers would have been in 1972 if the variables UCB/AWWCE, INEL and PCOV had been at their 1955 levels, assuming that this year had been one of full employment, as Okun had done in his calculation of the output gap[2]. According to our estimates, in 1972 unemployment among the insured would have been 2.5 percent instead of the 3.5 percent actually observed, if the three insurance related variables mentioned above had been at their 1955 levels. Since in 1972, 52,857 thousand persons were covered under the U.S. state insurance schemes, the above calculations imply induced unemployment of 529 thousand persons on average. With the overall U.S unemployment rate in 1972 at 5.6 percent and amounting to 4,840 thousand persons, the reduction by the 529 thousand induced

---

[1] One could compute the variances of the monthly seasonal adjustment factors for every year and use this as an independent variable to represent changes in the level of seasonal unemployment in annual data. See D. Smith, "Seasonal Unemployment and the Labour Market", in: *Employment Policy and the Labor Market*, Ed. by Arthur M. Ross, Berkeley, Calif., 1965, pp. 191sqq. Resource limitations prevented us from carrying out this analysis.

[2] See Arthur M. Okun, "Potential GNP: Its Measurement and Significance", in: *Proceedings of the Business and Economic Statistics Section of the American Statistical Association*, Washington, D.C., 1962, pp. 98sqq.

unemployed would have yielded an overall unemployment rate of 5.0 percent, which is about 11 percent lower than the 5.6 percent actually observed.

2. Cross-Section Analysis

The cross-section regression results are presented in Table 4. As can be seen, the dependent variable and the independent variables UCB/ AWWCE, INEL and PCOV are the same as the ones used in the time-series analysis. Therefore we need not further explain the rationale for their use here. The remaining independent variables were used to adjust for

Table 4 — *Cross-Section Estimate of Induced Unemployment, 1971*

$$\text{(8)} \quad UR_I = 5.653 + 9.793 \text{ UCB/AWWCE} - .049 \text{ INEL} - .415 \text{ PCEMP}$$
$$ \quad (1.78) \quad (2.27)^* \phantom{+ 9.793 \text{ UCB/AWWCE}} (3.09)^* \quad (3.30)^*$$
$$- .054 \text{ PCOV} - .177 \text{ AG/TOT} - .059 \text{ MFG/TOT} + .170 \text{ TRANS/TOT}$$
$$(1.17) \phantom{- .054 \text{ PCOV}} (2.39)^* (2.20)^* (1.96)^*$$
$$R^2 = .52$$

Notes: Figures in parentheses given t values. Asterisks indicate coefficients statistically significantly different from zero at the 5 percent level.

Source: UR$_I$ — U.S. Department of Labor, *Manpower Report of the President*, Stat. Appendix, p. 208.

UCB/AWWCE — U.S. Department of Labor, *Letter*, No. 1238, May 31, 1973.

INEL — calculated as the residual from an equation in which DENIALS is the dependent and PCEMP is the independent variable.

DENIALS — U.S. Departmant of Labor, *Unemployment Insurance Statistics*, April 1972, p. 14.

PCEMP — calculated as the percentage change in "Employees on Nonagricultural Payrolls" from 1970 to 1971, data from U.S. Department of Labor, Bureau of Labor Statistics, *Employment and Earnings*, Vol. 18, Washington, D. C., 1971/72, No. 11, pp. 126sqq.

PCOV — calculated by dividing "Average Monthly Covered Employment" from U.S. Department of Labor, *Letter*, No. 1238, May 31, 1973, by an estimate of labor force derived by dividing the insured unemployment count from the *Manpower Report of the President*, Stat. Appendix, p. 207, by UR$_I$.

AG/TOT — from U.S. Department of Commerce, Bureau of the Cencus, *General Social and Economic Characteristics, United States Summary*, PC (1) to C 1, Washington, D.C., 1974, p. 526.

MFG/TOT — *Ibid.*

TRANS/TOT — *Ibid.*

The data obtained from the census pertain to 1970, other data to 1971.

differences in the structural characteristics of the individual U.S. states, which on simple a priori grounds can be expected to influence the level of unemployment in 1971: the proportion of the labor force in agriculture (AG/TOT), in manufacturing (MFG/TOT) and the recent rate of growth in employment (PCEMP), 1970—71. A scatter diagram of observations brought to our attention that states with large transportation equipment manufacturing industries, such as Michigan and Washington, had particularly high unemployment rates in 1971. As a result we included the variable (TRANS/TOT) to reflect the proportion of the labor force employed in the transportation equipment manufacturing industries.

We have no theoretically or empirically well-founded a priori views on the expected signs of these standardizing variables. However, since agricultural employment tends to involve families and flexible work loads, the negative sign on the AG/TOT variable seems reasonable. Also, we would have expected unemployment to be lower, the greater the recent growth in employment (PCEMP). Only the negative sign for the manufacturing (MFG/TOT) coefficient is somewhat surprising, though it would be explained if the variance across states is dominated by differences in cyclically sensitive manufacturing industries that swamp the expected effect that overall dependence on manufacturing industries increases unemployment at the low point of the cycle as in 1971. As can be seen from Table 4, all coefficients are statistically significantly different from zero at the 5 percent level, except for the coefficient attached to PCOV.

The coefficient of greatest interest to this analysis is that of UCB/AWWCE. It has a t value of 2.27 and implies an elasticity of the unemployment rate among the insured with respect to UCB/AWWCE of .9 at the mean of UCB/AWWCE and UR_1 of .352 and 3.8, respectively. This elasticity is considerably below the 6.0 found in the time-series analysis. We hypothesize that this difference is due to changes in some social conditions which have lowered the cost of unemployment through time, such as lower probability of not finding a job at all resulting from the overall success of macroeconomic full employment policies, the availability of better welfare programs and changes in public attitudes towards work. These changes could not be quantified but may be assumed to have lowered the psychic and expected costs of unemployment in a probability sense during the period under observation. These influences may be assumed to have been the same in all states in 1971 so that the cross-section elasticity reflects more accurately than the time series on the pure induced unemployment effect of the benefit payments at the present. On the other hand, the conclusion drawn from the time-series results, that unemployment in 1972 would be 11 percent lower if all of the insurance related variables were at their 1955 levels, remains valid. However, the

Herbert G. Grubel and Dennis R. Maki

cross-section results do indicate that there are probably other important conditions and social policies which would have to be kept at their 1955 levels to achieve the suggested reduction in 1972 unemployment from a return to 1955 levels of insurance related variables.

III. Conclusions and Policy Implications

The results of our theoretical and empirical analysis imply strongly that unemployment benefit programs in the United States have induced substantial amounts of unemployment. While our precise elasticity estimates are likely to be changed by future refinements in econometric work, we believe that our findings are sufficiently reliable to permit us to reach the following policy conclusions.

First, the tax payers' cost of providing benefits for persons unemployed due to structural, cyclical or seasonal factors (SCS unemployment) is increased by the existence of induced unemployment. In 1971 the total transfer payments to unemployed persons came to $ 5,229.2 million[1]. But according to our time-series elasticity estimates, in that year approximately 11 percent of the unemployment was induced, so that only 89 percent, or $ 4,654.0 million went to the SCS unemployed for whom the program was initiated. Given an administrative cost of unemployment benefit programs of $ 778.6 million in 1971, the tax payers' costs came to $ 6,007.8 million to provide $ 4,654.0 million to the SCS unemployed, for a cost-benefit ratio of 1.3.

Such a ratio greater than one does not imply that the program should be abandoned. The justification for this and all transfer programs is that the marginal utility of the income of the tax payers is sufficiently below that of the recipients to yield a net social welfare gain in spite of administrative costs and inefficiencies. However, our analysis does suggest that the program should be reevaluated in the light of the ratio including the induced unemployment effect, which, to the best of our knowledge, has not been considered in any previous analysis.

In any public discussion of the merits of unemployment compensation plans the relevant costs and benefits to be considered are not average, but marginal at different levels of UCB/AWWCE. In principle, the marginal utility of transfer payments to SCS unemployed is a decreasing function of UCB/AWWCE, while the marginal induced unemployment effects are an increasing function of the UCB/AWWCE level, according to our time-series estimates. Consequently, there should be an optimum UCB/AWWCE ratio

---

[1] The transfer payments and administrative costs are from U.S. Office of Management and Budget, *The Budget of the United States Government, Appendix, Fiscal Year 1973*, Washington, D.C., p. 646.

where marginal costs equal marginal benefits. While we have no estimates of marginal benefits in terms of utility, we can provide a simple marginal benefit-cost calculation in terms of dollars resulting from a hypothetical one percent increase in the UCB/AWWCE ratio in 1971.

The additional benefits to the SCS unemployed are valued at $ 46.5 million, or one percent of the denominator of the 1971 ratio. The costs consist of increased payments to existing induced unemployed of $ 5.8 million while newly induced unemployment requires 6.4 percent of $ 5,229.2 million or $ 334.7 million additional payments. Assuming marginal administrative costs to be zero, the total marginal costs sum to $ 387.0 million, for a marginal cost-benefit ratio of 8.3.

Whether the contemplated one percent increase in the UCB/AWWCE ratio or any other marginal changes with such corresponding cost-benefit ratios would be justified on welfare grounds cannot be decided scientifically. The choice has to be made by the public and through the political process. Our analysis and estimates imply the need and ingredients for a public discussion about an optimal UCB/AWWCE ratio along the lines suggested. It is difficult to know what this ratio will be ultimately. However, we can venture the guess that if the current UCB/AWWCE ratio was considered to have been appropriate in the absence of full public appreciation of the cost of induced unemployment, then the ratio logically should be lower once these costs are included in the social calculus.

The second policy implication of our paper concerns the correct target for macro-economic employment policies. As is well-known, the target was set at 4 percent unemployment during the 1960s after much discussion about the social cost of inflation at various rates relative to the foregone output of goods and services associated with these inflation rates. One of the essential ingredients in the public discussion of the target unemployment rate was the "output gap" which resulted from the operation of the economy at levels of unemployment above 4 percent. This output gap, which represents the true social cost of unemployment, was estimated by A. Okun to have been about $ 50 billion in 1971, using his "Law" that productivity and labor force participation rates yield foregone output of 3 percent of GNP for every one percent unemployment[1]. The argument is that the social cost of a somewhat higher inflation rate was much smaller than the value of the lost output.

Our analysis implies that in 1971 the output gap would have been about 11 percent, or $ 5.5 billion, less than Okun's figure if the UCB/AWWCE, PCOV and INEL had been what they were in 1955, the base year of full employment underlying Okun's calculations. According to our

---

[1] See Okun, *op. cit.*

theoretical analysis, the $ 5.5 billion output gap caused by induced unemployment has as its counterpart the voluntary consumption of leisure and job search valued at this sum by the revealed preferences of the "unemployed." Therefore, in any social calculus the elimination of this part of the gap should be considered as involving no net social gain and, whatever the socially acceptable cost of inflation would have been at an output gap of $ 50 billion in the absence of induced unemployment, this should not be acceptable at the lower, adjusted figure of a $ 44.5 billion gap. In other words, changes in the ratio of UCB/AWWCE and in psychic and other costs of unemployment discussed above in recent years have shifted to the right the Phillips curve, derived without regard to these changes[1].

Recently, the validity of the concept of the Phillips curve trade-off has been challenged[2]. Whether these challenges will be found to be valid in the future need not concern us here. The rightward shift of the Phillips curve suggested by our preceding analysis involves an increase in the unemployment rate at which prices are stable. Since in the terminology of the challenges to the Phillips curve analysis, this rate is also known as the "natural rate of unemployment" it follows that this natural rate has risen as a result of the induced unemployment found in our study.

As in the case of the optimum ratio of UCB/AWWCE, the ultimate choice of an appropriate target of full employment policy must be decided in a public dialogue and by a political process. Again it is difficult to predict what the outcome of this process will be. However, if historically at a certain inflation rate the target rate was 4 percent unemployment in the belief that all unemployment was involuntary and any excess above 4 percent represented lost output and welfare valued according to Okun's Law, than at that same rate of inflation society should rationally choose a target level above 4 percent if all unemployment includes a substantial amount of voluntary unemployment and job search.

The third policy implication of our analysis is that all government programs designed to raise wages and employment, such as manpower training, increased labor market efficiency and employment of workers in

---

[1] For an argument that failure to recognize this shift of the Phillips curves in a number of large Western countries may have been responsible for the world inflation of 1972—73, see Herbert Grubel, *Soziale Sicherung und Weltinflation*, Kieler Vorträge, N. F., 78, Tübingen, 1974.

[2] See especially Milton Friedman, "The Role of Monetary Policy", *The American Economic Review*, Vol. 58, Menasha, Wisc., 1968, p. 10; and Edmund S. Phelps, "Money Wage Dynamics and Labor Market Equilibrium", in: *Microeconomic Foundations of Employment and Inflation Theory*, Ed. by *idem et al.*, New York, 1970, pp. 124sqq.

specifically created government jobs, will be successful only if the UCB/ AWWCE ratio and psychic and other costs of unemployment remain constant. Any increases in this ratio will raise induced unemployment and offset the gains in employment achieved by the government programs.

Fourth, our analysis has indicated that the tightening of eligibility rules and strict enforcement of these rules will tend to reduce the level of induced unemployment. However, there are important economic and political limitations to the success of this policy approach. The institution of better and more job-search documentation raises adminis- trative costs and the costs to the large proportion of SCS unemployed. Forcing persons to accept certain jobs they would not accept voluntarily causes inefficiencies, personal hardships and may be self-defeating as such persons become unemployed more frequently.

The final policy conclusion of our analysis is that induced unemploy- ment strengthens the case for a negative income tax or guaranteed minimum income to replace the plethora of modern welfare programs. This is so because one can consider that the induced unemployment results from very high marginal tax rates on working rather than receiving unemployment benefits. This is the analogous argument to welfare programs, which have received most of the attention in the negative income tax literature.

The preceding analysis of policy implications flowing from the exis- tence of induced unemployment implies the important point that the social welfare programs of governments are interdependent. The optimum target level of employment for macroeconomic policies depends on the UCB/AWWCE ratio, the level of eligibility enforcement, and the govern- ment policies to increase labor market efficiency and provide direct employment. The efficient and socially optimum levels of all of these social welfare programs have to be determined simultaneously.

*   *   *

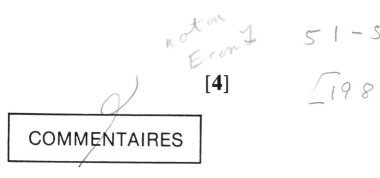

[4]

COMMENTAIRES

A Note on the Effects of Unemployment Insurance, Minimum Wage Legislation and Trade Union Growth on Reported Unemployment Rates in Canada, 1950-75

Herbert G. Grubel
and Dennis R. Maki

The paper analyzes the effects of the factors noted in the title on reported unemployment rates, both theoretically and empirically. The implications of the results for the natural rate debate and macroeconomic stabilization policies are briefly discussed.

In a previous paper[1], one of the authors presented theoretical arguments outlining why minimum wage legislation, unemployment insurance schemes and the activities of trade unions might affect the reported rate of unemployment. The empirical work in that paper used pooled cross section-time series data to estimate a reduced-form model, ignored the potential influence of trade unions, and concentrated on the effects of minimum wage legislation on differences in unemployment rates between provinces. This note uses annual time series data covering the period 1950-75 to estimate separate supply and demand equations, and from these estimates calculates the effects of minimum wages, unemployment insurance and trade union growth on reported unemployment rates for Canada as a whole[2].

Specification of the Model

The empirical model used is an augmented variant of the model used by Mincer[3] to investigate the effects of minimum wages on unemployment. It

• GRUBEL, Herbert G., Professor, Department of Economics and Commerce, Simon Fraser University, B.C.

MAKI, Dennis R., Professor, Department of Economics and Commerce, Simon Fraser University, B.C.

•• Research support under Canada Council Grant S75-1194 is acknowledged.

1 MAKI, Dennis R., "The Effect of Changes in Minimum Wage Rates on provincial Unemployment Rates, 1970-77", *Relations Industrielles,* Vol. 34, 1979, pp. 418-30.

2 The time period chosen was dictated on both ends by the availability of reasonably consistent data, as 1975 is the last year for which Labour Force Survey data are available by the "old" definitions, and Statistics Canada has revised data to conform with the "new" definitions back only to 1966.

3 MINCER, Jacob, "Unemployment Effects of Minimum Wages", *Journal of Political Economy,* Vol. 84, August 1976, pp. S87-104.

922

also bears a strong resemblance to the main equation of the model we previously used to investigate the unemployment effects of unemployment insurance[4]. The dependent variables are the labour force to population ratio
(L/P) and the employment to population ratio (E/P), with an additional
equation using the unemployment rate (U/L) also estimated as a cross-
check. Since one of the important theoretical arguments about the effects of
government policies and labour market institutions is that these influences
tend to interact, all equations were specified in multiplicative form, so that
by taking logarithms we obtain the following basic form of equation for
estimating purposes:

$$\ln DEP = a_0 + a_1 \ln B/W + a_2 \ln DSQL + a_3 T + a_4 T^2 +$$
$$a_5 \ln RTT + a_6 \ln RTT_{-1} + a_7 \ln UNION + a_8 \ln M/W$$
$$+ e$$

where DEP is the dependent variable (L/P. E/P or U/P), B/W is the ratio
of unemployment insurance to wages, DSQL is the rate at which applicants
for the receipt of these benefits are disqualified, T is a time trend, RTT is
the ratio to its own trend of constant dollar gross national expenditure,
UNION is the level of unionization and M/W is the ratio of minimum to
average wages[5]. The a's are coefficients to be estimated, and e is the error
term. Ordinary least squares were used for all estimations.

The expectation was that a_1 would be positive in the L/P equation,
negative in the E/P equation, and hence positive in the U/L equation, with
the opposite pattern of signs expected for a_2. The reasons for these theoretical expectations are contained in our earlier paper[6]. The coefficients of the
RTT terms were expected to be positive in the E/P equation and negative in
the U/L equation. The sign of these coefficients in the L/P equation
depends upon whether the discouraged worker or additional worker effect
dominates, an issue which is not clear in the Canadian context, so no sign
expectation was assigned. The coefficient of the minimum wage term was
expected to be negative in the E/P equation. Mincer[7] has shown that the effect of M/W on L/P (and hence U/L) is theoretically indeterminate. Since
we are using the unionization measure suggested by Kahn and Moriume[8],
the sign expectations for a_7 are the same as for a_8, for the same reasons. No
sign expectations were assigned for the coefficients of the time trend terms.

We also estimated the equations separately for males and females,
though the independent variables are in general not measurable sex-specific.
Estimation results are shown in Table 1.

---

    4 GRUBEL, H.G., D. MAKI and S. SAX, "Real and Insurance-Induced Unemploy-
ment in Canada", *Canadian Journal of Economics,* Vol. 8, May 1975, pp. 174-91.

    5 More detailed variable definitions and data sources are given in the appendix.

    6 GRUBEL, H.G., *et al., op. cit.*

    7 MINCER, J., *op. cit.*

    8 KAHN, L. and K. MORIUME, "Unions and Employment Stability: A Sequential
Logit Approach", *International Economic Review,* Vol. 20, February 1979, pp. 217-35.

TABLE 1

Regression Results, Annual Data, Canada, 1950-1975

Dep. Var.	Const.	B/W	DSQL	T	T^2	RTT	RTT_{-1}	UNION	M/W^a	R^2	d
Females											
L/P	3.786	-.105	-.0130	.00494	.00056	-.124	.151	-.209	.019	.997	1.34
	(12.21)	(-2.98)	(-1.66)	(1.42)	(4.57)	(-1.03)	(.94)	(-2.37)	(.24)		
E/P	3.933	-.121	-.0083	.00743	.00047	-.0165	.260	-.282	-.0030	.997	1.21
	(12.11)	(-3.26)	(-1.01)	(2.04)	(3.72)	(-.13)	(1.54)	(-3.05)	(-.04)		
Diff.[b]	-.147	.016	-.0047	-.00249	.00009	-.1075	-.109	.73	.022		
Males											
L/P	4.657	.0275	-.0026	-.0058	.00009	.0060	.197	-.058	-.033	.984	1.19
	(35.83)	(1.70)	(-.87)	(-4.50)	(2.31)	(.12)	(2.89)	(-1.55)	(-2.96)		
E/P	5.028	-.0436	.0103	-.099	.00023	.298	.395	-.225	-.295	.98	1.94
	(42.87)	(-2.98)	(3.82)	(-8.51)	(6.70)	(6.47)	(6.42)	(-6.61)	(-2.95)		
Diff.[b]	-.371	.0711	-.0129	.0041	-.00014	-.292	-.198	.167	.262		
Total											
L/P	4.339	-.0182	-.0063	-.0057	.00032	-.0144	.1888	-.1139	-.0496	.982	1.68
	(35.96)	(-1.24)	(-2.31)	(-4.84)	(8.70)	(-.31)	(3.08)	(-3.20)	(-3.57)		
E/P	4.614	-.0594	.0047	-.0075	.00035	.2174	.3360	-.2327	-.0400	.972	1.51
	(33.23)	(-3.51)	(1.49)	(-5.52)	(8.20)	(4.03)	(4.76)	(-5.69)	(-2.50)		
Diff.[b]	-2.75	.0412	-.0110	.0018	-.00003	-.2318	-.1472	.1188	-.0096		
U/L	-6.971	.9892	-.1990	.0601	-.0015	-4.243	-3.5611	3.0594	.1135	.970	2.90
	(-4.30)	(5.01)	(-5.44)	(3.78)	(-3.12)	(-6.74)	(-4.32)	(6.41)	(.61)		

Notes:

[a] *Separate M/W series are used for males and females, with the M/W series for the total equations being a weighted average of the two. See Appendix.*

[b] *Diff. is the difference between the magnitude of the coefficient in the L/P and E/P equations.*

General Results

The coefficients of multiple determination are uniformly high for all equations, as expected for time series data. The Durbin-Watson coefficients cover a wide range, with those for the main equations (L/P and E/P for the total population) probably toward the high end of the indeterminate range[9]. We reestimated these equations using Generalized Least Squares with rho estimated by the Hildreth-Lu technique, and found no qualitative difference between these results and those reported in Table 1[10]. Since the Labour Force Survey data for 1950-52 are probably not of the same quality as those for subsequent years, and since the substantial changes to the unemployment insurance system in 1971 may not have been adequately modelled, we tested for stability on the main equations of interest, using Chow tests. The results indicated no evidence of a structural break between 1952 and 1953[11],

9 The Durbin-Watson statistic is not tabled for as many regressors as are contained in our equations.

10 The Durbin-Watson statistic for L/P increased to 1.74 with a rho of 0.54, and for E/P it increased to 1.80 with a rho of 0.37. These results are available from the authors upon request.

11 The F values were 1.76 for L/P and 1.59 for E/P, with (3, 14) degrees of freedom.

but there was evidence of a break between 1971 and 1972[12]. Whether these results are due to inadequate modelling of the unemployment insurance program changes or to something else which was unique to the 1972-75 period cannot be determined.

Sign expectations were realized in all the "Male" equations, and except for a_1 in the L/P equation of the "Total" estimates, but several unexpected signs occurred in the "Female" equations (a_1 in both the L/P and E/P equations, a_2 and a_5 in the E/P equation). Possibly this is due to the fact that the independent variables (except M/W) were not measured specifically for females due to lack of suitable data.

Results for the Variables of Primary Interest

Confining attention to the "Difference" rows in Table 1, the results indicate that increase in unemployment insurance benefit levels or decreases in the disqualification rates for these benefits both increase unemployment. Similarly, increases in the level of unionization increase unemployment, with a substantially larger effect for males than females. The results for males and females separately indicate increases in minimum wages increase unemployment, again substantially more so for males than females; but paradoxically the sign of the difference for the total equation is negative, indicating that although increased minimum wage levels reduce employment, they reduce labour force even more. The cross-check equation using U/L as the dependent variable discloses a positive, but statistically non-significant, coefficient for the minimum wage term. Fortin and Phaneuf[13] also found statistically insignificant results for their minimum wage variable, a result they attribute to multicollinearity.

There are many ways to give some meaning to the magnitudes of the estimated coefficients. We will do so by asking the following counterfactual question: what would have been the average rate of unemployment in Canada during the period 1972-75 in relation to the one actually observed, if the key policy variables had been at the mean values observed in some base period, everything else remaining the same. We arbitrarily chose two base periods, 1952-55 and 1962-65. Using the earlier base period, the results indicate the unemployment rate would have been 1.1 percentage points lower, with changes in unemployment insurance accounting for 0.9 percentage points of this, unionization changes 0.8 percentage points, and minimum wages changes -0.6 percentage points[14]. Using the 1962-65 base period, the total difference would have been 2.2 percentage points, with unemployment insurance accounting for 0.3 percentage points, unionization 2.2 percentage points[15], and minimum wages -0.2 percentage points.

---

12   The F values were 4.20 for L/P and 4.64 for E/P, with (4, 13) degrees of freedom.

13   FORTIN, P. and L. PHANEUF, "Why is the Unemployment Rate so High in Canada?", Paper presented at the Meetings of the Eastern Economic Association, Boston, May 10, 1979.

14   The counterfactual L/P and E/P were estimated using the "Total" equations in Table 1, and then an implied U/L computed using a population of 16,363.25, the average over the 1972-75 period. Details of the calculation are available from the authors upon request.

15   The large difference between base periods in the effect ascribed to unionization is due to the fact that UNION was substantially lower in 1962-65 than in 1952-55.

Finally, if whatever secular changes are captured in the time trends were also held constant at base period levels (in addition to the unemployment insurance, unionization and minimum wage variables), both base periods yield similar results: the unemployment rate in 1972-75 would have been 2.6-2.7 percentage points lower than actually observed. If one based the same counterfactual computation on the cross-check equation using U/L as the dependent variable, the same overall estimate would obtain, but the U/L equation would attribute much more of the difference to isolated factors, and less to the time trend.

Conclusion

The main point arising from these estimations, which we have not noted elsewhere in the literature, is the possibility that trade union activity may have a substantial effect on the level of reported unemployment. The question deserves additional investigation.

BIBLIOGRAPHY

CLOUTIER, J., "The Distribution of Benefits and Costs of Social Security in Canada, 1971-75", *Economic Council of Canada Discussion Paper No. 108,* 1978.

FORTIN, P. and L. PHANEUF, "Why is the Unemployment Rate so High in Canada?", Paper presented at the Meetings of the Eastern Economic Association, Boston, May 10, 1979.

GRUBEL, H., D. MAKI and S. SAX, "Real and Insurance-Induced Unemployment in Canada", *Canadian Journal of Economics,* Vol. 8, May 1975, pp. 174-191.

KAHN, L. and K. MORIUME, "Unions and Employment Stability: A Sequential Logit Approach", *International Economic Review,* Vol. 20, February 1979, pp. 217-35.

KRUGER, A., "The Direction of Unionism in Canada", in R. MILLER and F. ISBESTER (eds.), *Canadian Labour in Transition,* Scarborough, Ont., Prentice-Hall of Canada, 1971, pp. 85-118.

MAKI, D., "The Effect of Changes in Minimum Wage Rates on Provincial Unemployment Rates, 1970-77", *Relations Industrielles,* Vol. 34, pp. 418-30.

MINCER, J., "Unemployment Effects of Minimum Wage", *Journal of Political Economy,* Vol. 84, August 1976, pp. S87-104.

SWIDINSKY, R., "Minimum Wages and Teenage Unemployment in Canada", *Canadian Journal of Economics,* Vol. 13, February 1980, pp. 158-70.

STATISTICS CANADA, *Canadian Statistical Review* (11-003), Various issues.

STATISTICS CANADA, *Canadian Statistical Review, Historical Summary 1970* (11-505), 1972.

STATISTICS CANADA, *Historical Labour Force Statistics* (71-201), 1973.

STATISTICS CANADA, *Statistical Report on the Operation of the Unemployment Insurance Act* (73-001), Various issues.

APPENDIX

Variable Names and Data Sources

L/P — Labour force participation rate, using the "old" Labour Force Survey definition, expressed as a percentage. Data from Statistics Canada, 11-505, p. 48 for

1950-71; more recent years from Statistics Canada, 11-003, various issues for the aggregate. Data disaggregated by sex for 1953-72 from Statistics Canada, 71-201, Feb. 1973; for more recent years from Statistics Canada, 11-003, various issues; and for 1950-52 from information obtained from Statistics Canada, Vancouver office, by telephone. Simple averages of quarterly data (five observations for 1952) were used to obtain 1950-52 values.

E/P — Employment to population ratio, expressed as a percentage. Same sources as for L/P.

U/L — Unemployment to labour force ratio, expressed as a percentage. Data from Statistics Canada, 11-505, p. 48 for 1950-71; more recent data from Statistics Canada, 11-003, various issues.

B/W — The ratio of average weekly unemployment insurance benefits to industrial composite average weekly wages and salaries. Benefits computed from total benefit payments and total weeks compensated, data for 1950-1971 from Statistics Canada, 11-505, p. 50; for more recent years from Statistics Canada, 11-003, various issues. Wage data for 1950-1970 from Statistics Canada, 11-505, p. 56; more recent years from Statistics Canada, 11-003, various issues. The average weekly wages and salaries series for 1950-56 was multiplied times 1.0004 to convert to 1960 SIC, the constant being estimated from the 1957-60 overlap period. The benefit-wage ratios for 1972 and 1973 were multiplied times 0.827, for 1974 by 0.820, and for 1975 by 0.835 to adjust for the fact that benefits became subject to income tax in 1972. These correction factors are based on information in J.E. Cloutier, "The Distribution of Benefits and Costs of Social Security in Canada 1972-75", Economic Council of Canada, Discussion Paper No. 108, p. 40.

DSQL — Disqualifications and disentitlements for unemployment insurance benefits, from Statistics Canada, 73-001, various issues, per 10,000 weeks compensated. Sources for data on weeks compensated noted under B/W.

T — A series of consecutive integers, zero in 1945. T^2 is simply T, squared.

RTT — The ratio to exponential trend of constant dollar Gross National Expenditure (GNE). Data on GNE from Statistics Canada, 11-505, p. 16 with change of base to 1971 for 1946-1960; Statistics Canada, 11-003 December, 1977, for 1961-76. The natural logarithm of GNE was regressed on a intercept and a series of consecutive integers using annual data for the period 1946-76. The difference between the actual and prediction values is 1n RTT, and 1n RTT_{-1} is the same variable lagged are period.

UNION — The ratio of union membership to non-agricultural paid employment, expressed as a percentage. Data on union membership for 1950-68 from Arthur M. Kruger, "The Direction of Unionism in Canada", in R. Miller and F. Isbester (eds.), *Canadian Labour in Transition,* Scarborough, Ont., Prentice-Hall of Canada, 1971, p. 94; and for subsequent years from *Labour Gazette,* March 1970, August 1971, July 1973, July 1974, August 1975, May 1976 and May 1977. Data for denominator from Statistics Canada, 11-505, p. 48 for 1950-71; more recent years from Statistics Canada, 11-003, various issues.

M/W — The ratio of coverage weighted minimum wages applicable to adult workers to average hourly earnings in manufacturing. Data for males and females separately are given in R. Swidinsky, "Minimum Wages and Teenage Unemployment in Canada", paper presented at Canadian Industrial Relations Association Meetings, London, Ontario, May 1978, p. 8. We took weighted averages of the male and female series, using relative labour force numbers as weights, to construct the M/W series used in the "total" equations in Table 1.

[5]

Excerpt from *Probing Leviathan: An Investigation of Government in the Economy* (1984), 59–85.

CHAPTER 3

THE COSTS OF CANADA'S SOCIAL INSURANCE PROGRAMS

Herbert Grubel

I. INTRODUCTION

It is unusual to start a paper with graphs, but this is the best way to set the stage for the following analysis. As can be seen from Figure 3.1, during the last twenty years Canada's inflation and unemployment rates have steadily increased. In addition, and economically disturbing, except for a temporary improvement during the world-wide raw materials boom of the early 1970s, there has been a pronounced downward trend in real income growth per person.

Figure 3.2 shows the growth in total government expenditures during the same period. As can be seen, accompanying the deterioration in the economy's performance indicators is a steep increase in government expenditures as a percentage of GNP. In data presented below it will be shown that over 40 percent of the increase in these expenditures can be explained by the growth in spending on social welfare. The main theme of this paper is that *growth in welfare spending has contributed substantially to the deteriorating performance of Canada's economy by depressing the output of actual and potential beneficiaries of welfare and by creating a disincentive to produce on the part of those taxed to pay for the benefits.*

60   *Herbert Grubel*

Figure 3.1

**Canada's Economic Performance
Five-Year Averages, 1961-81**

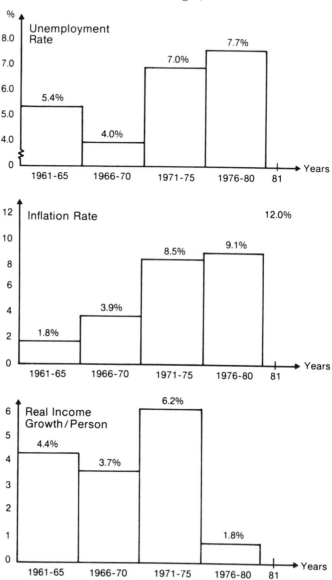

Source: *International Financial Statistics, 1981 Yearbook.*

The Costs of Canada's Social Insurance Programs   61

Figure 3.2

**Total Government Spending as Per Cent of GNP
Five-Year Averages, 1961-81**

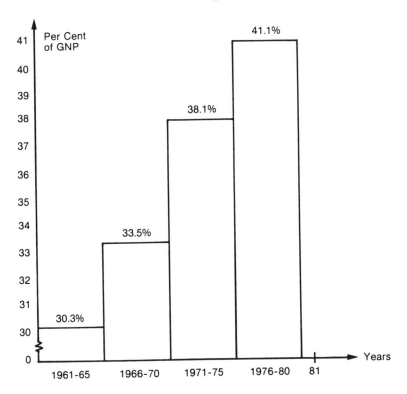

Source: *Economic Review, 1981.*

My emphasis in this paper should not be read as meaning that I believe Canada's problems are due solely to the growth in welfare expenditures. Blame, of course, also falls on monetary policies, excessive regulation, national energy and other policies. But the program of welfare expenditures represents an excellent case study of how liberal policy enthusiasm for fixing free markets has gone awry because of a blatant disregard of prices, incentives and the nature of man.

After presenting a brief rationale for social welfare programs, I review the recent growth in welfare expenditures and then discuss the unexpected side-effects of these programs that contribute to the deterioration of Canada's economic performance. In the concluding section I would have liked to offer solutions to these problems. Unfortunately, there are none. The best we, as a nation, can do is to make some better policy choices which include the unpleasant alternative of reducing direct government support for the needy as a prerequisite for a healthier and more dynamic economy and society.

II. RATIONALE FOR PUBLIC INSURANCE

The risk of losing one's capacity to earn, whether the result of accident, sickness, unemployment, old age or loss of assets, is an ever-present condition of life on earth. People have historically made all kinds of provisions to protect themselves from the incidence and consequences of these risks. They have modified personal behaviour patterns to avoid accidents and disease, and accumulated nest-eggs for income during hard times. A private insurance industry developed and permitted risk-sharing. The family and private charity flourished as people banded together in relatively small groups to cope with the calamities that could not be prevented or insured against.

Private insurance operations require that certain incentives be created to limit what is known as moral hazard effects. (Moral hazard means the tendency for people to modify their behaviour because insurance is available.) Otherwise, insurance-induced modifications in behaviour would result in larger increases in claims against the insurer. Thus, risk classes are set to determine levels of insurance premia and to discourage claims. Co-insurance is used to reduce nuisance and non-economic claims. Other institutions have also adapted to the reality of moral hazard behaviour. Private charity, by operating at a decentralized level, is able to limit moral hazard by the use of effective means tests and surveillance of claimants by methods that meet the group's standards of morality. It can be shown in a logically rigorous fashion that this private system of risk-reducing institutions tends to yield efficient results in the sense that individuals actually obtain the level of reduced risk they prefer and are willing to pay for it (Grubel, 1971).

Nonetheless, liberal critics of the free market process have found the private system of insurance deficient on several grounds. First, it is considered to be inefficient in that it requires private insurance companies to employ sales forces, portfolio managers and officers to police against moral hazard behaviour. It is argued that most of these expenditures could be saved by the use of universal, compulsory public insurance which also could reduce costs by exploiting economies of scale in administration. Second, private insurance fails to provide for such risks as unemployment and poverty after retirement. Third, private insurance is inequitable. It charges the highest rates to, and insists on the greatest degree of co-insurance from, the very people who frequently suffer from the insured risks and who, because of poor health and poverty, can least afford the costs of insurance. Healthy, well-to-do persons who can afford high premia and co-insurance rates typically enjoy low premia. Fourth, private charity forces dehumanizing means tests and procedures on the poor. Dickens' stories about crippled children being abused by their guardians and forced to beg and about the squalor of nineteenth century English work houses are symbolic of the shortcomings of private charity. The tendency for people to care for each other through several generations of a family living together, leads to dependence, exploitation and all kinds of horrors for which sociologists have found vivid terms.

On the above shortcomings, the inequity of private insurance looms largest as a motive for the public and uniform provision of many forms of insurance, but the dehumanizing effect of submitting oneself to means tests and facing continuous pressure to get off private charity's relief roles also explains public demand for the collective provision of insurance without such conditions.

The question of rights
Private methods for dealing with the risks of living have come under attack on grounds other than their inefficiency and inequity. In our time we have witnessed the rise of a philosophical movement promoting the view that the enjoyment of economic security is a right and that the state has an obligation to provide it.

The moral and natural rights philosophy which in eighteenth century England led Thomas Hobbes and others to argue that man has a moral right to a freely chosen government, provided the intellectual foundations for the French and American revolutions. It is now popular to apply much the same reasoning by which certain philosophers have defended the self-government right, to argue that the road from barbarism to higher levels of humanity and civilization can be travelled only through enshrining the right to economic security. A good society will not allow some unfortunate members to remain in need. This view has been expressed eloquently in Article 25 of the U.N. Declaration of Human Rights, which Canada signed in 1956:

> Everyone has the right to a standard of living adequate for the health and well-being of himself and of his family, including food, clothing, housing, and medical care and necessary social services, and the right to security in the event of unemployment, sickness, disability, widowhood, old age or other lack of livelihood in circumstances beyond his control.

I believe that today this philosophy is deeply rooted in the minds of a majority of Canadians.[1] It is important to appreciate this fact for the study of the growth and effects of Canada's social insurance programs as well as for designing potential changes in policies.

In conclusion, by concentrating on alleged inefficiencies and inequities, critics of private and free market means for dealing with life's risks have successfully attacked these institutions. In this attack they have been joined by those who see economic security to be a moral right of all citizens. In the kind of civilized society we want Canada to be, the state has an obligation to provide this security. Canada's politicians have responded affirmatively to these criticisms. As will be seen, they have fashioned a magnificent tapestry of programs for the provision of economic security. These programs eliminate inequitable risk classes, co-insurance provisions and means tests. Public insurance programs redistribute income and encourage the belief that the benefits are a right, not a privilege.

Need for utilitarian cost-benefit analysis

Before turning to the empirical part of my paper, I consider two important points raised by the preceding sketch. First, Canada's social insurance programs do not fare well in my critique, not because I believe they do no good, but because I find they do far more harm than good. The moral philosophers are certainly right—the fewer needy in a society, the better the society. Indeed, as we contemplate the size of welfare expenditures today, one cannot doubt that they do a lot of good for some and relieve the misery of many. Moreover, it is true that the operating cost of public insurance schemes per dollar of benefits provided is lower than that of private insurance. It is also true that savings in selling costs, management and economies of scale do exist.

Nevertheless, this paper shows that welfare programs have led to far higher costs than liberal critics of free markets have estimated and that philosophers tend to neglect entirely. The existence of the extra costs alone does not imply that welfare programs should be abandoned. After all, private insurance which would replace them also would incur large costs. The recognition of the existence and magnitude of the costs of social insurance merely suggests that it may be rational to modify terms at which public insurance is offered. Now that more evidence on the cost of welfare programs is available than when they were initiated, realistic and rational approaches to the design of the system should replace the original design that was largely motivated by emotion and forged in innocence of true costs.

Second, the cost-benefit analysis of Canada's social insurance system proposed below is, no less than the liberal welfare model, hallowed by a powerful philosophical tradition—the utilitarianism of Jeremy Bentham. Utilitarianism proposes that laws should not be based on absolute moral rights, but should all be subjected to a calculation of resulting gains and losses in the well-being of the members of society. Economists, with a well-known propensity for subjecting everything to cost-benefit analysis, are in this sense true Benthamites. Perhaps, if my findings and analysis are convincing, more utilitarians and economists will be hired in place of moral philosophers, lawyers and sociologists, by those institutions that formulate and administer Canada's social insurance programs.

III. SOME FACTS ABOUT WELFARE SPENDING

The complexity and scope of Canada's social insurance programs are often underestimated. Table 3.1, in which I list the programs under which Canada's federal, provincial and municipal governments are disbursing funds to the needy, should dispel any notion that Canada's social insurance arrangements are simple and lacking broad coverage. The table lists 47 programs, indicating for each the year when the program was inaugurated and expenditure levels for 1959, 1969 and 1979. For the major programs, the table shows the percentage growth rates between 1959 and 1979.

The data in Table 3.1 provide eloquent testimony to the rapid expansion of the Canadian welfare system. The number of programs has risen from 20 in 1959 to 43 in 1979. While this is not a precise measure, it is at least symbolic of the broadening of the social welfare effort during the period. The dollar value of expenditures rose from $2.7 billion in 1959 to $35.6 billion in 1979, or 12.9 times.

TABLE 3.1

Social Security Expenditures by Program ($ million)

	Year first in table	1959 $	1959 %	1969 $	1969 %	1979 $	1979 %	$ Growth 1959–79
1 Family Allowances	(1957)	475	17.2	560	7.4	2093	5.9	441
2 Youth Allowances and Quebec Schooling Allowances	(1965)			73	1.0	874	2.5	
3 Child Tax Credits	(1979)							
4 Old Age Security	(1957)	559	20.2	1297	17.1	4131	11.6	739
5 Guaranteed Income Supplement	(1967)			244	3.2	1234	3.5	
6 Spouses Allowance	(1976)					126	.4	
7 Canada Manpower Institutional Training Allowances	(1973)					117	.3	
8 Canada Manpower Industrial Training	(1967)			108	1.4	84	.2	
9 Registered Indians, Social Assistance	(1968)			22	.3	104	.3	
10 War Veterans Allowances	(1957)	55	2.0	96	1.3	236	.7	429
11 Veteran Disability and Dependent Pensioners	(1957)	151	5.5	223	2.9	437	1.2	289
12 CPP and QPP Retirement Beneficiaries	(1967)			7	.1	1055	3.0	
13 CPP and QPP, Surviving Spouse Pensioners	(1969)			20	.3	408	1.1	
14 CPP and QPP, Disability Pensioners	(1970)					229	.6	

No. & Program	(Year)							
15 CPP and QPP, Orphans and Dependent Children of Disabled Pensioners	(1968)			3		109	.3	
16 UIC, Unemployment Beneficiaries	(1957)	406	14.7	499	6.6	3917	11.0	965
17 UIC, Sickness Benefits	(1972)					156	.4	
18 UIC, Maternity Benefits	(1972)					200	.6	
19 UIC, Retirement Benefits	(1972)					15		
20 UIC, Fishing Benefits	(1972)					69	.2	
21 UIC, Persons in Manpower Training	(1972)					118	.3	
22 Workers Compensation, Temporary Disability	(1976)							
23 Workers Compensation, Pensions for Permanent Disability and Survivors	(1961)			69	.9	274	.8	581
24 Old Age Assistance	(1957)	85	3.1	104	1.4	494	1.4	
25 Blind Person Allowance	(1957)	60	2.2	13	.2	1		
26 Disabled Persons Allowances	(1957)	8	0.3	5	.1	1		
27 Unemployment Assistance	(1957)	31	1.1	29	.4			
28 CAP, Direct Financial Assistance	(1967)	62	2.2	34	.4	2179	6.1	
29 CAP, Homes for Special Care	(1968)			522	6.9	495	1.4	
30 CAP, Child Welfare	(1968)			91	1.2	165	.5	
31 CAP, Other Welfare Services and Work Activity	(1968)			78	1.0	462	1.3	
32 Vocational Rehabilitation of Disabled Persons	(1963)			60	.8	63	.2	
33 Registered Indians, Social Services	(1968)			8	.1	41	.1	
34 Mothers Allowances, Provincial-Municipal Cost-Shared	(1957)	41	1.5	8	.1			
35 Provincial Tax Credits and Rebates	(1974)					965	2.7	
36 Other Provincial Welfare Programs	(1957)	142	5.1	457	6.0	1582	4.4	1114

Continued overleaf

TABLE 3.1 (continued)

Social Security Expenditures by Program ($ million)

	Year first in table	1959 $	1959 %	1969 $	1969 %	1979 $	1979 %	$ Growth 1959–79
37 Hospital Insurance and Diagnostic Services	(1958)	64	2.3	812	10.7	3858	10.8	6222
38 Hospital Insurance and Diagnostic Services, Provincial Costs	(1958)	64	2.3	814	10.7	2631	7.4	4110
39 Medical Care Insurance	(1970)					1325	3.7	
40 Medical Care Insurance, Provincial Costs	(1970)					925	2.6	
41 Extended Health Care, EPF	(1978)					521	1.5	
42 Other Health Programs	(1957)	112	4.1	228	3.0	632	1.8	564
43 Worker Compensation, Hospital and Medical Care	(1957)	32	1.2	65	.9	198	.6	818
44 Other Hospital Care, Provincial	(1957)	234	8.5	451	5.9	835	2.3	357
45 Other Provincial Health	(1957)	70	2.5	426	5.6	1710	4.8	2442
46 Net Municipal Welfare	(1957)	35	1.3	84	1.1	339	1.0	969
47 Net Municipal Health	(1957)	75	2.7	95	1.2	210	.6	280
Total Expenditures		2762	100.0	7604	100.0	35619	100.0	1290
Total Number of Programs		20		33		43		220

Source: *Canada Yearbook 1981–82*, Table 8.16.

TABLE 3.2

Welfare Expenditures in Canada 1957–79

	Per capita expenditure in constant 1971 dollars	Annual increases in per capita constant dollars	Ratio of expenditures per $100 of personal income
1957	145	8.3	6.9
1962	174	0.5	7.9
1972	342	21.0	10.1
1977	502	4.4	11.3
1979	539	5.2	12.0
Average		6.1	

Source: *Canada Yearbook* 1980–81, Table 8.19.

Although the table records the growth of the system, the raw data it provides requires considerable further analysis. To convey a fuller appreciation of the growth in social insurance programs, Table 3.2 eliminates social insurance expenditures, on health, items 37–45 and item 47 of Table 3.1, leaving only welfare expenditures. Eliminating health expenditures makes the analysis of causes and effects of welfare spending simpler to follow.

As can be seen from Table 3.2, per capita expenditures in constant 1971 dollars rose from $145 in 1957 to $739 in 1979, an annual compounded rate of growth of 6.1 percent. Since per capita income during this period grew at only about half that rate, welfare expenditures rose from 6.9 to 12.0 percent of personal income.

Figure 3.3 shows major categories of government expenditures as a percentage of GNP for the years 1965–77, for which consistent data are available. This graph shows dramatically that social welfare expenditures rose more rapidly than any other category, both absolutely (by 5.7 percentage points) and in terms of rates from the base in 1965 (233 percent). Of the total increase in government expenditure noted in Figure 3.2, about 40 percent is accounted for by growth in welfare expenditures.

Figure 3.3 also shows that during this period defense expenditures

Figure 3.3

Government Expenditures as Per Cent of GNP
(Consolidated Federal, Provincial and Local)

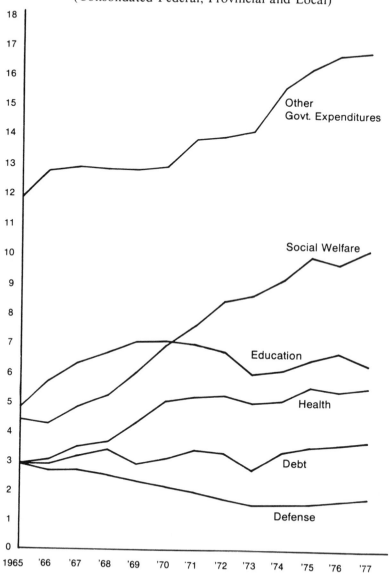

Source: Calculated from *Canada Statistical Yearbook*, various issues, Tables 22.1
          and 23.1.

fell by one half while education spending rose a miserly average annual rate of 1.5 percentage points or 25 percent on the 1965 base. Health expenditures rose at an average of 2.5 percentage points annually or 196 percent on the 1965 base. The largest category of government expenditures is a catch-all "other." It also rose sharply, but started from a much higher base. It contains many government services which might be categorized by some under the title social welfare. These include expenditures under programs for housing, agriculture and Indian affairs.

The adjustment of published welfare expenditure figures to reflect the welfare component of other spending programs is a difficult and contentious task and will not be undertaken here. The government presentation of statistics is subject to some manipulation, as may be seen from the treatment of defense expenditures. Until the early 1970s they were shown as such and exhibited a steady downward trend. They were then combined with domestic security expenditures to create a category entitled "Defense of Persons," which has shown a steady increase. To construct Figure 3.3 with consistent defense data, I had to consult different tables in government publications before and after the switch in nomenclature. I believe that by analogy, other government expenditures may contain substantial elements of social welfare spending that it is politic to hide.

G. Gilder (1981 estimated that in 1979 in the United States a welfare family of four received an *average* of close to $18,000 in government benefits and subsidies. This figure is meaningfully compared with the $9,000 annual earnings accruing to someone working full time at the minimum wage. I could not find similar calculations for Canada since there appear to be no data on the number of benefit recipients. A simple calculation may, nevertheless, usefully convey an idea of the per capita and per family level of Canada's welfare expenditures.

In 1979, Canadian social security expenditures totalled $36 billion. After subtracting the costs of health ($13 billion), family allowances ($2 billion) and UIC unemployment benefits ($4 billion), we are left with expenditures of $17 billion for retirement and welfare. By assuming that all two million Canadians over 65 were beneficiaries of the retirement programs, and that 10 percent of the remaining 20 million Canadians, received benefits, we calculate that $17 billion was spent on four million individuals. This would mean that in 1979 each welfare recipient received about $4,200 and a family of four received about $17,000. This figure is close enough to the one quoted by Gilder for the United States to give us some confidence, but it should be treated with great caution given the casual nature of the preceding calculations. Whatever the level of accuracy of this figure, there can be little doubt that per capita and family transfer payments have reached lofty heights in both Canada and the United States.

The above data document what most Canadians have believed for some time and have noted painfully at the end of April every year when income taxes are due. The Canadian system of welfare benefits has grown rapidly, is very generous to its beneficiaries, and costs taxpayers a great deal of money.

What are the causes of growth in welfare expenditures? Is there simply an increasing willingness of the middle and wealthy classes to share wealth with the needy, as some social workers, politicians and intellectuals argue? Or is there something to the widespread belief that the welfare system involves a great deal of cheating and generates its own need? The purpose in writing this paper is to provide answers to these questions.

IV. MORAL HAZARD

Most Canadians would agree that in 1965 the level of welfare in Canada was, by general standards, reasonable. True, the needy, poor and wretched of the earth were with us, but the combination of government welfare expenditures together with family and private charities provided these groups with the essentials. Twelve years later, in 1977, real per capita government welfare expenditures had risen threefold from 1965 levels. Despite this enormous expansion in per capita support levels, the needy, poor and wretched appear still to be with us. Few Canadians have strong personal experiences with welfare recipients and our knowledge comes largely from the CBC and the testimony of social workers. I tend to distrust the objectivity of both sources of information, but their testimony is the most persuasive available. Statistics on income and wealth inequalities are notoriously difficult to construct and interpret, but they basically support the CBC's and social workers' views that the vast growth in welfare expenditures has not created a correspondingly more equal society. What, if anything, has gone wrong?

Relation to welfare cost growth

The answer to this question is obviously complex and a full answer that would meet the most rigorous standards for evaluating evidence may never be possible. I do defend, however, the hypothesis that a very significant proportion of the growth in welfare expenditures has been due to what popularly is known as welfare "cheating," known in the insurance industry as "moral hazard," and interpreted by economists as rational behaviour towards changes in relative costs and opportunities introduced by the welfare system itself. In other words, the growth in expenditures is due largely to the broadening and deepening of demand for welfare services that would not have occurred in the absence of their availability. This is a case of supply engendering much of its own demand.

At the outset of the analysis I find it useful to allocate the observed growth in expenditures to different, easily assignable causes. To do this I show in Figure 3.4 the level of welfare expenditures in 1965 at $2.4 billion. The upward sloping lines from the 1965 origin indicate the levels of expenditure that would have been necessary to maintain real services per recipient at their 1965 levels. I have assumed that total need varies proportionally with the general population, the share of the aged in the population and the general rate of inflation. Accordingly, we see that expenditures of $7.7 billion in 1977 would have provided for delivery of the same level of real services per needy person in 1977 as was provided in 1965.

Because during the 1965–77 period real income per person in Canada rose substantially, it can be convincingly argued that the need to increase benefits declined proportionately, since public charity is supposed only to provide a minimal safety net for the needy. By the same token, others would argue that higher incomes permit a more generous treatment of the needy and that benefits should increase more rapidly than income. In Figure 3.4 I reflect the view which may well appeal to most Canadians' sense of fairness, that the needy should receive a *constant proportion of average incomes*. As can be seen, on this basis and after adjusting for inflation and changes in the age distribution of the population, in 1977 welfare expenditures should have totalled $14 billion. The true amount Canada spent in that year was $21 billion, or 50 percent more than my standard. I submit that this extraordinary growth was caused by the operation of moral hazard.

The dynamics of moral hazard

Moral hazard is a term used in the insurance industry to describe the

74   *Herbert Grubel*

Figure 3.4

Social Welfare Expenditures
in Canada

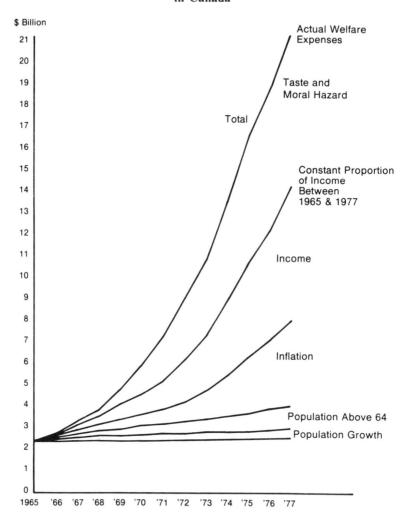

Note: $WE_{p,i} = (WE_{65} \cdot P_i)/(P_{65})$, where WE is welfare expenditure, P indicates adjusted
for population growth, 65 refers to value in 1965, i is the year = 66, 67, ...,77.
Further adjustments are made by multiplying $WE_{p,i}$ by $A_{65,i}/A_{65}$ where A is
population aged 65; and so on for each variable. The final value adjusted for
population, age, inflation (I) and income per capita levels (Y) is:
$WE^* = (WE_{65} \cdot P_i \cdot A_i \cdot I_i)/(P_{65} \cdot A_{65} \cdot I_{65})$

phenomenon that whenever a class of risks is insured, the incidence of the hazard increases. For example, restaurants insured against fire damage burn down more often that those that are not. Persons with dental insurance make more frequent visits to the dentist than those who do not have the same coverage.

Unfortunately, though moral hazard is a catchy term to describe the phenomenon, it is misleading. Only a few insured risks lead the insured to engage in outright cheating, which violates universal standards of morality, as for instance when someone torches a restaurant. Most increases in damage to insured property are due to more subtle changes in behaviour that economists identify as rational responses to changes in relative prices. For example, restaurant owners tend to become less careful about the removal of hazardous rubbish and kitchen grease simply because the return to expenditures for such services is lowered by the insurance. People with dental insurance have fewer cavities for shorter periods, replace lost teeth sooner, and have fancier replacement work done than those without such insurance coverage, for the good reason that their dental work costs them less.

Moral hazard behaviour is induced also by government insurance designed to pay benefits to those who suffer from unemployment, single parent status, blindness, other physical and mental handicaps, old age and many other conditions. The potential beneficiaries under these programs have one of the strongest of incentives to refrain from employment, because the schedule of benefits dramatically lowers their effective returns from work.

For example, a single mother who could earn $5 an hour or $200 a week working full time might, given the welfare system, be left with as little as $1.25 per hour. The welfare system taxes her $2.75 on each hour worked. (To arrive at this figure I assume that after work-related expenses, paying a babysitter and taxes, the disposable income from work is $150 a week. If the government pays the single mother $100 a week in support, the net gain from work is only $50 a week, or $1.25 an hour.) Many people who would find it worthwhile to work for $5 an hour would not do so for $1.25 an hour. Furthermore, by not working the single parent can earn additional income through the increased availability of discretionary time, to do informal and casual work for pay, learn skills and do work around the house that would otherwise have to be bought. Similar incentives, of course, affect all recipients of benefits when the benefits are conditional on not working.

76   *Herbert Grubel*

The impact of moral hazard behaviour on welfare expenditures in recent years has grown because of changing public attitudes and beliefs, as well as changes in relative prices. As was noted above, increasingly large sections of the community have accepted the idea that social welfare benefits are a right. This view is sometimes supported by the argument that most beneficiaries have in the past, as taxpayers, paid in advance for the funds they now claim.

Measurements of effects

Few people, not even socialists, moral philosophers or lawyers would deny today that moral hazard incentives of welfare programs exist and operate in the manner described above. What is in dispute is the magnitude of the effects. To decide the dispute over magnitudes, measurement is necessarily of the utmost importance. Unfortunately, little direct and reliable evidence is available.

One of the first direct measures of moral hazard effects was published by Grubel and Maki (1975) in connection with Canada's unemployment insurance program. We found that the 1972 increase in unemployment insurance benefits relative to wages, together with other liberalizations in the program concerning eligibility for benefits, led in 1975 to unemployment rates 1.5 percentage points above the 5.0 percent would have prevailed in the absence of the 1977 changes in the UIP.[2] This study of the unemployment insurance program, was possible because of the availability of data collected by the UIC. Such data, unfortunately, are rarely available for other social insurance programs. Therefore, all that can be done instead is to outline the typical changes in behaviour called forth by the availability of insurance to support the thesis that much of the recent growth in welfare expenditures is due to moral hazard.

Behaviour modifications

Some of the behaviour modifications stimulated by increasingly generous unemployment insurance follow:

1. Employers are quicker to lay off workers during slowdowns in business because they know benefits prevent extreme hardship, and allow workers to seek temporary employment without penalty and take holidays while awaiting recall.

2. Workers are more prone to leave when they are dissatisfied with the package of work conditions, pay, etc. because benefits cushion their income while they search for new jobs. Employers and workers often collude to disguise quits as lay-offs since to do so costs the employers nothing, and creates good-will among workers, and this collusive behaviour is not closely controlled by the authorities.
3. Once on unemployment insurance benefits, the worker is induced to extend job search time. Workers can set higher quality standards for the job they will accept and reduce the intensity of their search. They resort to many well-known techniques for resisting government pressures on them to accept job offers or for preventing offers from being made.[3]
4. Benefits are equivalent to government subsidies for seasonal workers and industries. In the absence of such subsidies, seasonal industries would be less prevalent in Canada and average unemployment would therefore be lower.
5. Benefits are equivalent to subsidies for people who prefer to live away from rapidly growing labour markets. In recent years, though there were labour shortages in the West, unemployment benefits permitted people to remain in remote areas and economically declining regions.
6. Benefits raise the effective wage rate earned while working. As a result, people with secondary interest in labour force participation, such as mothers, the young and elderly, are induced to enter the job market for short periods, quit after eligibility for benefits has been established, and contribute to the measured unemployment rate.

Because so much is known about the effects of unemployment insurance, the above list stands alone with little additional comment. On the other hand, it may be tempting to argue that moral hazard behaviour in the case of unemployment is a unique situation and tends to be high because co-insurance is very low while most other genuine welfare programs, such as aid for such groups as the blind, single mothers, etc., are associated with high levels of co-insurance and leave little room for what the English call fiddling. After all, it is hard to imagine someone going blind or becoming a single parent in order to become eligible for relatively miserly benefits. This line of argument misses the subtle effects of moral hazard behaviour.

Many people think of welfare aid for single parents as funds supporting a widow with five children who lost her husband in an industrial accident. However, reality tells a different story. The majority of beneficiaries of aid to single parents are young mothers with a single child. The ranks of the latter group have been swelled greatly in recent years by such benefit-induced changes in behaviour as the following:

1. More children are born out of wedlock because of the widespread awareness among young parents that the single mother will be supported by the state.
2. people move geographically for many reasons, but in the past, mobility was reduced by the desire to keep several generations of a family together for mutual assistance, including help with the raising of children if, for any reason, a parent became single. The availability of benefits for single parents has eased restraints on geographic mobility and left many single mothers unable to work since there are no babysitting grandparents nearby.
3. Sociologists have found that in families with low-income fathers, disputes that would otherwise be simple quarrels may lead to separation and divorce. This occurs because a mother experiences little and often no reduction in net income when she shows her husband the door, while a departing father leaves knowing the state will look after his family. This explains why the number of single parents reaches such high proportions in New York's Harlem, where wages are low, and at the other extreme in Sweden, where welfare benefits are high.
4. Since eligibility ceases upon marriage or remarriage, many relationships between single mothers and potential husbands remain informal, and in many jurisdictions, surreptitious.

The preceding short review of benefit-induced changes in behaviour in the case of the unemployed and single parents is designed merely to provide some rough indications of the types of adjustments that social insurance programs call forth and that have increased the cost of operating them. This kind of behaviour is as diverse as are people and it is ubiquitous, affecting every welfare program. Unfortunately, direct evidence is scant on the quantitative effect of moral hazard behaviour, except in the case of unemployment insurance, and even in the case of unemployment insurance the measured effects document only the reaction to recent liberalization of the program, not the program itself. Therefore, regarding the increase in welfare expenditures from 1965 to 1977, which I find excessive, attribution of this excess to moral hazard rather than another reason must remain indirect and circumstantial. Readers must, in the end, trust their own intuition and draw on personal experiences in reaching a final judgement on the validity of my hypothesis and the resultant need for policy changes.

V. COSTS THROUGH CHANGES IN THE NATURE OF SOCIETY AND HIGH TAXES

The availability of the social welfare system has other important influences on economic and social behaviour that most people identify as inducing extra costs on society. These can only be sketched here, but they may be more important than the expansion of demand for benefits and the subsequent financial outlays created by the types of moral hazard behaviour noted above. These changes are sometimes obvious and in other cases rather subtle.

For instance, attitudes towards work, education and savings are changed because the traditional penalties of failure are much reduced. One obvious influence is revealed by employers' complaints about the poorer work habits of the young, which are likely correct on average. Also, budget studies show that people include public pensions and medical benefits in their planning for retirement and emergencies, reducing correspondingly their private savings. On the other hand, more subtle effects occur when people make decisions for a lifetime. In Sweden, Lindbeck (1980) notes that universities have trouble filling engineering classes because this type of training demands serious effort whereas they face overcrowding in easier fields of study.

Another less apparent change is the growing social and political tension between those holding traditional values and paying high income taxes and those of the younger generation holding the new values, for whom welfare benefits and personal behaviour patterns are a matter of right. There are grave social and political consequences of this split in the community. Aid to people with marginal ability and willingness to work, such as single parents and the blind, engenders a sense of frustration and dependence. It is difficult to find the extra energy and resourcefulness to learn new skills, develop work habits and face the discomfort of working when the effective pay rate, the premium earned over and above the level of available benefits, is lowered so much by the availability of welfare benefits. Single parent support programs increase the number of children who are raised with only one parent in the home. Many of the crime problems of Harlem are attributed to the effects which this welfare program has had on generations of black families living there. The traditional multi-generation family relationship is broken up as welfare programs reduce intergenerational dependence. This may be welcomed for the extra mobility and personal freedom it sometimes brings but on the other side of the coin is the harm done by reducing the influence of grandparents and increasing the influence of television on the formation of character and values of young people.

Welfare programs have led to a vast proliferation of laws and regulations that invite fiddling to allow citizens to maintain their relative standard of living. This erosion of general standards of honesty has serious and as yet unconsidered consequences both for individual mental health and for the preservation of those standards of human interaction without which civil society can hardly survive. "Everyone is doing it" and "I've paid my taxes" are the easy rationalizations used.

In sum, social insurance programs erode the traditional values, constraints, penalties and institutions of society, the loss of which threatens the viability of that society. Even if many such changes taken individually are welcomed by some Canadians, especially those among us who often, for romantic reasons, dislike free market solutions to economic and social problems, these same Canadians would shrink from the prospect of the sum of these social changes bringing about a new type of society with unpredictable and potentially highly undesirable characteristics. There remain serious doubts about the productivity of a Canada in which the work ethic is replaced by the social attitudes induced by the welfare state.

Impact of taxation

The effect of benefits on recipients is possibly less serious for the economy than the impact of the taxes raised to pay for the benefits. The continued growth of unemployment and the rise in numbers of dependent single parents, retired and the disabled persons induced by social insurance shrinks the tax base. As a result, given the progressivity of Canada's tax structure, increasingly high marginal tax rates are needed to raise revenues. The hardest hit are the productive middle classes, with effects that only now are entering into society's consciousness.

Traditional economic theory teaches that taxation may or may not decrease work effort, depending on the relative size of the income and substitution effects. This may well be true for taxes used to pay for defense and roads, but it is not similarly true for taxes used to supply otherwise privately supplied services. Under these conditions the substitution effect is clearly cut and these taxes reduce work effort. Let me explain. When the government initiates a pension program and at the same time taxes me to pay for it, my wealth position is unchanged because the reduction in my flow of income is matched by the reduced obligation to provide support for my parents or save for my own retirement. All that is left is a tax-reduced return to effort and a guaranteed benefit that is independent of my own effort.

The traditional view of the incentive effect of taxation has tended to downplay the potential magnitude of all substitution effects because it was believed that most people had only limited opportunities to vary their working hours. This neglects three important long-run adjustments.

The first adjustment is made possible by the social insurance programs noted above. Sick leaves, absenteeism, temporary unemployment, early retirement, and work-related injuries all present opportunities for the enjoyment of leisure without significant loss of income. Germany and Sweden every year are setting new records in the number of work days lost through sickness and absenteeism even though the people of both countries are enjoying increasing levels of health by everyone's medical standards.

Second, young people rationally and in increasing numbers choose occupations which allow more opportunity to earn income in kind. Executives refuse promotions requiring geographic mobility because after tax income increases fail to compensate for the untaxed costs of settling in a new community. It is well known, for instance, that executives are increasingly unwilling to move from Vancouver to eastern locations even for significant promotions.

Third, there has developed in Canada a large underground economy, which has been estimated to be about one quarter of the size of the officially recorded economy (Mirus and Smith, 1981). It provides ready opportunities for strictly illegal activities, but for the purpose of the present analysis it is important to note that it consists in large part of work done in the home, for barter or for money which is not reported to the income tax authorities. Opportunities for such work are especially great for temporarily unemployed people who are recorded as sick or absent for unexplained reasons.

The preceding analysis suggests that there exists a synergistic link between the size of moral hazard, tax rates and the underground economy. Encouraged by a growing indifference to traditional values and the law, these developments feed upon and reinforce one another, thereby lowering incentives to work, decreasing productivity and changing the nature of Canadian society.

Implications for the future

Descriptions of life in the socialist paradise of Eastern Europe make depressing reading for most Canadians. Not only are living standards lower than in Canada, but still more depressing are the pictures of the drabness of everyday life, the omnipresence of the state and the hopelessness of ordinary citizens. I believe that through the expansion of the welfare state in Canada, our society is encouraging such conditions here. The blunting of incentives to work, savings and risk-taking has proceeded at a steady rate from both ends of the social scale — it removes penalties for failure as well as imposing high tax penalties on success. This decay has entered our perceptions only slowly, it takes more than one generation to accept the realities of a new economic and social environment and to learn that economic security is a citizen's moral right. In Canada, the second generation is now coming to the fore.

As in Eastern Europe, the protection of the achievements of the rights ideology justifies state paternalism and ever increasing regulation. Fortunately, our police institutions are still strongly steeped in democratic traditions, but troubles loom as the underground economy draws away increasing resources and reduces the tax base. It will not be a nice country to live in when there are three sharply distinct classes of people in the country — one class living off social insurance benefits, another working in the legitimate sector, paying high taxes and being only marginally better off in terms of consumer goods than the welfare section, and finally, a third class given over wholly to the underground economy and enjoying non-taxable incomes and high living standards.

VI. POLICY CONCLUSIONS

The sketch of historic trends in the growth of Canada's social insurance scheme just presented is unpleasant, but who would doubt its validity? Projections from the described trend into the future probably would be excessively alarmist. There must be a slowdown in the growth of the welfare state, if just because 100 percent of GNP is an absolute ceiling for the claims of the state. However, this is no basis for being sanguine.

Nothing in the above analysis of moral hazard as a main cause of the rapid growth in the demand for social insurance has not been known in principle and predicted by the opponents of the welfare state from its inception, and yet growth of the programs has been irresistible. Nevertheless, I believe that the beginning of the 1980s is an opportune time to re-examine these arguments in light of the experience of twenty years of welfare state expansion and of the economic crisis in unemployment, inflation and slow growth that has appeared in tandem with the welfare state.

None of this is to say that I have *proved* in this paper that the economic crisis is *caused* by the welfare state. Undoubtedly many other forces have contributed to the development of the crisis, from government policies of monetary inflation and social regulation to exogenous technical change and the global population explosion. If, like the lemming, we hide from reality and do not act until someone succeeds in proving absolutely that the welfare state is the *cause* of economic malaise, we may well be doomed to the fate of Eastern Europe. My analysis is a plea to move the Canadian system of social insurance from its pedestal as the political sacred cow that no one dares criticize, let alone touch. We need to have our intellectuals, business leaders and politicians openly discuss the trends and issues presented here. We must end the idea that anyone wanting to question the wisdom of the welfare state model is necessarily a fascist and a successor of Genghis Khan, bent on destroying the achievements of Western civilization and its system of moral rights.

VII. RECOMMENDATIONS

Unfortunately, there are no "solutions" to the problems posed by the existence of economic risks in the world which do not bring problems of their own. Private and market methods for dealing with risk leave many Canadians unhappy about resulting inequities, indignities and the suffering of some. The government approach to dealing with risks has the costs noted above. The mistake made by many critics of the market's means of distributing and allocating risk is to compare its shortcomings with the idealized perfect working of a mythical government-run system. We need to compare the results of both approaches in the real world, not someone's conception of their ideal norms.

When there are no "solutions" to problems, it is necessary to choose rationally between the available alternative ways of dealing with them. In the case of economic risks, there are no methods for eliminating them. We can only choose ways that minimize the costs of insuring against them.

In my view, the state provision of economic security is a distinctly inferior method for dealing with economic risk. The entire preceding analysis of the costs of the welfare system serves to support my judgement. In comparison, free market solutions are superior through their preservation of private incentives for self-protection, the reliance upon a dynamic and efficient private insurance industry with a strong self-interest in the control of moral hazard, and the reliance on private charity for dealing compassionately with unfortunately situated people and for limiting moral hazard. Thus, I believe that the true welfare of Canadians would be served by turning away from the collective provision of insurance and returning to the decentralized choices of individuals.

NOTES

1. I recently attended a colloquium sponsored by the Liberty Fund at which academic lawyers, sociologists, political scientists, moral philosophers and economists discussed the history and issues surrounding constitutional guarantees of human rights. After lengthy discussions and after the economists had pointed to the growing evidence of the very serious costs of welfare spending and taxing, 60 percent of the intellectuals at the colloquium remained convinced that Canadians had the "right" to the economic benefits mentioned in the U.N. Charter and that the state had an obligation to deliver them. None of the economists present voted with the majority.

2. Studies of unemployment compensation programs in other countries modelled after the Grubel-Maki study came up with analogous results. See the proceedings of a conference on this subject sponsored by the Fraser Institute, Grubel and Walker (1978).
3. One such technique involves going to mandated job interviews with a two-day-old beard and in old clothing over which some alcohol has been poured.
4. For a technical analysis of these issues in a world with complementary and substitute government services, see Lindbeck (forthcoming).

REFERENCES

Economic Council of Canada. *Reforming Regulation 1981.* Ottawa: Government Publishing Centre, 1981.

Gilder, G. *Wealth and Poverty.* New York: Basic Books, 1981.

Grubel, H.G. "Risk, Uncertainty and Moral Hazard." *Journal of Risk and Insurance,* March 1971.

————and Maki, D. "Real and Insurance Induced Unemployment in Canada," *Canadian Journal of Economics,* May 1975.

————and Walker, M., ed. *Unemployment Insurance: Global Evidence of Its Effects on Unemployment.* Vancouver: The Fraser Institute, 1978.

Lindbeck, A. "Tax Effects vs. Budget Effects on Labour Supply." *Economic Inquiry* (forthcoming).

————. "Work Disincentives in the Welfare State." Summer Paper 164, Institute for International Economic Studies, University of Stockholm, 1980.

Locke, J. *Second Treatise of Civil Government.* Laslett, ed., Cambridge: Cambridge University Press, 1960.

Mirus, R. and R.S. Smith. "Canada's Irregular Economy." *Canadian Public Policy.* VII, 3, Summer 1981.

[6] [1986]

Herbert G. Grubel*

Government Deposit Insurance, Moral Hazard and the International Debt Crisis

After the occurrence of major economic problems governments typically enact policies to prevent such problems in the future. Unfortunately, these policies often involve government interference in market processes. Typically they are designed to deal with circumstances that have a low probability of occurring again in the future. As a result, costly preventative measures are in place for long periods, produce avoidance behavior which adds to the costs and therefore yield low and often negative social returns. I believe that in the aftermath of the LDC debt crisis of the 1980s there exists exactly such a temptation for governments to increase government regulation and control without corresponding benefits.

However, I believe that these conditions can be prevented if governments react to the debt and other crises by initiating policies which improve rather than reduce the effectiveness of competition and market processes. In the case of the debt crisis, such a policy involves requiring the insurance of all bank deposits by private companies. Such a policy would lead to the internationalization of externalities, the existence of which underlies the perception of the debt problem as an issue for public concern.

In Section I of this paper I present a simple model of insurance drawing heavily on a paper I had published in 1971. It focuses on the phenomenon of moral hazard and leads to some speculation about the apparent need for public insurance for bank deposits, which exists in a number of major countries. Section II uses this model to analyze some of the problems which the U.S. deposit insurance scheme has encountered. In Section III I discuss the feasibility of creating an international deposit insurance program operated by the private sector.

I. Insurance and Moral Hazard

Insurance is an economic and social institution which permits members of society to spread the risk of being afflicted by a certain hazard. If we assume that the introduction of an insurance scheme does not alter behavior, the economics of insurance is a simple matter. Annual premiums in competitive equilibrium would be at a level sufficient to pay costs of administration and risk capital and, most fundamentally, the costs of the damages which are expected to occur during the year. Such expected damages would be calculated by taking the average of past years. Un-

---

*The analysis of this paper draws heavily on a manuscript which Ed Kane made available to me. He also provided useful comments on an earlier draft.

certainty would require that premiums contain a charge for building up a contingency reserve. Premiums would be lowered by any earnings from investments of contingency reserves. Important for later analysis is the institution of reinsurance of risks. It basically involves a system whereby insurance companies take out insurance to cover the risks of their own activities. It permits individual firms to spread their exposure very widely across different types of risk and different regions.

In the real world, however, the introduction of insurance has the effect of altering the behavior of the insured. In the specialized language of the industry, this phenomenon is known as moral hazard behavior. For economists, this is a misleading descriptive term. The changes in behavior are influenced somewhat by standards of morality, but the basic cause of these changes is that the insurance alters incentive structures through the changing of relative prices. Generally, it leads to willfully or voluntarily increased risk-taking.

A well-known illustration of moral hazard behavior involves the fact that restaurants and stores with fire insurance coverage tend to suffer from fire damage more often than those without. More controversial, but also more important, is the moral hazard phenomenon accompanying social insurance. Elsewhere I have used the concept in the specification of econometric tests, which show that unemployment rates in Canada and the United States are an increasing function of the generosity of insurance programs. Of course, moral hazard is also a problem in the insurance of bank deposits against the insolvency and illiquidity of deposit institutions.

1. Moral Hazard in Banking

Economists have no difficulties understanding how insurance changes relative prices and therefore leads to rational alterations of behavior. Persons who make deposits at a bank without insurance have strong incentives to keep themselves informed about the financial condition of the bank. The banks in turn know about this and pay corresponding attention to the composition of their portfolios and to providing a flow of clear information about their ongoing policies and financial conditions. In market competition product differentiation among banks would tend to make them choose portfolios with different risk characteristics and pay interest on deposits that compensates depositors for the degree of risk inherent in these different portfolios. Under these conditions private institutions would develop and lower the cost of information facing individual depositors. These institutions would gather and sell independent and reliable information about banks' financial conditions.

It is clear that with insurance, much of this behavior is changed because it does not yield any returns. Fully insured depositors have no effective incentives to pay attention to the condition of bank portfolios. In fact, incentives are perverse. Since investigations are costly, they result in lowered wealth for depositors. At the same time, the insurance and the absence of depositors' concerns relax banks' incentives to manage their portfolios in the interest of depositors and to advertise their condition. The returns to competition based on risk-adjusted deposit rates are eliminated. Competition takes the forms well known from the study of imperfect market models. Another effect of the insurance is the disappearance of the market for the independent gathering and dissemination of information. The outcome of these and many other marginal changes in the behavior of a wide variety of economic agents leads to the increased incidence of bank failure following the introduction of deposit insurance.

2. Controlling Moral Hazard

The existence of moral hazard does not prevent the development of insurance facilities. Instead, it causes insurers to institute methods for the control of the phenomenon. In the case of deposit insurance these methods consist of using coinsurance, setting risk-related premium rates and collecting and distributing information.

Coinsurance

The use of coinsurance simply stipulates that the payment for damages is limited to a certain percentage of the total or that a certain deductible sum is not included. For example, consider a system where 10 percent of a deposit is lost if a bank fails. Under these conditions, depositors face again the same kinds of incentives to keep themselves informed about the condition of the bank that they do when there is no insurance. It is clear, however, that the strength of this incentive is an increasing function of the size of the coinsurance deductible.

Under competition among insurance companies the size of coinsurance can be chosen by buyers of insurance. The greater the coinsurance is, the lower are the premiums charged. Experience of the insurance companies and competition assure that the premiums for each level of coinsurance cover the rate of losses. All of these facts are known to most people who, as buyers of property insurance, have been faced with the choice of different deductible and premium rates. As a result of competition there is a tendency for this system to lead to efficient outcomes in that peoples' premiums on average cover the cost of the losses in the coinsurance class they have chosen.

There is no reason why different banks could not opt for different coinsurance levels on the deposits they insure. Banks' premium levels would differ accordingly. Those offering large deductibles would face lower premiums than those offering small deductibles. To cover operating costs, the former can function on narrower spreads between lending and borrowing rates than the latter. Consumers would then be able to choose from a spectrum of coinsurance and earnings levels that best suited their preferences.

Risk Classes

A second method for controlling moral hazard used by insurers involves the setting of risk-related premium rates. Thus, buildings with sprinkler systems and concrete walls have lower fire insurance rates than those without. Heavier and faster automobiles cost more to insure than do the light and slower ones. Young males pay more for automobile insurance than do women with young children. Under competition private insurance companies set premium rates for such identifiable risk classes according to loss experience, which assures that each class pays for the true cost of insuring it.

Setting risk premiums and classes in this manner reduces moral hazard as it eliminates subsidies inherent in class-less systems and charges each buyer the true cost of risky activity. For example, teenage automobile drivers face high insurance premiums and therefore some of them cannot afford to drive. As a result, overall accident rates are lowered and the degree of moral hazard is decreased. In addition, the risk-related premium system encourages the use of loss-reducing substitutions such as the installation of sprinklers in buildings and the use of safer cars. It also reduces the problem of adverse selection to be discussed below.

In bank deposit insurance the practice of setting risk-related premiums would have the analogous effect of inducing portfolio adjustments and information flows that lead to efficient outcomes. For a general economist it is difficult to envision the details of such risk-class systems and the adjustments that they might induce. Risk classes based on different types of portfolio assets are the most obvious. But one can also imagine classes that are a function of the type and volatility of deposit classes, which influence the riskiness of banking. Kane [1985] emphasizes the fact that the electronic revolution in information technology makes possible risk survey techniques that previously had been unthinkable for the banking industry.

It should be noted here that the establishment of the number and type of risk classes is itself a matter determined by the market. Insurance companies develop this method for the control of moral hazard to the point where the marginal cost equals marginal benefits. New information and technology change these margins all the time. The recent introduction of special life-insurance rates for non-smokers was due to such changes.

Adverse selection, which is a serious problem in the administration of all insurance systems, occurs as the buyers of insurance attempt to obtain coverage at rates that are less than the true expected cost of losses. The establishment of risk classes overcomes some of the problems of adverse selection as the insured are charged different rates according to certain criteria. Unfortunately, there are strong private incentives to cheat, as when a person with a newly diagnosed heart disease attempts to buy life insurance while hiding the pathology. Insurance companies use investigative methods to protect themselves against such adverse selection. Such protection is often expensive and limits the establishment of risk classes. However, under competition, one would expect again that the companies push such investigative activities and the establishment of different risk classes to the margin where cost and benefits are equal.

One of the great problems of the private insurance industry has been that, under the system just described, some potential buyers of insurance appear to be unable to obtain any coverage. This situation arises when existing information and technology have led to the establishment of a particularly risky group, such as male teenage drivers of automobiles. The economic premiums for this group may be so high that no sales are made and for all practical purposes this is interpreted as reflecting the total non-availability of insurance. In democracies, such groups of allegedly non-insurable people have a tendency to use their interest group power to get politicians to force insurance companies into offering insurance at what amounts to subsidized rates.

Elsewhere [1971] I have argued that Knight's famous distinction between risk and uncertainty is an invalid dichotomy. Hazards are non-insurable when the cost of moral hazard control measures together with remaining expected loss rates lead to the setting of economic premiums at which there is no market for the insurance. Profit insurance is characteristic of this type of insurance. Loss rates with different moral hazard control systems can be established in principle and it would be in the interest of the insurance companies to do so. The reason why they don't is that with the methods for moral hazard control available, the economic cost of premiums for profit insurance would be too high for anyone to buy it. These considerations suggest that the establishment of a viable private deposit insurance is an empirical question. We return to this issue in Section III.

Information

A third method for the control of moral hazard involves the collection and distribution of information relevant to the loss rate from the insurance offered. Thus, insurance companies spend substantial sums on the investigation of those who want to buy insurance in order to establish risk classes, as we noted above. In addition, however, they also tend to investigate compliance with conditions under which the insurance was sold, as persons are likely to find out if they purchase life insurance as non-smokers and then smoke heavily. Insurance companies also carry out investigations to protect themselves against outright fraud, such as arson of insured property or suicide in the case of life insurance.

Information gathered in such investigations is used primarily for the benefit of each company. However, there also exist industrial associations to which these companies report some of their findings and from which in turn they obtain information. For example, the Insurance Bureau of Canada is such an industry agency which compiles detailed statistics on automobile insurance levels, accident rates and costs and more. This information is published and is used widely not only by the industry but also by governments as well as the producers and consumers of automobiles. This information-gathering activity of private insurance industries is important for the subsequent analysis and interpretation of the debt crisis of the 1980s.

Insurance companies have additional methods of preventing moral hazard behavior. They encourage the use and development of accident preventing materials and processes, as when they get involved with laboratories that develop and test electrical safety equipment. Insurance companies also advise clients on safe packaging and shipment. They become involved in advertising compaigns against health and accident hazards, such as drinking and smoking.

In sum, the preceding analysis suggests that insurance is an industry like any other where the profit motive tends to result in the efficient allocation of resources. The individual cost of accidental losses is reduced by the collective sharing of the risk. Changes in behavior affecting the incidence of accidents as a result of the availability of insurance are limited through economically efficient means of moral hazard control. Whatever moral hazard cannot be eliminated leads to an increase in insurance rates. These become so large as to prevent the sale of any coverage except in cases where the economic cost of insurance is so great that it is economically inefficient to have it sold in private markets. This condition gives rise to a so-called market failure only if the non-availability of this insurance results in negative externalities. If this is the case, the government should subsidize the buyers of this form of insurance. The failure of the private sector to provide certain types of socially desirable insurance therefore is not a sufficient argument in favor of its provision by the government.

II. Problems with Government Deposit Insurance

The bank deposit insurance system of the United States was set up during the 1930s. It is a complex system run partly by special agencies and partly by the Federal Reserve Board. This is not the place to review the details of operation of the U.S. system. The main objective of this section is to make the case that the international debt crisis of the 1980s was due to the fact that the system was run by government agencies rather than by a private industry.

The U.S. insurance system was set up by the government in the 1930s because the large-scale and pervasive bank failures of the Great Depression had added to the country's economic troubles and, obviously, there had been no adequate private insurance system to prevent these externalities. Kane has argued that the absence of such private insurance, in the analytical framework presented above, was due to the following. Under the technological conditions of the time, information gathering and moral hazard control would have been so limited and moral hazard so great that the provision of insurance could have taken place only at such a high cost that there would have been no market for it. In addition, he argues that deposit insurance is different from all other insurance in that it involves a special systemic risk.

Systemic risk in the banking field arisis from the fact that a deep recession tends to affect all banks simultaneously. Under such extreme conditions there might be so many bank failures that historic loss experiences are made irrelevant and private insurers' resources are inadequate to cover all losses. Such conditions are unlikely to affect other forms of insurance, except perhaps during periods of war, and such contingencies are usually excluded from private property and life insurance contracts. While the systemic risk explanation in a sense is a subset of the more general cost explanation advanced above, for the present purposes of analysis it is not necessary to settle the historic issue with a logically rigorous and empirically supported argument.

1. Insurance as a Political Matter

Whatever may have been the ultimate causes in the 1930s, the important fact is that presently the U.S. deposit insurance system is owned and operated indirectly by federal and state government-sponsored corporations. The modern theory of interest group and agency behavior suggests what should be the outcome of this institutional arrangement. The insurance system is used to further the interests of politicians and of the industry. Kane's [1985] book and much of the literature he cites are devoted to documenting this situation. Of course, in ways well known from the study of agencies, the alleged motives of behavior are much more noble. All actions are defended on the grounds that they prevent monetary instability or collapse and therefore the development of a great economic tragedy for all Americans and the world.

There are two main ways in which the policies of the government insurance agencies have served the interest of the industry. First, the full coverage of the majority of all deposits has provided the industry with the opportunity to advertise this condition and therefore to deflect efforts of depositors to monitor the banks' portfolios. The supervisory responsibility of the government agency has been perceived by the public to be a sufficient protection from mismanagement and fraud. No independent private monitoring business has developed.

The reliability of the government insurance effort was perceived to have been especially great since it was backed by both the monetary authority and the government's taxation capacity. In fact, the supervision of federally chartered banks is undertaken by the monetary authority itself.

It seems obvious that with such backing and with public confidence in the government's determination to prevent a major banking crisis, the public insurance agencies did not have to accumulate as large a contingency reserve as private insurers would have had to. As a result, premiums for banks have been below their true actuarial value, to the benefit of the owners of banks. More generally, the banking industry has been uneconomically large at the expense of competitive financial intermediaries because the government subsidy implicit in the low insurance rate encouraged this result.

Much of the interest in deposit insurance reform in the United States in recent years is due to the fact that independent estimates of the insurance agencies' contingent liabilities and actual reserves suggest that they are either insolvent or close to that condition. This fact may be interpreted as indirect evidence of the preceding proposition that the insurance system has been operated not as an economically viable institution but as one that served the interests of the industry it was supposed to have insured and regulated. Kane describes in his book the methods used by the U.S. insurance agencies in dealing with a recent spate of bank failures. His main conclusion is that these methods are designed primarily to avoid political embarassment for the government and to protect the accounting position of the insurance agencies. He suggests that these motives have resulted in the de facto nationalization of U.S. banks and through it the subsidy of bank share holders.

The second way in which the government deposit insurance system has served the interest of the banking industry is through its failure to use market instruments for moral hazard control. It is true that the insurance authorities are required by law to supervise the management of bank operations to assure their economic safety. Regulatory guidelines are in place for this purpose and inspectors and fine structures are used to effect compliance. However, the task set for the insurance agencies by the legislature has been impossible to carry out effectively. To assure that the risk of bank failure is eliminated would mean that the control agencies would have to examine every transaction by the banks and in effect have better judgements on their economic viability. U.S. bank supervisory authorities may have succeeded in reducing outright fraud and criminal activities in the industry by making them more expensive. But the recent record of bank failures suggests that, especially during a period of rapid innovations in the banking business, the regulators were not up to the task.

Because of the authorities' reliance on regulatory supervision there is no coinsurance for depositors and premium rates are not risk related. If I may speculate about the causes for the absence of these control mechanisms I would suggest that a deductible is politically not very popular. A recent cartoon in a leading U.S. newspaper reflects this idea. In this cartoon a bank customer is told by the teller of a bank: "Yes, your deposit is federally insured, but only up to six dollars. Now, how do you like that?"

In addition, especially dynamic banking firms would be expected to prefer and lobby for a system without coinsurance and risk-rated premiums, since it would permit them to obtain indirect subsidies by increasing the return on their activities. One could also invoke theories of agency behavior in explanation, such as that the centralized control system requires more agency manpower and resources, which in turn raises rent to its political and managerial leaders. Whatever may be the reasons, the fact is that in spite of the urging of experts during the design of the system and in recent years that these moral hazard control mechanism be used, they have been and are absent.

In fact, however, the problem of moral hazard is even worse than is suggested by the absence of such mechanisms. The system has demonstrated in recent years that when the chips are down and banks are in trouble, only a relatively small proportion of small banks are allowed to fail. Large banks inevitably are bailed out by clever maneuvers that save most of the equity of owners at the present or future cost of taxpayers. These policies set precedents that cannot but further increase moral hazard. They vindicate the actions of those banks that in the past managed their affairs aggressively and brought high returns and dividends to their owners while they disregarded the accompanying risks because they knew that these risks would ultimately be borne by the insurance system and the government.

It makes an interesting study to discover how private market institutions have developed to exploit the inflexible regulations of the government insurance scheme. Thus, in order to lower the cost that accompanies efforts to avoid the ceiling on the maximum amount of insured deposits (recently raised to $100,000), there are now brokers who use electronic information systems to place large depositors' funds in the appropriate number of institutions. In addition, bankruptcy court laws treat deposits matched by an owner's corresponding obligation as claims that rank ahead of other categories. Through clever legal and accounting maneuvers some large depositors have in fact succeeded in having their assets protected beyond the legal maximum in any case of bank failure (1).

Finally we should note that the government operation of the deposit insurance system has failed to generate the kind of information which private insurance companies surely would have demanded from their clients. It is entirely conceivable that under a private system there would now exist universal and readily accessible ratings for banks analogous to the bond ratings of Dun and Bradstreet. And we would expect banks to use such ratings in their competition for markets. In addition, private insurers would have been much more alert to the effects of technological change and deregulation on the creditworthiness of banks than the public authorities have been.

2. Implications of a Public Deposit Insurance Scheme for the Debt Crisis

In the light of the preceding analysis, one of the most important results of the fact that the United States has a public deposit insurance scheme is the following. After the middle 1960s U.S. banks established a large presence abroad in order to participate in the rapidly developing Eurocurrency and global money markets. The deposit insurance law excluded deposits made at these U.S. bank branches abroad, even though it should have been obvious that the results of their activities impinged directly on the liquidity and solvency of their domestic parents. In this sense, the foreign branch business affected directly the probability of U.S. domestic bank failure and therefore the responsibility of the deposit insurance agencies.

In fact, the interrelationship of domestic and foreign banking business went beyond the profits and losses transferred from foreign branches. It had been established fairly early during the development of the Eurocurrency business that host countries such as the United Kingdom expected foreign head offices of U.K. branches to accept responsibility for their operations beyond that implicit in the strict interpretation of corporate liability. As a result, it is quite certain that failures of foreign branches would have involved U.S. banks directly and in ways which should have called for corresponding, protective action by the deposit insurance authorities. Yet, these actions did not take place.

The failure of the U.S. bank deposit insurance agencies to act in the light of these international developments resulted in an implicit subsidy of these foreign bank operations by the U.S. government. This subsidy, which permitted the banks to operate on narrower spreads between lending and borrowing rates, enabled them to attract more deposits from

---

(1) See Kane [1985] for further explanations and examples.

the regulated U.S. environment and make more loans to borrowers who otherwise would have had to do business in traditional, supervised banking markets. As a result, loans to developing countries grew more rapidly and by more than they would have in the absence of the subsidy.

The preceding analysis suggests that the U.S. taxpayers have implicitly subsidized the loans made to developing countries during the period leading up to the debt crisis. They have also subsidized the depositors, who received higher rates of return than they could have in other markets without having to worry about the safety of their deposits. It is ironic, of course, that a sizeable fraction of these deposits were owned directly or indirectly by rich OPEC interests. Therefore, in a sense the system contributed to the prolonged maintenance of the cartel's power.

3. Lack of Information

There appears to be now some agreement among observers that one of the important factors contributing to the rapid growth of Third World debt has been the absence of knowledge about its size during the crucial years (1). This state of affairs came about because the development of Eurocurrency banking was accompanied by an escape of banks from the domestic environment which previously had assured disclosure of lending activities to regulatory authorities. The new bank business itself did not generate the equivalent type of information because confidentiality was an instrument of the competitive struggle for what seemed to be very lucrative investments. By the time international cooperative efforts were made to assemble and publish the total debt positions of individual countries, the damage had already been done. It was a little like closing the barn door after the horses had gotten out.

In the debate over the merit of public and private deposit insurance it is useful to contemplate whether such a lack of information about the exposure of all banks would have taken place if there had been private deposit insurance systems in the United States and other major countries. I would suggest that under a private system the information would have been available much more promptly and that therefore the debt crisis would have been avoided. In the first place, a private system would surely have blown the whistle on the implications of the growth of the Euro-banking business. This would have prevented the implicit subsidy of this activity and its growth would have been slower. In addition, private insurers would have routinely collected and interpreted information about the indebtedness of individual countries. The profit-oriented operation of coinsurance and of risk-adjusted premiums would inevitably have generated this information.

Perhaps the preceding analysis overstates the role which a private deposit insurance system could have played in the prevention of the inter-

---

(1) See Devries [1985]; Guttentag, Herring [1985]; and Smith, Cuddington [1985], for expression of this view.

national debt crisis of the 1980s. On the other hand, the arguments appear to have enough merit to suggest that the possible prevention of such a crisis in the future represents one more argument in favor of private as against public deposit insurance systems. Certainly, the case study of the debt crisis reveals once more the relative inflexibility of public institutions in a world of rapid technical and economic change. Because of their size and political character, such institutions are known to be very slow in responding to changes in circumstances that were not envisaged at the time that legislators created the institutions.

III. Private Insurance and International Banking

The preceding analysis suggests that governments of the major industrial countries should consider the passage of laws which require that all bank deposit institutions operating under their jurisdiction must purchase deposit insurance. This law would apply to banks engaged in domestic as well as international business. Under these conditions, private insurance companies would begin to offer such insurance. It is clear from the above that such a policy would not only serve to improve the efficiency and stability of domestic banking. It would also decrease the probability that in the future technical and regulatory changes would lead to crises like the recent one involving the developing countries' debt. There are a number of objections to this idea.

1. Systemic Risk

The first objection is that private insurance companies would be willing to enter into this business only if there were some way of dealing with systemic risk. An alternative way of putting this point is to say that insurance companies would charge extremely high premiums in order to compensate themselves for the systemic risk, so that deposit institutions in competition with other financial intermediaries could not "afford" the insurance.

The validity of this position depends on one's interpretation of the nature of systemic risk. Elaborating on the points made about it above, one may say that it consists of the consequences of national illiquidity and of an overall dramatic decline in the value of banks' assets. Under the proposed system of private deposit insurance the provision of liquidity for the banking system as a whole would remain the responsibility of the central bank. Recent experience with central banks suggests that they are fully aware of their responsibilities in this field and that they can be relied upon to carry out these responsibilities in the future. Undoubtedly, the growing acceptance of illiquidity as a cause of the Great Depression adds to the willingness of central banks to stand by this policy.

This leaves the risk of an overall dramatic decline in all bank asset values. It should be noted that this is significantly different from the systemic risk which accompanies the failure of a large bank, which in turn would create insolvency for potentially many other banks and therefore the system as a whole. Deposit insurance reduces this risk to a negligible level. In fact, this is exactly its purpose. It is also highly likely that the policing function of the private deposit insurance scheme will lower the likelihood of a dramatic reduction in the asset values of a significant proportion of all banks which would endanger their solvency. Under these conditions I find it difficult to envision a scenario that would bring about such a crisis. However, the answer on this point is ultimately an empirical one and I must live with the possibility that my conclusions are wrong.

2. Credibility of the Insurers

A second objection to the proposal for private deposit insurance is that the exposure of the insurers would be so large that public confidence in their ability to cover losses would be in doubt. This view puts great weight on the history of insurance companies which have prospered for prolonged periods, only to fail when they were really needed because of some large losses. The heavy regulation of the insurance industry in many countries has of course been motivated by these events. In the case of private deposit insurance such a scenario would be especially plausible if there were events triggering a system-wide crisis. This is so even if one accepts the arguments made in the preceding paragraph that the likelihood of such a catastrophe is very small in the light of the existence of central banks and the monitoring functions of the private insurance companies.

In assessing the validity of this fear of insurance company failure we must note that this industry routinely uses markets for reinsurance to distribute all risks widely across regions and industries. As a result, insurance companies specializing in deposit insurance would have only very limited exposure to this particular risk. However, there are several policies available to governments to reduce the potential lack of confidence in the insurance companies.

One of them has been suggested by Kane [1985]. It involves a general, but vague and uncertain governmental promise that public resources would be available for the rescue of the system perhaps after a specified percentage of industry assets had gone into liquidation. Kane suggests that this approach is both realistic and credible since it represents the continuation of the present policy. While it does so, the private insurance system with all of its moral hazard and information control mechanisms assures the efficient administration of the insurance. This approach will not appeal to purists who fear the longer-run moral hazard implications of governmental involvement. However, at the practical level of policy making, such a governmental commitment to the maintenance of stability is inevitable. Moral hazard or not, governments are the providers of insurance against large-scale risks of this sort, often of their own making, and it is possible that on efficiency grounds they should be.

A second approach has been suggested by Ely [1985]. He suggested that the private insurance system be owned by the banks themselves, who would pledge substantial portions of their equity for this purpose. Variants of this basic approach can readily be envisaged. The government might stipulate that the deposit insurance industry consist of mutual companies for each of which the equity must be at least, say 40 percent of insured deposits, with some specified percent of this equity coming from all banks in proportions determined by their size. The rest of the equity would come from private insurance companies.

Presumably, the large equity base would make these insurance companies holders of vast sums of assets. A stipulation could force a reinvestment of these funds in the banks that contributed them as equity. In the case of insolvencies, these insurance-owned deposits would represent a priority claim (or in fact would be insured). At the same time, the funds and income on them would not be lost to the contributing banks and the system. Under such conditions banks themselves would have a great stake in assuring the operation of efficient moral hazard controls, reinforcing the incentives of the owners of the insurance companies.

A modification of the preceding arrangements would leave in place a government insurance program, but it would have very low limits on the size of deposits insured. Private insurance would then be required to cover deposits in excess of this maximum. This idea is mentioned by Kane and may have the merit of political feasibility in that it guarantees the deposits of very large numbers of voters with limited resources and a possible distrust of private market institutions.

3. International Aspects

Ideally, international agreement would lead to the introduction of such private deposit insurance systems in all major countries. However, the success of the scheme does not depend on its universal or even widespread adoption. This may be seen by considering what would have happened in recent years if it had been in existence during the development of the Eurocurrency business. One would expect that the spread of U.S. banks abroad would have been monitored by the insurance companies and that they would have adjusted their premiums on domestic activities according to the increased risk exposure. Alternatively, they might have offered appropriate coverage to the U.S. banks' foreign branches.

Such new premiums would have meant higher operating costs for U.S. banks in the international business where competitors might not have such a domestic insurance scheme. However, such higher costs would not have meant a necessary competitive disadvantage since presumably depositors would be willing to pay for the greater safety of their assets in U.S. banks. We may be quite certain that under such circumstances both the insurance companies and the banks would have launched publicity campaigns about the risks of the growing loans to developing countries and would have made much of the existence of their insurance.

The systemic risk of deposit insurance was discussed above in the context of U.S. conditions. Of course, it exists also for other countries and the world as a whole. Therefore, it would seem to be a useful gesture as well as a financially viable idea for international organizations to participate in the equity financing of basic insurance or reinsurance systems. After all, the IMF, BIS and European Monetary Agreement are

guardians of international monetary stability and the creation and maintenance of a private deposit insurance scheme would serve these objectives.

In closing I would like to note that a private insurance system would
probably develop into an effective lobbying force for the rationalization
of domestic banking systems. An aspect of irrationality in the present
setup that I have discussed elsewhere [Grubel, 1983] is the non-payment
of interest on required reserves. This institution represents a very high
tax on value-added in banking, which has greatly encouraged the growth
of the Eurocurrency business as a method for avoiding this tax and has
led to the non-economic development of rival financial intermediaries.
Reserve requirements may have been an efficient tax in the past, but
they are so no more in the age of computers, satellites and jet aircraft.
It should not be unreasonable to assume that a private deposit insurance, had it existed in the past, would have given great publicity to the
way in which this tax has pushed U.S. banks abroad and led to the
increase in insurance premiums for the U.S. public.

IV. Summary and Conclusions

This paper examines a shortcoming of the banking industry which was
revealed by the recent debt crisis of the developing countries. This
shortcoming is the existence of government-owned and -operated bank
deposit insurance corporations in the United States and elsewhere. The
main thesis of this study is that this government insurance system has
failed to use the kinds of moral hazard controls which a private system
would have employed and which would have prevented the development of
the crisis.

A private deposit insurance scheme would have been much more alert to
the consequences of technological change and deregulation, which have
been the main indirect causes of the growth of international banking and
the excessive indebtedness of developing countries. There would have
been risk-adjusted premiums that surely would have reflected the increased riskiness of deposits and would have prevented the implicit subsidy of foreign depositors under the present system. The profit-oriented
scheme would also have generated information about the indebtedness of
countries and thus would have provided warning signals much earlier
than has in actuality been the case.

The analysis of the shortcomings of the existing system leads to the rec-
ommendation that governments abandon or modify public schemes to encourage the development of a private deposit insurance system. There
are many advantages to such a policy, not least of which is that it encourages the internalization of an externality through the appropriate
use of market mechanisms. I argued that such a private system would
not only be technically more efficient. It would also reduce sharply systemic risk in the future, just as it probably would have prevented the
recent debt crisis or at least have curtailed its magnitude.

There are a number of real and perceived obstacles to the implementation of private deposit insurance programs. Systemic risk and the implications it has for the possible adequacy of the equity base of the insurance companies are the most important. There is considerable uncertainty about the importance of these problems. Central banks would retain responsibility for system liquidity and governments would be certain to remain the ultimate guarantors of financial stability. This role they play under the current system as well, and the private insurance system would be certain to reduce the expected need for such actions, as was argued in the context of the current crisis. In addition, there are methods available for risk pooling and access to equity, which could be built into the system without destroying its basic market-oriented character.

The analysis presented here leaves many questions unanswered and may be naive in its faith in the superiority of market over government-operated insurance programs. However, the logic of the case appears to be strong enough by any standards to merit the attention of governments and international organizations interested in developing efficient mechanisms for the prevention of crises of the sort that have recently rocked the world's financial community.

References

DEVRIES, Margaret, "Historian Traces Origins and Development of Fund Involvement in World Debt Problem". IMF Survey, Jan. 7, 1985, pp. 2-5 and Jan. 21, 1985, pp. 18-20.

ELY, Bert, "No Deposit Reform, No Return to Stable Banking". The Wall Street Journal, March 5, 1985, p. 8 (See also letter to the editor May 2, 1985, p. 9).

GRUBEL, Herbert G., "Risk, Uncertainty and Moral Hazard". The Journal of Risk and Insurance, Vol. 38, No. 1, March 1971, pp. 99-106.

--, "Interest Payments on Commercial Bank Reserves to Curb Euro-money Markets". In: Fritz MACHLUP, Gerhard FELS, Hubertus MÜLLER-GROELING (Eds.), Reflections on a Troubled World: Essays in Honour of Herbert Giersch. London 1983, pp. 117-135.

GUTTENTAG, Jack M., Richard HERRING, "Commercial Bank Lending to Developing Countries: From Overlending to Underlending to Structural Reform". In: Gordon W. SMITH, John T. CUDDINGTON (Eds.), International Debt and the Developing Countries: A World Bank Symposium. The World Bank, Washington 1985, pp. 129-150.

KANE, Edward J., The Gathering Crisis in Federal Deposit Insurance. Cambridge, Mass., 1985.

SMITH, Gordon W., John T. CUDDINGTON (Eds.), International Debt and the Developing Countries: A World Bank Symposium. The World Bank, Washington 1985.

The Taxation of Windfall Gains
on Stocks of Natural Resources

HERBERT G. GRUBEL / Simon Fraser University and
Nuffield College, Oxford
SAM SYDNEYSMITH / Vancouver

As the first main point of this paper we argue that the supply of natural resources is price elastic so that, unlike in the case of land, the taxation of profits due to unexpected price increases leads to inefficiencies. We argue that the precedent setting taxation of windfall profits in Canada causes the truncation of the upper part of the probability distribution of returns expected by investors. As a result they can be expected to lower investment in natural resource industries and keep their funds in other, socially less profitable employment. As a second main point we show that taxation of companies through the forced sale of natural resources in Canada at prices below world opportunity costs causes further welfare costs through the induced overconsumption of these products in Canada.

En premier lieu, nous montrons dans cet article que l'offre dans le domaine des ressources naturelles est sensible à des variations de prix, de sorte qu'un impôt sur les profits, suite à une hausse inattendue dans le niveau des prix n'est pas efficace; cependant ceci ne s'applique pas au cas du sol. Une telle taxe sur les profits imprévus au Canada réduit la probabilité des rendements élevés attendus par les investisseurs. En conséquence, on devra s'attendre à ce que les investisseurs réduisent leurs investissements dans le secteur des ressources naturelles et les orientent dans des secteurs socialement moins rentables. En second lieu, nous montrons qu'en forçant les compagnies à vendre les ressources naturelles en deça des coûts d'option mondiaux, il va se créer au Canada, des coûts sociaux additionnels à cause de la surconsommation induite de ces produits.

In Canada and provinces like Alberta and British Columbia, which are important producers and exporters of raw materials, foods and fuels, the large 1973–74 increases in the relative prices of these goods in the world have led to the demand for the taxation of the windfall gains of the producers of these goods and for the establishment of dual price systems which would keep prices to domestic consumers below world prices. In this paper we discuss the economic efficiency and welfare implications of such policies by the construction of a simple analytical model. As such, the present study cannot

CANADIAN PUBLIC POLICY—ANALYSE DE POLITIQUES, I: I
winter/hiver 1975   Printed in Canada/Imprimé au Canada

14 / Herbert G. Grubel and Sam Sydneysmith

and does not pretend to evaluate the entire range of considerations about federal-provincial relations, multi-national corporations, income distribution effects, national security and past taxation practices which must ultimately enter into a social cost-benefit analysis of these policies. Furthermore, only passing reference will be made to actual legislation enacted or proposed because of the rapid changes taking place in this area continuously. The main objective of the paper is to present a set of economic principles which underly these policies and which often are forgotten in arguments over many political and social aspects of the particular policy recommendations of the day. The principles to be developed have universal validity and should be considered by all governments which are tempted to tax windfall gains of domestic producers and subsidize domestic consumption of goods in which they are net exporters.

The plan of the paper is to present first a model of economic rent in a framework of comparative statics, then to extend the model to include dynamic considerations of investment in new capacity. In Part III we analyse the problem of dual pricing. All of the analysis uses the oil industry as an example, though other products such as copper, uranium, lumber, wheat and fish could be used instead. Where there are important differences for the analysis between renewable and non-renewable resources we will discuss them.

I   A MODEL OF ECONOMIC RENT – COMPARATIVE STATICS

Henry George has popularized the now well-known argument that profits from the ownership of land can be taxed away without affecting the allocative efficiency of the price system in a market economy. George's ideas underly a large proportion of the proposals to tax away profits from other non-renewable resources, such as oil, gas, metals and minerals, the prices of which have risen so dramatically in 1973–74. Initially, we develop a model to make the strongest possible case for the taxation of profits from oil reserves by treating oil as if it were identical to land. In Part II we use this model, to establish with precision in what sense oil and other non-renewable resources differ from land and to analyse whether or not George's argument is applicable to those resources other than land.

Let us begin our analysis by considering that on a given date in 1972 Canada's oil production consisted of a certain amount, the quantity of which was fixed unalterably by decisions of producers in the time period before that date in order to maximize profits at the given Canadian and world price for oil. Competition from substitute energy sources and oil producers in the rest of the world assured that at this given price of oil the output yielded only 'normal' profits, presumably requiring no particular public attention. Now let us assume that on the evening of this crucial date after all production facilities had shut down for the night an unexpected increase in the Canadian and world price of oil took place. As a result, the output of oil on that day yielded unexpected profits for the producers from their sales on the next day, equal to the quantity of oil times the increase in the price. This profit is also known as 'windfall profit' and, according to some analysts, represents economic rent.

Economic rent has the property that it can be taxed away without the introduction of any social costs or inefficiencies. In our example, the oil producers were assumed to be unable to change output after the price increase and therefore in no way were their output decisions changed by a tax which appropriated the windfall profits for the government and therefore left the price for producers at the level expected when the output decisions were made. The tax did not lead to a reallocation of resources from the one the free operation of the market would have produced. The only effect was that oil producers' profits were smaller by the amount of the rent and forced to stay at the 'normal' level existing before the rise in the world price of oil. The tax revenue of the government can be used to supply public goods, change the income distribution or reduce taxes. Even though the Canadian public pays a higher price for oil, the higher payments are returned to it through the government and at the same time the oil price provides a signal to Canadian consumers to be more economical in the use of this resource whose value in exchange for other goods in the world has risen. The overall public benefits from having this higher consumer price for oil will be discussed in some detail in Part III below.

The preceding argument in favor of the taxation of rent on oil is equivalent to that made by Henry George in favor of a tax on land, which he assumed to be available in given, limited supply for all times. It is logically valid, given the assumptions. It has always been popular, especially with people who do not own land. However, its empirical relevance to the case of oil depends crucially on the question whether or not the supply of oil is given and limited for all times as is that of land. If the supply curve for oil is responsive to prices and therefore indicates that more oil is supplied at higher than lower prices, then the taxation of the windfall profits induces the misallocation of resources in the economy and leads to a reduction in public welfare. In the next section of this paper we argue that the supply of oil and all natural resources is indeed price elastic in anything but the shortest run and that therefore the taxation of rent results in welfare costs the nature of which will be explained and which in a rational social calculus must be weighted carefully against the alleged benefits derived from it.

II   ECONOMIC RENT IN A DYNAMIC WORLD

Alfred Marshall has developed a widely accepted theory of the firm according to which it is useful to distinguish analytically three different time periods over the length of which supply elasticities differ for reasons to be explained. These three periods are the short, medium and long run. Applied to the case of oil, we can describe these supply responses as follows.

In the short run supply is by definition totally fixed. Operationally, this short run may be very short for oil. To the extent that there exists any slack capacity at all in existing pumping and delivery facilities, it lasts only as long as it takes to order engineers to increase pumping speed and workers to work overtime. As soon as there is any increase in supply at all we find ourselves in the medium term, according to Marshall's analytical framework. In this

16 / Herbert G. Grubel and Sam Sydneysmith

medium term more full-time workers are hired, more maintenance is applied to pumps and transportation equipment to permit running them at continuously higher speed and pressures. By the application of more resources new wells and fields are brought into production more quickly. The shutting down of fields is delayed as at the higher price of oil it is profitable to continue to operate low-yield pumps which at the lower price did not cover variable cost of operation. Certain qualities of oil with high levels of sulfur and other impurities and low viscosity are recovered and processed profitably. Secondary recovery methods using water under pressure and steam to force more production are employed in wells where the facilities exist but operation at the low price is not profitable.

Economists and even experts in the oil industry do not know by how much oil production can be increased in Canada in the medium term by these methods. There simply have been no past price increases as dramatic as these in the 1973–74 period to permit generalizations from historic experience. However, for our purposes of analysis, it does not matter here that we give precise estimates of the supply response in the medium term. As long as it is logically and empirically plausible that higher oil prices create incentives to use the above list of methods to increase supply in the medium term it follows that the supply curve is price responsive and the taxation of windfall profits leads to economic losses.

These losses occur for the following reasons. At the initial, low price for oil and under the existing cost of using these methods for increased production, the size of reserves, interest rates and expected future prices of oil, it was not profitable for the oil companies to use these methods. There exists the possibility that this lack of profitability to the oil companies has been induced by government policies, such as unrealistic depletion allowances and other tax concessions or by market imperfections, such as the oligopolistic nature of the industry. We will deal with this possibility below and here assume that the lack of private profitability in the use of these medium term measures for increasing supply reflects the lack of social profitability.

Now when the price of oil rises unexpectedly, as it did in 1973–74 as a result of the activities of the organization of oil-exporting countries, with the cost of using these methods, interest rates and the size of reserves remaining unchanged, it follows logically that it must then be privately and socially profitable to use these medium term methods to augment supply. But if the government taxes away the increase in the price of the oil, private incentives for raising output are removed. As a result, resources which should have been drawn into raising oil output by the medium term methods are prevented from moving and remain in their initial, lower yielding employment. The social loss is equal to the difference in the yield of these resources in the original employment and in the foregone high yield in the production of oil.

In principle, this loss can be avoided by permitting oil companies to sell output obtained through the use of these medium term methods at a higher price than oil produced at the original level of output with the traditional methods. In practice, such a scheme would be difficult to administer, especially in the face of depletion, a phenomenon which we have disregarded thus far to keep the analysis simple. As reserves in existence at the time of the price increases are depleted, less and less oil can be produced profitably at the low price using the original methods. Employment of the medium term technology tends to retard or speed up depletion and in practice it is extremely difficult to attribute output through time to 'reserves' in existence at a certain point in time and to original and medium term production methods.

Economically more important than the medium term supply response is the long run. In Marshall's analytical framework the long run is characterized by the ability of firms to increase fixed plant and equipment. The expansion of productive capacity in this manner takes longer than the application of medium term methods because the financing of the outlays and the design, manufacture and installation of capital goods involves months or years as compared with the short time required to hire additional labor or increase the operating speed of existing machines. In the case of the oil industry the long run is characterized primarily by finding and developing new oil fields but also involves capital-intensive secondary recovery methods like water pressure and steam applied to otherwise depleted fields. Geological surveys, drilling and the construction of water and steam delivery systems and of transportation facilities from fields to markets are known to take years, especially as in recent times the exhaustion of convenient locations caused exploration activities to be shifted to more remote areas and into more difficult climatic zones and terrain such as the Arctic and the Continental shelves.

In a world in which worldwide population and industrialization are growing and existing deposits are depleted, oil companies are continuously in the process of exploring for, discovering and bringing into production new oil fields. The rate at which this activity takes place is determined by a process which, in the tradition of recent theorizing about investment decisions in an uncertain world may be modelled as follows. At any given moment in time executives of oil companies gather the best available information on the probability of success in drilling wells in all parts of the world, the cost of drilling, the cost of transporting oil to markets once it has been found, the likely price of oil in the future, the cost of acquiring drilling rights from the government, existing and likely tax treatment of income and expenditure, future interest rates, exchange rates, the likelihood of confiscation by governments, sabotage by insurgents, etc. Typically, the results of estimating the influence of all of these factors on the profitability of exploration activity in a country like Canada results in a probability estimate with a certain mean and variance. For example, the best guess, or mean of the distribution, may be for a 10 per cent after tax rate of return on the investment of, say, one billion dollars in 1975 in Canada, but there are also non-zero probabilities for rates of return above and below this mean, including very high positive and negative rates. High negative rates of return may be realized if all of the above determinants of the rate of return come out adversely at the same time: dry wells may abound, the construction of pipelines may be held up, the development of a cheap alternative energy source may depress the price of oil, the cost of borrowing capital may soar, a socialist government may confiscate without compensation all oil properties, etc. On the other hand, it is not difficult to imagine what combination of circumstances might lead to rates of return much above the most likely 10 per cent rate. A similar probability

18 / Herbert G. Grubel and Sam Sydneysmith

distribution would exist for contemplated expenditures above or below the hypothesized one billion in a given period. It is difficult to generalize about how different levels of expenditure affect the mean and variance of the distribution. In practice the choice of the expenditure is determined by the cost and availability of capital to the firm in the market, which in turn depends on the probability distribution. We abstract in this analysis from the complicated, but reasonably well understood process by which a firm's owners decide on their optimum level of borrowing, investment and indebtedness under exogenously given probability distributions of returns and supply schedules of capital by assuming that the firm maximizes stockholders' equity by borrowing and spending one billion dollars at a certain rate which makes it profitable to undertake the investment project with a certain expected return distribution.

Oil companies typically are operating in many regions of the world and can be assumed to form probability distributions of returns for every contemplated project. If they face two projects with equal expected rates of return, they prefer the one with the smaller range of expected outcomes, or as it is commonly referred to, the less risky project. On the other hand, higher returns can compensate for greater riskiness in this sense. In global operations firms are likely to take into account interdependencies of likely profit rates. Thus two neighboring Latin American states are more likely to elect socialist governments and expropriate foreign holdings simultaneously than one country in Africa and one in Latin America. For this reason, *ceteris paribus*, global company earnings are less risky by investment in one country in each of the continents than in the two Latin American countries. For our purposes of analysis it is important only to establish that in principle a representative oil company faced a certain probability distribution for a one billion dollar investment in Canada during the period of say 1975–77, and that in attempts to maximize global income with an acceptable level of risk, it had planned to invest this one billion dollars in oil exploration and production in Canada.

Now consider what would have happened to the investment plans of this firm after the price increases in 1972–73 and in the absence of any government intervention. If the price increases had been expected and incorporated in the probability distribution for 1975–77 returns formulated in 1971, it would not be changed. Investment might still rise because higher profits on existing reserves lowered the cost of capital to the firm either through increasing the availability of internally generated funds or through lower costs of borrowing in capital markets. If the price increases had not been expected, then the distribution is changed and its mean is likely to shift upward. Combined with the lower cost of capital we would find a higher investment than the one billion dollars originally contemplated for the period. It may be reasonable to assume that the price changes in 1972–73 were not fully reflected in the probability distribution for the 1975–77 period formulated in 1971. While they were expected with a non-zero probability in any careful analysis in 1971, after they had taken place in 1972–73, they should have influenced the probability distribution for the 1975–77 period perceived in 1973. For these reasons we conclude that the price increases of 1972–73 would have led oil companies to revise upward their investment expenditures in Canada and all other parts of the world. As a result, we are justified in concluding that there exists a long-run supply curve for oil which is an increasing function of the price of oil. By analogy with the arguments presented above in the context of intermediate term methods of increasing output, this privately profitable increased investment is socially efficient, since it yields an expected rate of return higher than that available from using the resources elsewhere.

Now it is a simple matter to use the preceding model and analyse the consequences of an increase in the price of oil combined with a government tax on excess profits in Canada. First, such a tax prevents the lowering of the cost of capital and the upward shift of the probability distribution of expected rates of return. Consequently, the incentives to increase investment during the hypothetical 1975–77 period above the one billion dollars planned originally are removed. Social losses are incurred because the resources remain in their lower productivity employment in other industries. Second, for future times the probability distribution of expected rates of return, *ceteris paribus*, will be truncated at the upper end and shifted to the left as a result of the precedent-setting action of the government which indicates to oil companies that it is prepared to tax away profits accruing when combinations of fortuitous circumstances produce very high rates of return. Since this policy leaves all other risks unchanged, the lower tail of the distribution stays the same and the mean of the expected rate of return is lowered. Consequently, given the oil companies' unchanged investment alternatives in some other countries, oil companies maximizing profits with acceptable risks rationally will reduce their investment in Canada below what it would have been in the absence of the government tax. If the level of investment in Canada without the tax would have been socially optimal, then the new level of investment is below the social optimum. Canada loses by keeping resources employed in activities with a lower social yield or by failing to attract foreign capital whose social yield exceeds its cost. It should be noted that this change in the perceived probability distribution of expected returns takes place even if the government exempts future production from newly discovered fields from this tax. The precedent of the government's activities must affect expectations in the future and the upper tail and mean of the distribution must be adversely affected.

Through time, the lower rate of investment in Canada relative to the rest of the world changes the relative expected success rate for drilling in favour of Canadian prospects since promising areas abroad are explored more quickly. As a result, the probability distribution of expected returns in Canada shifts upwards and to the right. Eventually, investment in Canada will again increase as risk-adjusted rates of return from investment in all parts of the world are equalized by the oil companies. However, this fact does not eliminate the losses incurred by the temporarily lowered rate of investment and the change in the expectations induced by the government's action.

The preceding analysis can be summarized as follows. First, we established the important fact that at the initial equilibrium at pre-1972–73 output there exists a long-run supply for oil, which in contrast with the short-run supply and with the supply for land is not perfectly unresponsive to prices.

20 / Herbert G. Grubel and Sam Sydneysmith

Because of the investment necessary to discover and bring into production new oil fields, the supply-price relationship is positive and the same as in manufacturing. Second, the imposition of a certain tax per barrel equal to the increase in price is treated by producers like a cost of production which leaves the profitability unchanged at the previous equilibrium level. Third, the truncation of the expected rates of return distribution caused by the precedent-setting taxation of excess profits causes the new long-run supply to be less price responsive than the original one. This implies that for any given rate of depletion of existing stocks and for any given non-taxed future oil price increase, the supply response of Canadian oil producers will be smaller than it would have been in the absence of the tax. All of the above consequences of the taxation of windfall profits from oil reserves lead to inefficiencies in the allocation of resources if the level of investment in Canadian oil prospects would have been efficient in the absence of the tax. How correct is the last assumption?

Three important arguments have been made suggesting that in the past investment in oil exploration in Canada has been too high and that therefore the tax on output corrects for existing excessive investment incentives. We now turn to a brief analysis of these arguments and make the case that if these incentives exist, they should be eliminated directly and not through the imposition of a new distortion in the industry.

The first argument suggests that there has been past overinvestment because of excessive depletion allowances, the provision of tax shelters for wealthy investors and the protection of domestic oil prices through quotas on imports. There is little doubt that in recent decades the oil industry in North America has benefited from subsidies of this sort, though it should be noted that society received a return from them in the form of discovered reserves in excess of those which more neutral tax-treatment would have yielded. These larger reserves were considered to be necessary for national security and independence from imports. Whatever the merit of these objectives was at the time of their initiation or in retrospect, if now they are deemed to be obsolete, then the correct policy is to remove them. If this were done, investment would be reduced from its excessive level and other undesirable consequences such as the tax avoidance feature of depletion allowances and the income distribution effects of quotas would be removed simultaneously. The tax on output can achieve the desired reduction in investment incentives, but it leaves the undesirable feature of the original distortions.

The second argument states that the oil companies are multinational enterprises which can use internal transfer pricing to show taxable profits in countries with lowest taxes or, in some versions of the argument, in countries of corporate headquarters. As a result, Canada and other countries in which oil is taken out of the ground do not have the opportunity to tax the profits made from this oil. Furthermore, incentives are created for overinvestment in countries where tax avoidance of this sort can take place relative to countries where higher effective local tax rates are in force.

It is not clear whether the preceding argument is supported by facts. International double taxation agreements have led to the elimination of outright tax havens; the US tax laws of multi-national corporations actually encourage reporting of profits abroad wherever a foreign country has lower than US tax rates since the higher US tax has to be paid only upon repatriation of the earnings. Non-repatriated foreign earnings taxed at the lower foreign rate thus represent an interest-free loan, the existence of which creates incentives to bias profit reporting in favor of foreign countries. Canadian corporate profit rates are about equal to US rates and may be lower. Because of differences in Canadian and US definitions of income and costs it is extremely difficult to obtain unambiguous answers to the question of relative effective tax rates. However, whatever the facts may be, if there are tax havens and inefficient transfer pricing practices of multinational companies the best cure to these ills is again to eliminate them directly through international tax agreements and legislation regulating transfer pricing. To the extent that these measures are needed, they will have important effects on all foreign investment while the tax on output considered here discriminates against the oil industry, creating a new non-neutrality and therefore inefficiency.

Since the oil companies are largely owned abroad, increased profits from high oil prices accrue to foreigners, rather than Canadians, even if tax havens did not exist and transfer pricing was efficient. Therefore, the tax on output only assumes that Canadians receive what belongs to them. This argument is in principle the same that we made above in the case of the owners of oil reserves generally. The problem is one of efficiency and whether it is in Canada's interest to generate a permanently smaller elasticity in the supply of foreign capital, which the precedent setting tax brings about. In the future, foreign investors will make available less capital for any given expected profit rate since the Canadian government has shown that it will tax away profits produced by especially fortuitous sets of circumstances. To the extent that there are investment opportunities which should have been made with the help of foreign capital for the benefit of the Canadian economy and they are not made, the Canadian public suffers as a result of the tax. If the argument is more generally directed against foreign ownership of Canadian firms, then again the objective of less foreign investment should be dealt with directly through appropriate legislation. Singling out of the oil industry or even all resource industries creates inefficient distortion.

The third argument considers that oil is an industry like fishing, in which investors entering the industry calculate only their private profits and neglect the negative impact their investment has on all of the firms already in the industry. For example, a fisherman newly entering the industry earns a certain profit sufficiently large to encourage him to stay in the industry, but his catches reduce the returns to all fishermen already in the industry. Under such circumstances the sum of the losses to others resulting from his activity reduces the overall social return to the marginal fisherman's investment and may actually turn it negative. Society thus ends up with socially excessive investment in industries such as fishing.

Analysis of this kind of problem has shown that it is due to the existence of a resource, such as the fish in the sea, for which property rights have not been determined. Every fisherman treats the fish as a free good, which they are to the individual, but which they are not to society as a whole. In ordinary competitive markets producers typically have to bid and pay for all of the

22 / Herbert G. Grubel and Sam Sydneysmith

resources used in the production process so that the problem of overinvestment for the reasons just analysed does not take place. The solution to the difficulties in industries like fishing therefore is for a government or group of governments to establish property rights where there are none, as for the fish in the sea, by auctioning off fishing rights in quantities leading to socially optimum investment levels. Fishing without these rights then is prohibited. In technical terms such auctioning of fishing rights and limitation of entry leads government to appropriate the rent from the natural resource for the public as a whole and prevents this rent from being dissipated and wasted through overinvestment by private industry.

There is some resemblance between the case of fish and oil resources. If there were one oil field being tapped by a number of different companies simultaneously, then the rate of recovery of oil by one would affect the rate and total recovery by all others. The pool of oil is a common resource for which, under our assumptions, property rights have not been defined properly and incentives exist to overinvest in pumping facilities to obtain as much of the pool as possible before competitors exhaust it. Another example establishing a similarity between fish and oil is where a technological breakthrough has suddenly made it profitable privately to drill under the polar ice cap in regions where seismological surveys have predicted a high probability of deposits. Without property rights for the seabed in these regions the private firms acting individually would be tempted to overinvest. The potential fields might be discovered at great cost a number of times and there would be more producing wells than a single firm owning exclusive property rights would have found profitable.

The similarity between fish and oil resources just sketched is real. But the problem of controlling overinvestment in oil is much easier than it is in fishing because it is simple to define property rights for drilling and discovered reserves of oil and nearly impossible for ocean fishing. International agreements to limit fishing in the open seas have been notoriously difficult to negotiate and maintain. On the other hand Canada and other national governments have successfully sold exclusive regional drilling rights to competitive bidders and have otherwise set out comprehensive laws clarifying property right issues in case of common pools, etc. To the extent that the problems associated with the common property resource oil have not been solved and there continues to be overinvestment, the best solution is to continue work on perfecting the laws. The imposition of a tax on oil production as discussed above would leave unsolved the common resource property problems, which would continue to lead to overinvestment in certain regions and projects even while the tax reduces overall investment in the industry.

In sum, if it is true that in recent years government policies or particular market institutions have caused overinvestment in Canada's oil industry, then economic theory suggests that the causes of this overinvestment should be eliminated directly, not through a tax on current oil production from proven reserves, which according to our analysis would lead indirectly to lower investment rates in the future.

In closing this section of the paper we wish to discuss very briefly the merit of two other arguments which suggest that reduction in private investment in oil supplies is desirable. The first argument is that Canada is running out of resources and the present generation owes it to the future to be more economical in their use. This proposition is based on a failure to understand the working of a price mechanism and of interest rates in market economies, which in the past have led to ever increasing wealth and living standards in spite of the fact that at all times economic activity has involved the exploitation of scarce resources. Profits and interest rates have provided strong incentives for the accumulation of capital and the preservation of resources, properly balanced with the maintenance of appropriate current living standards. There is every reason to believe that this process will continue in the future if markets are left alone and the public as a whole is able to vote how much wealth should be passed on to future generations through appropriate spending and savings decisions. The Canadian public should be cautious about entrusting decisions about conservation to idealists and vocal minorities.

The second argument is that the government can step in and make up the gap in private investment left as a result of the tax. Government involvement in this manner is welcomed by some people who dislike the operation of the free enterprise system and who believe that the government can provide the service more cheaply than the monopoly-ridden private oil industry. This argument involves many ideological issues as well as empirical judgments, which cannot be discussed here. However, it may be worth mentioning in this context that it is extremely costly and time-consuming to assemble the technical expertise now working for the international oil companies. Even the Soviet Union has found it advantageous in recent years to enlist the help of these companies. Many students of bureaucracies doubt that governments can operate in the long run as efficiently as these companies which in many ways are strong competitors and forced by the market into operating efficiently. If the Canadian public does not like the forms which some of this competition takes, such as excessive numbers of gas stations, advertising gimmicks, etc., then these undesirable aspects of monopolistic competition should be corrected through appropriate legislation or the encouragement of genuine competition.

III   THE QUESTION OF DUAL PRICING

Let us assume now that in spite of the existence of economic losses considered above it has been decided that the windfall profits of oil producers from the 1972–73 world price increases should be taxed away in the expectation of social and political benefits exceeding the pure economic costs. We then face the alternative of having the federal or provincial governments collect all of the rent first, by a per unit tax per barrel of oil produced equal to the increase in the world price or, second, by collecting an export tax of an equal amount and forcing the oil producers to sell to domestic consumers at the original lower world price. Under both systems the windfall profits are returned to the Canadian public and taken away from the producers.

The second method has great political appeal since it avoids unpopular increases in consumers' prices and in costs of Canadian producers who thus

24 / Herbert G. Grubel and Sam Sydneysmith

become more competitive in export markets, *ceteris paribus*. We shall now use the analytical framework developed above to discuss the economic cost associated with choosing the second alternative of having dual prices.

Under the assumption that in the long run the demand for petroleum is negatively related to price, the long-run effect of letting the domestic price rise is a reduction in domestic consumption by a certain, positive amount. As a result, exports increase by this amount and yield added income to Canada equal to the number of barrels exported times the world price per barrel, of which a portion is in the form of export taxes. In effect, the Canadian public has been induced by the higher price for oil to economize on its use and to consume instead other goods, the relative price of which has fallen in Canada and in trade with the rest of the world. Underlying this adjustment process are the following changes in the public's receipts and expenditures. Canadian consumers are left with an amount of cash income equal to what they saved by not spending it on oil and which they now can spend on other goods providing equal satisfaction. However, because of the rise in price of oil, consumers have to spend more money on the amount they continue to buy. This increased expenditure goes to the government in the form of taxes on domestic consumption which, under the assumption made at the beginning of this section, is equal to the rise in the world price of oil. This revenue is returned to the public in the form of government services, public goods or reduced taxes and therefore does not constitute a net loss. There remains, however, a loss of welfare which is known in technical economics as consumer surplus. We cannot develop this concept here but we show its nature and magnitude rigorously in the Appendix to this paper. Suffice it here to state that this lost consumer surplus is equal to only one half of the government's export tax receipts so that there remains a positive net gain to consumers equal to the remaining one half of the tax receipts, considering that the government returns all of these export tax receipts to the public in the form of either government services, public goods or reduced rates of taxation. If the price of oil is not allowed to rise, this net gain is foregone and it represents in effect the social cost of maintaining the domestic price below the world price.

The preceding analysis implies that Canadians can always be made better off by maintaining parity between domestic and world prices of export commodities. However, the size of the gain depends on the degree of price responsiveness of long-run domestic demand. We do not know this degree for petroleum products, but many experts believe that higher prices for gasoline and heating fuel will lead to many adjustments by consumers which will ultimately result in substantial savings. For example, there will be substitutions of small for big cars, public for private means for commuting to work, more efficient appliances and better house insulation. Consumers will also be induced to switch to other energy sources, such as coal and electricity generated from atomic power, which will result in lower demand for petroleum products.

We may speculate about the size of the value of the gain from the uniform price system for petroleum products in Canada. If the increase in world crude oil prices in 1972–73 was approximately 100 per cent, from $3 to $6 per barrel, then consumers' prices for refined products can be expected to increase by a smaller percentage since a substantial part of the market price of gasoline consists of value added in refining, transportation and marketing and of taxes. Let us assume that the crude oil price increases result in a 20 per cent increase in prices to consumers. If the above mentioned adjustments result in an equi-proportionate decrease in consumption, then Canadian demand for crude oil in 1975 would be 662 million barrels instead of 827 million barrels, assuming a 5 per cent national annual growth rate in demand and a consumption of 714 million barrels in 1972.[1] The 165 million barrel savings in 1975 would be exported and yield $495 million export taxes at the assumed tax rate of $3 per barrel. According to our theoretical analysis, the net gain to Canada after subtraction of the foregone consumer surplus would be $248 million per year. Other figures can be easily derived by changing assumptions underlying our calculations, but it seems to us that after rounding, the $250 million figure for 1975 is a reasonable guestimate. The gain would accrue every year, though the amount would decline as the 1972 stock of reserves became reduced and would cease when the stock was exhausted.

The one-price system would also avoid the creation of difficult administrative problems in the future if, as we argued in Part II, newly discovered fields must be permitted to charge higher prices for crude oil. Furthermore, once the dual price system has been in effect for a prolonged period of time, vested interests are likely to oppose any change and may force the government into payment of outright subsidies to domestic consumption once the 1972 stock of reserves is insufficient to meet growing domestic demand at the old price.

The higher domestic prices for petroleum products accompanying the one-price system would evoke a number of costly and inconvenient adjustments in the Canadian economy along the lines suggested above in connection with our discussion of the long-run sources of savings in the consumption of crude oil. If the price of petroleum products has risen permanently in the world, these adjustments are inevitable unless the Canadian government commits itself to subsidize domestic prices indefinitely. Such commitment seems unwise since the subsidies would have to be raised through taxes from the same public to which the subsidies are paid and there would be the added costs of administration and the efficiency losses detailed above.

The preceding calculations should be considered illustrative only, involving a number of guesses which could be turned into reliable estimates only at great cost. Furthermore, events in this field are moving with such speed that very frequently estimates are made obsolete between production and publication of research by unforeseen and unforeseeable price changes. However, our analysis suggests that the costs of dual pricing of oil may easily become quite large. They have the further characteristic of being incurred year after year as long as the system is maintained. In contrast, the adjustment costs incurred by consumers and producers in moving to permanently higher prices

1 Source: *An Energy Policy for Canada: Phase 1, Vol. 1, Analysis*, (Ottawa: Information Canada, 1973). This source indicates a daily consumption in 1972 of 2.6 million barrels of crude, .13 million barrels of LPG gas and .05 million barrels of net exports of refined products. In estimating annual consumption we treated gas and refined products as if they were crude oil.

26 / Herbert G. Grubel and Sam Sydneysmith

are necessary only once. However, as is well known, adjustment costs are an increasing function of the speed with which they are incurred. For example, a large and sharp increase in fuel oil prices would induce a large and sharp increase in demand for insulating material and call forth shortages and higher prices until the insulating material industry could expand supply capacity. A slower increase in heating oil prices and derived demand for home insulating material would enable supply to grow in step with increasing demand and the temporary price increase and resultant public hardships could be avoided. To the extent that adjustment costs are a function of the speed of changes it would be socially desirable to slow down the rate of increase in domestic petroleum prices below that which the market would have produced on its own.

Such a slowed rate of domestic price movements towards the world price has the added advantage that more evidence on the true long-run supply price would become available. It may well be that the economic and political developments in 1972–73 have caused world petroleum prices to overshoot their long-run average and that they will be lowered again by the substitutions by consumers and suppliers of rival fuels discussed above. If this were to happen, new adjustment costs would be incurred by Canadians who had acted on the higher price. These costs could be avoided by government policies which slow down but do not prevent the rise of domestic prices to the ultimate world price for petroleum products.

The existence of adjustment costs more generally provides a rationale for government action to insulate domestic prices from large fluctuations in world prices. In principle therefore, dual prices for petroleum, and some other products in which Canada is a large exporter such as wheat and milk, are justified as temporary measures to internalize the externalities arising from price instabilities. The problem with such government price stabilization policies is that historically they have often developed into permanent instruments of control and subsidization operated inefficiently and inflexibly to the long-run detriment of the public.

High petroleum prices would reduce the real income of many Canadian families already living at the poverty level. These families should be compensated for this loss in real income by corresponding increases in transfer payments now available under a variety of public assistance programs. This direct manner of helping the poor is considerably less costly to the public as a whole than is the maintenance of inefficiently low petroleum product prices for reasons discussed above.

IV SUMMARY AND CONCLUSIONS

In this paper we have shown that Henry George's argument about the absence of allocative inefficiencies from the taxation of rent is applicable to natural resources such as oil only in the very shortest decision period. In the intermediate and long run the supply of oil, unlike that of land, can be increased through investment. Taxation of windfall profits from already discovered oil reserves decreases the availability of internally generated finances of oil companies and as a precedent-setting government policy affects the upper tail of the probability distribution of expected returns from oil investment in

Canada. Both of these results of the taxation of rent cause oil investment to decrease and the long-run supply curve for oil to be less price responsive than it would have been in the absence of the tax. We concluded that Canadian welfare is reduced by the tax because it prevents investment resources from flowing into oil investments, which as a result of world oil price increases have become socially more profitable than the next best alternative use of these funds in Canada.

We dealt with a number of arguments in support of the view that reductions in the investment in the oil industry are desirable. We showed that the existence of excessive depletion allowances, foreign ownership and taxation and the common resource problem may have resulted in past overinvestment. However, economic theory suggests that this overinvestment should be corrected by removal of the distortions which originally caused it, not by the introduction of a new distortion in the form of the windfall profits tax.

In the concluding part of this paper we dealt with the possibility that one form of taxing oil companies is to force them into selling their product domestically at the price prevailing before the recent increases in the world price. While such a policy is politically appealing it causes inefficiencies in the Canadian economy which we showed to be substantial and perpetual under a reasonable set of assumptions about the world, while the social adjustment costs are only once and for all.

The principles, costs and benefits of taxing windfall profits on exploitable oil revenues developed in this paper are applicable to all Canadian natural resources, whether they are non-renewable, such as ores and minerals, or renewable in time, such as fish, forests and grains. As the world population and scarcities continue to grow, in the future Canada will find herself frequently in the position where world prices for her staple exports relative to manufactures increase, result in windfall profits to resource owners and cause higher living costs for Canadians. This paper suggests that the politically expedient taxation of these profits and the establishment of dual prices incur potentially high social costs through inefficiencies in the allocation of resources in the longer run.

APPENDIX

In this appendix we present a geometric analysis which serves to give greater precision to the verbal arguments presented in the text and permits us to demonstrate the nature and magnitude of the welfare cost associated with the dual pricing of oil, given the decision that it is in the interest of the Canadian public to tax windfall profits.

In Figure 1 we measure the quantity of oil in barrels per time period and the price of oil per barrel in dollars along the horizontal and vertical axis, respectively. The supply of oil is assumed to be OS barrels per time period equal to the maximum output from existing oil fields regardless of the price of oil and abstracting from any problems arising from depletion. Under this assumption the supply curve for oil is the vertical line SS. The domestic demand curve for oil is shown as DD. It indicates that consumers purchase more oil per time period the lower the price. Canada, as a relatively small country may be assumed realistically to face a world price of oil of OW_0 dollars, at which any quantity can be bought or sold without affecting the price. This fact is reflected in the horizontal world demand curve W_0W_0. Under these assumed conditions the equilibrium relationships involve Canada producing OS barrels of oil, OA_0 of which are consumed domestically and A_0S are exported. The oil producers' revenue is equal to $OSLW_0$, which before the price rises in

28 / Herbert G. Grubel and Sam Sydneysmith

1973–74 did not attract particular public attention and may be considered as representing costs of production and 'normal' profits.

Let us now analyse the implications of an exogenous rise in the world price of oil from OW_0 to OW_1, generating a world demand curve for Canadian oil equal to W_1W_1 in Figure 1. Everything else remaining the same, under the preceding set of assumptions in the new equilibrium with the price at OW, Canadian domestic consumers demand OA, and exports are A_0S per time period. That is, FI barrels not consumed domestically are available for export. The revenues of oil producers in the new equilibrium are W_0BCW dollars above their levels in the initial situation, W_0GFW dollars coming from Canadian consumers, GBCF dollars from the rest of the world. This increased oil producers' revenue is also known as economic rent or windfall profits.

Next, let us consider that the government imposes a tax on oil producers equal to W_0W_1 per barrel, which is equal to the increase in the world price. Figure 1 shows readily that under the assumed conditions domestic consumption, exports and total production remain the same as before. The tax does not lead to a reallocation of resources from the one the free operation of the market would have produced. The only effect is that oil producers' profits are smaller by the amount of the rent and forced to stay at the 'normal' level existing before the rise in the world price of oil. The tax revenue of the government can be used to supply public goods, change the income distribution or reduce taxes. Even though the Canadian public pays higher price for oil, the higher payments are returned to it through the government and at the same time the oil price provides a signal to Canadian consumers to be more economical in the use of this resource whose value in exchange for other goods in the world has risen.

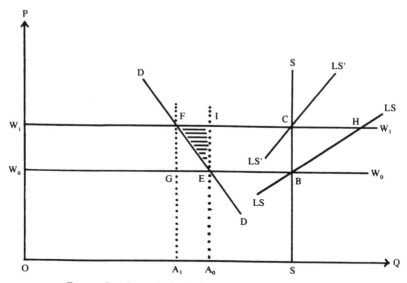

FIGURE 1   Demand and supply in the long and short runs

In the main body of this paper our concern has been to argue that in the intermediate and long run the supply curve for oil is not perfectly elastic, but has a positive slope. We have shown such a supply curve in the line LS–LS. The imposition of an excise tax of W_0W_1 on oil shifts upward the long-run supply curve to LS'–LS', as is well known from the theory of public finance. In Figure 1, LS'–LS' is shown therefore to intersect the world price line at point C. In sum, the tax prevents the increase in output of CH which would otherwise have taken place and leads to a social loss equal to the difference in the productivity of the resources required to produce the output CH but which by the tax are prevented from moving away from their previous employment and into oil production and discovery.

If, in spite of this loss of efficiency, it is deemed to be in the public interest to tax the windfall profits, the tax can take two alternative forms. First, there is a tax on all output, giving rise to a tax revenue of W_0BCW_1, of which $GBCF$ is in the form of an export tax and the rest is domestic excise tax revenue. Under this tax scheme the domestic and world prices are equal and domestic consumption is OA_1, given the domestic demand curve DD. Total social welfare from the produced oil OS is equal to the area $OSCW_1$ under the assumption that the tax revenue is returned to the public in the form of public goods or reduced taxes.

Second, the domestic price remains at OW_0 so that domestic consumption stays at OA_0. The windfall profits are appropriated by an export tax of $EBCI$ on A_0S of exports and by forcing the oil producers to sell OA_0 output for OA_0EW dollars domestically which is worth OA_0IW_1 at world prices. However, the welfare gained by the public from having a price of OW_0 rather than OW_1 is only OA_0FW_1, the integral under the relevant part of the demand curve above OW_0, leaving a loss of welfare equal to EIF compared with the welfare enjoyed under the regime of a uniform domestic and world price. The area EIF is also equal to the consumer surplus triangle GEF (assuming a linear demand curve) or one half of the export tax revenue which could have been earned from increased exports of A_1A_0 made possible by reduced domestic consumption in response to a higher price of OW_1.

[8]　　[1982]

Towards a Theory of Free Economic Zones

By

Herbert G. Grubel

Contents: I. Analytical Description of Free Economic Zones. — II. The Political Economy of the Free Economic Zones. — III. Welfare Effects of Free Economic Zones. — IV. Free Economic Zones for Other Industries? — V. Summary and Conclusions.

I n this paper I present a theory capable of analysing the welfare effects of a wide variety of institutional innovations which have in common that they involve the deregulation of, or the lowering of tariffs and taxes on, a range of economic activities that can be effectively separated from the regulated, taxed and protected industries of which they are a part. The partial deregulation of economic activities in this manner will be shown to lead to the expansion of trade, but also to involve potential costs of locational diversion of trade and negative externalities. In the context of the debate over deregulation the development of free economic zones can be seen as a practical compromise that generates powerful local interest groups pushing partial deregulation against the well-known interest groups opposing general deregulation.

In this study I could draw on a limited stock of published research, none of which deals directly with the problems considered to be central in this study, but which provides some useful instutitional information[1].

In the first part I provide a descriptive analysis of free economic zones. Part II presents the political economy and Part III the welfare effects of free economic zones. In Part IV I speculate about the possibility

Remark: Many people have helped me to refine the arguments and find empirical illustrations presented in this paper. I would like especially to thank Walter Block, John Chant, Max Corden, Steve Easton, Sid Fancy, John Helliwell and Lars Svensson. I also benefited from discussions during seminars at the Universities of Mannheim, Zürich, St. Gallen and Pennsylvania; at the German Military Academy in Hamburg, UNIDO in Vienna, the Institut für Weltwirtschaft in Kiel, the HWWA-Institut für Wirtschaftsforschung in Hamburg and the Institute for International Economic Studies in Stockholm.

[1] The economics literature dealing with the free trade zone phenomenon is limited to three theoretical papers, Hamada [1974], Rodriguez [1976] and Hamilton and Svensson [1980], and the more institutionally oriented papers by Wall [1976], Fernstrom [1976], Ping [1979] and Diamond [1979]. This literature has failed to create a comprehensive theory of free trade zones capable of assessing their welfare effects and suggesting tests for empirical study.

40   Herbert G. Grubel

of using the free zone concept for the partial deregulation of other heavily regulated industries. The paper closes with a summary and conclusions.

I. Analytical Description of Free Economic Zones

Free Trade Zones

Free trade zones are areas separated from the surrounding host country's territory by fences or other barriers into which goods from abroad can be brought without quota restrictions or the payment of tariffs and excise taxes, and without being subjected to exchange controls, and to the majority of statistical reporting requirements and regulations aimed at the protection of consumers. Goods can be stored, used in manufacture, exhibited, assembled, sorted and sold in such zones in processes that are subject to the host country's normal laws governing environmental protection, workers' safety and employment conditions. Profits and wages earned in the zones are taxed at regular rates. Goods can be exported as freely as they are imported. However, when goods are brought into the zone's host country, they are subject to the normal import quotas, duties and excise taxes.

In practice free trade zones may be as small as a retail store in an airport or as large as the territory of Hong Kong and they may serve the simple function of warehousing or may contain a broad spectrum of industries. The essential feature of free trade zones for economic analysis is that they lower the host country's level of protection through the reduction of tariffs, quantitative barriers and administrative hindrances to trade[1].

For example, a firm imports goods into the free trade zone, processes or assembles and then exports them. The firm saves the duty on these imports and for these goods the host country's tariff revenues and there-

---

[1] When a free trade zone consists of only a warehouse, it is often called simply a "bonded warehouse". In the United States in recent years factories, such as the one assembling Volkswagen automobiles in Pennsylvania, have been declared free trade zones. In some instances, as in Panama, the free trade zones consist of a large area containing industries of many types. There are also free trade zones devoted to retail stores only, as at many international airports and harbors. According to our definition, Hong Kong represents one very large free trade zone. The Hanseatic cities of Northern Europe and the Free Cities of Germany, similarly used to be large free trade zones.

In developing countries we find also so-called "industrial estates" and "export processing zones". They have all of the characteristics of free trade zones as described in the text but in addition, they often provide subsidized services and facilities to occupants. One such service of great value often provided is an agent that deals with the host country's bureaucracy in the name of the zone's occupants [UNIDO, 1980].

fore average tariff rates are lowered[1]. Many countries have rules under which certain goods imported are assessed at a certain rate, but if these same goods are embodied in a product that has a certain domestic value-added percentage, then they enter at a lower tariff rate. Activities in free trade zones often contribute this required percentage of domestic value added and therefore indirectly lead to the lowering of tariff rates[2]. When imports are subject to quota restrictions, then they can be stored in free trade zones and imported whenever quotas become available. As a result, the effective import restrictions implicit in a given quota are lowered.

Importers value highly other effective duty reducing benefits provided by free trade zone operations. For example, defective goods can be destroyed in the zone before a shipment is imported into the host country and duty is assessed. Free trade zones serve as show-rooms for customers[3]. In addition there are savings in costs of dealing with customs and tax authorities which for small firms often are relatively large.

At the end of 1979 there existed 344 tax-free trade zones, free ports and similar designated areas on 72 countries of the world. In the United States there were about 50 such zones and plans existed for the creation of many more. It was estimated that in 1979 about $ 100 billion of total world trade of $ 1,300 billion went through free trade zones. Forecasts are that by 1985 about $ 300 billion or 20 per cent of world trade would pass through such free trade zones [Diamond, 1979].

Free Banking Zones

Euro-Currency Banking. — It is now widely accepted that one of the primary causes of the rapid growth of Euro-, Asia- and Latin-American currency banking since the 1960s is the exemption which this type of

---

[1] The savings for the exporter and therefore the practical reduction in duty burden from operating in the free trade zone usually is only equal to the opportunity cost of the duty paid since in most countries a system of duty drawbacks returns customs paid on all exported intermediate inputs. However, it should be noted that the economic effect of these savings for exporters may be quite significant since they are relevant to the export activity's value-added base. Therefore it is important to evaluate all of the reductions in protection in terms of the concept of effective protection as developed by Corden [1971].

[2] This characteristic of U.S. tax laws explains why several foreign automobile assembly plants in the United States have been made into free trade zones.

[3] In Hamburg oriental carpet dealers regularly take customers to their large warehouses in the duty free zone. In New York a free trade zone on a dock serves as an exhibition ground for sellers of machinery, to where customers can bring samples of goods for a demonstration of the processing capabilities of the equipment. Diamond [1979] provides an extensive list of benefits for exporters and importers located in free trade zones in a form useful for agents promoting a free trade zone. The sources of reduced operating costs noted here are merely samples designed to make the general point.

banking enjoys from the taxes implicit in minimum reserve requirements. That this is so can readily be seen by consideration of the following simplified example.

Consider a bank located in Montreal which pays interest on deposits at the annual rate of 8 per cent and therefore pays $ 8 on a $ 100 deposit. Faced by an assumed 15 per cent reserve requirement, this bank can lend out only $ 85 of the deposit and if the loan rate is 10 per cent, it earns $ 8.50. Under these conditions, the $ 100 intermediation business brings the bank net operating revenue of $ 8.50 — $ 8 = $ .50. Assuming that operating costs for labor, etc. constitute $ .45, the before income tax net profit is $ .05 per $ 100 deposit.

Now assume that this bank opens a branch in London, England, and persuades its customers to do business there in return for a marginally higher deposit and marginally lower loan rate. For the sake of simplicity we assume that this margin is so small that in the present calculation it can be disregarded. Under these assumptions and remembering that there are no legally required reserves on foreign currency deposits for banks located in London, the net operating margin of the Montreal bank branch on a $ 100 deposit is $ 10 — $ 8 = $ 2, which is four times that the parent bank could earn in Montreal. If labor and other costs are the same $ .45 per $ 100 of intermediation in London as in Montreal, the London branch shows a before income tax net profit of $ 1.55. Shifting business from the taxed and regulated home base to the free banking zone in London therefore implies an increase in the bank's net profit margin of over 3,000 per cent[1]. Analogous increases in net profit margins are available to banks in most countries on deposits and loans made in foreign currencies.

The preceding example illustrates the strenght of the incentives facing banks to enter the Euro- and other regional currency business and explains why this type of banking has grown from practically nothing in the 1960s to over $ 1,500 billion in 1980. For our purposes of analysis it is important to note that it involves a partial deregulation through the lowering of an implicit tax on a type of business that can be kept separate from the regular and regulated other business in two ways. First, the deregulation applies to business transacted in a geographically defined area, just like

---

[1] In fact, the spread between lending and borrowing rates in Euro-currency markets in individual currencies is narrower than that found in the currencies' home countries by an amount equal approximately to the implicit cost of the respective countries' reserve requirements. In effect, customers are reaping a large share of the benefits of the taxes saved. Portfolio balance considerations of banks, lenders and borrowers prevent perfect arbitrage between the rates in domestic and Euro-currency markets. However, the illustrative calculations are indicative of the strength of the incentives facing banks to escape domestic regulation, which persist as long as lending and borrowing spreads are determined in the domestic markets.

in the case of free trade zones discussed above, but with the important difference that in practice all of the rest of the world is the free economic zone[1]. Second, the deregulation applies to a certain type of business, namely foreign currency deposits, even though it may take place within a geographic territory where the banks' other business is fully regulated.

Free Banking Zone in New York. — In the year 1981, after many years of negotiation, a free banking zone was opened up in New York [Cheng, 1981] and if it is successful, more such zones will be created in other U.S. centers of finance. The basic idea behind the establishment of these zones is the removal of reserve requirements on banks in order to induce the return to the United States of some of the business that has been lost to the rest of the world through Euro-currency banking. The problem faced in the establishment of these zones is how to prevent massive shifts of domestic business into them, which would produce serious inequities between ordinary banks and those operating in the zones. In addition, such shifts would raise the reserve-deposit multiplier and create problems for U.S. monetary policy. The solution to these problems adopted is that banks are freed from U.S. reserve requirements only on deposits in large denominations owned by others than U.S. residents. This particular method for the separation of deregulated from regulated business is likely to limit severely the growth of business in the U.S. free banking zones, though in the end their chances for success involve an empirical question which only actual operation of the zone can provide[2].

Free Insurance Zone

Lloyds of London. — During the great wave of regulatory fervor in the postwar years all industrial countries have imposed increasingly more severe restrictions on the operation of insurance companies. During this period Lloyds of London grew rapidly because it constituted a haven free from regulation.

Lloyds has attracted mainly two types of business from other countries. First, there are the special risks for which there are few or no ex-

---

[1] Germany is the exception since that country's banking laws require the maintenance of reserves on deposits in all currency denominations. As a result, Germany harbors practically no Euro-currency banking business.

[2] It should be interesting to discover how enforceable is the foreign residence requirement in preventing shifts of domestic business into the zone, given the well-known ease with which funds can be funnelled through foreign branches and subsidiaries. Also, given the low cost of information transmission it is likely that new institutions can be developed which permit effective circumvention of the legislation restricting U.S. residents from use of the zone.

perience ratings, such as the cancellation of Olympic Games broadcast opportunities and the cancellation of computer leasing contracts. Second, there are the very large risks of insuring super-tankers and large-scale industrial projects. Lloyds has not attracted from other countries the standard fire, accident and life insurance business for which the local availability of agents is of paramount importance.

It is clear from the preceding description that an effective separation of regulated and deregulated insurance business has taken place in the world. Routine business involving large numbers of relatively small accounts has remained under the control of national regulatory authorities largely because transactions costs of dealing with Lloyds are too large. Special and very big risks, on the other hand, have been shifted to Lloyds either because in the case of special risks the advantages of deregulation are great or in the case of very large routine risks the transactions costs for the insured multinational enterprises are small.

The New York Free Insurance Zone. — In 1980 New York opened a free insurance zone [Decaminada, 1979; The Economist, 1979]. Similar zones may well be established in other U.S. cities. In the New York zone resident insurance companies can underwrite risks that require a minimum annual premium of $ 100,000 without obtaining the permission of regulatory authorities of the State of New York. In addition they can underwrite many special risks which have been identified by the authorities and whose common characteristic is that regulators in the past have been unable to ascertain promptly and reliably that premiums charged and other conditions of the contract protect the consumer and assure viability of the underwriters. Because of the regulatory delays and costs such risks in the past have been insured by Lloyds.

The intent of the New York free insurance zone is clearly to return some of the business that has been lost to the deregulated environment abroad by offering similar deregulation to New York firms. But through the specification of the nature of deregulated business, an effective separation between regulated and deregulated sectors is assured. Some doubts have been raised about the likely success of the New York insurance deregulation experiment [The Economist, 1979] on the grounds that the success of Lloyds has been due not only to a favorable regulatory environment but also to the special expertise and financial structure of the firm[1]. It remains to be seen how successful will be the New York free insurance zone in exploiting the benefits of deregulation and accumulating the required expertise.

---

[1] Partners in Lloyds face unlimited personal liabilities.

Free Gambling Zones

The State of Nevada constitutes a free gambling zone. It was created in 1931 when the sparse population of the state and its distance from centers of population amounted to the effective separation of markets. Only well-to-do people who could afford to travel to Nevada would be exposed to the risk of deregulation while the masses of ordinary citizens continued to be protected by the regulatory umbrella.

The establishment of gambling casinos in Atlantic City was approved and undertaken in the same spirit as Nevada's, though the strength of the possible discrimination between regulated and deregulated customers is much weaker. Still, in contrast with totally free gambling in New Jersey, limited free gambling in Atlantic City significantly reduces the exposure of ordinary citizens to the temptation of the activity. Already existing proposals for the establishment of other gambling centers in the United States suggest that if Atlantic City is successful, they will be established not in large urban centers but in relatively small resort centers where access by ordinary citizens is limited.

In Europe, where for a long time there has been less regulation of gambling than in the United States, big-time organized gambling through roulette and card games has been permitted only in casinos located in famous 19th century spas such as Baden-Baden and Monte Carlo frequented by royalty and gentry and where access is rather difficult for ordinary citizens. British gambling clubs require membership fees that represent a barrier to use by local residents of moderate means.

Free Enterprise Zones

It is widely accepted that the decay of city cores in Britain and the United States is due to a very significant degree to regulation of business, which affected especially small business and the employment it provided traditionally [Butler, 1980]. In Britain legislation has been passed that led to the designation of some depressed urban areas as Free Enterprise Zones. In these zones a number of burdensome types of regulation and taxation have been eliminated. The U.S. Congress is debating legislation that would permit the establishment of such zones in depressed U.S. cities.

The need to create effective separation between regulated and deregulated business has given rise to as yet unresolved problems in the formulation of the U.S. legislation and has led to problems with the British zones since discrimination in essence is based on geographic location. As a result, the borders of the zones create strong discontinuities. They have induced some business to move from outside the zone into it. In the process they have created a belt of depressed activity and real estate values around the zones. In addition, the zones can develop into tax-havens for large firms. It remains to be seen whether it will be possible to create legislative mechanisms that allow the effective discriminatory deregulation and tax reductions to be channeled properly for the achievement of the stated objective of stimulating the establishment of *new* small enterprises without generating costly additional regulation.

II. The Political Economy of the Free Economic Zones

The preceding description of the types, characteristics and growth of free economic zones raises the question why they have been permitted to develop in the past when there was generally strong faith in the need for and ability of regulation to improve free market institutions. Furthermore, the question arises why they are growing so rapidly in number in recent years when, after widespread realization of the high cost of regulation, efforts to achieve general deregulation have been stalled? In this section I will provide provisional answers to these questions arguing first that free economic zones are an instrument for selective deregulation and second, that they generate powerful interest groups which assure political success.

Selectively Targeted Deregulation

Regulation is basically a blunt instrument. For example, foreign trade restrictions bring costs to all regions of a country while often benefiting only a few. This proposition holds in the case of tariffs on automobile components, which benefit an industry that is often concentrated regionally, but the tariffs raise the cost of automobiles and automobile assembly, harming the interests of other regions, including some which under free trade might have a comparative advantage in automobile assembly. Similarly, regulation often provides paternalistic protection for consumers whether they need it or not. For example, in the insurance underwriting business for large tankers, it is reasonable to assume that the buyer does not need the state's protection concerning rates charged and the fiscal soundness of the insurer, while there is a much stronger case for protecting the public from the sellers of life-insurance policies that use unethical selling techniques and invest customers' funds fraudulently or unwisely. Also, the case for protecting the uneducated and poor from the temptations of gambling is certainly greater than that for protecting the wealthy[1].

---

[1] None of the above examples are to be interpreted as making an absolute case for regulation. I think that the argument about the need to protect the poor but not the rich from the temptations of gambling is paternalism of the worst sort since it is combined with elitism.

The preceding examples suffice to make the case that regulation is basically a blunt instrument that cannot readily be applied to meet the special requirements of regions and groups of people. Seen in the light of this characteristic of regulation it is clear that free economic zones represent an instrument for the selective application of deregulation, permitting in principle the development of an optimum pattern by regions and classes of customers.

However, free economic zones are a useful instrument for selective deregulation only if two conditions are met. First, there must be a need for it and second, it must be technically feasible to achieve a separation of the regulated and deregulated market. In the case of the examples cited above, these two criteria appear to be met, except in the case of free enterprise zones where it is not clear that it is technically feasible to limit deregulation to the economically relevant firms.

Interest Group Backing

It is well known that the deregulation of some U.S. industries has been stalled because the deregulation lowers the welfare of some firms and workers clearly and by a substantial amount so that it is worthwhile for them to form well-financed interest groups lobbying with politicians and presenting them with a credible threat of the loss of blocks of votes in case their industries are deregulated. The beneficiaries of the deregulation, on the other hand, usually are large in number and would gain very little each from deregulation. As a result, they have no incentives to form interest groups and lobby with politicians for deregulation. Consequently, even in cases where it is widely accepted that the sum of small benefits exceeds the large costs to a few, the political process of deregulation is often stalled.

The preceding model of the political economy of regulation, however, can be used to explain why in the case of industries where complete deregulation is stalled, partial deregulation through the creation of free economic zones has been accomplished successfully. The reason is simply that the free economic zones generate benefits sufficiently large and concentrated for some firms, workers and local governments that it is profitable for them to form interest groups for lobbying with politicians in favor of the zones. The costs created by the zones, on the other hand, tend to be small and diffuse and therefore do not generate strong interest groups and political opposition.

The preceding considerations can be illustrated by reference to a free trade zone. When the Volkswagen company considered establishing an assembly plant in Pennsylvania, local workers, small businesses and governments stood to benefit a great deal and they formed a powerful lobby that succeeded in obtaining legislation which granted free trade zone status to the VW assembly plant. The producers of automobile parts in Michigan whose level of protection was lowered through the free trade zone suffered only marginally and in ways which were difficult to establish quantitatively. If they tried to lobby against the Pennsylvania zone, they obviously did not succeed because they were unable to generate a credible voting threat.

In the case of the free banking and insurance zones the pattern of interest group pressures was even more in favor of their establishment because most of the firms in the zones are branches of existing U.S. firms, which expect no reduction in business done in the regulated sector in the United States and instead expect to gain at the expense of foreign firms and by bringing home business that had been lost to partial deregulation abroad. As foreigners have no votes in U.S. elections, opposition from these interests was ineffective and the main battle was in persuading domestic firms unable to open branches in the zone that the planned techniques of discrimination would be successful in preventing loss of business from the regulated sector[1].

III. Welfare Effects of Free Economic Zones

The creation of free economic zones raises welfare through the more selective application of regulation according to the requirements of different regions and groups of customers. In real terms, the deregulation lowers costs of protection and of transactions, permitting welfare gains through the expansion of trade and specialization. Free economic zones are likely to have dynamic effects on the supply of work, technology and entrepreneurship.

However, free economic zones also may reduce welfare through the locational diversion of trade and investment and through the generation of negative externalities. In addition, there are welfare effects of an indeterminate sign due to the redistribution of tax revenue between governmental jurisdictions.

Theoretically, the overall, net welfare effects of free economic zones are indeterminate. Only empirical studies can lead to estimates of net benefits and it is doubtful that some of the effects can ever be measured[2].

---

[1] The New York free banking zone was long delayed by opposition from U.S. banks which were prevented by federal law from opening branches in the zone and which feared that the zone would divert business away from them.

[2] Perhaps it will be possible to employ the methodology used in the empirical study of the effects of trade diversion and creation in connection with economic integration. In these

Real Economic Effects

As was shown above, the creation of a free trade zone amounts to the lowering of the level of protection of the host country. It is well known from the theory of international trade that such a lowering of protection leads to increased levels of trade and specialization, which in turn results in higher community welfare. This proposition is illustrated with the help of the standard Heckscher-Ohlin model in the figure, where the small home-country's import good X and export good Y are measured along the horizontal and vertical axes, respectively. In initial equilibrium production is at point P_0 on the production possibility locus XY, where the protection-distorted domestic relative price line TT' is tangent and the relative price of the traded good is equal to the marginal rate of transformation in production. Trade takes place along the world price line WW' and permits attainment of welfare level C_0, where the domestic price level is equal to the marginal rate of substitution for consumers.

Trade Creation and Locational Trade Diversion

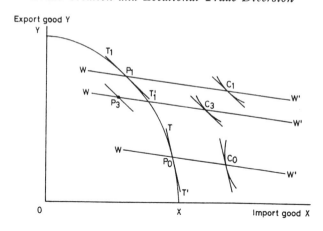

The lowering of protection due to the creation of the free trade zone is assumed to result in the new domestic price ratio T_1T_1' with the new equilibrium output at P_1 and consumption at C_1 after trade at the unchanged world price WW'. The core of standard international trade theory consists of establishing rigorously that consumption point C_1 must imply a higher level of welfare than C_0. It follows therefore that if the creation of

---

studies externalities and tax effects have also been ignored or treated as residuals. Hodjera [1978], Johnson [1976] and Grubel [1980] have attempted cost benefit studies of regional free Euro-banking centers.

a free trade zone leads only to the lowering of protection and has no other effects, a small country must gain welfare through the increased specialization in production which exploits its comparative advantage. However, the lowering of protection through the creation of a free trade zone does have another effect which requires amendment of the standard model and results.

Locational Trade Diversion

The elimination of protection in the free trade zone may induce production to take place in an inefficient location, resulting in extra costs of production that lower the level of welfare below that which the country could attain if the same reduction in protection had been available uniformly to all firms regardless of location. Two examples may serve to illustrate this important point. First, when bank intermediation business is induced to shift from Montreal to London through the absence of the reserve requirement tax, several extra real costs of doing business are incurred because the London branch of the Montreal bank has to be staffed and supervised over great distances from the parent's headquarters. Lenders and borrowers incur extra costs of communication or travel or perhaps just legal complications by dealing in London rather than in Montreal, where by assumption in the absence of free banking in London they would have done their business at least cost. These added social costs of Euro-currency banking must be offset against the social gains which accrue because the smaller spread between lending and borrowing rates in London induces some extra lending and borrowing and makes capital markets more perfect. It should also be noted that the private incentives for doing business in London rather than Montreal remain in spite of these extra social costs, for otherwise the shift of the business would not take place.

As a second example consider the Swiss village of Nandans, which is located in a high valley between Switzerland and Austria. Because of difficult access from Switzerland in the 19th century this village was granted exemption from Swiss excise taxes and tariffs. In essence, it is a free trade zone which attracts much business through offering low prices especially in heavily taxed and protected gasoline and cosmetics. The economic waste created by this free trade zone is readily apparent as one envisages heavy gasoline trucks slowly lumbering up the steep mountain road to the village. These trucks are followed by long lines of private passenger cars. Once in the village the gasoline is transferred into the tanks of the passenger cars via the pumps of tax-exempt gas stations. After this transfer the cars and trucks return to the lowlands for regular, productive work. It is clear, that the free trade zone induced business in

Nandans is privately profitable, but that it involves a relatively substantial waste of real resources.

In terms of the model in the figure, the inefficiencies caused by the locational diversion of business are shown by production taking place at point P_3, which is inside the efficient frontier. While trade still takes place at the world price line WW', the point of consumption C_3 must necessarily be below C_1 because the only difference between the two situations is that C_1 is reached without the inefficiency cost of the locational diversion of business. Whether or not C_3 is on a higher indifference curve than C_0 is an empirical question that depends on the relative magnitude of the gains from trade creation and the losses due to the locational diversion of trade. However, it cannot be ruled out on logical grounds that because of locational diversions of trade free trade zones result in a net loss of welfare by the criteria of the standard trade model[1].

Defensive Deregulation

At this point of the analysis it is important to introduce a distinction between what might be called offensive and defensive free economic zone creation. When a free trade zone is created in a country we have the offensive case for which all of the preceding conclusions about trade creation and diversion are relevant. However, the creation of the free banking and insurance zones in New York involve a defensive act in the sense that they are a response to prior deregulation abroad in the form of Euro-currency banking and Lloyds of London, as described above. Therefore, these U.S. free zones reverse some of the locational diversion of trading that the prior deregulation had produced and they are more likely to be raising welfare than are the offensive zones.

Generally, the preceding analysis suggests that the costs of trade diversion are likely to be the smaller the more free economic zones there are. In the limit, the number of zones will be so large as to include all of the country's territory and in effect universal free trade is achieved with zero costs of trade diversion.

---

[1] The results of the analysis focusing on the concepts of trade creation and locational trade diversion are strongly reminiscent of results obtained in the analysis of the effects of economic integration [Lipsey, 1960]. In fact, we have here simply another case of the second-best and reconfirmation of the basic principle that partial movement towards free competition does not necessarily result in greater welfare. However, the results of second-best policies are ultimately an empirical matter and in this context it may be useful to note that most studies of the effects of European integration concluded that trade expansion dominated by far trade diversion effects. However, only actual studies of free trade zones from this point of view can establish whether the beneficial effects of integration also prevail in the case of free trade zones. No such studies have been brought to my attention.

In this context it is worth noting that the "underground economy", which recently has become the object of much study [Feige, 1979; Mirus and Smith, 1981] is a form of free economic zone, which involves welfare gains and losses that are analogous to those of free economic zones just discussed. Deregulation that causes economic agents to leave the underground economy are defensive and can lead to a lowering of existing costs of locational diversion costs. Free gambling zones may well have this result if they induce gamblers and the suppliers of gambling services to give up their illegal activities, creating social savings in the form of less crime and corruption.

Capital Flows

Free economic zones generally, but free trade zones in developing countries especially, can give rise to capital flows which have potentially important welfare implications. As is well known, regulation and protection in many developing countries represent serious barriers to the inflow of capital, even if local labor productivity would otherwise make such investment profitable. The establishment of a free trade zone which removes these barriers can induce the inflow of capital which raises the productivity of local labor, may generate dynamic linkage effects and gives rise to income tax revenue from the profits of foreign firms, all of which translates into gains in welfare for the host country. At the same time, the owners of capital in the rest of the world gain since their private yields are increased.

The growth in world welfare caused by the more efficient global allocation of capital is in addition to that of the gains due to the more efficient allocation of given resources in each country discussed in the preceding section. However, as in the case of the effects involving given resources, the flow of capital can result in costs of locational diversion. For example, foreign capital which has located in the Philippines' Bataan free trade zone might have located elsewhere in Philippines if deregulation had been uniform for the whole country. If this is the case, the productivity of the capital is lower than it would have been if it had located in the most efficient place. In the extreme, if the foreign capital comes from a regulated environment, the true social productivity in that zone may be lower than what it was in its country of origin. Again, as in the case of the analysis of the effects with given resources, the net welfare effects of capital flows induced by free economic zones on the host and home country are a function of the empirically determined relative effects of creation and diversion.

Dynamic Effects

All of the preceding arguments about the welfare effects of free economic zones are essentially static in the sense that they considered the results of induced changes within the analytical framework of given resource endowments, technology and the efforts of workers and entrepreneurs. This approach misses what in the longer run may be the most important source of benefits of free economic zones, the dynamic effects. While they are notoriously difficult to predict or even to identify, their importance was stressed in empirical studies of the effects of integration and they underlie the widespread interest in supply side economics in the 1980s. The dynamism generated by selective deregulation has already manifested itself in the more rapid and frequent innovations in banking and insurance services offered, in Euro-currency banking and by Lloyds of London, respectively. It has been due to the fact that only commercial and technical feasibility determined their introduction and regulatory processes could not prevent or even delay them. The well-known past innovations in the free banking and insurance zones are likely to be followed by more and free zones in other industries should result in similar acceleration of innovation.

External Diseconomies

There exist two competing theories of the reasons for regulation. The first suggests that it is the outcome of democratic political processes which enable special interest groups to enrich themselves at the expense of the general public and overall total welfare [Wolf, 1979; Cairns, 1980]. To the extent that free economic zones lower trade barriers under this model they injure only special interest groups and increase overall welfare. Therefore, the estimates of welfare gains due to free trade zones must be revised upward in a way that can never be rigorous.

Under the second model, protection is imposed to eliminate some market failure. Lowering of trade barriers through free economic zones thus leads to the reappearance of external diseconomies and a social cost that has to be included in the welfare analysis presented above.

The impact of the external diseconomies can logically consist of the following extremes. First, the external diseconomies are confined to the host country, as for example might happen if through lowered protection of an import-competing industry the country loses the security benefits of domestic agriculture or of a defense industry. Under these conditions the welfare calculus for the host country has to be adjusted downward. The calculus for the rest of the world requires no adjustment. Second, the external diseconomies accrue mainly to the world as a whole and only minimally to the host country. For example, Euro-currency banking is feared to have raised the probability of a major global financial crisis because in the absence of national regulatory controls these banks have invested imprudently large amounts relative to their capital base to individual borrowers of doubtful ability to repay [Grubel, 1979]. Whatever may be the merit of this argument in practice, it serves to illustrate how deregulation of banking in Euro-currency markets can result in negative externalities for the world while most of the benefits from the deregulation accrue to the few financial centers hosting the Euro-currency banks. In such cases the welfare calculus of the effect of free economic zones must be amended in obvious ways that are not pursued here.

Finally, it should be noted that if the methods used for discriminating between regulated and unregulated sectors are working imperfectly, business which should be regulated escapes into the deregulated sector. For example, it may not be possible to exclude people from free gambling zones who through excessive losses become public burdens, or firms with imperfect knowledge may be induced to do business with deregulated banks and insurance companies that is not in their long-run interest and leads to social losses. The negative external effects of such imperfect separation of regulated and unregulated markets must be entered into the social welfare calculus of free economic zones.

Tax Revenue Effects

Free economic zones cause a redistribution of tax revenue between governmental jurisdictions that permit some to lower taxes and require another to raise them (or change expenditures without corresponding changes in taxation). The resultant welfare effects are well known from the public finance literature and will not be pursued here. Instead, the following is limited to a brief taxonomy of the major tax revenue effects.

The local government jurisdiction hosting the free economic zone gains income directly if it is the landlord of the zone and raises charges to land users upon establishment of the economic zone[1]. If the local government has an income tax, revenue is raised by the growth in factor incomes accompanying the free economic zone trade expansion and as the tax base is broadened through the migration of capital into the zone from

---

[1] If the owner of the land wishes to maximize his income, he will charge for the use of the land an amount that is analytically equivalent to the economic rent which accrues to the occupant. A duty-free camera retail store at an airport, for example, faces a downward sloping demand curve and sets the price at an output level and accompanying price where marginal revenue equals marginal costs, with all inputs available at constant prices from the regulated sector and the rent being determined as a residual. In this extreme case, all of the benefits from deregulation accrue to the airport authority and the local government owning

the host country and abroad. Overall increased activity and wealth raise excise and property tax revenues of the local jurisdiction.

The senior government of the country hosting the zone suffers a loss of tariff and other revenue generated by regulation equal to that avoided by firms locating in the free economic zone. In addition, there is a shrinking in the income tax base as factor incomes are lowered in industries which contract because of lower protection. Offsetting these losses are higher factor incomes and therefore income tax revenue from export industries and the broader tax base created by the flow of foreign capital into the zone. The rest of the world loses tax base through the outflow of capital.

The most important conclusion emerging from this brief overview is that the local government hosting the zone always gains tax revenue and it should therefore not be surprising that local governments typically are prime promoters of free economic zones. Senior governments, on the other hand, are likely to lose revenue unless the trade expansion and foreign capital inflows are large enough to offset the losses. This may well be one important reason why some senior governments, such as that of Canada, oppose the creation of free trade and economic zones.

IV. Free Economic Zones for Other Industries ?

Free Investment Zones

After the analysis of the nature and welfare effects of free economic zones, it may be useful to consider application of the principles developed to other industries which are well known to suffer from heavy regulation. I will do so here for the investment and drug-medical industries.

Paternalism in the regulation of capital markets of the world is very strong, having moved from an initial concern with the accuracy of information disclosed about investment projects to where some governments

---

it. Capital, managers and labor of the store are paid only their opportunity cost in the regulated sector.

If landlords charge rent above the monopolistic optimum, the level of business done in the tax free store will also be less than optimum. I have noted that in some countries duty free airport stores charge prices that appear to be above the optimum and therefore appear to transact very little business. The question arises whether in these cases the stores exploit a very inelastic demand curve, the determinants of which may not be obvious to the casual visitor or whether landlords have set rents too high in ignorance of the elasticity of demand.

On the other hand, it is also possible for landlords to charge less than the optimum amount. In this case the entrepreneur leasing the store enjoys economic rents, which may imply non-desirable income distribution effects. To avoid non-optimal outcomes, the owners of land on which free economic zones are established should set charges through competitive bidding.

Herbert G. Grubel

have taken it upon themselves to evaluate the economic merit and risk of projects. Inevitably, the legislative requirement to have all capital issues approved by the bureaucracy has resulted in additional costs and delays and in effect requires government officials to do things for which they are not particularly well qualified. Doubts have been expressed that these costs are worth the benfits to investors [Kalymon, 1978].

As in the case of insurance and banking, there is room for disagreement over the net social benefits of regulating capital markets and there exist powerful interest groups benefiting from the regulation. Complete deregulation is therefore unlikely and it may be worth considering partial deregulation through the establishment of free investment zones. In such zones borrowers would not be required to obtain government approval of prospectuses accompanying the issue of new securities. Investors' protection would consist of the remaining applicability of laws which make it a criminal offense to misrepresent facts in prospectuses. Basically, however, investors would be required to have their decisions guided by the principle of "caveat emptor", which would induce them to study prospectuses carefully, use the services of private firms specializing in such evaluations, or both. And, of course, they always have the option of not buying securities in the zone at all.

It may well be that in equilibrium there would be dual capital markets. Risk averse and untrained investors would purchase securities in regulated markets and would be willing to pay the premium and accept delays involved. Firms in relatively stable industries, such as utilities, might find the costs and delays in getting approval acceptable and would be the main suppliers of securities in these regulated markets. In the unregulated zones, on the other hand, securities would be sold to investors with a preference for risky but potentially high return securities and with special skills in evaluating investments. Small and newly created firms in industries where new investment opportunities tend to develop quickly, such as high-technology and resource development, would supply securities and gain greatly in their ability to exploit new opportunities quickly and cheaply.

Free Medical Zones

It is well known that the regulation of drugs, hospitals and medical doctors has resulted in excess costs because the political and bureaucratic incentive structure puts too much weight on the prevention of problems with new products and treatments relative to the cost incurred by delays or cancellations in the introduction of new products and treatments[1].

---

[1] See Grabowski [1976] and Wardell [1979] for studies which indicate that the U.S. cost of obtaining permission to market a new drug was $ 50 million on average in the middle 1970s

There exist in fact free drug and hospital zones in Mexico, some Eastern European countries and in the Swiss Canton of Appenzell[1]. Patients from many countries take advantage of these facilities, often after treatments in their home-countries were unsatisfactory. Because public health-insurance programs in most countries do not cover treatment in such zones abroad, access has been limited to wealthy persons.

The creation of free medical zones in industrial countries would be defensive in the sense defined above and could be achieved simply by setting aside areas within which most of the existing regulation of drugs, treatments and doctors are inapplicable. Patients who consider use of the facilities in the zones would have to rely on their own judgement and that of their doctors and relatives as to the merit of the risks and potential benefits offered. They would have also as protection the desire of firms in the zone to continue in business, which would prevent them from offering drugs and treatments that are ineffective or carry excessive risk in use Perhaps it would be useful to require that all consultations between firms in the zone and patients be recorded on video tape as evidence that patients had been given full explanations of risks, benefits and costs and had consented to treatment under free will and in possession of their facilities.

It is clear from the preceding considerations that free investment and medical zones do not offer an opportunity for the separation of markets in the same way as do the free banking and insurance zones. In these latter types of zones use is restricted easily to customers who through their size and other characteristics clearly have very little need for the paternalism of the state. In the case of free investment and medical zones it is not possible to use objective criteria to limit access to those who obviously do not need protection. In the case of the medical zone, in fact, arguments can be made that potential users are in special need of state paternalism. For these reasons perhaps the suggested creation of free investment and medical zones has little chance of being implemented in the near future.

---

and involved testing over several years. As a result, life-saving drugs that had been proven effective and safe in Europe have become available in North America only after several years and after much unnecessary suffering and deaths. Some so-called "orphan drugs" are never marketed because expected sales levels would not permit the recovery of the required $ 50 million investment in obtaining government approval, even though, by all medical standards such drugs are effective and safe.

[1] Appenzell is the home of many clinics using "natural" treatment methods for many ailments. Medical doctors can practice and use their titles obtained abroad without having to pass examination required in other Swiss cantons. According to casual observations by Swiss economists, the Canton of Appenzell has attracted many patients from abroad for a long time and business has not been impeded by expensive law-suits or scandals.

However, in principle, the case for free investment and medical zones is much like that for free gambling zones and there may well come a time when like in the case of gambling the costs of regulation become so great that relatively small and politically independent areas will encourage the creation of such free investment and medical zones because of the large local benefits they promise.

V. Summary and Conclusions

In this paper I have described several recent and diverse institutional innovations which have in common that they permit the selective deregulation of economic activity by location or type of customer or both. It was shown that such selective deregulation, referred to conveniently as the creation of free economic zones, generates powerful interest groups which can succeed politically where attempts at complete deregulation are stalled because of some doubts about the merit of the action and because vested interests oppose it politically.

The welfare effects of the free economic zones are theoretically indeterminate. There are gains from the expansion of trade, encouragement of innovation and increased freedom of choice for producers and consumers. Welfare losses may arise from the locational diversion of trade and externalities, including some due to the imperfect separation of regulated and deregulated sectors. Some free economic zones created in New York are defensive in the sense that they are in response to zones created abroad and the accompanying diversion of trade. Such zones are likely to reduce rather than increase the cost of locational diversion of trade.

If the already existing free economic zones are successful commercially and costs in terms of locational diversion and externalities are small, further free economic zones are certain to be created and new industries included. The selective deregulation of the investment and medical industries may be primary candidates for such new initiatives.

References

Butler, Stuart M., *Enterprise Zones.* Washington 1980.

Cairns, Robert D., *Rationales for Regulation.* Economic Council of Canada, Technical Report Series, No. 2, Ottawa 1980.

Cheng, H.-S., "From the Caymans". Federal Reserve Bank of San Francisco, *Weekly Letter*, February 13, 1981.

Corden, W. M., *The Theory of Protection.* Oxford 1971.

Decaminada, Joseph P., *An Analysis of the New York Insurance Exchange and "Free Zone".* Memo of The Atlantic Companies, New York, May 31, 1979.

Diamond, Walter H., *Free Trade Zones Offer Worldwide Opportunities.* Area Development Series, University of Miami, December 1979, pp. 33—47.

The Economist, "New York's Insurance Industry". London, November 17, 1979, pp. 114—115.

Feige, Edgar L., "How Big is the Irregular Economy?". *Challenge,* Vol. 22, December 1979, pp. 5—13.

Fernstrom, John R., *The Establishment of Free Trade Zones in Promoting Industrial Development.* Thesis for the Industrial Development Institute, University of Oklahoma, 1976.

Grabowski, Henry G., *Drug Regulation and Innovation: Empirical Evidence and Policy Options.* American Enterprise Institute for Public Policy Research, Evaluative Studies, 28, Washington 1976.

Grubel, Herbert G., *A Proposal for the Establishment of an International Deposit Insurance Corporation.* Essays in International Finance, No. 133, Princeton 1979.

—, "A Proposal to Establish an Afro-Currency Market in Nairobi". In: John S. Chipman and Charles P. Kindleberger (Eds.), *Flexible Exchange Rates and the Balance of Payments: Essays in Memory of Egon Sohmen.* Studies in International Economics, Vol. 7, Amsterdam 1980, pp. 297—309.

Hamada, Koichi, "An Economic Analysis of the Duty-Free Zone". *Journal of International Economics,* Vol. 4, 1974, pp. 225—241.

Hamilton, Carl, and **Lars E. O. Svensson,** *On Welfare Effects of a "Duty-Free Zone".* Institute for International Economic Studies, University of Stockholm, August 1980, processed.

Hodjera, Zoran, "The Asian Currency Market: Singapore as a Regional Financial Center". *IMF, Staff Papers,* Vol. 25, 1978, pp. 221—253.

Johnson, Harry G., "Panama as Regional Financial Center: A Preliminary Analysis of Development Contribution". *Economic Development and Cultural Change,* Vol. 24, 1976, pp. 261—286.

Kalymon, B. C., *Financing of the Junior Mining Company in Ontario.* Ontario Ministry of Natural Resources, February 1978.

Lipsey, R. G., "The Theory of Customs Unions: A General Survey". *The Economic Journal,* Vol. 70, 1960, pp. 496—513.

Manhattan Report Special Edition, *A Forum on Urban Enterprise Zones — Reversing the Decline of Our Inner Cities.* International Center for Economic Policy Studies, April 1981.

Meade, J. E., *The Theory of Customs Unions.* Amsterdam 1955.

Mirus, Rolf, and **Roger S. Smith,** "Canada's Irregular Economy". *Canadian Public Policy,* Vol. 7, 1981, pp. 444—453.

Ping, H. K., "Birth of the Second Generation of Free Trade Zones". *Far Eastern Economic Review,* May 18, 1979.

Rodriguez, Carlos A., "A Note on the Economics of the Duty Free Zone". *Journal of International Economics,* Vol. 6, 1976, pp. 385—388.

Time, "Free Enterprise Oases". New York, July 14, 1980, p. 43.

United Nations Industrial Development Organization (UNIDO), *Export Processing Zones in Developing Countries.* UNIDO Working Papers on Structural Changes, No. 19, UNIDO/ICIS. 176, [New York], August 18, 1980.

Viner, Jacob, *The Customs Union Issue.* Carnegie Endowment for International Peace, Studies in the Administration of International Law and Organization, No. 10, New York 1950.

Wall, David, "Export Processing Zones". *Journal of World Trade Law,* Vol. 10, 1976, pp. 478—498.

Wardell, W., "More Regulation or Better Therapies?". *Regulation,* Vol. 3, 1979, pp. 25—33.

Wolf, Jr., Charles, "A Theory of Non-Market Failure". *Journal of Law and Economics,* Vol. 22, 1979, pp. 107—139.

*   *   *

Excerpt from *Management of Success: The Moulding of Modern Singapore* (1989), 373–98.

17

SINGAPORE'S RECORD OF PRICE STABILITY, 1966–84

HERBERT G. GRUBEL

During the first twenty years of its independence Singapore enjoyed one of the best records of price stability and high economic growth in the world. This chapter* analyses how this record was achieved. It does so in the first part by organizing available data around some basic and widely accepted theoretical models. These are the quantity theory of money and its extensions into a world of fixed, and then flexible, exchange rates in a Mundell world with perfect goods and capital-market arbitrage.

The next part of the chapter considers Singapore's budget policy and public-sector borrowing requirements to establish why monetary and exchange-rate policies were free to be used in the pursuit of price stability in time periods when most of the countries of the world had lost this freedom. In the final part I discuss the use of a form of incomes policy in Singapore since 1972, addressing the difficult questions about the need for it and whether it may not have done more harm than good. The chapter ends with some speculation about the reasons why the Singapore Government pursued price stability in an otherwise strongly inflationary world.

THE RECORD ON PRICES: A MONETARIST EXPLANATION

Singapore's economic achievements can best be appreciated by comparison with the record of performance of the rest of the world. For this purpose Fig. 17.1

---

* This chapter was written while I held the position of Distinguished Fellow of International Banking and Finance at the Institute of Southeast Asian Studies in Singapore in the Fall of 1985. I would not have been able to write this chapter without information and many analytical insights I gained from discussions with Kernial Sandhu, Lim Chong Yah, Teh Kok Peng, Ng Chee Yuen, and Lee (Tsao) Yuan. Chris Rieger also helped me with data and the taming of the computer. None of these individuals are responsible for the analysis and conclusions presented here.

373

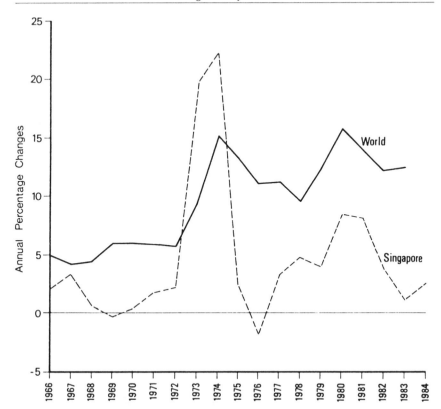

Fig. 17.1. Inflation rates (CPI) for Singapore and the non-communist world, 1966–84. *Source:* International Monetary Fund, *International Financial Statistics, 1985 Yearbook* (Washington, D.C., 1985).

shows inflation rates of Singapore and of the non-communist world during the years 1966–84. The statistics are for consumer prices, and the world index is that compiled by the International Monetary Fund using national incomes as weights. As can be seen, during this period Singapore had a consistently lower inflation rate than the world, except in 1973 and 1974. The averages were 4.7 and 9.7 per cent for Singapore and the world respectively.

What makes this record of price stability even more remarkable is that it was achieved without any apparent sacrifice of economic growth. The real growth rates of Singapore and the non-communist world are shown in Fig. 17.2. Singapore's growth averaged 9.9 per cent annually while that of the world averaged only 3.5 per cent. As can be seen from the figure, Singapore's growth was above that of the world in every year, even though the fluctuations were highly correlated.

How can this record of price stability and rapid economic growth in Singapore be explained? I believe that this question can best be approached by using a

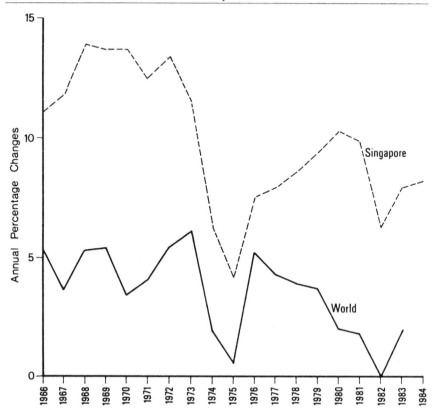

Fig. 17.2. Real GDP growth rates for Singapore and the non-communist world, 1966–84. *Sources:* Department of Statistics, *Yearbook of Statistics, 1984/85* (Singapore, 1985); International Monetary Fund, *International Financial Statistics, 1985 Yearbook* (Washington, D.C., 1985).

theoretical model to organize the large quantities of data which in principle are relevant to the determination of consumer prices. The model that I shall use is the very old quantity theory of money, which has enjoyed a renaissance during the 1970s, but which has not yet been applied to Singapore.[1]

The Monetarist Equation

Following Friedman (1969) and Friedman and Schwartz (1963) we start our analysis with the following familiar identity:

$$M * V = P * Q$$

where M is the money supply, V is the income velocity of circulation of money, P is the price level, Q is national income, and * is the multiplication sign. Taking logarithms of the equation, differentiating with respect to time and rearranging yields:

$$gP = gM - gQ + gV$$

where $gx = (1/x) \, (dx/dt)$; $(x = P, M, Q, \text{ and } V)$.

This equation says that during any given time period such as a year, the rate of change in prices is equal to the rate of change in the money supply minus the rate of change in the demand for money, which is assumed to be equal to the growth rate in real output, plus the rate of change in the velocity of circulation of money. For example, if in a given year the money supply is increased by 10 per cent and real income, and therefore the demand for money, rises by 6 per cent, then the inflation rate is 4 per cent if the velocity of circulation remains unchanged.

A set of statistics relevant to an empirical test of this theory is found in Fig. 17.3. One time series graphs the annual percentage changes in the consumer price index (CPI), lagged one year. The second takes the difference between the annual percentage growth rates in the money supply and the real gross domestic product (GDP). The definition of the money supply used here is that of currency in circulation and demand deposits, which are commonly referred to collectively as M1. The test applied here assumes that the velocity of circulation has remained constant.

An inspection of Fig. 17.3 shows that the two time series move together remarkably well. When there was large excess money-supply creation, inflation was much above average. During most of the years when excess money supply was created at tolerable rates, inflation was at tolerable rates. Given the many abstractions from reality which characterize the quantity theory of money, this visual experiment lends strong support to the general proposition that Singapore's inflation rate was determined predominantly by the excess creation of money during the period under observation.

The Experience with Inflation, 1973–74

The explanatory power of the theoretical model is particularly evident in the inflationary episode of 1973–74, which stands out in both Fig. 17.1 and Fig. 17.3. During these two years, the world suffered through the effects of petroleum price increases caused by the Organization of Petroleum Exporting Countries (OPEC) and food-price rises attributed to a series of bad harvests in several major food-producing countries. The graph for Singapore shows clearly that the excess creation of money took place *before* these external price increases. In fact, Singapore's money supply increased by an unprecedented 35.5 per cent in 1972 while OPEC raised prices only in 1974. During that latter year the world money supply increased by 13.4 per cent. For these reasons we should not be surprised to find that in 1973 and 1974 Singapore's inflation rate exceeded that of the world by a substantial margin, as is evident from Fig. 7.1.

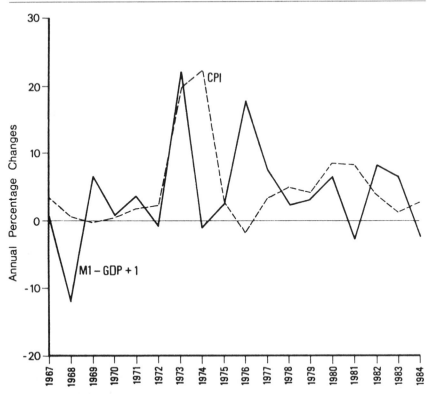

Fig. 17.3. A monetarist model of Singapore: percentage changes in the consumer price index and M1 – Gross Domestic Product (leading one year), 1967–84. Calculated from data provided by the Department of Statistics, *Yearbook of Statistics 1984/85* (Singapore, 1985).

Of course, as with any theory, the monetarist model is a highly simplified representation of the real world. As such, it does not imply that only excess money creation causes inflation or, conversely, that excess money creation always leads to inflation, or that it does so with lags of consistent length. It only implies that money-supply creation is the single most important determinant of inflation over longer periods. From this perspective, we may note the large excess money-supply creation in 1975 that is clearly evident in Fig. 17.3. It resulted from an increase in M1 of 21.5 per cent and an increase in real income of only 4.1 per cent. The impact on inflation in the following year had not been as pronounced and immediate as in the 1972 episode of excess money creation. However, there were relatively large price increases in 1980–81, which represent the second serious inflationary episode during the period under examination. These delayed effects of the 1975 excess money creation are consistent with the quantity theory of money since, after the 1972 wage determination, the Singapore economy was subject to an incomes policy administered by the National Wages Council. This policy kept wages below their market equilibrium, as will be discussed below. It delayed and spread out the effects of excess money creation but could not eliminate the increases predicted by the quantity theory of money in the longer run.

In sum, from an inspection of Fig. 17.3 one may reasonably conclude that, at the most fundamental theoretical level, Singapore's record of price-level changes is explained by monetary policy. Inflation was high following periods of excess money creation and low when the money supply more nearly equalled demand for it.

Implications

In the mid-1980s this finding does not come as a surprise to many people, mostly because of the widespread acceptance of the monetarist model as a valid explanation of inflation. However, this acceptance is of rather recent origin and is not entirely universal. During the 1960s and 1970s many battles were fought between Monetarists and Keynesians, who insisted that monetary policy was ineffective in the creation of full employment and irrelevant to the determination of inflation. Even in the 1980s there exists a vocal group of so-called Post-Keynesians who continue this dispute, although the grounds have shifted somewhat. Post-Keynesians accept the obvious correlation between the quantity of money and inflation, but they insist that the money supply is merely accommodating inflationary pressures that stem from exogenous increases in wages and other costs of production.[2]

In the following I assume that Fig. 17.3 stands as sufficient evidence for the basic proposition that Singapore's record of price stability during the period under study is due to the creation of appropriate quantities of money. This allows me in turn to question how the Singapore Government was able to pursue this non-inflationary policy when many other countries are alleged to have been unable to do so for a number of technical reasons. In particular, I shall discuss how the exchange-rate regime initially was inconsistent with an independent monetary policy and led to the inflationary episode of 1973–74, and how in 1972 the adoption of a floating exchange-rate system created national monetary sovereignty for Singapore.

THE EXCHANGE-RATE REGIME

Under the Bretton Woods agreements signed in 1945 the non-communist countries of the world, including Singapore, functioned under the so-called parity exchange-rate system. This system was characterized by a general commitment to fixed exchange rates by all national governments. Under this commitment exchange rates fluctuated routinely around a narrow margin of less than one percentage point. Major exchange-rate adjustments were permitted when fundamental economic conditions required, but there was a strong presumption that such requirements would be rare and the required changes would be small. In the early 1970s this system broke down under stresses, which can readily be understood by consideration of the kind of situation which confronted Singapore at the time.

Singapore is an extremely open, small economy.[3] As a result, it cannot influence world inflation and interest rates. When the Singapore Government maintains a fixed exchange rate, any increases in the prices of its internationally traded goods are reflected fully and very quickly in Singapore dollar prices for these goods. As a result, there is a strong tendency for Singapore's CPI to move together with that in the rest of the world.

By analogy, nearly perfect capital arbitrage at all times establishes world interest rates in Singapore. Under fixed exchange rates, attempts by the monetary authorities to have Singapore interest rates lower than those in the rest of the world lead to massive capital outflows and consequently unsustainable official reserve losses. Interest rates that are higher than world level cannot be established because very large capital inflows require the monetary authorities to buy foreign exchange with Singapore dollars. The resultant excess supply of money in turn puts upward pressures on prices and generates unsustainable trade deficits.

The well-known Mundell (1968) model has resulted in enhanced understanding of the problems encountered in managing small countries' economies. In particular, it has shown what must be the results of attempts to achieve smaller inflation rates domestically than in the rest of the world. As the money supply is made to grow at a rate consistent with low domestic inflation, there are upward pressures on interest rates and arbitrage capital flows into the country. Furthermore, the somewhat slower rate of domestic inflation increases international competitiveness and, therefore, improves the trade balance. Eventually, the country's balance of payments becomes so favourable and foreign-exchange reserves grow so large that an appreciation of the exchange rate is expected and attracts massive speculative capital inflows. Exchange-rate controls are not able to stem this tide of balance-of-payments surpluses so that sooner or later a crisis develops and some basic changes in policy or institutions have to be undertaken.

Loss of Monetary Sovereignty

The crisis takes effect through the excess supply of foreign exchange which, under the fixed exchange-rate regime, needs to be purchased by the government. The government pays for the foreign exchange with central-bank deposits, which represent the base on which monetary expansion takes place. Open market operations and increases in bank-reserve requirements can be used to sterilize some of the rise in these central-bank deposits. However, eventually the capital inflows become so large that sterilization becomes impossible. The government loses control of the money base and inflation follows. Final equilibrium is achieved only when the country creates money and accepts inflation at the rates prevailing in the rest of the world. In this sense, it is said, small countries with fixed exchange rates do not have national monetary sovereignty.

The Mundell model implies that national monetary sovereignty can be achieved only if the small, open country adopts a floating exchange-rate system. If it does so it can have domestic inflation smaller than that in the rest of the world by letting its exchange rate appreciate at rates equal to the difference between the world and desired domestic inflation rates. For example, if the world inflation is 10 per cent and the desired domestic inflation is 3 per cent, then the exchange rate must be allowed to appreciate at an annual rate of 7 per cent.

Singapore's Experience in the Light of the Model

Singapore's history makes an excellent case-study of the Mundell model. As Fig. 17.1 shows, Singapore had achieved lower price increases than those prevailing in the world during the years of fixed exchange rates from 1965 to 1973.[4] The results predicted by the theory are traced in Fig. 17.4, which shows annual foreign-capital inflows and additions to the stock of international reserves, all expressed as a percentage of GDP.

In 1968, 1971, 1972, and 1973 international-reserve gains constituted about 15 per cent of GDP annually. After abandonment of the fixed exchange rates in 1972, the annual rates of reserve gains were halved. The reasons for the high rate of reserve gains before 1972 were that the authorities were required to purchase large amounts of foreign exchange to meet the excess supplies generated in the private market at the fixed rate. The excess supplies were the outcome of large trade surpluses which resulted from the increasing international competitiveness of the country's productive sector. This competitiveness in turn was the result of the restrictive monetary policy in preceding years and its success in restraining domestic costs and demand.[5]

The large central-bank purchases of foreign exchange were also caused by substantial capital inflows in response to high interest rates and the profitability of investment initially. Later they were enlarged by the growing expectation of an upward valuation of the Singapore dollar. After 1972 capital inflows remained high and exceeded the levels of the preceding years. However, the smaller level of reserve gains in the later years implies that the trade surplus had shrunk significantly.

To appreciate the problems created by the large gains in international reserves, it may be useful to consider some absolute figures for 1971. During that year the reserve gains came to S$969 million, while the entire increase in the M1 money supply was only S$254.3 million, S$185.6 of which consisted of notes and coins, which by Singapore law have to be backed by foreign exchange. Similar figures characterize developments in 1972 and 1973.

However, most telling is the fact that in 1972 and 1973 the commercial banks' deposits with the Monetary Authority of Singapore (MAS), the high-powered

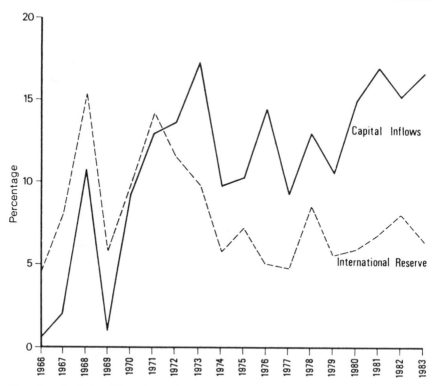

Fig. 17.4. Capital and international-reserve gains (as percentages of the gross domestic product), 1966–83. Calculated from the Department of Statistics, *Yearbook of Statistics 1984–85* (Singapore, 1985).

base which determines the growth of the money supply, jumped by 59 and 55 per cent respectively. During the preceding four years it had risen only at an average of about 11 per cent per year.[6]

Prices and Exchange Rates

The Mundell model implies that under flexible exchange rates the difference between world and Singapore inflation rates should be equal to the change in the value of the Singapore dollar. This proposition is tested in Fig. 17.5, which shows the ratio of the world to the Singapore price level, the Singapore-U.S. dollar exchange rate, and a Singapore dollar exchange-rate index. This index, taken from Lee (1984), is the average of the Singapore-dollar exchange rates against its main trading partners with each rate weighted by 1971 trade levels. To facilitate comparisons, both exchange rates and the price ratio were calculated from a base of 100 in 1971.

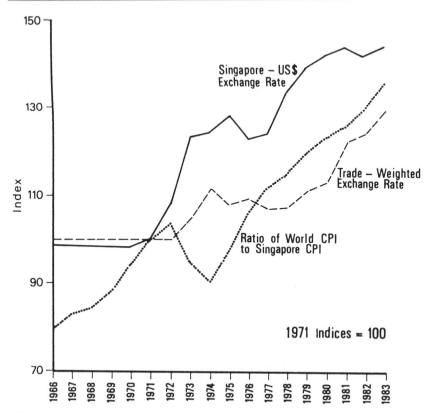

Fig. 17.5. Singapore prices and exchange rates, 1966–83. Calculated from data provided by the Department of Statistics, *Yearbook of Statistics 1984/85* (Singapore, 1985).

The graph reveals clearly that in the pre-1971 period a growing gap opened between the Singapore and the world price levels, which was unmatched by an exchange rate appreciation against the dollar.[7] This lack of exchange-rate adjustment resulted in exchange-market disequilibrium, trade surpluses, capital inflows, excess growth of the money supply, and the inflation in 1973–74 analysed above.

However, the graph also shows that, after the exchange rate became flexible in 1973, the price and trade-weighted exchange rate lines moved together, and in 1983 they had reached very nearly the same level. These developments are exactly as predicted by theory, which is all the more surprising since the world price index reflects developments in many countries which are not Singapore's trading partners and which therefore are not reflected in the exchange-rate index. As a result, the price- and exchange-index lines cannot be expected to coincide completely, even if the theory is correct.

The nearly parallel movement of the U.S.-dollar exchange rate with both the price ratio and the weighted exchange-rate index is also as predicted by the theory. This is so since the United States is both Singapore's major trading partner and carries much weight in the calculation of the world index of inflation. The relatively wide gap in the levels of the price ratio and the U.S. exchange rate in the early 1970s suggests that in 1971 the latter was at a corresponding dis-equilibrium level. This proposition is accepted by most economists. In fact, it was the inability to eliminate this disequilibrium within the fixed exchange-rate regime which led to the adoption of the flexible exchange-rate system in 1973.

Conclusions

The main purpose of the present section has been to argue that Singapore's record of price stability can best be explained in the framework of Mundell's model of the small, open economy. Between 1966 and about 1970 attempts to maintain a more stable price level than that prevailing in the rest of the world led Singapore into a growing disequilibrium as the exchange rate was fixed and the resultant under-valuation of the currency raised trade competitiveness and encouraged investment and speculative capital inflows. In 1972–73 this disequilibrium resulted in loss of control over commercial banking reserves, an explosion of the money supply, and in 1974–75 to the most serious inflation in the new country's history. However, the adoption of a managed float for the exchange rate in 1973 enabled the Singapore Government to resume its pursuit of price stability without the creation of a self-defeating disequilibrium. Since this time Singapore has enjoyed, and has exercised, monetary sovereignty "to maintain a strong and stable Singapore dollar aimed at sustaining confidence in the domestic economy and mitigating external inflationary pressures, as well as safeguarding export competitiveness" (Monetary Authority of Singapore 1985). In the process, the value of its currency has appreciated at almost the same rate at which world inflation exceeded Singapore's domestic price increases.

MONETARY POLICY FREE FROM
OTHER RESPONSIBILITIES

An important technical condition necessary for the achievement of price stability is that monetary policy be independent of the budgetary needs of the government. It is well known that this condition did not exist in the post-war years in many newly independent countries, which often started socially desirable expenditure programmes without sufficient tax revenues to pay for them. Some used the printing presses of central banks to overcome the revenue shortfalls and thus directly co-opted the use of monetary policy for price stability. Many, however, sold bonds to finance the deficits.

In principle, under these conditions the money supply can be managed to achieve price stability. But the sale of government securities, *ceteris paribus*, puts upward pressures on the domestic rate of interest. The political response to such developments has typically been to instruct the central bank to maintain low and stable interest rates. This can be achieved only by extra money-supply increases. Through this indirect process budget deficits incapacitate monetary policy and lead to inflation.

It may be worth noting that the preceding analysis is relevant for countries which have fixed exchange rates, foreign-exchange controls, and regulations repressing the normal functioning of financial markets. Countries with relatively free markets and exchange rates during the 1970s found that the upward pressure on interest rates could also be mitigated by capital inflows. We now know that these countries ended up with very large foreign debts.

Singapore in its short history escaped the need to finance government expenditures in excess of revenues by direct or indirect financing or by incurring large foreign obligations. The reason for this state of affairs is found basically in the political and economic ideology of both the country's rulers and the people who have accepted their leadership. However, for a full understanding of the special case of Singapore and its relevance for other countries, it is important to examine the process by which budgetary balance was achieved and which left monetary policy free to pursue price stability.

No Expensive Welfare Programmes Undertaken

First, the government has rejected the idea that the state is responsible for the creation of a comprehensive social-security net and for the equalization of incomes through direct-taxation measures and the subsidization of consumption goods for the poor. This philosophy is reflected in the following quote from a speech by S. Rajaratnam, then Senior Minister in the Singapore Government:

> We want to teach the people that the government is not a rich uncle. You get what you pay for .... We want to disabuse people of the notion that in a good society the rich must pay for the poor. We want to reduce welfare to the minimum, restrict it only to those who are handicapped or old. To the others we offer equal opportunities and it is up to them what they make of [them]. Everybody can be rich if they try hard. (Vasil 1984, p. 168)

As a result of this philosophy the Government of Singapore has avoided the initiation of large spending programmes such as have burdened so heavily the budgets of most of the developing countries that gained independence in the post-war years and which have led to large deficits in many industrial countries in the 1980s. Thus, Singapore has no unemployment insurance programme.[8] Spending on outright public assistance to indigent handicapped and the old absorbed only about 0.5 per cent of total government spending in Singapore during the 1980s (Lee [Tsao] 1985).

No Burden Placed on Private Capital Markets

Secondly, the Government of Singapore has on average maintained equality between expenditures and revenues. It therefore has not had to burden private capital markets with large sales of government securities. In order to document this the annual net borrowing requirements of the government are considered. For most countries this would simply be equal to the growth in the government's debt. Fig. 17.6 shows this statistic, expressing it as a percentage of gross national product (GNP) in order to keep it in proper perspective to the growing economy. Fig. 17.6 also shows Singapore's official foreign debt, which is included in the total. As can be seen, this component of the debt is negligibly small and will be disregarded in the following analysis.

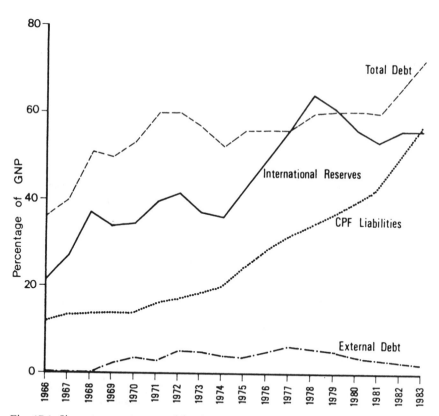

Fig. 17.6. Singapore government debt, international reserves, and Central Provident Fund liabilities (as percentages of gross national product), 1966–83. Calculated from data provided by the Department of Statistics, *Yearbook of Statistics 1984/85* (Singapore, 1985).

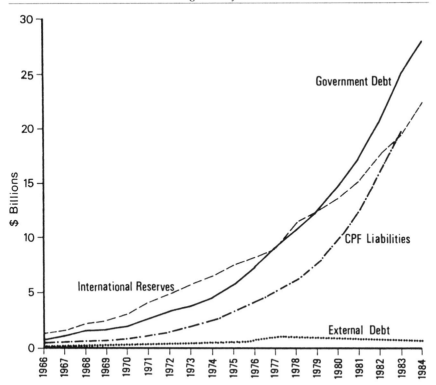

Fig. 17.7. Singapore government debt, international reserves, and Central Provident Fund liabilities (in Singapore dollars), 1966–84. Calculated from data provided by the Department of Statistics, *Yearbook of Statistics 1984/85* (Singapore, 1985).

According to Fig. 17.6, the government debt has risen rapidly as a percentage of GNP during the entire period, reaching a peak of about 80 per cent in 1984. This is quite a high growth rate and ratio by international standards.[9] In Singapore, however, it is inappropriate to consider the growth of the debt as a measure of the government's borrowing requirements because of the existence of the Central Provident Fund (CPF). Before we discuss the CPF's influence on borrowing requirements, it is necessary to sketch briefly the basic characteristics of the system.

The CPF serves as the agent of the government in administering a programme of forced savings for the people of Singapore.[10] Under this programme all workers have to pay a specified percentage of their current earnings into this fund, and the contributions are matched by a levy on employers. The rates of contribution have risen gradually and in 1983 reached the level of 25 per cent from both employers and employees. The funds in individual accounts are owned by the contributors and are paid out when the beneficiary has reached the age of fifty-five, the normal retirement age in Singapore. Some of the funds may be withdrawn for specified purposes such as the financing of housing and medical expenses. In Fig. 17.6, the liabilities of the CPF, including interest earned on portfolio investments, are shown as percentages of the GNP.

Cash contributions to, and other income of, the CPF, net of out-payments, are invested in government securities. The CPF system therefore has been a very important source of funds for government expenditures that are not covered by current revenues. In fact, as Fig. 17.6 shows, there has been a relatively constant gap between the size of CPF liabilities and government debt throughout the period. This crucial statistic is shown with more precision in Fig. 17.8. There we see the government's net borrowing requirements, which are equal to the respective year's growth in domestically held debt less the growth in the liabilities of the CPF. The average annual borrowing requirements have been 2.4 per cent

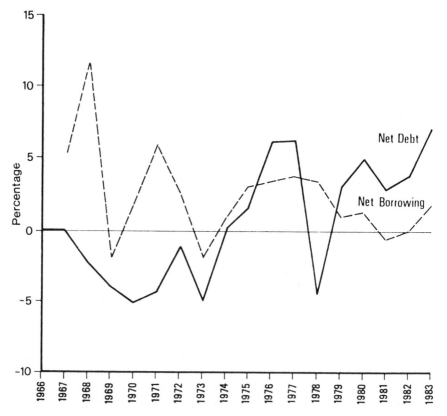

Fig. 17.8. Net borrowing requirements and net debt growth (as percentages of gross national product), 1966–83. Calculated from data provided by the Department of Statistics, *Yearbook of Statistics 1984/85* (Singapore, 1985).

of GNP. The time profile of the series shows them to have been relatively much higher before than after 1974. However, within these two periods there does not appear to be a trend.

In sum, the preceding analysis shows clearly that the Singapore Government during the period under review has succeeded in keeping within manageable range the need to borrow funds from the domestic capital market. It has done so by the avoidance of large expenditures on social welfare and income-redistribution schemes, and by being able to draw on the very large forced savings from the CPF. As a result, monetary policy in Singapore has been left free to pursue the main goal of price stability.

Small Deficit Spending

The third ingredient of Singapore's economic policies which permitted the pursuit of price stability is found in its relatively low level of deficit spending. Large deficit spending carries with it the danger of a loss of confidence in the government's ability to service its debt. Inability to service debt usually is expected to lead to inflation or steep increases in taxation. Because typically the public expects the government to have to take such steps sooner or later, large deficits induce domestic wealth-holders to shift assets abroad and foreigners to become reluctant to invest in the country. Monetary policy maintaining high interest rates can be, and has frequently been, used to reduce capital flight of this sort because higher domestic interest rates can compensate wealth-holders to some degree for the risks of future inflation and higher taxes. If the monetary-policy instrument is used for this purpose, it is not available for the pursuit of price stability.

Before turning to Singapore's record in this matter it may be useful to discuss briefly the difference between deficit spending and net borrowing requirements. Normally the two are highly correlated, but they need not be. This can best be seen from the following analogy. Government, like individuals, can for some time spend in excess of income by going into debt. During this period expenditures equal receipts. We have seen in the preceding section that this condition has indeed held in Singapore during the period under study. However, such spending cannot go on without limits because sooner or later creditors ask questions about the debtor's ability to repay. In the Singapore context the big creditor who might ask this question is, of course, the CPF, which holds such a large proportion of the government's debt, as we have seen above.

Credit-worthiness of individuals as well as governments is determined by two basic characteristics. What are the future income prospects and what assets does the wealth-holder have? On both accounts, Singapore's standing is excellent. Budget statistics assembled by Lee (Tsao) (1987) and Seah (1983) show that annually more than 40 per cent of government expenditures have gone for development projects such as the airport, harbours, freeways, public housing and industrial-estate developments, water, sewer, electricity, and telephone systems, as well as modern schools and universities. It is not possible to provide hard data, but there is little doubt that the reproduction or market value of the public-sector's assets in 1984 exceeds by far the $28-billion debt.

However, since there is no market for the majority of the government's investments in infrastructure, the relevant question concerns the ability to derive from them sufficient cash flow to meet the debt-service costs.[11] Since these investments have contributed significantly to the increase in the productivity and income of Singapore citizens, they have thus raised the taxation capacity of the people. But have they done so sufficiently?

Before we attempt to answer this question, let us consider the second determinant of wealth-holders' credit-worthiness, namely the amount of their liquid assets. The Government of Singapore has working balances and accounts receivable. We disregard them here and consider only foreign-exchange reserves in the form of gold and foreign currencies. In principle, these can readily be turned into cash and used to retire domestic and foreign debt. The remaining net debt is the one which has to be serviced by taxation.

In Fig. 17.6 the levels of the debt and international reserves are shown, both in terms of percentages of GNP. In 1966 the debt exceeded reserves, but the gap narrowed continuously until for a short period around 1974 the Government of Singapore owned liquid assets in excess of its entire debt. Since then, the gap has opened up again, but not dramatically so. In other words, these data imply that the Government of Singapore until 1974 had financed all of its current and development expenditures by current revenues and at the same time had run a surplus to add to its foreign asset holdings.[12]

Fig. 17.8 shows the additions to Singapore's net debt alongside the net borrowing requirements, both expressed as a percentage of GNP. The former time series reveals in greater detail the developments discussed in the preceding paragraph. As can be seen, before 1974 the additions to the net debt were negative; thereafter they were positive. For the full period they averaged 0.54 per cent of GNP annually.

These data allow us to return to the question as to whether public investment has been large enough to create sufficient taxation capacity for the service of the debt in the future. While the concept of taxation capacity is operationally imprecise, it may be said with confidence that increases in debt-service needs have been so small and investment and income growth have been so large that there has not been, and there will not be for the foreseeable future, any need to be concerned about the government's ability to service its debt.

In sum, the preceding analysis has shown that Singapore has managed its economic affairs in such a way that both net borrowing requirements and the growth of the net debt have been well within manageable ranges. As a result, the government has been able to use monetary policy freely to pursue the goal of price stability. In this, Singapore's experience stands in stark contrast with that of many other countries of the world during the period under study and should be noted as an important aspect of the state's early history.

INCOMES POLICY

A group of economists who call themselves Post-Keynesians, and who count John Kenneth Galbraith as one of their members, argue that monetarist theory is highly misleading as an explanation of national price behaviour. In their view, monetary authorities are not really free to vary the amount of money they create. Instead, they are driven to the creation of money by the economically and politically overwhelming need to avoid unemployment, which would otherwise result from increases in the costs of production due to union wage demands and foreign price increases. In other words, the ultimate causes of inflation are increases in the costs of production, which are independent of monetary policy. Therefore, governments that control these cost increases can have price stability without unemployment. The main instrument for the control of costs is an incomes policy.

There are different approaches to incomes policies, ranging from outright wage controls, which require the government to set rates for many categories of workers, to a system called Tax-based Incomes Policies (TIPs), favoured by Post-Keynesians, which uses tax incentives to direct private behaviour into socially desirable channels. Sweden has for many years operated a system for determining wage increases which appeals to many economists. It involves a consultative process among representatives of private-sector employers, employees, and the government. This tripartite group is charged with the task of examining the expected growth in the nation's real output during the next contract period and of reaching agreement on how this output is to be shared among the three interest groups. Agreements reached by this group are legally binding.

The National Wages Council

Since 1972 Singapore has had an institution called the National Wages Council (NWC).[13] The NWC is constituted much like the Swedish wage-setting agency. It consists of representatives of employers, employees, and the government, and it considers likely future growth in output and other economic developments. However, wage increases can only be recommended by the NWC: they do not have the force of law as they do in Sweden. But in practice the NWC recommendations have been followed by all major bargaining units in Singapore, and in effect have provided a floor to annual wage increases.

No discussion of the history of price developments in Singapore can be complete without an analysis of the influence of the NWC. Unfortunately, however, any such analysis is bound to be inconclusive, much as is the continuing debate between Post-Keynesians and Monetarists. The problem is that the existence or absence of incomes policies influences a wide range of behaviour and institutions. There appears to be no method for establishing what unions would have done in the absence of the NWC. Would there have been strikes and wage settlements different from those that actually took place? How would the government have reacted to such strikes? If wages had been higher, would they have produced unemployment or would the monetary authorities have increased the money supply and created inflation? Would the inflation have resulted in ever increasing demands for nominal wage increases to assure real wage growth, leading in the end to ever increasing inflation rates – as happened in the United Kingdom until Mrs Thatcher took office?

Obviously I cannot provide answers to these counterfactual questions that are in any sense based on objective economic analysis. Instead, I offer the following observations which have determined the conclusions that can be found at the end of this section.

Some Observations and Speculations

During the 1950s and 1960s unions in Singapore were militant and called frequent strikes. In 1961 there were 116 strikes resulting in the loss of 411,000 man-days. Since then, strike frequency has declined continuously. In the four years 1968–71 there were only eleven strikes. However, in 1972 there was an upsurge to ten strikes in one year. Since 1978 there has been none at all (Department of Statistics, *Yearbook of Statistics*, various years).

The causes of this reduction in strike activities have several interpretations. One of the most widely accepted is that before independence strikes were part of a communist strategy to gain political power and an electoral majority in Parliament. The reasoning was that strong labour unrest and economic turmoil would induce votes for the Communist Party since it was most likely to be able to control its members in the unions. When the communists were purged or co-opted into the People's Action Party, the usefulness of strikes as an instrument of power politics was ended. It also meant that a new, less militant union leadership came to power.

Undoubtedly union militancy was also reduced by the success of the economic policies which came into effect in 1965 and which produced the very rapid growth with price stability discussed above. The wage increases which accompanied this economic growth were unprecedented in Singapore's history and by the standards of other developing countries. Under those conditions union leaders almost certainly had great difficulties in persuading their members that strikes and political changes would produce even better results. This explanation of the decline in strike activity is supported by the fact that, when in 1972–74 rapid inflation threatened real wage levels and gains, strike activity rose again to twenty-five occurrences during those three years.

It will be recalled from above that Singapore enjoyed price stability between 1966 and 1972 and that the subsequent inflation is adequately explained by monetarist theory and the weakness of the international monetary system, which resulted in excess money creation. Also, we must remember that during this period employment grew rapidly and the unemployment rate fell continuously and strongly. This suggests that in these years unions did not push for or obtain the excessive wage increases which would have produced cost increases and the results emphasized by Post-Keynesian analysis. Obviously, an incomes policy was not needed, and there was none.

Given these facts, the establishment of the NWC is justified only if at the beginning of the 1970s there was a pronounced increase in the willingness and ability of the unions to obtain excessive wage increases. We noted above that the rapid growth of income and productivity continued after 1974 so that one would not have expected a change in union attitudes stemming from this influence. The upsurge of strike activity in 1972–74 seems to be explained adequately by the inflation, and it does not seem reasonable to interpret it as a basic return to militancy. These considerations lead me to the conclusion that the NWC was not needed in Singapore to assure the absence of labour-market stability and cost push. Correct monetary and development policies were the ultimate causes of Singapore's record of price stability.

Did the National Wages Council Cause Harm?

In this concluding section I propose and defend the following thesis: the NWC not only was not needed but probably has done some damage to Singapore's strategy of economic growth with price stability.

The most basic argument which leads me to this thesis is very general. It is that the determination of equilibrium wage rates is very difficult because of many and highly uncertain influences on it. Under such conditions, the innumerable and decentralized decisions of individual market participants, and even of some unions and large employers, are more likely to arrive at the correct wage rates on average and through time than is any group of individuals, however capable, informed and well-meaning they may be.

In a decentralized system, mistakes in the assessment of future developments made by wage bargainers in reaching settlements are relatively quickly corrected by market signals and pressures. Thus, firms that pay too much lose competitiveness, market share, and employment. Workers in such firms who want to save their jobs have to take cuts in wages. Firms that pay too little gain market share, need more workers, and have to pay higher wages to get them. Through this adjustment process, average wage rates are also flexible since they are the mean of the rates determined at the decentralized level. In contrast, centrally determined wages do not have this flexibility. Once set, they are very difficult to change, partly because of the unwieldy wage-setting process and partly because the issue is politicized. Politicians can ill afford to rescind wage increases once they have been granted.

Some Empirical Evidence

The preceding general analysis finds support in Singapore's statistics. Fig. 17.9

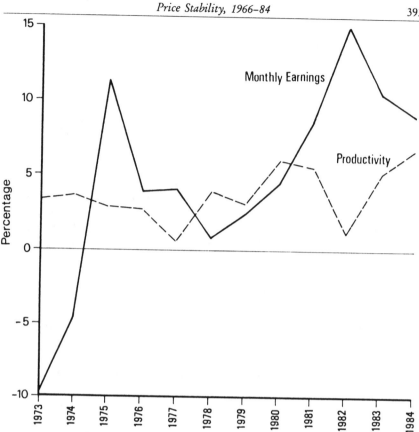

Fig. 17.9. Real monthly earnings and productivity (annual growth rates, CPI deflated), 1973–84. *Source:* Ministry of Trade and Industry, *Interim Report of the Economic Committee* (Singapore).

shows real wage and productivity gains between 1973 and 1984, the starting date of the series having been determined by data availability. At the beginning of the period wage increases were smaller and then much greater than productivity gains. This was the period of rapid inflation and subsequent price stability which were discussed above. Under such disturbances, wage setting typically is erratic and produces the kind of under- and overshooting we observe. It seems that after its creation in 1972 the NWC did not succeed in smoothing this adjustment, although we cannot know what the pattern would have been otherwise.

After 1977 and until about 1981, under the influence of the NWC guidelines real wages were kept below real productivity growth. Such conditions typically create an excess demand for labour, and they did so in Singapore. There was widespread job-hopping and employers complained of difficulties in finding workers. National policy was to permit the excess demand to be met by foreign workers. This relieved the labour shortage and the low real wages probably were close to equilibrium.

During the 1977–81 period public dissatisfaction with real-income growth became widespread since a most spectacular economic boom was obviously going on and workers were not sharing in it. The NWC and others blamed the lagging real wages on a market failure, claiming that the country had been caught in a "low-wage trap". To eliminate it, they recommended a sharp increase in real wages. During the four-year period 1981–84 deliberate wage increases were granted far in excess of productivity gains, as can be seen from Fig. 17.9. During this period the government also raised CPF contribution rates and real labour costs rose a staggering 48.7 per cent. All this was justified by the idea that the low-wage trap required a non-market incentive which would encourage entrepreneurs to introduce more labour-saving and productivity-raising capital and technology.

A Critique of Events and a Rationale for Policies

The preceding considerations lead me to the following critical evaluation of NWC wages policies. After 1977 wages were kept too low by the NWC recommendations. In the absence of the NWC wage guidelines, domestic workers' wages would have risen more quickly, the substitution of capital for labour would have gone on continuously, labour productivity would have grown correspondingly, and the pressure to allow foreign workers into the country would have been smaller. There would have been no low-wage gap and no subsequent experimentation with extremely high real-wage increases. From the perspective of this interpretation of the actions of the NWC, it is ironic that its policies initially produced labour-market disequilibria which were then blamed on market failures, and then led to further actions which created a potentially even more serious problem of excessive real-wage levels.

When real wages are too high, there are incentives for too much substitution of capital for labour and the use of too much labour-saving technology. The economy then suffers from what is widely known as technological unemployment. The people replaced by machines are unemployed but, given typical wage-setting behaviour, are unwilling to work at wages below those earned by the employed. At such wages, there simply are not enough other inputs and capital available to generate full employment.

The danger is that in Singapore such unemployment will develop and will again be blamed on market failures. By the mid-1980s, there were signs that the role of the NWC might be diminished and primacy of the market in wage determination might be restored. One can only hope that there will not develop a new impatience with market processes since probably the high-wage policies have already led to the introduction of inappropriate amounts of capital and types of technology. The adjustment process to appropriate wage levels, capital, and technology may well take several years.

The preceding analysis has undoubtedly been facilitated by the benefit of hindsight and it should not be interpreted as asserting that a free labour market would have functioned completely smoothly. However, the history of the NWC does illustrate the dangers of letting collective decisions take the place of the market in complex processes such as wage setting. A country which engages in monetary and exchange-rate policies consistent with price stability and which does not give excessive powers to special interest groups in the economy, such as unions and large employers, has no need for an incomes policy.[14]

SUMMARY AND CONCLUSIONS

In this study an attempt has been made to shed light on Singapore's outstanding record of price stability and economic growth in the period 1966–84. The monetarist model of a small, open economy has served as a useful device for the organization of the large body of empirical material available. The study has shown that stable prices prevailed whenever increases in the supply of money were within a relatively narrow range around increases in the demand for money. The inflationary episode of 1973–74 was preceded by a massive increase in Singapore's money supply. This was seen to have been caused by fixed exchange rates and a buildup of the inevitable pressures encountered by any small economy attempting to maintain a lower inflation rate than that prevailing in the rest of the world. The adoption of a managed exchange rate since 1973 has permitted monetary policy to pursue the goal of price stability.

Singapore's stable prices are also attributable to the fact that budgetary policies and the government's borrowing requirements have been such that monetary policy has been left free entirely for the management of a stable price level. The final section of the study dealt with incomes policy. The conclusion was reached that this policy was not necessary in Singapore since monetary policy was perfectly capable of assuring price stability. The incomes policy, it was argued, has resulted in periods of disequilibrium wage changes, the adverse consequences of which may be haunting the Singapore economy for an indefinite time in the future.

This study, of course, has many limitations. The monetarist model cannot explain all fluctuations in prices, and the study has failed to discuss the myriad other influences on annual price changes. However, perhaps the most serious shortcoming of this study is that it does not explain why the Government of Singapore has used the monetary and fiscal policies necessary for price stability just when most governments in the rest of the world have been running large budget deficits and creating large inflationary amounts of money.

I wish I could remedy the last deficiency of this study. Unfortunately, however, answers to the question raised are not likely to be found in the realm of economic analysis. It is almost a truism to say that Singapore's leaders did not fall for the facile policy recommendations of Keynesianism, which promises more rapid real growth and lower unemployment by the simplistic devices of printing more money and large deficit spending. The basic and interesting question is why they were not seduced by the siren song of this ideology? I have been told that traditional Chinese Confucian values and attitudes are an important part of the answer, but such an answer is only partial. Why did these values and attitudes survive in Singapore when in Europe and North America their previous dominance was swept away?

Answers to this question might result in important insights about the future of Singapore, especially the critical issue of whether the next generation of Singapore citizens and leaders will still be holding these values and attitudes, even though they have known nothing but stability and prosperity. Or will they, like every new generation, want to do even better than their elders and abandon their reliance on the market?

NOTES

1. There are a number of studies of demand and supply functions for money in Singapore, most notably by Lee (1985) and Simkin (1984). However, their focus is not on a history of inflation. Closest to the present study in coverage and selection of issues comes the fine paper by Lee [Tsao] (1987).
2. These theories are found in the *Journal of Post Keynesian Economics*, which is published by M.E. Sharp, Inc., Armork, New York. However, there are also many critics in the United States and Great Britain, too numerous to mention here, who have focused their attention on developments in recent years when monetarist equations have had less explanatory power in some countries than they did in the past. Defenders of the monetarist approach suggest that these problems are due to widespread financial deregulation and innovation driven by unprecedented progress in electronics technology. They are alleged not to destroy the validity of the monetarist analytical approach for the longer run.
3. In recent years the value of Singapore's exports plus imports has been about three times that of its gross national product. By this standard the Singapore economy ranks as the most open in the world. Only Hong Kong comes close to this index of openness. Among the industrial countries, Canada ranks at the top with exports plus imports representing about 60 per cent of national income.
4. The Smithsonian Agreement, signed in December 1971, is often considered to represent the date at which exchange rates became flexible. In fact, however, the Agreement had brought primarily a realignment of major exchange rates and attempts were made to maintain them for nearly a year. It was only in early 1973 that most countries officially abandoned their commitments to specific rates and floating began in earnest. The trade-weighted exchange rate for the Singapore dollar, which is defined to be 100 in December 1971, in fact was still at 100 at the end of 1972.
5. See the next section for a documentation of this effect. Fig. 17.5 and the discussion show that the ratio of the world to the Singapore price level rose 20 per cent between 1966 and 1971 while the exchange rate was unchanged.

6. Lee and Jao (1982) argue that the holding of government securities by the private sector in Singapore is so small that the MAS cannot engage effectively in open-market operations to make monetary policy. If this is true, it had further complicated the problem of sterilizing the massive foreign-exchange purchases which were required under the fixed exchange-rate regime. For additional comments on the role of the MAS see Chapter 16.

7. There is no trade-weighted index for the period before 1971 but, because of the great overall stability of exchange rates in the world during those years, it may be reasonable to assume that it was in fact very close to 100 during the period.

8. Unemployment insurance programmes can become heavy fiscal burdens. In Canada in 1982 spending on unemployment insurance benefits was equal to 3.5 per cent of GNP, and it has not declined significantly with the return of economic prosperity. For an analysis of the interaction between unemployment benefits and the rate of unemployment see Grubel and Bonnici (1986).

9. In 1980 the U.S. federal debt was equal to 27 per cent of GNP. In 1985, after the much discussed deficit crisis of five years, the ratio had risen to 45 per cent.

10. This section draws heavily on the *Report of the Central Provident Fund Study Group* prepared by the Department of Economics and Statistics, National University of Singapore in 1985.

11. Lee [Tsao] (1987) noted that the Singapore Government has followed persistently the practice of having infrastructure investments pay for themselves whenever feasible technically and economically. For example, the Singapore airport departure tax of S$12 per person in recent years raised significant revenue from the approximately three million annual visitors.

12. This policy leads to an inefficient intertemporal allocation of resources between generations. Economic theory suggests that additions to the private and public capital stock should be financed through borrowing so that the resultant market-clearing interest rates provide correct signals about the scarcity of current and future resources, influencing private savings and investment behaviour correspondingly. In other words, the Singapore policy of financing public investment leaves future generations with too much capital, by the standards of neo-classical economics.

13. In this section I rely heavily on Lim (1981, 1984).

14. This does not mean that labour markets cannot be made more flexible and efficient by appropriate government policies. For a proposal to do so through the encouragement of bonus pay systems see Grubel and Ng (1986).

BIBLIOGRAPHY

Department of Economics and Statistics, National University of Singapore. *Report of the Central Provident Fund Study Group.* Singapore, 1985.

Department of Statistics. *Economic and Social Statistics: Singapore 1960–1982.* Singapore, 1983.

———. *Yearbook of Statistics 1984/85.* Singapore, 1985.

Friedman, Milton. *The Optimum Quantity of Money.* London: Macmillan, 1969.

Friedman, Milton and Anna J. Schwartz. *A Monetary History of the United States, 1867–1960*. Princeton, N.J.: Princeton University Press, 1963.

Grubel, Herbert and Josef Bonnici. *Why Is Canada's Unemployment Rate So High?* Vancouver: The Fraser Institute, 1986.

Grubel, Herbert and Ng Chee Yuen. "Bonus Pay Systems and Wage Flexibility in Singapore". *ASEAN Economic Bulletin* 2, no. 3 (1986): 186–94.

International Monetary Fund. *International Financial Statistics, 1985 Yearbook*. Washington, D.C., 1985.

Kapur, Basant Kumar. "Exchange-Rate Flexibility and Monetary Policy". In *Papers on Monetary Economics*. Monetary Authority of Singapore, 1981.

Lee Sheng-Yi. "Some Aspects of Foreign Exchange Management in Singapore". *Asia Pacific Journal of Management* 1 (1984): 207–17.

_____. *Demand for and Supply of Money in Singapore, 1968–82*. Taipei: Chung-Hua Institution for Economic Research, 1985.

Lee Sheng-Yi and Y.C. Jao. *Financial Structures and Monetary Policies in Southeast Asia*. London: Macmillan, 1982.

Lee (Tsao) Yuan. "Comment on the paper 'Social Security Systems in Singapore'". Paper presented at the Fourth Annual Conference of the Federation of ASEAN Economic Associations, 5–7 November 1985, Singapore.

_____. "Economic Stabilization Policies in Singapore". In *Economic Stabilization Policies in ASEAN Countries*, edited by Praduma B. Rana and Florian A. Alburo, pp. 123–53. Singapore: Institute of Southeast Asian Studies, 1987.

Lim Chong-Yah. *Commentary on Economics and Current Affairs*. Singapore: Federal Publications, 1981.

_____. *Economic Restructuring in Singapore*. Singapore: Federal Publications, 1984.

Monetary Authority of Singapore. *Papers on Monetary Economics*. Singapore: Singapore University Press, 1981.

_____. *Annual Report*. Singapore, 1984/85.

Mundell, Robert. *International Economics*. New York: Macmillan, 1968.

Seah, Linda. "Sources of Finance for Economic Growth in Singapore 1965–75, with Special Reference to the Public Sector". Ph.D. dissertation, Department of Economics and Statistics, National University of Singapore, 1983.

Simkin, Colin. "Does Money Matter in Singapore?" *Singapore Economic Review* 29 (1984): 1–15.

Vasil, K. Raj. *Governing Singapore*. Singapore: Eastern Universities Press, 1984.

KYKLOS, Vol. 40 – 1987 – Fasc. 2, 163–175

Capitalism Needs Risk-, not Profit-Sharing

HERBERT G. GRUBEL*

In the last few years the idea of profit sharing has experienced somewhat of a renaissance, at least among intellectuals in North America, as a result of publications by MITCHELL [1982a, 1982b], NIGHTINGALE [1983] and especially WEITZMAN [1984, 1985]. This new literature applies some modern theoretical concepts and new empirical insights to a body of knowledge that has a long tradition and has been reviewed in the classic by LESIEUR [1958].

The application of these new ideas has concentrated on the analysis of the effects of profit-sharing schemes on macroeconomic stability and unemployment, especially in a world of inflation. The new literature has failed to provide new insights into the incentive effects and operational alternatives of profit sharing schemes. In particular, it has not confronted adequately the question why profit-sharing schemes have not been adopted widely in the past, in spite of their appeal to a number of intellectuals and to the current flock of analysts.

This question is addressed here by setting out the operational features of a general system of risk-sharing. The resultant analytical framework is used to draw a fundamental distinction between systems that share profits and those that share risks. It is then shown that profit-sharing systems result in a direct and fundamental alteration of the incentive structure which drives SCHUMPETERian entrepreneurs and which is seen by many as the main source of economic progress in free market economies.

* Professor of Economics at Simon Fraser University, Vancouver, B.C. – I acknowledge gratefully comments made on an earlier draft of this note by JOHN CHANT, STEVE EASTON and DENNIS MAKI.

163

HERBERT G. GRUBEL

Systems for the sharing of risk, on the other hand, are shown to produce increased real wage flexibility. They may therefore be presumed to increase the ability of the economy to deal with random shocks and thus reduce the magnitude and frequency of fluctuations in unemployment. The model used for this purpose also implies that risk-sharing systems can be applied to other commercial contracts, such as oil-drilling licenses and construction agreements. Used in these contexts, risk-sharing increases opportunities for different expected return distributions available in the market and thus can increase welfare.

I. A GENERAL RISK SHARING SYSTEM

A generalized risk sharing system requires that periodic contracts between employers and employees of a given firm specify the following relationship. *First,* there is the expected monthly wage Y_e payable over the life of the employment contract. This wage is assumed to be determined by the same factors with and without the introduction of the bonus pay system[1].

Second, there is the core pay ratio c. It determines the fraction of any periodic pay period wage, here assumed to be the monthly, which is payable as a fixed and predetermined sum at the end of the month much like normal wage compensation. It is between zero and one.

Third, there is the bonus pay period, which may be of any length greater than one of the periodic pay periods. For illustrative purposes it is assumed here to be one year and thus cover twelve monthly payments. Under the preceding assumptions, the core pay C for the bonus pay period is

$$C = (c*Y_e)*12 \qquad (1)$$

1. Total national income and therefore wages are likely to be raised by risk-sharing systems if they result in a lower average unemployment rate through time. This has been the main argument for the use of risk sharing schemes advanced in the recently published literature noted in the introduction. In addition, there may be gains due to greater efficiency as workers share in its gains through profit sharing. This has been the main argument for profit sharing in the earlier literature cited above. To keep the analysis simple, we abstract from these gains here.

RISK- VERSUS PROFIT-SHARING

Fourth, there is the expected bonus B_e which is payable at the end of the bonus pay period:

$$B_e = Y_e*12 - C \qquad (2)$$

The operational features of such a system can be seen readily with the help of a simple example. Assume that a worker's normal monthly pay Y_e is $1,000 under a contract covering 2 years. It is agreed that the core pay ratio c is 0.8. Under these conditions the worker can expect 12 monthly payments of $800 and a core pay C of $9,600. The expected bonus at the end of the first year is $2,400.

Fifth, there is the actual bonus B_a payable at the end of the period:

$$B_a = B_e + SR_i*[X_i(A - E)_i]*B_e \qquad (3)$$

where SR_i is the share ratio, X_i are weights, A are actual and E are expected values of parameters deemed to be i determinants of the firm's net profits and therefore 'ability to pay'. Positive influences enter with a plus and negative influences with a minus sign in the equation. A typical set of these determinants would be indices of the firms's output prices and labour productivity (both entering with a plus sign) and input prices (entering with a minus sign). Weights attached to these determinants are a function of the relative importance of prices and productivity in the firm's performance.

If the share ratio is zero, actual and expected bonuses are always equal and all of the risks of unexpected changes in the determinants of the firm's performance fall on the firm's owners, just as they do when there is no risk sharing. If it is one, all of the differences in the expected and actual value of the determinants affect only workers' bonuses. In practice, the share ratio may be expected to be between zero and one for each of the determinants of the firm's performance, depending on the preferences of the parties to the contract.

The essence of risk-sharing systems is immediately apparent from the preceding. Actual is equal to expected bonus pay whenever in equation (3) the values of A and E are equal, that is, the determinants of the firm's performance turn out to have been at their expected levels. If actual and expected values of these determinants differ, the workers' bonus pay, and therefore full compensation, share the excesses or shortfall with the firm's owners in a proportion determined by the share ratio.

HERBERT G. GRUBEL

It should also be noted that the size of the core pay ratio c has important implications for the operation of the bonus pay system. The smaller is c, the smaller are workers' monthly payments and the larger is the expected bonus at the end of the bonus pay period. A low c tends to bring hardships to workers who have to get along with small monthly pay and end up borrowing funds in anticipation of the bonus. A high c, on the other hand, raises the probability that bonuses at the end of the period are negative. Such negative bonuses require that workers make cash payments to the firm which tends to result in hardships. For these reasons, c has to be chosen to balance the effects of excessively high and excessively low levels of the core pay ratio.

II. RISK- AND PROFIT-SHARING COMPARED

In a profit-sharing system the actual bonuses paid workers at the end of a contract period are a function of the residual of the firm's operation during the period. The general bonus pay system described above becomes a profit-sharing system if the components of the last term in equation (3) exhaust all influences on the profitability of the firm, the share ratios are the same for all and the weights reflect exactly the relative contribution of each to the level of profits. Therefore, profit-sharing is a special case of general risk-sharing systems[2].

The great advantage of the profit-sharing system is its simplicity. It does not require the specification of an agreement on the determinants of a firm's ability to pay wages. This tends to facilitate negotiations and operations. This is the point emphasized by WEITZMAN and the older literature on profit-sharing. It may easily dominate all other considerations. However, in my view this simple system also has *three* major disadvantages.

First, the profit-sharing system forces the contracting parties to share all types of risk. This is potentially very important since there are two basic types of risks. Using KNIGHT's [1933] terminology, there is genuine risk that is exogenous to the firm and its management. It can be assessed on the basis of experience. Examples of such risk are the distribution of

2. Readers may find it useful to study the *Appendix* for a numerical example of how actual bonuses are calculated under a profit- and a general risk-sharing system.

RISK- VERSUS PROFIT-SHARING

expected prices for energy inputs and the prices of the firm's output. Such distributions may be developed from forecasting models and the use of historic data.

Drawing further on KNIGHT, the other major type of hazard is determined to a large extent by the actions of the owners, managers and workers of the firm. It is known as uncertainty and, because it is endogenous to the policies initiated by the firm, it cannot be forecast from past observations. Uncertainty typically surrounds the success of investment in new products and processes but may also be associated with decisions to expand or contract operations.

KNIGHT's distinction of the two types of risk is important because workers are likely to have different attitudes towards each. They tend to be more willing to accept a sharing of the risks due to exogenous influences than they are in sharing those due to endogenous events. The general risk-sharing system outlined above makes it possible for workers to exclude or give lower weight to endogenous than to exogenous influences on the size of their bonuses. Profit-sharing does not give workers this option.

In addition, there are numerous determinants of firms' profits, which are potentially subject to manipulation by accounting and similar procedures. Under the profit-sharing system employees need to protect themselves against loss of income due to such manipulation. Such protection tends to be costly and resisted by employers, especially if it means that all accounts must be open to inspection by employees. Under the general risk-sharing system such administrative complications can be avoided since it is possible to make bonuses dependent entirely on data generated outside the firm.

Second, profit-sharing systems do not lead to an explicit specification of the determinants of the firm's performance as do general risk-sharing systems. In the negotiations for profit-sharing contracts presumably the influences of output prices and input costs on profits are discussed, but they need not be articulated fully and written into a contract. Full articulation of and agreement on these matters are likely to increase cooperation and trust between the contracting parties, which under certain conditions can be important ingredients in the success of sharing systems and labour relations more generally.

At the same time, however, contracting parties may also choose to exclude certain determinants of performance from detailed analysis and

HERBERT G. GRUBEL

empirical verification. More generally, the increased flexibility of the risk-sharing system is likely to lead to increased welfare as both employers and employees will choose contract patterns that most suit their own preferences and the characteristics of their firms.

Third, and most important, the profit-sharing system is in much greater conflict with the efficient operation of a dynamic free market than is the general risk-sharing system. In the age of SCHUMPETER [GIERSCH, 1984] the important role of the entrepreneur as the driving force behind economic growth has again become recognized. As BIRCH [1979] has shown, entrepreneurs starting new firms in large numbers have been one of the most dynamic elements of the US economy during the post-war years.

It is well known that the failure rate among these entrepreneurs is very high and that the profits of those who are successful must be large enough to compensate all new entrepreneurs through sufficiently high expected returns for their risk-taking. Profit-sharing reduces the variance of the distribution of expected returns from entrepreneurial activities since it results in a division of both gains and losses between workers and entrepreneurs. However, the sharing of losses is limited by the entrepreneurs' net worth and the need to pay a minimum income to workers while gains and positive bonuses are potentially without limit. Therefore, profit-sharing also is likely to reduce the expected, risk-adjusted average return to entrepreneurial activities. To the extent that the supply of entrepreneurial activites is sensitive to the risk-adjusted rate of return, profit-sharing results in a decrease in the supply of entrepreneurial risk-taking.

The importance of this decrease in risk-taking is an empirical question. However, there is a strong presumption that the effect exists and that it is important. The chance to become rich has always been one of the main driving forces behind the foundation of new firms. But even in large, existing firms managers and owners are driven into innovation and risk-taking by the chance to get rich and famous. Entrepreneurial capitalism with profit-sharing generally is a lot like a lottery which stipulates that the really large wins have to be shared with the neighbors. Fewer such lottery tickets are likely to be sold under these conditions than if winners can keep all of the big prizes.

In a dynamic world of entrepreneurs profit-sharing also has undesirable consequences for labour markets and allocative efficiency. Thus, workers who were employed by the entrepreneurs who fail simply re-enter the labour market and tend to find work promptly. On the other hand, workers lucky enough to have a profit-sharing contract with successful entrepreneurs enjoy incomes above the equilibrium supply price. This condition affects allocative efficiency since the excessive labour costs reduce profits and therefore opportunities for the expansion of the firms' operations. Fewer additional workers are hired in a world with than without profit-sharing. More generally, one can expect to see the development of conflicts between management which aims to maximize profits and expand output and workers that wish to maximize economic rent on their incomes. Only the former objectives are consistent with the inter-temporal efficiency of a Schumpeterian market economy.

Furthermore, if such firms are unionized, wage rates in excess of equilibrium may have to be paid to all new employees. As a result such firms tend to hire workers with correspondingly high human capital. As a result, the non-distorting rent of the original employees would eventually be turned into a wasteful overemployment of human capital.

Presumably, these misallocative effects of profit-sharing can be minimized by the periodic renegotiation of contracts, which WEITZMAN envisages in his model. However, it is clear that such renegotiations can be interpreted as being attempts to take away the fruits of extra risk-taking which the workers consider themselves as having earned. One would therefore expect that workers would resist strenuously the renegotiations of profit sharing contracts by successful firms.

All of these disadvantages of the profit-sharing system are present to a much smaller extent in the general bonus pay system outlined above. The influence of discretionary entrepreneurial risk-taking on profits can be isolated explicitly and given any desired weight in the determination of bonuses and expected wages. Entrepreneurs can retain for themselves the expected benefits and costs of their specific risk-taking function in the firm. At the same time employees are able to retain their traditional distance from the role as the bearers of entrepreneurial risks. Yet, the sharing of the exogenous risks associated with output price and input cost uncertainties leads to more stable employment and profits and the host of micro- and macroeconomic advantages discussed in the papers cited above.

HERBERT G. GRUBEL

III. SHARING OF RISKS IN NON-LABOUR CONTRACTS

The model or risk-sharing outlined above can be used not only in wage contracts but also in a wide range of other contracts where prices are set on the basis of expected, exogenous developments. Consider, for example, bids made for oil drilling rights on public land. The value of the bid is determined by expected developments of oil prices and costs of production, as well as the assessment of geological evidence. The latter involves the main entrepreneurial function, which is subject to large elements or moral hazard and therefore non-insurable.

However, the level of output prices and input costs is almost totally beyond the control of the bidder for drilling rights. There would therefore seem to exist the opportunity for the two parties in the contract to share the risk of the uncertain price and cost developments. In such a contract the owner of land could invite bids for oil drilling rights, specifying a matrix of output and input prices and bids would be entered for each combination[3].

Under such a system, the private risk of oil exploration and development is reduced and, given the market price of risk, the firm should be willing to pay a higher price for the right to explore and develop the oil field. In return for accepting some of this risk, the owner of the land obtains a higher income.

However, the total social risk of the oil venture is not changed by the different arrangements for sharing it among the private parties. An increase in welfare arises only if the two parties have different attitudes towards risk and therefore one or both parties to the contract can move to a more preferred portfolio composition.

Presumably, the innovative contracting system discussed here gives rise to the possibility for such welfare gains since it raises the set of opportunities available to the parties. In the case where one of the contracting parties is the government, there is a presumption that it has

3. For example, an oil company might bid a certain sum for a specific drilling right under the assumption that the price of oil is $20 a barrel. This sum is payable upon winning the bid. However, the company simultaneously commits itself to paying extra sums at the end of every quarter if the price of oil is higher and will get back money if the price os lower. The proportion of oil-price changes which is thus shared between the two parties in the contract is equivalent to the share ratio in the wage contracts analyzed above. It determines the level of the bid and initial cash payment offered.

RISK- VERSUS PROFIT-SHARING

greater risk diversification opportunities than private firms [ARROW and LIND, 1970]. In addition, the government may be able to reduce the externalities costs associated with the rigidity of prices. Increased transactions costs are unlikely to be large enough to outweigh the welfare gains from the different risk-sharing opportunities[4].

Risk-sharing contracts of the sort discussed here are used quite widely in the private sector and are in these instances of obvious benefit to all contracting parties. It is therefore ironic that the government has shown such a reluctance to use these contracts in situations where they would result in potentially large positive externalities.

IV. SUMMARY

In sum, the analysis of general risk-sharing systems showed that profit-sharing represents a special case of the more general systems. General risk-sharing systems are more efficient than profit-sharing systems in that they permit contracting parties to exclude or treat differently certain types of risk, especially those which are endogenous to the firm and its management and therefore subject to moral hazard. Most important, general risk-sharing systems make it possible to exclude the returns from entrepreneurial risk-taking from share arrangements with workers. This feature makes general risk-taking consistent with the efficient operation

---

4. These principles may be worth considering here in the context of the problems which the conventional bidding for timber rights from the US government has created for the forest industry in the Pacific Northwest in the 1980s. In the late 1970s forest companies had bid for timber cutting rights in expectation of continued inflation and growing demand for forest products. These expectations were dashed with the recession of 1981–1982 and the subsequent restoration of price stability. However, since the forest companies had paid for the timber cutting rights, they were faced with debt payments far in excess of levels consistent with normal returns to capital. The consequences of this situation have been bankruptcies and unemployment in the industry with multiplier effects on the entire region.

Under the conditional contract system government revenues from the sale of timber cutting rights would have been lower, but the costs of social assistance programs would have been lower and tax revenues would have been higher in subsequent periods. The result would have been greater stability of government net revenue and possibly even a higher average net return from the timber holdings: The firms and workers of the region would have had more stable profits, employment and incomes.

HERBERT G. GRUBEL

of dynamic SCHUMPETERian market economies. Risk-sharing systems can also be used to increase the efficiency of contracts between parties other than employers and employees and they are most likely to raise welfare when one of the contracting parties is the government.

This study complements the main traditional explanation for the scarcity of profit-sharing systems in the real world, which is that workers do not like them. In modern terminology, workers already employed are 'insiders' [LINDBECK and SNOWER, 1986]. Profit-sharing requires them to accept greater income instability in order to reduce the average level of employment for the benefit of 'outsiders'. It is this fact which has led GRUBEL and SPINDLER [1984] to suggest the need for tax measures designed to raise private incentives for the acceptance of profit-sharing plans. Such incentives can be created by the application of revenue-neutral lower tax rates on bonus relative to core income. Such tax incentives probably also are needed to make general risk-sharing systems acceptable to workers.

APPENDIX: ILLUSTRATION OF PROFIT- AND RISK-SHARING

The essential difference between the profit- and risk-sharing system is brought out in the following numerical illustration.

Consider a firm with the following profit (TP) function:

$$TP = Q_O * P_O - Q_L * P_L - Q_I * P_I$$

where Q are quantities, P are prices and the subscripts refer to output, labour and inputs, respectively. Illustrative index values for quantities and prices are inserted into the preceding equation and assumed to differ such that they result in normal and high bonus payments, the latter under two different scenarios:

Normal	$20 = 50*2 - 10*5 = 30*1$	Profit Index 1.00
High 1	$30 = 50*2.2 - 10*5 - 30*1$	1.50
High 2	$30 = 60*2 - 12*5 - 30*1$	1.50

Under *profit-sharing* an illustrative actual bonus formula is:

$$B_a = B_e + SR(API - EPI) * B_e$$

where API and EPI are the actual and expected profit indices. The actual bonus formula gives rise to the following numerical results, assuming SR to be 0.5, B_e to be $2,400 and the above values for the determination of profits:

Normal	$B_a = 2,400 + 0.5(1.00 - 1.00)*2,400 = 2,400$
High 1 and 2	$B_a = 2,400 + 0.5(1.50 - 1.00)*2,400 = 3,000$

RISK- VERSUS PROFIT-SHARING

It is noteworthy that under the assumed profit sharing system the bonus payment does not differentiate between causes of higher profits since it treats them as a residual. Therefore, it provides to workers the same bonus when the higher profits are due to an increase in output prices (high 1 result) and when they are due to the net effect of increased sales with unchanged output prices and increased use of labour for both advertising work and greater production (high 2 result). The latter profits increase may be considered to be the typical outcome of an entrepreneurial decision and therefore different in nature to the exogenous increase in output prices in the first example.

Under *risk-sharing* an illustrative actual bonus formula is:

$$B_e = B_e + SR*Be*[X(OPIA - OPIE) - Y(IPIA - IPIE)]$$

where OPIA and IPIA and actual price indices for output and input, respectively and the OPIE and IPIE are the expected indices; X and Y are weights given to the input and output prices in the determination of the actual bonus. Assuming the share ratio and expected bonus to have the same values as above and X and Y to be 5 and 0, respectively, the numerical profit values from above give the following results:

Normal $B_a = 2,400 + 0.5*2,400[5(1.00 - 1.00) - 0(1.00 - 1.00)] = 2,400$
High 1 $B_a = 2,400 + 0.5*2,400[5(1.10 - 1.00) - 0(1.00 - 1.00)] = 3,000$
High 2 $B_a = 2,400 + 0.5*2,400[5(1.00 - 1.00) - 0(1.00 - 1.00)] = 2,400$

Under this particular risk sharing system workers share in extra profits due to an exogenous increase in the price of outputs. However, all extra profits due to the returns on entrepreneurial activities are not shared with workers. Of course, the risk sharing formula can be designed to make the workers also share in the returns to entrepreneurial activities. Therefore, risk-sharing systems that specify determinants of bonuses can include all of the characteristics of profit-sharing systems. But the latter cannot be made to differentiate between exogenous and endogenous influences on profits.

For readers familiar with WEITZMAN's work it is interesting to note that the general risk formula presented here gets rid of WEITZMAN's result that profit-sharing always keeps the marginal cost of labour below its price because additional labour costs are lowered by the reduced bonus payments required on the inframarginal units. This somewhat puzzling result is at the centre of WEITZMAN's main conclusion that risk-sharing systems would generate excess demand for labour and therefore full employment. General risk-sharing systems can be set up in such a way that they avoid this feature, which is not in the best interest of workers already in the firm.

HERBERT G. GRUBEL

REFERENCES

ARROW, KENNETH and LIND, ROBERT: 'Uncertainty and the Evaluation of Public Investment Decisions', *American Economic Review*, Vol. 60 (1970), pp. 364–378.

BIRCH, DAVID C.: *The Job Generation Process*, Cambridge, Mass.: MIT Program on Neighborhood and Regional Change 1979.

GIERSCH, HERBERT: 'The Age of Schumpeter', *American Economic Review*, Vol. 74 (1984), pp. 103–109.

GRUBEL, HERBERT and NG, CHEE YUEN: 'Bonus Pay Systems and Wage Flexibility in Singapore', *ASEAN Economic Bulletin*, March 1986.

GRUBEL, HERBERT and SPINDLER, ZANE: 'Bonus Pay Systems for Greater Economic Stability, *Canadian Public Policy*, Vol. X (1984), pp. 185–192.

KNIGHT, F. H.: *Risk, Uncertainty and Profits*, London: London School of Economics and Political Science, Series of Reprints of Scarce Tracts No. 16, 1933.

LESIEUR, F. G.; *The Scanlon Plan: A Frontier in Labor-Management Cooperation*, Cambridge, Mass.: Technology Press of MIT 1958.

LINDBECK, ASSAR and SNOWER, DENNIS J.: 'Wage Setting, Unemployment and Insider-Outsider Relations', *American Economic Review*, Vol. 76 (1986), pp. 235–239.

MITCHELL, D.J.B.: 'Gain Sharing: An Anti-Inflation Reform', *Challenge*, July-August, 1982a.

MITCHELL, D.J.B.: 'Gain Sharing Plans: In Quest of a more Stable Economy', *Public Affairs Report*, Bulletin of Government Studies, University of California, Berkeley, October, 1982b.

NIGHTINGALE, D.V.: *Profit Sharing Handbook*, Don Mills, Ont.: Profit Sharing Council of Canada 1983.

WEITZMAN, MARTIN L.: *The Share Economy*, Cambridge, Mass.: Harvard Univ. Press 1984.

WEITZMAN, MARTIN L.: 'The Simple Macroeconomics of Profit Sharing', *American Economic Review*, Vol. 75 (1985), pp. 937–954.

SUMMARY

The analysis of general risk-sharing systems shows that profit-sharing represents a special case of the more general systems. General risk-sharing systems are more efficient than profit-sharing systems in that they permit contracting parties to exclude or treat differently certain types of risk, especially those which are endogenous to the firm and its management and therefore subject to moral hazard. Most important, general risk-sharing systems make it possible to exclude the returns from entrepreneurial risk-taking from share arrangements with workers. This feature makes general risk-taking consistent with the efficient operation of dynamic SCHUMPETERian market economies. Risk-sharing systems can also be used to increase the efficiency of contracts between parties other than employers and employees and they are most likely to raise welfare when one of the contracting parties is the government.

174

[11]

Reflections on a Canadian Bill of Economic Rights*

HERBERT G. GRUBEL/Department of Economics,
Simon Fraser University

This paper proposes that if and when attempts are made to write a modern constitution for Canada, thought be given to the inclusion of clauses designed to constrain the legislative power of parliament in the sphere of economics. Balanced budgets, price stability, expropriation of property by price legislation and the absence of government monopolies are suggested as Canadians' economic rights. The paper analyses the origins of the need for such rights and discusses likely difficulties in making the constitutional clauses operational.

Cet article propose que, dans l'éventualité et au moment où une nouvelle constitution canadienne sera rédigée, les auteurs pensent à inclure des clauses destinées à contraindre le pouvoir législatif du parlement dans le domaine de l'économie. Comme droits économiques pour les Canadiens, nous suggérons des budgets équilibrés, une stabilité des prix, l'expropriation des propriétés par législation et l'absence de tout monopole gouvernemental. L'article analyse aussi d'où vient la nécessité de tels droits et étudie les difficultés probables, lorsqu'on tentera de rendre opérantes les clauses constitutionnelles.

The analysis of the economic implications of changes in the British North America Act and its transformation into a Canadian Constitution has had a long history. This undertaking has been given renewed vigor in recent years as a result of federal-provincial disputes over the distribution of rents from natural resources and of attempts by the federal government to link 'Patriation of the Constitution' with a strengthening of federalism at the expense of provincial power.[1]

While much has been written *about* the economic implications of the policy initiatives accompanying the patriation of the constitution, there has been a total absence of discussion about the merit of 'putting economics *into* the constitution.' Yet as Canada is to attempt to write and adopt a modern, model constitution, there exists a unique opportunity to include in it a Bill of Economic Rights to complement the proposed Bill of Human Rights.

In the following paper I set out some basic reasons why constitutional guarantees of economic rights are desirable, drawing on recent insights into the interrelationship between

* Earlier drafts of this paper benefited from useful comments made by W. Block, A. Breton, R. Lipsey and Z. Spindler, even though Breton's views were not at all sympathetic to my ideas for constitutional changes. E. McWhinney provided some perspectives on economic rights in constitutions of other countries and in history. While working on this paper I was supported by a BC Government grant from the Program of Excellence.

1 See Breton (1974), Safarian (1974), (1980), Walker (1978), Brecher (1980).

CANADIAN PUBLIC POLICY – ANALYSE DE POLITIQUES, VIII:1:57–68
winter/hiver 1982 Printed in Canada/Imprimé au Canada

0317–0861/82/0013–0057 $1.50 © 1982 Canadian Public Policy – Analyse de Politiques

58 / Herbert G. Grubel

politics and economics developed by economists and political scientists.[2] I then present a draft of a bill, explaining briefly the backgound giving rise to the need for each clause.

The following analysis has a neo-conservative orientation. It is my conviction that the people of Canada are better served by a greater reliance on markets rather than on politicians and bureaucrats to solve economic and social problems. This conviction is not based on the uncritical acceptance of free market doctrines, but, as will be shown below, on the interpretation of recent history which shows that many of the policies initiated in an attempt to eliminate undesirable consequences of free markets have themselves resulted in costs that are greater than those they were supposed to eliminate.[3] Most of the costs of these policies cannot be avoided by modification or intensification because the very nature of the political and bureaucratic process in the economy must always produce unexpected costs.[4]

Of course, there are many people who disagree with the premises and conclusions reached in this paper. I hope that as a result they will be encouraged to propose their version of a Bill of Economic Rights. There should emerge from such an exercise a deeper understanding of the facts and issues that will be helpful to a possible Constitutional Assembly in writing a Canadian constitution.[5]

I THE ECONOMIC AND PHILOSOPHICAL BACKGROUND

The main advance of free market solutions to economic and social problems occurred during the 18th and 19th centuries, when memories of the economic and social stagnation of the preceding centuries of mercantilism were strong in the minds of the public. The era of primary reliance on markets produced economic development, social and economic mobility of people, personal freedom and increased longevity at rates and to levels unprecedented in the history of mankind. But free markets have always had their critics who found faults with the system and compared its performance with that of an ideal of their own choice.

In the 19th century romantic socialists, who still have many followers today, believed that sharp income differences, unfettered competition, great uncertainty, and the existence of

2 See Courchene (1980) for a discussion of the trend towards the politicization of economic life in Canada and the costs that it has brought. A number of US journals, such as *The Public Interest*, *Public Choice*, *Regulation*, *The Journal of Law and Economics*, in recent years have published many articles analyzing the interaction between politics and economics. J. Buchanan and G. Tullock (1965) in the United States and T.E. Borcherding (1977) and Z. Spindler (1980) in Canada have produced basic scholarly work in this field. Also relevant is Lipsey (1979) and Brennan and Buchanan (1980).

3 See Cairns (1980) for a review of the literature of the effects of government regulation in the Canadian context. An influential US publication on this subject is Weidenbaum (1979). The Economic Council of Canada (1981) presents a politically balanced and technically sound analysis of the issues.

4 See the magazine *Challenge* for analysis in support of further and better intervention. In Canada the Institute for Policy Analysis in Toronto publishes treatises that support increased government interventionism.

5 The members of such a Constitutional Assembly could be selected by the following process based on democratic principles; it would avoid many of the difficulties associated with having members chosen by existing legislatures or in a conventional election. If, for simplicity's sake we assume there are 20 million eligible voters, then each of 10,000 regional assemblies will consist of 100 delegates elected by a first set of 20 voters. These 100 delegates in turn would elect from their group 5 delegates to be sent to 500 second-round regional assemblies of 100 delegates each. The final steps consist of a national assembly of 2,500 delegates elected by the second-round assemblies, which in turn would select the 125 members of the group charged with the task of drafting a new constitution that ultimately is to be submitted for ratification to Canadian voters. The delegates will tend to be independent individuals with a minimum of obligations towards economic, social and regional interest groups, selected on the basis of their character and abilities judged at each round by a peer group small enough to assess these qualities with reasonable reliability.

scarcity are all due not to the nature of man and the environment but to the ownership of private capital and free markets. Romantic socialist ideals have led to Marxism and, in turn, to the many Communist nations with centrally planned economies. Few people living in Western countries in the last quarter of the 20th century need to be convinced that while these centrally planned economies have eliminated most free market institutions, they have not achieved the aims of romantic socialism and that the failures of that system are greater than those of the free market system it replaced.[6]

Recent decades have seen the evolution of the ideal of the mixed economy, where free markets are abandoned or interfered with wherever and whenever democratically elected governments decide that it is in the public interest to do so. This idea has strong intellectual appeal and is rooted in the modern scientific tradition, which led to increasing control of the *natural* human environment through the accumulation of knowledge about the laws of nature. In this tradition it appears logical that the *economic and social* environment of man could be and should be similarly subjected to a scientific analysis and manipulated into the service of man. Some supporters of the mixed economy idea are simply pragmatists without consistent vision of an ideal society. Other supporters see the mixed economy as an evolutionary step towards the ideal of romantic socialism.

Economists once studied primarily how the market works and interacts with social and political forces. In the tradition of the natural sciences, in recent decades they have turned more and more to the construction of models that simulate the actual and idealized operation of market systems with the goal of subjecting them to what is known as social and economic engineering. The development of mathematical models capable of computer manipulation has been considered an important contribution to the success of this engineering, and explains the high prestige mathematical economists have enjoyed since the 1950s.[7]

Since the Second World War, partly as a result of important advances in modelling the economy after the 'natural laws' discovered by Keynes, partly as a result of the obvious success of science and engineering in increasing output, and partly as a result of the imperfections of the free market system allegedly revealed by the Great Depression, Western countries were ready to start experiments in economic engineering designed to 'perfect' the free market system. There was little effective opposition to these experiments because the dominant intellectuals of the time were caught in the euphoria created by the success of the natural sciences. Economists were far from unhappy with the prospect of the increased power and influence they expected to have as scientific advisors. Politicians and bureaucrats looked forward to being the guardians of the great experiments, which promised them greater power and prestige than they could expect ever to have under a free market system. People with compassion for the poor and other disadvantaged looked forward to the opportunity to do good on a larger scale through welfare programs financed with money raised by taxes rather than from the traditional voluntary contributions.

While the supply of social and economic engineers represented a formidable alliance with great intellectual and moral strength, the movemement obtained the large numbers of votes necessary in democracies from all those who expected to gain from the spread of the mixed economy. The greatest strength of the demand for economic and social engineering was reached uring the 1960s and early 1970s. when politicians in Canada began policies that would produce 'A Just Society.'

6 For a most revealing account of conditions in the Soviet Union see Smith (1977).
7 Most Nobel prize winners in economics, with a few exceptions such as M. Freidman, F. von Hayek, G. Myrdal, and A.W. Lewis, were pioneers in the mathematical development of economic theory. Hayek (1964) has analyzed the problems raised by excessive formalism in economics, which he called scientism.

60 / Herbert G. Grubel

Outcome of Experiments

The economic and social engineering experiments of the 1960s and 1970s have come under increasing scrutiny during the late 1970s and into the 1980s because they did not move societies significantly closer towards the romantic socialist ideal and because they appear to have been accompanied by unexpected social and economic costs. Inflation, high levels of unemployment and slow economic growth have strongly interfered with the economic engineering programs designed to improve on the free market's performance with respect to income equality, overall high standards of living, the provision of jobs, income and health security and the preservation of the environment. In fact, in several areas in which free markets were judged to be deficient by these performance criteria, the economic engineering policies have made conditions worse. In my view, most of the economic and social engineering experiments have failed. The problem now faced by society is what to do about those failures.

One approach is to improve the quality of the engineering. The natural sciences provide the rationale for this approach. Researchers in science labs learn from failure about the strength of materials and properties of molecules and particles. In a similar manner, it is argued, faulty economic experiments can teach us how to do better the next time. This approach is supported by the powerful alliance of economists, politicians, compassionate individuals and expectant beneficiaries who have such a strong self-interest in the initiation of experiments.

The second approach, advocated here, is a permanent, significant reduction in economic engineering of Canada's free market economy. The rationale for this approach is based on the following considerations. Many of the economic and social engineering experiments have failed because they were based on faulty analysis of economic processes. It is not possible to derive economic laws by the study of the operation of free markets and expect them to hold up when the economic environment is changed. For example. it is an undisputed fact that when markets were free, periods of low unemployment coincided with inflation. But this correlation between inflation and unemployment is not in the nature of a scientific law which can be used to engineer a permanent reduction in unemployment by government policies of creating permanent inflation and optimizing on a Phillips curve trade-off. As is well known now, only a few years after the government experiment was put into effect during the 1960s the conditions that gave rise to the observed events of the past were destroyed. The unemployment-inflation relationships were due to the existence of *temporary* and unexpected increases in demand and prices, not permanently higher levels.[8] Similarly, higher farm product prices were noted to have some positive relationship with high farmers' incomes. But as soon as the government legislated permanently higher product prices for farmers during the 1950s and 1960s, it changed the environment. The resultant excess supplies resulted in the need for supply restrictions and a nullification of the efforts to raise farmers' incomes permanently.[9]

The basic and insuperable problem is that in economics it is impossible to carry out laboratory experiments to establish the vaiidity of laws derived by the observation of nature. The economic and social engineering policies of the 1960s and 1970s in fact are equivalent to laboratory experiments. It is true that human history contains episodes in which almost all of the modern experiments have been tried — excessive increases in money supplies,

---

8 A history of the evolution of the idea of the inflation-unemployment trade-off is contained in Friedman's (1977) Nobel Laureate address.

9 For a case-study of price fixing in the milk industry see Grubel and Schwindt (1977). The Economic Council (1981: chap. 6) discusses marketing boards generally.

government deficit spending, the fixing of prices[10] — but so strong was and partly still is the faith in the scientific approach that the failure of these experiments was interpreted as having been the result of faulty administration, obvious human errors or too little scope for intervention — all of which a new and better informed generation of engineers allegedly can avoid. Unfortunately, there is a strong alliance of numerous individuals who benefit from continued and ever greater engineering of the free market economy. Therefore, there is a great probability that these people will periodically obtain a majority in parliaments and be in the position to continue the engineering experiments. In this position of power, they disregard historic and current evidence that they must fail and instead cling to the faith that they can move the system towards the ideal of romantic socialism.

The preceding interpretation of current and likely future events leads me to propose that the alliance of supporters of economic engineering be restrained by constitutional limits from making laws designed to interfere directly with the market economy. Constitutional restraints on the freedom of legislators have received strong support in the past from philosophers who have noted the weaknesses of parliamentary democracy reaching all decisions by simple majority voting.[11] The fear of politicians' short-run considerations of expediency, and of the selfish interests of a majority gaining at the expense of the minority, have resulted in clauses in most modern constitutions guaranteeing free speech and underly the demands for a Canadian Bill of Human Rights. The following proposals for a Canadian Bill of Economic Rights are designed in a similar manner to protect from political expediency and from the tyranny of the majority the very existence of the free market economy and the democratic freedoms that can flourish only in conjunction with it. They are not designed to entrench established rights of a ruling class because a democratic, free market economy is characterized by greater economic, social and political mobility than any socio-economic system ever tried by any country as large as Canda. A Bill of Economic Rights is needed not because the free market produces an ideal economy and society but because there is such strong evidence that still worse results are produced by unconstrained economic and social engineering experiments inspired by the ideals of romantic socialism or by the simple pragmatism of wanting to fix obvious wrongs.

As will be seen below, the proposed Bill of Economic Rights will not interfere with the obligation of the government to provide for external and internal security, to regulate the money supply, to define property rights that assure limits on the pollution of the environment and to raise taxes to pay for these public services. I do not propose the withering away of the state which anarchists would recommend. My argument is purely and simply a reaction to the excessive social and economic engineering of the post-war years. In a sense it is completely in the tradition of liberal pragmatism that has so many supporters who believe that economic wrongs can be corrected through legislation without adherence to the ideals of romantic socialism simply by pragmatic cost-benefit analysis of every policy. In this tradition, the social and economic engineering policies of recent decades should be evaluated and dealt with if their costs are greater than their benefits.

10 Carr (1976) contains an analysis of efforts to control inflation by wage and price controls which has many references to the failure of such policies in the past.
11 The need of constitutional controls on the majority has been argued in the Federalist Papers, by J.S. Mill and many other philosophers. McWhinney (1981) reviews the history of constitutional clauses in many countries that deal with economic matters. See also Brennan and Buchanan (1980) and Wagner and Tollison (1980) for US proposals to have such constitutional restraints placed on politicians.

II THE BILL OF ECONOMIC RIGHTS

Before setting out the Canadian Bill of Economic Rights, it is useful to consider the following three points.

First, constitutional clauses can always be overturned by mechanisms specified in constitutions, such as a two-thirds majority vote in the US Congress. A similar provision is under discussion for the Canadian constitution. This means that if economic and social conditions change in the future and require a rewriting of the Bill of Economic Rights, this can be done. The main objective of the Bill as set out here is to protect the system of free markets from encroachment by simple majorities that attempt to provide legislative benefits at the expense of minorities or of the country as a whole in the longer run. If this protection appears unnecessary or expectations for better policies arise in the future, the clauses can be changed.

Second, there are instances in Western democracies where constitutional guarantees have been violated or changed even without explicit legal processes. There are dictators in Latin American countries openly violating human rights guaranteed in constitutions. In the United States, the judiciary has changed through time the interpretation of constitutional provisions and permitted increased economic engineering. (Anderson and Hill, 1980) Legislators and bureaucrats have numerous ways of circumventing laws and constitutions. The Carter administration in the United States demonstrated this when it officially overestimated revenues and underestimated expenses to show a legislatively mandated balance in the 1980 budget. Nothing can be done to prevent these violations of basic human and economic rights. In spite of this, of course, most countries have constitutions because it is believed that their existence does make a difference, even if they cannot assure anything.

Third, while constitutional clauses can always be changed, as was noted above, they should be designed to last for as long a time as possible. For this reason they cannot contain specific prescriptions and limitations on economic legislation, just like the Human Bill of Rights does not prescribe in detail how certain freedoms are to be safeguarded. Technology and science, including economics, constantly change the economic and social environment, requiring, and making possible, different responses to the problems of the day. For these reasons, I will not present specific ways in which the government has to achieve balanced budgets, price stability and so on. Instead, I will discuss how in the light of conditions and knowledge in the early 1980s these rights can be safeguarded.

The proposed specification of the Canadian Bill of Economic Rights has the disadvantage that it will impose on the judiciary and technical experts the duty of deciding how individual clauses have to be implemented. This appears to be an inevitable cost of trying to safeguard human and economic rights through the constitution and it does not mean that the inclusion of a Bill of Economic Rights into the Canadian constitution is an empty gesture. On the contrary, if it is accepted after widespread discussion by an assembly and ratified by a referendum, it will signal to Canadian politicians the mood of the people, strengthen the hands of politicians and bureaucrats wanting to preserve it in action and make violations more difficult.

1 Balanced Budget Clause

CANADIANS HAVE THE RIGHT TO BE FREE FROM BURDENS IMPOSED BY CURRENT AND PAST DEFICIT SPENDING FOR PUBLIC CONSUMPTION.

Background: Canadian parliaments in recent years have enacted legislation leading to expenditures in excess of tax revenues, partly in the belief that permanent deficit spending would reduce unemployment permanently (see Friedman, 1977) and partly because expenditures can be made to provide benefits to people who are likely to deliver votes. The economic results of deficit spending have been that some of the loanable funds and savings generated by the private sector go to the purchase of government securities rather than to firms for the use of real capital formation and to individuals for the financing of mortgages. The resultant smaller capital formation has reduced economic growth and the available housing stock.[12] This displacement of private by public borrowing and reduced capital formation would have been even more severe if the Bank of Canada had not been required to increase the money supply at an accelerating rate to keep down interest rates. But the accelerating money supply increases have resulted in increasing inflation rates, which can be seen to have been caused at least indirectly by deficit spending.

Deficit spending causes the growth in government debt. In recent years, this growth took place at a rate exceeding that of the overall economy while at the same time the accelerating inflation resulted in rising interest rates. Consequently, the expense of servicing the public debt has become an increasingly large part of the government budget, raising the deficit and requiring higher taxes. These higher taxes in turn have had detrimental effects on work and savings incentives.

The benefits of deficit spending, on the other hand, have turned out to have been transitory only. Unemployment cannot be reduced permanently by the creation of excess demand and all government services provided to the public ultimately have to be paid for by a reduction in income in the private sector.

Discussion: It is impossible for governments in practice, and it is not desirable for the sake of cyclical stability, to balance budgets during every period covered by a budget. Therefore, budgets should be balanced over full business cycles, with deficits during recessions balanced by surpluses during the expansionary phases of business cycles.

It is no simple technical task to set expenditure and tax levels in an uncertain environment to attain the stated objective of balanced budgets over business cycles. Moreover, there is the question of what should be done if over one cycle there were net imbalances. Should they be carried forward to the next cycle or cycles?

Another problem associated with the balanced budget clause is the fact that for the sake of economic efficiency government investment should be financed by borrowing so that capital markets convey the appropriate signals to savers and investors about the overall social rate of capital formation. But what are government investment and government consumption expenditures? Spending on education, medical care and defense can be interpreted as investments in human capital, health and national security.

Undoubtedly, there are other practical problems in the implementation of the proposed balanced budget clause. Yet, the basic meaning and the intent of the clause appears to be clear, and if it is, then ways can be found to translate the principle into operational procedures by technicians and the courts. The Economic Council of Canada can be required to define officially the peaks and troughs of business cycles, much like the National Bureau for Economic Research in the United States, and provide forecasts that serve as official guides for estimates of government revenues and cyclically determined expenditures. The Council also can set out, after appropriate public discussion, categories of investment and consumption expenditures. Judicial review of these Council actions and of government fulfillment of its obligations will not be entirely free of political considerations, but it is likely to result in

12 The 'crowding out' hypothesis is in strict contrast with the basic Keynesian model and has been argued in Carlson and Spencer (1975). For skeptical views on this effect see Stein (1976) and Purvis (1980).

64 / Herbert G. Grubel

exactly the kind of practical restraints on politicians that the Bill of Economic Rights is intended to provide.

2 Price Stability Clause

CANADIANS HAVE THE RIGHT TO A STABLE PRICE LEVEL.

Background: Even though the monetary history of all countries over many centuries has shown that inflation is always caused by excess money creation,[13] most economists during the 1960s and 1970s recommended that moderate amounts of excess quantities of money be created because they believed that the resultant moderate rates of price increases would lower unemployment permanently. The targets of unemployment set under this policy soon became targets for expansionary monetary policy, which did not remain moderately excessive but, as is well known now, required acceleration in the rate of increase in the money supply to achieve any lowering in the unemployment rate.

The political process determining these policies favors the continued acceleration of money supply growth because any *deceleration* leads to economic stagnation, high unemployment rates and other social costs, which make the cure for inflation seem worse than the disease itself. *Steady growth rates* lead to unemployment rates excessively high in the light of expectations raised during the period when it was believed that there was stable inflation-unemployment trade-off.[14] The time between elections in Canada is short relative to the time required for the deceleration of the money supply to lower inflation rates. Therefore, no government can afford to stick with these policies long enough to achieve price stability. Instead, the need for reelection creates strong incentives for renewed acceleration of inflation and resultant lower unemployment rates and faster growth. The final result of these policies will either be a hyper-inflation and well-known accompanying traumatic economic and social effects, or more policies such as wage and price controls which move the Canadian economy towards the socialist planning model, with all of the costs and loss of freedom these policies are known to entail.

Because of the fact that the costs of price stability attainment and maintenance appear in the short run while the benefits can only be seen in the long run, the democratic process that causes politicians to face voters frequently and disregard the longer run cannot be trusted to achieve and maintain price stability and can only be constrained by the constitution.

Discussion: As in the case of the balanced budget clause, the price stability clause raises many important problems of implementation. The most important of these are the following. Is price stability to be measured by the behavior of the consumer price index, the GNP price deflator or an index that reflects changes in the quality of goods on the market? How often should these indices have their basket weights revised? (See Gordon, 1981)

There are cyclical fluctuations in individual commodity prices as well as indices. Over what period of time should price increases and reduction net to zero?

While it is one thing to establish that historically and in most countries inflation is correlated with excess money creation, it is quite another to conclude from this that the control of a particular monetary aggregate assures price stability. Exogenous technical change as well as changes induced by the controls themselves can destroy historic correlations between

13 For Canadian studies on this subject see Courchene (1976) and Laidler and Parkin (1975). Also see Mayer (1978) for a background.
14 Barber and McCallum (1980) argue the case about the high cost of reducing inflation through monetary policy restraints.

monetary aggregates and inflation rates. So how in practice would the Bank of Canada assure monetary growth consistent with price stability?

The diagnosis of money as the basic cause of inflation is in vogue presently, but there are many economists who believe that the concentration of economic power in Canada causes cost-push inflation to which the money supply is merely accommodating to prevent excessive unemployment of resources. This diagnosis of the cause of inflation leads to the conclusion that price stability is achieved most efficiently by controls on wages and prices, which make it possible to keep down the money supply growth that historically has been associated with price stability. Should monetary policy therefore be supplemented by or even subordinated to direct controls on wages and prices?

The answers to the above questions are found partly in technical economic analysis and partly in politically determined perceptions of an ideal society. As in the case of the balanced budget clause, the Economic Council of Canada can be required to make technical assessments of most of the issues of implementing the price stability clause, with the desire of the people for stable prices as expressed in the constitution guiding the judiciary and technicians whenever political issues intrude on their decision. At the very least, the constitutional clause will strengthen the position of the Governor of the Bank of Canada when in the future a prime minister urges increases in the money supply to finance unexpectedly large expenditure deficits that otherwise would raise the interest rate to politically uncomfortable levels just before an election. Under these conditions the Governor, backed by the Economic Council and other technicians can more readily refuse the prime minister's request by pointing to the constitutional requirement to maintain a stable price level.

3 Rights to Private Property Clause
CANADIANS HAVE THE RIGHT TO OWN PRIVATE PROPERTY AND TO PROTECTION FROM EXPROPRIATION WITHOUT DUE PROCESS OF LAW AND THE LEGISLATION OF PRICES AND WAGES.

Background: Canadian governments in recent years have increasingly become involved in determining prices of commodities and services produced by the private sector in order to change income distributions or achieve other objectives deemed to be in the social interest. Examples of price determination in this spirit are rent controls, minimum wage legislation, agricultural marketing boards and energy prices. Governmental price setting is politically appealing in that it seems to alleviate economic hardships for certain groups of people with great voting power at the expense either of corporations that have few votes, or of large numbers of individuals each implicitly paying such small amounts that they have no incentives to engage in organized protest. The latter condition exists for buyers of agricultural products whose supply is managed by marketing boards.

Economists are almost unanimous in their condemnation of income redistribution through such price setting because in the longer run it always results in more economic hardship than do the free market conditions. Thus, high minimum wages cause unemployment, (see Walker and Grubel, 1978) low prices of energy and apartments reduce supplies and cause much higher prices later,[15] high prices for agricultural products result in excess supplies and the creation of output controls which lower farmers' incomes. (See Grubel and Schwindt, 1977.) Moreover, through the legislation of prices some Canadians are singled out for taxation and essentially capricious expropriation. For example, rent control forces the owners of apartments to subsidize renters and energy price legislation results in subsidies paid by the owners

15 See Watkins and Walker (1977) on energy, Block and Olsen (1981) on rent control.

of some types of natural resources to the general public. Such forms of taxation undermine long-standing Canadian rights to private ownership, equal treatment of income and wealth under the law and the right to fair compensation if the state appropriates private or corporate assets for public purposes.

If Canadians want higher incomes for low-skilled workers and farmers or to help low income earners to pay for the high costs of apartments and energy, then they should have their politicians vote open and direct income subsidies and simultaneously raise taxes explicitly on the incomes of those who were chosen to pay for the subsidies, without discrimination concerning the source of income.

Discussion: All government taxes and expenditures have effects on the incomes earned by Canadians. Thus, high excise taxes on alcoholic beverages lower consumption and reduce the incomes of specialized factors of production serving the industry. Consumers faced with higher produce prices suffer a reduction in real income, the more so if their tastes run towards the consumption of alcohol. Does the private property clause mean that the government cannot impose any product-specific taxes?

Unions and professional organizations are government sanctioned institutions that can and do raise the incomes of their constituents at the expense of other groups in the economy. Why are farmers and renters therefore not allowed to organize and exercise their power in the same way?

The answers to these questions are more technical than those that arise in the context of balanced budgets and price stability. There is an important difference between legislating minimum or maximum prices of goods, services and labour and imposing excise taxes to discourage the consumption of goods that have socially undesirable properties. This difference is that in the latter case government involvement stops with the setting of the tax, whereas in the former case the legislated disequilibrium prices result in chronic excess demand or supply and inevitably require further legislation to eliminate the undesired consequences, usually involving subsidies or direct, coercive policies to restrict supply and competition.

Farmers and renters under the property rights clauses have the right to organize just like unions and professionals to gain strength in bargaining over prices. The clause merely denies the right to legislatures to respond to pressures from the boards and renters' associations to legislate prices. Wage rates are determined by collective bargaining between unions and employers, not by the government.

Government Monopoly Clause

CANADIANS HAVE THE RIGHT TO PURCHASE THEIR GOODS AND SERVICES FROM PRIVATELY OWNED FIRMS OPERATING IN MARKETS FREE FROM MONOPOLIES GRANTED BY THE GOVERNMENT.

Background: So-called natural monopolies like the post office, railroad, airlines, and telephone companies were brought under government ownership or control in the belief that private operation for profit would result in excess profits and higher consumer prices. Many economists now agree that the fear of these costs is exaggerated because all industries have competition from substitute products and the risk of entry by competing firms is great.[16] Most important, however, is that public ownership and regulation have resulted in economic and social costs that are greater than those unregulated and privately owned monopolies would

---

16 Cairns (1980) contains a review of the evolution of thinking on the need for and merit of controls on public monopolies. See also Economic Council of Canada (1981).

have produced. This is so because public ownership and regulation lead to the politicization of prices, output decisions and technological change, as a result of which incentives for work and efficiency have been dulled and special interest groups have been served. Consequently, the public receives inferior goods and services at higher prices than are warranted by technology and demand with overall adverse welfare effects greater than those which free markets would have produced.

Discussion: In contrast with the preceding constitutional clauses, the monopoly clause is relatively uncontroversial and technically unambiguous. The biggest practical problems of implementation arise from the change of the existing system of publicly granted monopolies to competition. Vested interests such as unions and managers of the post office or of monopoly truck routes will oppose the changes because they will reduce their power and incomes. But it is precisely in the political struggle pitting the unorganized public interest against the powerful vested interests that the constitutional clause can be the decisive factor in the outcome.

III SUMMARY AND CONCLUSIONS

In expectation of the opportunity to enact a modern constitution for Canada, there has been much public debate about the economic implications of some proposed amendments and the inclusion of a Bill of Human Rights. There has been an absence of debate over the merit of including an amendment defining a Bill of Economic Rights. This omission is puzzling since in recent years there has been a thorough re-examination of the effects of economic and social engineering aimed at improving the free market system in the light of romantic socalist ideals as well as liberal pragmatism. This re-examination has resulted in the widely accepted conclusion that such engineering in many instances has failed badly in the sense that it has resulted in economic and social costs exceeding those that had existed when markets were free. Insights into the democratic political process which encourages this engineering have led to demands for constitutional restraints on legislation by simple majority in the field of economics.

In this paper I have outlined very tentatively a set of constitutional clauses in this spirit to provoke discussion in preparation for a possible Canadian constitutional assembly in the future. The list of clauses is not exhaustive, the background explanations merely scratch the surface and there are many problems of a legal nature and relating to enforcement and existing legislation which have not been discussed. The problem is simply too big for one paper and one author, but I hope that a discussion of the issues can take place among intellectuals and politicians and help prepare public opinion for the creation of a Canadian Bill of Economic Rights in the future.

REFERENCES

Anderson, T. and P.J. Hill (1980) *The Birth of the Transfer Society* (Palo Alto, Calif.: The Hoover Institution)

Barber, C.L. and J.C.P. McCallum (1980) *Unemployment and Inflation: The Canadian Experience* (Toronto: Canadian Institute for Economic Policy)

Block, W. and F. Olsen (ed.) (1981) *Rent Control: Myths and Realities* (Vancouver: The Fraser Institute)

Borcherding, T.E. (ed.) (1977) *Budgets and Bureaucrats: The Sources of Government Growth* (Durham, North Carolina: Duke University Press)

Brecher, I. (1980) 'Reflections on Being 'Out of Joint with the Times',' *Essays in Public*

Affairs, September (Montreal: Concordia University, School of Community and Public Affairs) 1:1.

Brennan, G. and J.M. Buchanan (1980) *The Power to Tax* (New York: Harper and Row)

Breton, A. (1974) *The Economic Theory of Representative Government* (Chicago: Aldine)

Buchanan, J. and G. Tullock (1965) *The Calculus of Consent* (Ann Arbor: University of Michigan Press)

Cairns, R.D. (1980) 'Rationales for Regulation,' Ottawa, Economic Council of Canada, Technical Report No. 2, October.

Carlson, K.M. and R.W. Spencer (1975) 'Crowding out and its Critics,' *Federal Reserve Bank of St. Louis Review*, December, pp 2–17.

Carr, J. *et al.* (1976) *The Illusion of Wage and Price Controls* (Vancouver: The Fraser Institute)

Courchene, T.J. (1976) *Money, Inflation and the Bank of Canada* (Montreal: C.D. Howe Research Institute)

—— (1980) 'Towards a Protected Society: The Politicization of Economic Life,' *Canadian Journal of Economics*, November, pp.556–77.

Economic Council of Canada (1981) *Reforming Regulation* (Ottawa: Government Publishing Centre)

Friedman, M. (1977) 'Nobel-Lecture: Inflation and Unemployment,' *Journal of Political Economy*, June, pp.451–72.

Gordon, R.J. (1981) 'The Consumer Price Index: Measuring Inflation and Causing It,' *The Public Interest*, Spring, 63.

Grubel, H. and R. Schwindt (1977) *The Real Cost of the B.C. Milk Board* (Vancouver: The Fraser Institute)

Grubel, H. and M. Walker (ed.) (1978) *Unemployment Insurance: Global Evidence of its Effect on Unemployment* (Vancouver: The Fraser Institute)

Hayek, F.A. von (1964) *The Counter-Revolution of Science: Studies on the Abuse of Reason* (New York: Free Press of Glencoe)

Laidler, D. and M. Parkin (1975) 'Inflation: A Survey,' *Economic Journal*, December.

Lipsey, R. (1979) 'An Economist looks at the Future of the Market Economy,' paper presented to the XV Annual Nobel Conference on the Future of the Market Economy, Gustavus Adolphus College, St. Peter, Minnesota.

Mayer, T., *et al.* (1978) *The Structure of Monetarism* (New York: W.W. Norton)

McWhinney, E. (1981) *Constitution Making. Principles, Process, Practice* (Toronto: University of Toronto Press)

Purvis, D. (1980) 'Monetarism: A Review,' *Canadian Journal of Economics*, February, XIII:1.

Safarian, A.E. (1974) *Canadian Federalism and Economic Integration*, Constitutional Study prepared for the Government of Canada (Ottawa: Information Canada)

—— (1980) 'Ten Markets or One? Regional Barriers to Economic Activity in Canada,' Ontario Economic Council, Discussion Paper Series.

Smith, J. (1977) *The Revisions* (New York: Ballantine Books)

Spindler, Z. (1980) 'Oligopolistic Behavior and the Theory of Representative Government,' *Public Choice*.

Stein, J. (1976) *Monetarism* (Amsterdam: North Holland)

Wagner, R.E. and R.D. Tollison (1980) *Balanced Budgets, Fiscal Responsibility, and the Constitution* (Washington: Cato Public Policy Research Monograph No.1)

Walker, M. (ed.) (1978) *Confederation at the Crossroads* (Vancouver: The Fraser Institute)

Watkins, C.G. and M. Walker (1977) *Oil in the Seventies* (Vancouver: The Fraser Institute)

Weidenbaum, M. (1979) *The Future of Business Regulation* (New York: AMACOM)

Constitutional Limits on Government Spending Deficits and Levels in Canada

Herbert G. Grubel

Introduction

In this essay I propose a bold but sensible course of action: that Canada's federal and provincial governments enshrine restrictions on government spending deficits and levels in their respective constitutions. A violation of the requirements would automatically invoke dissolution of the legislature concerned and require an immediate election. Although severe in nature, I believe this proposal is absolutely necessary. It is motivated primarily by the postwar growth of spending and by the large fiscal imbalances that have existed since the mid-1970s. In my view, these developments deprive Canadians of their economic rights and threaten the stability of the economy and possibly the future of democracy in Canada.

If given substance, this proposal will eliminate excessive spending levels and deficits, thus protecting the economic right of Canadians, that is, the right to enjoy the fruits of their labor and investments and also eradicating a potential threat to the democratic system of government in Canada. The growth of spending in recent years has reduced the income of Canadians because it is wasteful and hence effectively decreases the efficiency of the economy.

I gratefully acknowledge the useful comments on the first draft made by Irene Ip, David Keating, John McCallum, and participants at a seminar at Simon Fraser University in March 1991. I am also grateful for the valuable insights provided by James Buchanan and James Davidson concerning the movement for constitutional spending limitations in the United States. The National Taxpayers Union of Washington graciously supplied me with relevant literature.

My second motive for writing this proposal is that it would invalidate federal fiscal mismanagement as a justification for Quebec independence, as recently argued by Pierre Fortin.[1] The adoption of constitutional spending restraints would destroy this argument, thereby assisting Canada in its search for unity.

The third motivation for this proposal is that the restraints would eliminate the need for cooperation and harmonization of fiscal policies between the federal and provincial governments. The institutionalization of such a system, which the federal government proposed in the fall of 1991, may be expected to meet much resistance from provincial governments reluctant to surrender any of their fiscal sovereignty to a central authority. However, the constitutional spending restraints I suggest for both levels of government would effectively eliminate the need for such controversial coordination.

The imposition of constitutional restraints on the fiscal freedom of a democratically elected government involves a fundamental change in the nature of parliamentary democracy, which requires careful consideration and justification. The first part of this essay provides such a review at the level of the philosophy of government and the nature of democracy. The second section places the justification for restraints into the context of the recent problems of the federal government, which I see to be the seemingly intractable propensity to engage in deficit spending and the growth of spending as a percentage of national income.

I argue, further, that these developments imply a growing inefficiency in the allocation of resources and a reduction in the rate of economic growth. Spending deficits crowd out private investment and require ever-increasing rates of taxation. Reduction in private income without corresponding improvement in the supply of public goods and income distribution is a blatant violation of the fundamental economic right to the enjoyment of the returns from one's economic activity. In addition, there is the risk that this development

---

1 Pierre Fortin, "Quebec's Forced Choice" (Remarks prepared for the Conference on the Future of Quebec and Canada, Faculty of Law, McGill University, November 16–18, 1990).

threatens the very existence of traditional democratic institutions. The incomes and rights of future generations are thus violated as well.

The growth of overall government spending and the persistence of deficits results from the actions of unconscionable politicians who cater to powerful special-interest groups for the purpose of obtaining their support in upcoming elections. The power of these groups, and that of the bureaucracy, is a consequence of largely irreversible changes in the technological environment, which have lowered the costs of organization and political lobbying. This power can be controlled only through changes in the rules of the game governing the behavior of Parliament: the Constitution. By imposing on legislators a budget constraint, and thereby limiting the funds available for distribution, legislators cannot be tempted to dole out the dough to every group that asks.

Subsequent sections of this study present specific proposals for restraint provisions and discuss general problems encountered in their design. Problems of implementation are serious but not insuperable. The discussion of these problems, as well as the existence and successful operation of such restraints in many U.S. states, suggests that the benefits far outweigh the difficulties, costs, and risks involved.

Quebec's demands for more power and the consequent federal government proposals for the revision of the Constitution have opened a window of opportunity for the inclusion of spending restraints in this document. Let us hope that Canadians will make use of this occasion to protect their future.

The Role of Constitutional Restraints in Democracies

Proponents of constitutional limitations on government must address one fundamental issue: Why do democratically elected governments require such severe limits on their freedom to govern? After all, according to conventional wisdom, Parliament is supreme, serves the general well-being by enacting legislation that raises the operating efficiency of a free enterprise economy, and thus reflects the will of the people. Furthermore, if Parliament enacts laws of which the majority of the public disapproves, including laws that result in excessively high levels of spending and deficits, the democratic election process assures voters the ability to express their dissatisfaction at the ballot box. Through their votes, citizens can elect a new government that will do away with the offending legislation. Sadly, the democratic process does not function as effectively as conventional wisdom would have it. As I outline below, the game must be given parameters.

The Protection of Fundamental Rights, Minorities, and the System of Democracy

The justification of constitutional limits on parliamentary supremacy involves profound issues about the nature of humanity and the purposes and actual functioning of government. These issues were widely discussed in Canada during the 1970s, shortly before the Constitution was patriated and the Charter of Rights and Freedoms was enacted.

In a nutshell, the argument for general constitutional restraints on the government in power is that we need to ensure that it does not encroach on the fundamental rights of human beings, that the minority is protected from exploitation by the majority, and that the democratic system will not be threatened by policies that endanger its very existence. The argument gains strength from a recent change in public perception of government and bureaucracies. According to this view, politicians and bureaucrats alike serve not the public interest but their own.[2]

---

2 For the first studies of these issues, see James Buchanan and Gordon Tullock, *The Calculus of Consent: Logical Foundations of Constitutional Democracy* (Ann Arbor: University of Michigan Press, 1962); and William Niskanen, *Bureaucracy and Representative Government* (Chicago: Aldine-Atherton, 1971). Scholarly reviews of a wider range of arguments in support of constitutional spending restraints are contained in Aaron B. Wildavsky, *How to Limit Government Spending* (Berkeley: University of California Press, 1980); and Advisory Commission on Intergovernmental Relations, *Fiscal Discipline in the Federal System: National Reform and the Experience of the States* (Washington, D.C., July 1987).

The need to protect fundamental human rights and the need to prevent the exploitation of the minority by the majority have been recognized and justified most eloquently by the fathers of the U.S. Constitution. They argued that, without such protection, the quality of life of the governed would be destroyed by the slow but cumulative effects of laws restricting fundamental human rights and freedoms. Each of these laws would be adopted by simple legislative majorities, justified by the political and economic problems of the moment, and would be seen to be correct in the light of the ideological preconceptions of the party in power. To protect against such a process, the U.S. Constitution prohibits Congress from "passing any laws which...infringe the freedom of speech" or deny citizens the right to receive a fair trial, to own private property, or to bear arms. Most modern governments of the world are restrained by such constitutional clauses. The Canadian Charter of Rights and Freedoms, for instance, restricts Parliament similarly, except that private property rights and the right to bear arms are not included.[3]

The third justification for constitutional restraints on legislatures is that they protect the democratic system from demagogues and dictators. Autocratic regimes throughout history, but particularly in seventeenth- and eighteenth-century Europe, stayed in power by suppressing both dissent and political opposition. They did so by censorship of speech and publications and by jailing citizens without trial, all of which could have been outlawed by the presence of the appropriate restraints in a respected constitution.[4] In the next section

---

3   The proposals for constitutional reform launched by the federal government in the fall of 1991 include a short reference to the possible enshrinement of private property rights. In Herbert Grubel, "Reflections on a Bill of Economic Rights," *Canadian Public Policy* 8 (Winter, 1982): 57–68, I argue the merit of such a constitutional clause and consider it to be part of a "Bill of Economic Rights," which includes protection against the burden of public debt payments and excessive levels of spending. The need for such a broad Bill of Economic Rights is increased by the existence of the Charter of Rights and Freedoms and the proposed creation of a Bill of Social Rights.

4   Thus, the constitutional right of Americans to bear arms, which in recent years has aroused so much controversy because of the high rate of homicides using firearms. The Fathers of the Constitution believed that this right would facilitate popular uprisings against autocratic governments and would thereby protect democracy against the possible development of dictatorial governments.

I argue that we must protect our democratic system from the threat
of destruction posed by excessive spending and deficits. I believe
this menace represents one of the most important arguments in favor
of constitutional limitations.

The constitutions of many countries contain provisions that
permit those constitutions to be amended to reflect changing economic, technical, and social conditions.[5] Efforts by Canada's federal
government to add such provisions have opened a window of
opportunity for including financial restrictions.[6] The adoption of
formal amendment procedures will mean that constitutional spending restraints can also be changed. Nevertheless, the merit of constitutional restrictions is that they are more difficult to change than
mere statutes. The resulting process permits the opinions of minor-

---

5 Constitutions define the rules of the game by which politics is played. Changes
   in these rules in response to technological innovations are analogous to changes
   in the rules of ordinary games of sport and entertainment in response to shifts in
   the particulars of the games, as when racing cars become too fast or when
   insufficient excitement is created by rules limiting goal scores.

6 The U.S. Constitution can be amended by a constitutional convention. Such a
   convention can be called by either of two methods: by a majority vote of two-
   thirds of both houses of Congress, or by a call from two-thirds of the state
   legislatures, or 34 of the present 50. Constitutional amendments proposed by a
   convention called by either method must be ratified by the legislatures of at least
   three-quarters of the states, or 38, before becoming law.
       The writers of rules for the rewriting of constitutions must carefully balance
   the need for periodic reviews and revisions, and the consequent loss of continuity
   in the rules, which would damage legislative efficiency if constitutional reforms
   took place too often.
       The same balancing act is required in writing the conditions under which
   constitutions would permit states or provinces to opt out of a federation. On the
   one hand, it is necessary to prevent provinces from opting out and then renego-
   tiating terms whenever they can benefit individually, as Alberta might have been
   tempted to do after the increase in the world prices of energy during the 1970s.
   On the other hand, the ability of provinces to opt out by a well-defined process
   tends to limit the tendency of the central government to usurp power, and thus
   preserves the union.
       For this reason, it might be useful to permit independence of a Canadian
   province after two popular referendums held at a two-year interval and after
   approval by about 60 percent of eligible voters. If such a rule had existed in the
   Canadian Constitution, much of the crises of recent years, which came about
   because of some Quebecers' demands for the independence of Quebec, could
   have been prevented.

ities and general concerns about long-run consequences to have more influence on changes before they are enacted, especially in contrast to the short-run considerations of politicians, which currently dominate spending decisions.

Precedents in the Use of Constitutional Fiscal Restraints

In my view, it is important that all proposals for institutional and legal changes be examined not only in the light of the kind of fundamental principles discussed in the preceding section, but also in the light of historic precedent. For this reason, I will consider briefly the nature and performance of fiscal restraint clauses in existing constitutions.

The U.S. Constitution contains no restraints on spending levels and deficits.[7] However, the constitutions of 49 U.S. states limit deficit spending and ten limit taxes and expenditures. In addition, as of January 1990, 12 states had statutory limits on taxes and spending.

---

7 The absence of such a clause has an interesting explanation, which has been given to me by James Davidson. Thomas Jefferson as the U.S. ambassador to France, observing the fiscal irresponsibility of the French court, had written to his colleagues from France about the merit of constitutional restraints. However, at the time that the U.S. Constitution was written, financial markets and the absence of a central monetary authority had made it seem impossible for the government to incur large spending deficits. The obligations of the government at that time were selling at 15 percent of their nominal value.

According to Wildavsky (*How to Limit Government Spending*, p. 45), James Madison noted in the Federalist papers the importance of special-interest groups in the functioning of democracy, though he did remark on the danger of having small interest groups gain too much influence. However, Madison believed that the large geographic size of the United States would raise the cost of organization for small groups and that, as a result, only large ones could organize. Their size would assure that the influence an interest group could exert on legislation would reflect a common, shared opinion of a sizable portion of the population. Accordingly, there was no need to be concerned about the implications of modern public choice theory. The prohibitive costs prevented small groups from obtaining legislation favoring them at the expense of the general public. Nor could the collective effect of small interest groups increase spending substantially or block tax increases needed to balance the budget.

The restraint provisions vary greatly in detail from state to state, making some more effective than others. For example, the effectiveness of restraint depends largely on whether school district budgets are part of a state's accounting system or if each school district can float its own obligations. Some differences depend on whether capital expenditures are included in the spending limits or not.[8]

It is interesting to note that restraints in U.S. state constitutions did not exist until the mid-nineteenth century. They were introduced at that time because the depression of 1837 had forced many states into bankruptcy. Limitations on either taxation or spending were adopted by a substantial number of states between 1970 and 1985, largely in response to the rapid growth in state expenditures during this period.[9] The history of U.S. state spending limitations suggests that severe financial crises of governments or excessively rapid growth in spending can provide the stimulus needed for the enact-

---

Note 7 - cont'd.

The growth of government spending during the postwar years and the persistence of deficits since the 1970s prompted the creation of several nonprofit organizations that have lobbied for the convocation of an assembly to propose limits on spending levels and imbalances in the U.S. Constitution.

The efforts of these organizations and other parties resulted in a vote in the House of Representatives on July 17, 1990, whereby 279 members voted in favor and 150 against a balanced-budget amendment, just seven votes short of the two-thirds majority required for passage. In 1990, 32 of the 34 states required to force the convention of a constitutional assembly had called for such an action. Political observers believe that Congress will pass a balanced-budget amendment once it becomes clear that the state legislatures can muster the votes for the creation of a constitution-writing assembly; Congress would rather not face the risk that such an assembly would extend its agenda into risky and uncharted territory.

8 Detailed descriptions of the U.S. state limitations are found in Advisory Commission on Intergovernmental Relations, *Fiscal Discipline in the Federal System*; and Connecticut Public Expenditure Council, *Tax and Spending Limitations for Connecticut: Needed Discipline or Excessive Constraint?*, Public Policy Report, vol. 2 (December 1990).

9 Naomi Caiden, "Problems in Implementing Government Expenditure Limitations," Appendix C, in Wildavsky, *How to Limit Government Spending*, contains a review of the history of state limitations on levels of deficits and spending with relevant references to the literature up to the late 1970s. There is some evidence that the economic performance of states is a positive function of the strength of the constitutional limits on spending deficits and levels.

ment of constitutional restraints. In the next section, I argue that, on these grounds, conditions are now right for the enactment of such restraints in Canada.[10]

The Dangers of High Deficits and Spending Levels

In this brief review of the recent Canadian history of deficits, the debt, and spending levels, I argue that the existing and prospective deficits and spending levels directly cause reductions in income, general welfare, and the rate of economic growth. They do so by discouraging work and investment, encouraging emigration and capital flight, creating social tensions, and threatening personal liberties. As a result of these developments, society at large suffers both currently and in the future. In addition, high spending levels increase the risk of economic and social upheavals, the consequences of which are hard to predict but sure to be both far-reaching and disconcerting.

High Deficit and Debt Levels

Figure 1 illustrates the development of the net debt of the federal government and of the provincial and municipal governments and hospital boards of Canada between 1961 and 1990. The debt, of course, represents the cumulative effect of spending imbalances, rising and falling as a result of deficits and surpluses, respectively. Debt is expressed here as a percent of national income, or gross

---

10 Proposals for the creation of a Federation of European States within a decade or so are now being discussed widely. A common constitution will have to be written and adopted by all member states. This prospect has prompted Buchanan and Bernholz to propose the inclusion of spending restraints in the new constitution, as can be seen in James Buchanan, "Europe's Constitutional Opportunity" (manuscript, Center for the Study of Public Choice, George Mason University, Fairfax, Va., 1990); and Peter Bernholz, "Institutional Aspects of the European Integration," in Herbert Grubel and Silvio Borner, eds., *The European Community after 1992: Perspectives from the Outside* (Houndsmill: MacMillan, 1991).

Figure 1:   *The Evolution of the*
Government Sector's Net Debt, 1961–90

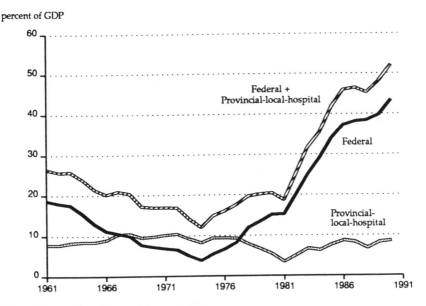

percent of GDP

Note: Data are on a National Accounts basis.

Source: Canada, *Canadian Federalism and Economic Union: Partnership for Prosperity* (Ottawa: Supply and Services Canada, 1991), p. 32.

domestic product (GDP), in order to facilitate economic interpretation of the data.[11]

---

11 The discussion in this section uses the definition of debt found in Canada, *Canadian Federalism and Economic Union: Partnership for Prosperity* (Ottawa: Supply and Services Canada, 1991) — that is, net debt, or gross debt minus government assets. This section also assumes a national accounts basis rather than flow of funds. There are important differences in the levels and rates of growth of debt according to which definition is used. However, discussion of these differences goes beyond the scope of this essay. Basically, the growth rates and implicit size of deficits are much the same by all definitions.

Strictly speaking, the debt, as a percentage of GDP, falls if the growth rate of the deficit is less than the growth rate of nominal GDP. For this reason, the growth rate of nominal debt and therefore the absolute size of the annual imbalances are understated by the figures shown. Especially between 1961 and the mid-1970s, the decrease in the debt as a percent of GDP was caused mostly through growth in GDP. Thus, during the 1961–74 period, the value of the net debt rose from $13 billion to $25 billion, even though it fell from 18 to 5 percent of GDP, as Figure 1 shows.

A Short History of Canada's Debt

A few comments will help put these figures into perspective. First, the collective net debt of the provincial and local governments and hospital boards generally remained at a constant level throughout the period examined.[12] This trend will not likely hold up in the near future because, as of 1991, large provincial deficits have started to emerge, most notably in Ontario, where deficits of about $10 billion have been announced for the next three years. The net debt will also rise because of the budgetary measures of the federal government, which has curtailed transfer payments to provincial governments without corresponding reductions in mandatory spending or increases in taxation powers.

Second, the growth of the federal net debt as a percentage of GDP has been rapid only since the mid-1970s and has slowed somewhat since 1986. Budget projections by the federal government predict that the growth will become zero by the mid- to late 1990s. However, the recession of the early 1990s has raised serious doubts about the reliability of this forecast.

Third, as Figure 2 reveals, an important aspect of total public sector spending has shifted. Between 1970 and 1990, spending on goods, services, and capital formation remained unchanged at about 22 percent of GDP. Transfers to persons and business were 9.2, 13.0, and 14.9 percent of GDP in 1970, 1980, and 1990, respectively. But the largest increase in spending paid for interest on the public debt, absorbing 3.6, 5.4, and 9.4 percent of GDP during these three years. A substantial proportion of the growth in this particular category of spending is attributable to increases in interest rates that could not be influenced by the government of Canada.

---

12 These figures hide the dramatic increase in spending on goods, services, and capital formation by provincial and local governments and hospital boards from 10.5 to 17.3 percent of GDP in 1960 and 1990, respectively, while federal government spending for the same purposes actually fell from 6.7 to 4.9 percent of GDP. See Figure 3 for these data.

**Figure 2:   *The Evolution of Total Public Sector
                Expenditures and Taxes, 1960–90***

percent of GDP

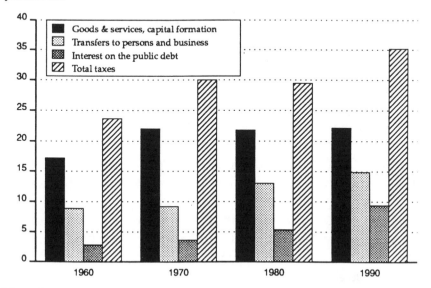

Note: Data are on a National Accounts basis. The total public sector includes the federal,
        provincial, and local governments, the hospital sector, and the Canada and Quebec
        Pension Plans.

Source: Canada, *Canadian Federalism and Economic Union: Partnership for Prosperity* (Ottawa:
        Supply and Services Canada, 1991), p. 32.

The Costs of High Debt

In my view, the data on the growth of the debt and the implicit level
of deficit spending that underlies it are together indicative of a
fundamental crisis of democracy in Canada. For nearly 15 years,
deficit spending has been maintained during periods of economic
boom — times when, traditionally, deficits are eliminated and surpluses are generated. I am skeptical that efforts to eliminate the deficit
will be successful. Nothing has changed in the political process that
produced 15 years of deficits to make me believe that the combined
levels of government will actually achieve smaller overall deficits.

The large debt and expected continuation of deficits pose a
problem for the Canadian economy for two basic reasons. First, the

financing needs of a debt-ridden government use up a substantial part of the nation's savings, and thus interest rates and the cost of capital go up. As a result, private capital gets crowded out of the picture, or, if more capital is borrowed abroad to fill in the gaps, obligations to foreigners are raised. Under either scenario, the real future income of Canadians drops.[13]

The second problem posed by a large debt is that the need to service the debt creates undesirable incentive effects. In fiscal year 1989/90, payments on the debt issued by the federal government represented 6 percent of GDP, 34.1 percent of budgetary revenues, and 37.4 percent of spending on transfer and exhaustive expenditure programs.[14] Further growth in these figures will inevitably result in an exhaustion of the taxation capacity of the nation; beyond a certain critical point, taxation can cripple a nation.

In countries where taxation approaches such a critical level, the incidence of tax evasion and avoidance rises drastically. These changes in the behavior of taxpayers shrink the tax base, and hence produce a need for even higher tax rates and further erosions of the base: a vicious cycle ensues. Ultimately, taxpayers are driven to force changes in a decrepit taxation system through the political process or by means of revolution.

Economic Effects of High Taxes

The most devastating economic effects of increased tax rates come about through the reduction in incentives to work, save, and invest. Emigration becomes an inviting option for capital and the most

---

13 Government debt obligations have a tendency to make citizens consume less and save more, knowing that they have to service the government debt in the future. This argument was made prominent by Ricardo and was revived recently by Robert Barro. In its extreme formulation, it implies that government deficits do not crowd out private investment. Evans reviews the empirical evidence and finds that it "can at most suggest that Ricardian equivalence is a good approximation" and that "Ricardian equivalence is not blatantly inconsistent with the data" (Paul Evans, "Is Ricardian Equivalence a Good Approximation?" *Economic Inquiry* 4 [October 1991]: 626–644).

14 Canada, Department of Finance, *Quarterly Economic Review, Special Report: Fiscal Indicators and Reference Tables* (March 1991), p. 30.

productive members of society, especially if, as in the case of Canada, a culturally similar country with lower taxes is well known and accessible. These developments invariably reduce the rate of economic growth, the ultimate determinant of both private living standards and the ability of government to finance spending on public goods and social welfare programs.

The widely held Keynesian view suggests that the size of the debt is immaterial to a country's well-being because funds to service the debt are taken away and returned to the citizens of the same country. The validity of this proposition disappears with high levels of deficits and debt, which cause public debt to be held abroad, because foreigners must ultimately be paid by the transfer of real goods and services, which, in turn, directly reduces the living standards of Canadian citizens. In the present context, the main shortcoming of this proposition stems from the neglect of the negative effects on incentive described above. Such an omission is inappropriate for an accurate analysis of a situation involving the high levels of debt developing in Canada.[15]

The Cost of Reducing Expenditures

As we approach the taxation saturation point of the Canadian economy, two economically and socially detrimental efforts will be made

---

15 Deficit spending is also unethical. It violates the rights of future generations, who are without voting rights or are not yet even born. Even if the debt remains at the present level, they face the prospect of having to pay 6 percent or more of their income in the form of taxes just to meet the interest due on deficits incurred by earlier generations. These debt payment obligations are in addition to tax burdens arising from the need to make payments to pensioners as well as those that they face to finance the government operation, health care, and education for their own generation.

Many Canadians consider it to be amoral to saddle future generations with such heavy debt burdens; they argue that, to a considerable degree, the debt they inherit will be matched by stocks of both real capital and knowledge capital. In fact, the burden of debt on future generations has not been discussed widely, and, in my view, it does not carry much weight in the justification of constitutional restraints on deficit spending. Nevertheless, reduction of this unethical burden on future generations may be seen as an additional benefit to be garnered by constitutional limits on deficit spending.

to reduce spending. First, essential types of government spending on infrastructure and the education and health-care systems will be restricted. These restrictions will produce even more negative effects on economic growth and social conditions.

Second, attempts will be made to lower interest payments on the debt and shrink the real size of the debt through money supply increases and inflation. This approach has been used successfully in the past. However, in today's world of integrated capital markets and highly sophisticated investment managers, the Bank of Canada cannot possibly follow this course of action. Inflationary increases in the money supply would result in lower interest rates for only a fleeting period of time. Actions of both lenders and borrowers in capital markets would quickly increase nominal interest rates to reflect the expected higher inflation rates. As a result, debt payments as a percent of GDP would remain virtually unchanged.[16]

An alternative approach to lowering the interest rate involves the use of direct controls. These would have to be complemented by strict foreign-exchange controls in order to avoid international capital flight. Such controls do work but only with highly undesirable consequences for freedom, income distribution, and efficiency of capital markets. In particular, Canadian pension funds and their owners would suffer reductions in wealth and pension incomes.

In sum, the continued growth of government debt will inevitably lead to higher taxes. These in turn will reduce economic growth and erode the supply of government services; emigration of both people and capital will be encouraged; history and foreign experiences would predict a risk of increased inflation and the dangerous

---

16 Nevertheless, the temptation to inflate away the debt problem will always be with us. For a scholarly analysis of the dilemma posed by persistent deficits and the incentives it creates for politicians, see Thomas Sargent and Neil Wallace, "Some Unpleasant Monetarist Arithmetic," *Federal Reserve Bank of Minneapolis Quarterly Review* 5 (1981): 1–17. The widely held view that inflation is a lesser evil than unemployment and slow growth fuels the temptation to use inflation for the elimination of the debt burden. During 1990 and 1991, the Bank of Canada's high interest rate policy, which was aimed at limiting inflation, was criticized by many prominent economists and politicians holding this view.

use of direct controls. All of these developments involve undesirable reductions in the living standards of Canadians and the violation of fundamental economic and social rights.

High Spending Levels

The level of government spending in Canada increased sharply between 1960 and 1990, as can be seen in Figure 3. Federal spending rose from 14.5 to 18.6 percent of GDP in 1960 and 1990, respectively, which represents a 28.3 percent increase in the share of GDP. However, this general picture of the overall growth in spending levels hides some important and disturbing facts. Federal spending on real goods and services, which tends to raise productivity, dropped 27 percent as a share of GDP. During the same period, transfer payments, which have significant negative effects on effort and productivity, increased 29 percent as a share of GDP.

Furthermore, the facts about federal spending levels tell only part of the story. Provincial and municipal governments and hospital boards also raised outlays. Spending on real goods and services and on transfer payments, rose 65 percent and 186 percent, respectively, as a share of GDP.[17]

In 1991, the federal government introduced legislation to limit spending on items other than debt service to 3 percent per year in nominal terms, which is likely to force a reduction in total spending as a percent of GDP. This spending restraint is welcome. However, it remains to be seen whether or not the government has the determination to follow through on its intentions, and if future governments, possibly consisting of different political parties, will retain it. As in the case of the approach to deficits, I have seen no changes in the political system, which created the growth and high levels of

---

17 These spending figures must be interpreted with care. Much of the increase in real spending represents medical care and education expenditures required by federal programs and financed through revenue sharing. Much of the transfer spending was also made mandatory by federal government programs and financed by corresponding payments to the provinces.

Figure 3:   *Comparison of Federal and Provincial-Local-Hospital Sector Expenditures and Taxes, 1960 and 1990*

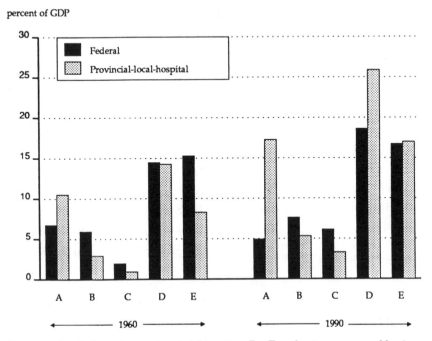

percent of GDP

Key: A = Goods & services and capital formation; B = Transfers to persons and businesses;
      C = Interest on the public debt; D = Total expenditures; E = Total taxes.

Note: Data are on a National Accounts basis.

Source: Canada, *Canadian Federalism and Economic Union: Partnership for Prosperity* (Ottawa:
          Supply and Services Canada, 1991), p. 32.

recent decades in the first place, that would make me optimistic that spending levels will decrease substantially in the near future.

Public Choice
Interpretation of Spending

According to the traditional view about the nature of government, the high spending levels just discussed must reflect the will of the people. Similarly, all programs must raise the efficiency of the economic system and produce a publicly preferred distribution of income. In recent decades, however, a modern theory about the nature of governments, commonly known as the theory of public choice, has questioned the validity of the traditional view. This theory has been able to explain the existence of a wide range of government programs and policies, which, in the view of most dispassionate observers, are detrimental to the public interest. These include marketing boards, rent controls, minimum wages, and tariffs, as well as excessively high unemployment insurance benefits[18] and subsidies to a wide range of industries.

According to the modern view, these programs and policies come about because unethical politicians attempt to secure the voter loyalty of special-interest groups by granting them legislated benefits, the costs of which are too small, when taken individually, to generate any sort of organized opposition from the general public that must ultimately pay for them. Modern technology, by effectively lowering the costs of massive organization, has resulted in an historically unprecedented growth in such interest-group legislation.

Niskanen provides an additional explanation of the rapid growth of government spending.[19] He argues that bureaucrats have strong incentives to increase the size, number, and scope of the spending programs they oversee, since their personal income and status increases proportionately with the size of the expenditures they administer. Bureaucrats can achieve these self-interested goals by providing biased interpretation of information and by facilitating a symbiotic relationship between politicians and special-interest

---

18 For further theoretical and empirical evidence on this analysis, see Herbert Grubel, Dennis Maki, and Shelley Sax, "Real and Insurance-Induced Unemployment in Canada," *Canadian Journal of Economics* 18 (May 1975). This paper provides a study of the reasons for the growth in the cost of unemployment insurance payments in Canada. The findings were confirmed by the Economic Council of Canada and received a further official stamp of recognition in the Forget Commission Report on the Canadian Unemployment Insurance System. In Herbert Grubel, "The Costs of Canada's Social Insurance Programs," in George Lermer, ed., *Probing Leviathan* (Vancouver: Fraser Institute, 1984), I applied the analytical tools used in the explanation of the growth in demand for unemployment insurance to explain the growth in other social insurance spending.

19 Niskanen, *Bureaucracy and Representative Government.*

groups. The ability of bureaucrats to achieve these objectives has also increased as the cost of communications and information has come down.

The increased spending attributable to the activities of special-interest groups and bureaucrats has produced a large and growing waste of economic resources; consequently living standards and growth rates have dropped. These reductions represent a violation of the fundamental economic right of all Canadians to enjoy the fruits of their labor, investment, and risk-taking. The proposed constitutional restraints on spending levels, as outlined in this essay, can ensure that Canadians will once again enjoy this economic right.

High Spending and Economic Growth: Some Evidence

Strong evidence exists to support the case that government spending reduces the economic growth rates of individual countries. Lindbeck, in a number of studies, documents the decline of Sweden's economic fortunes, which resulted from an increase in costly social programs in recent decades.[20] High government spending and taxation accompanied Britain's economic decline between the end of World War II and the election of Margaret Thatcher in the 1970s. Only the fiscal restraint of Thatcher's regime reversed this trend. Somewhat less known is that Germany's outstanding record of economic growth during the postwar years was accompanied throughout by low levels of both spending and taxation. Since the 1970s, Germany's spending and taxation programs have been among the highest while

---

20 During the mid-1960s, before the initiation of its famous welfare and tax programs, Sweden had been among the top three countries in the world in terms of per capita income and real growth rates. Twenty years after the start of these programs, Sweden moved into the middle rank of countries in the Organisation for Economic Co-operation and Development (OECD) according to per capita income. This position was reached as a result of a reduction in the rate of growth, which put it last among the OECD countries. See Assar Lindbeck, "Swedish Industry: In a National and an International Perspective," *Scandinaviska Enskilda Banken Quarterly Review* 3 (1988): 60–71; and idem, "The Swedish Experience" (Institute for International Economic Studies, Stockholm University, Seminar Paper, no. 482, December 1990).

its economic growth rates have been near the lowest of the OECD countries.[21]

The preceding evidence on the correlation between government spending and economic growth is backed by scientific studies involving large numbers of countries undertaken by Marsden,[22] Reynolds,[23] and Rabushka.[24] Additional evidence stems from a study of U.S. states, 49 of which had balanced budget requirements in 1984 and a smaller number of which had limitations on spending levels. This study concluded that "the higher the level of state and local taxes, the lower the rate of economic growth."[25] Olson analyzed the different rates of economic development of Germany and the United Kingdom during the postwar years.[26] To a large extent, he attributes Germany's comparatively better economic performance to the destruction of all German special-interest-group legislation following the loss of the war.

---

21 Argentina, New Zealand, and Australia were among the countries with the highest per capita incomes until they vastly expanded the role of government in the economy and, in particular, raised spending and taxation programs and incurred large spending deficits. Since then, economic growth rates in these countries have stagnated and their per capita income levels have dropped behind that of many other countries.

The point about the detrimental effect of high spending and taxation on growth is reinforced by the experience of a number of countries that have succeeded in attaining high growth rates while maintaining policies of low spending and limited deficits. Examples of countries with these characteristics are Singapore, Hong Kong, Taiwan, and South Korea, the so-called little tigers of Southeast Asia.

22 Keith Marsden, "Links Between Taxes and Economic Growth: Some Empirical Evidence," World Bank Staff Working Papers 604 (Washington, D.C.: World Bank, 1983).

23 Alan Reynolds, "Some International Comparisons of Supply-Side Policy," *Cato Journal* (Fall 1985).

24 Alvin Rabushka, "Taxation, Economic Growth and Liberty," *Cato Journal* (Spring/Summer 1987).

25 Richard Vedder, "Do Tax Increases Harm Economic Growth and Development?" in *Taxpayers Resource Book*, vol. 2 (Washington: National Taxpayers Union Foundation, 1989), p. 87. For a detailed review of this study, see ibid.; and Advisory Commission on Intergovernmental Relations, *Fiscal Discipline in the Federal System*.

26 Mancur Olson, *The Rise and Decline of Nations: Economic Growth, Stagflation and Social Rigidities* (New Haven: Yale University Press, 1982).

Gambling with Canada's Future

The high government spending deficits and levels of recent years have been caused, to a considerable degree, by the efforts of special-interest groups to cater to politicians' and bureaucrats' selfish motives. The effectiveness of these groups in recent decades developed as a result of the lower costs of communication and transportation caused by technological innovations. Much of the resulting spending does nothing to increase the welfare of the average Canadian. On the contrary, it is a wasteful practice that lowers the living standards of current and future generations of Canadians. In addition, high levels of spending of this nature produce no gains in the quality of life or, indeed, in any other social, nonmeasurable aspects of life.

The lowered income of Canadians generated by this wasteful spending reduces the fundamental economic right of Canadians to the fruit of their labor and investment. In the long run, however, more than a violation of economic rights is involved. The practical difficulties of dealing with the deficit increase the temptation of governments to resort to inflation or direct controls to assure economic stability. These temptations constitute a growing threat to the very existence of the system of freedom and democracy.

How great is this threat to the system? On the one hand, Canada has had a long history of stable, democratic government. One would hope that chances are good that social and political instabilities can be avoided. On the other hand, the history of the world is full of instances in which these very conditions have brought on political chaos and the loss of democratic and personal freedoms. Hitler's rise to power in Germany was, to a considerable degree, due to the economic and social dislocations brought about by the hyperinflation of the 1920s. Excessive spending and deficits during the interwar period in China, Hungary, and Austria caused serious economic, social, and political problems. In recent times, the economic and social instabilities in Latin America, as well as the rise of military dictatorships in that area of the world, are all related to irresponsible government deficit spending and the resultant inflations.[27]

Canada's future is highly uncertain. The federal government may or may not be able to control the growth of spending and deficits with sufficient speed to avoid the dangers that come with ever higher levels of debt and interest payments. There may exist methods unknown to me — and therefore not reviewed in this paper — by which Canadian governments can avoid the costly consequences of high and growing levels of debt payments. And even if spending and deficits do continue to grow and the predicted slowdown of economic growth and cut in social services take place, thus lowering the standard of living, it might not be a complete disaster — the people of Canada may still have the fortitude to maintain their tradition of democracy.

In my view, however, it is abundantly clear that the continuation of past trends raises the probability that some or all of the undesirable developments will take place. The proposed constitutional limits on government spending deficits and levels are a promising way out of a difficult situation; they constitute an insurance policy against the occurrence of such calamities in Canada. They will protect not only the present generation but also future generations against the consequences of yet unforeseen conditions that might favor the growth of government spending and use of deficits in the future.

The Need for Constitutional Fiscal Restraints

The merit of constitutional restraints on government spending deficits and levels depends to a considerable degree on whether or not

---

27 The experience of Argentina is particularly telling in this respect. Its government turned one of the most prosperous and stable countries of the world into one of the lowest performers of all the middle-income countries. Democratic institutions and liberty were violated repeatedly by military juntas that attempted to restore a semblance of economic stability and prosperity, all justified on the grounds that democratically elected legislatures were unable to solve the economic problems.

the trends in spending and deficits discussed above are considered permanent. I first discuss this issue by reviewing the role of Keynesian and socialist economic doctrine, which spread during the postwar years. The second part of this section deals with the impact technical change has had on the effectiveness of special-interest groups and the consequent inability of the political system to control spending and deficits.

The War of Ideas in Economics

Buchanan and Wagner argued that, before the 1970s, deficits and excessive spending by Western governments were constrained by public opinion, which they considered to be equivalent to an unwritten constitutional restraint on the political system.[28] The basis of this public opinion was a strongly held common belief that for private persons to incur debts was both immoral and detrimental, and that this same moral stricture applied to governments.

This traditional, unwritten constitution against deficits began to break down rapidly during the postwar years as a result of an almost universal acceptance of the validity of Keynesian economic theory. According to this theory, deficits do no harm to the economy and society: interest payments on public debt are nothing but transfer payments that require taking money away from some people and giving it to others.

Moreover, according to this theory, deficits actually have beneficial effects. When they are incurred during recessions and are matched by surpluses during booms, they reduce the length and severity of unemployment over the full business cycle. More important in breaking down the public strictures of deficits was the spread of the Keynesian idea that permanent deficits can be used to increase aggregate demand and reduce unemployment permanently through the exploitation of the well-known Phillips curve tradeoff between employment and inflation.

---

28 James Buchanan and Richard Wagner, *Democracy in Deficit: The Political Legacy of Lord Keynes* (New York: Academic Press, 1978).

The ultimate victory of these Keynesian ideas about the multiple benefits to be derived from deficits was achieved during the 1960s and 1970s, when economists trained in these doctrines reached positions of power as advisers in governments in Canada and the United States. Because of the newfound, widespread public acceptance of the ideas, politicians could act on the advice of these economists and vote for large and lasting deficits — all without facing the risk of retribution by the electorate.

The development and widespread acceptance of the ideology of socialism and communism during the postwar years also had considerable influence on the increased acceptability of high spending levels in Canada and other Western countries. The Great Depression, combined with the apparent economic and social successes of communist countries in Eastern Europe, provided the fuel for profound reassessments of the merit of free markets. Sophisticated models were developed to show that government spending could deal with the serious pathologies of capitalism and could create a more equitable society with high and stable growth, all at the cost of a small loss in personal freedoms.[29] The widespread acceptance of these ideas increased the election chances of politicians who promised increased government spending for income security and equality, thus expanding the problem of uncontrolled spending.

Buchanan and Wagner cite the breakdown in traditional public values in their proposal for the introduction of spending restraints in the U.S. Constitution. However, I am not convinced that much emphasis should be given to these developments as justification for constitutional restraints in the Canadian Constitution. On the one hand, since the 1970s many of the central propositions of Keynesian economics have become discredited. More recently, the abandon-

---

29 In the wake of *perestroika* and the resultant revelation of the failure of communism, new research has revealed many references to the views expressed by former leading economists and intellectuals. For example, Paul Samuelson's influential introductory economics textbook asserted, in many editions, that communist economic policies had the merit of producing greater income equality and economic growth and stability than the free market could provide and that their only demerit was the loss of freedom of individuals.

ment of the communist system in Eastern Europe has discredited the ideology on which it was based. Therefore, politicians may soon be facing the traditional public disapproval of spending deficits and the wrath of voters revolting against high spending levels. If too much emphasis had been placed on the missing public stricture as justification for restraints, pundits would be telling us that the need for restraints was gone.

On the other hand, deficits and the growth in spending are still out of hand in Canada. Ideologues of the left are rationalizing the failure of Keynesianism and the East European regimes, and want to see these failures as the result of tactical errors that could be avoided in the future. The history of intellectual movements suggests that the lessons of the past eventually will be forgotten and traditional arguments in favor of deficits and high government spending will once again become respectable, most likely in some new formulation. Therefore, there is merit in constitutional restraints, public disapproval of spending deficits or not, if only to make it more difficult to revive such policies some time in the future.

Special-Interest Groups and Bureaucracies

The most persuasive argument in support of constitutional spending limits is the increasing power of special-interest groups and bureaucrats, as discussed above. Special-interest groups, bureaucrats, and politicians have existed ever since the first government was formed, yet they never exerted undue influence until recently. Why did they not raise spending and taxes and create detrimental economic effects long ago? Is their recent rise to power likely to peak or be reversed at some time in the future? Are there no countervailing forces to reduce their power? The answers to these questions are important. If a natural process could be counted on to reverse recent trends, the argument in favor of limiting the power of these groups through constitutional clauses would be weakened considerably.

First, the power of these groups has risen as a result of a considerable drop in the costs of communication and travel. These technological developments have lowered the real cost of organizing special-interest groups and of their lobbying efforts with politicians. Second, most modern elections are won by such slim margins that no politician can afford to lose the support of any interest group, however small and however outrageously self-serving its demands might be. Mix these two factors together and you get the makings for financial disaster.

The electronic media, in particular, have increased the effective power of interest groups, which have become masters at manipulating radio and television to serve their own purposes. With the help of the media, an interest group can readily generate an avalanche of mail to lawmakers and thus influence legislation. During the past few years, several spending and taxation programs of the Mulroney government aroused the fury of special-interest groups, which attacked the government with the support of the media. As a result, several programs were scuttled or altered drastically, and the Progressive Conservative party's support in opinion polls suffered severe setbacks.[30]

It is important to note that the public choice and bureaucracy model of government spending and deficits does not cite any changes in the morality of politicians or bureaucrats as responsible for the observed developments. Politicians and bureaucrats in office during recent times are likely to have the same, if not higher, moral standards as their predecessors. The technological advances responsible for the increased power of special-interest groups are not

---

30 Examples of these programs were taxation of government benefits paid to pensioners with high incomes, the reduction of passenger services provided by VIA Rail, and lower contributions to women's groups designated to finance lobbying with the government. All of these government initiatives had widespread support among economists and other analysts of the efficiency and costs of government programs.

One of the ironies of modern interest group politics is that, in the 1970s, the Trudeau government organized some special spending programs to provide financing for the formation of such groups. According to Peter Brimelow (*The Patriot Game* [Toronto: Key Porter Books, 1988]), the Liberal party adopted this strategy in the hopes that it would be possible to remain in power by ensuring the voting and financial loyalties of new interest groups through appropriate legislation.

reversible or likely to be offset by other technical changes.[31] For this reason, constitutional limits on spending and deficits represent the most promising approach to dealing with the consequences that these technological advances have had on the political system, economic rights, and the prospects for a democratic system in Canada.[32]

Creating Restraint Provisions

In this section, I present some ideas to show how constitutional spending restraints could be made operational. Practical application will not be an easy task, for the following reasons. First, there exists a bewildering variety of theoretical models of how to bind legislators

---

31 The Canada-U.S. Free Trade Agreement has curtailed the power of some special-interest groups by increased competition. For example, the benefits of agricultural supply management and of the union membership of supermarket employees have been curtailed and may be eliminated by crossborder shopping. Free trade has brought into the open the otherwise hidden cost of the benefits accruing to these interest groups at the expense of the public. In my view, this development, though rarely discussed, is one of the most important benefits of the Free Trade Agreement.

32 An important idea in the study of economics maintains that competition exists in all markets, including the market for political favors to special interest groups. In such markets the potential gains from participants are limited by the budget constraint, which limits the total benefits that all of the special interest groups can obtain together. In the end, efforts by any one group to increase its benefits come only at the expense of other interest groups, which in turn devote most of their efforts to defend gains already won. This competition model has been used by Gary Becker ("A Theory of Competition among Pressure Groups for Political Influence," *Quarterly Journal of Economics* 97 [August 1983], p. 37) to argue that there is little reason for concern about the power of interest groups and the damage they can do collectively to the economy.

The validity of this conclusion depends on the existence of a budget constraint provided by public censure of deficits and high spending levels. The history of economic ideas and the actual deficits and spending in Canada suggest that this unwritten budget constraint has been weak in recent decades. The proposed constitutional limits are designed to assure the existence of a budget constraint and to force the outcome predicted by Becker's model.

to limits. The federal government will have to choose one course of approach and stick to it.

Second, all possible approaches involve tradeoffs in means, ends, and risks; they cannot be avoided. Legislators should therefore expect that implementation of the spending limitations will require time-consuming negotiations involving many ideological, legal, and technical problems.

Third, by becoming entangled both intellectually and emotionally in designing the details of restraint procedures, one could easily become despondent about the likelihood of finding acceptable and workable solutions. We should therefore try to remember that existing U.S. restraint systems work effectively and that acceptable solutions to the problems do exist.

Fourth, simplicity and transparency in the operation of restraint procedures are more important than economic purity or technical elegance. Constitutional restraints must serve as well as be seen to be serving the interest of all Canadians. Reasons for the choice of particular procedures must be explainable in simple terms. If possible, detailed rules for implementation should be in legal statutes rather than the constitution itself, where only main principles and basic guidelines should be presented.[33]

To simplify the discussion, I have limited my consideration to one model that appeals to me and that can serve as a basis for extensions and modifications. I provide references for literature that reviews alternatives.

---

33 The operation of this principle may be seen most readily in the case of the constitutional guarantee of freedom of speech. Many times in U.S. history, legislatures passed laws to prohibit people from yelling "fire" in crowded theaters and, what was somewhat more controversial, prohibit the sale of pornographic material. The judiciary has been required to decide whether or not these and other laws violate the constitutional mandate of freedom of speech. A constitutional clause could not have foreseen the difficulties and would have been too unwieldy if it had attempted to specify all possible cases of laws to which the freedom of speech abuse might apply. Similarly, flexibility and strength of basic purpose should be embodied in the wording of constitutional spending restraints.

One Restraint Proposal

An Outline

Spending Limits

> *Spending by the government of Canada must not exceed a specified percentage of national income, which implies that it cannot grow at a rate faster than the growth in national income.*

In operational terms, this means that rates of planned annual spending increases, in real terms, must not exceed the average annual growth rates of real income during the preceding five years plus a rate equal to the expected rate of inflation during the year.

Prohibition of Deficits

> *The government of Canada must not incur spending deficits over the full business cycle.*

In operational terms, this means that planned annual tax revenue increases each year must equal the average annual growth rate of tax revenue during the preceding five years. Because spending grows at the same rate, the budgets of one complete business cycle will be balanced on average.

In any budget year, actual spending and actual revenues can differ as a result of cyclical fluctuations. When actual revenues exceed actual outlays, the surplus goes into a rainy day fund. When actual spending exceeds actual revenues, the shortfall can be withdrawn from the rainy day fund.

When the rainy day fund exceeds 10 percent of annual spending, the surplus funds must be returned to taxpayers through appropriate reductions in the following year's tax liabilities. If the rainy day fund balances are drawn down and threaten to become completely depleted, the next budget must raise tax rates or broaden the tax base to eliminate any projected deficits.

Suspension of Requirements

The limits on spending and deficits can be suspended for a maximum of two years by a resolution in Parliament passed with a two-thirds majority.

Penalties

If total spending exceeds the specified percentage of national income or the rainy day fund is exhausted, an election must be held two months later.[34]

Choice of Spending Levels and Rates of Increase

The concept of an optimum spending level involves some fundamental assumptions about the role of government in society. A thorough discussion of the range of ideological views is not possible here and, furthermore, is unlikely to yield useful results. Pragmatically, the spending levels in existence could form the basis for a debate about desirable levels for both the short and long run. I can envisage the adoption of a spending limit as a percentage of GDP, equal to that of the last five years. Provisions can be made to reduce it by some percentage, say 25, during the following ten years.

The selection of this long-term target is crucial, and a lengthy public debate should precede its enshrinement in the Constitution.

---

34 In reactions to the proposed penalty, several Canadians have suggested to me the desirability of other forms of penalty. One example would make members of the party or of the cabinet in power ineligible for re-election during the mandated election. Another popular suggestion would reduce the pension rights of such members of Parliament.

At the same time, it should be remembered that the selection could be altered, as the Constitution will almost certainly contain a formula for amendment.

Once a desired level of government spending, as a percent of national income, has been achieved, annual spending can increase only at the rate at which national income increases. However, the existence of business cycles, and divergences in the prices and productivity of the private and public sector are likely to make the implementation of this simple rule economically inefficient.[35] In my view, the solutions for these time-specific problems should be included in statutes rather than the Constitution.

Expenditures for Inclusion

To be helpful to politicians, the establishment of a spending limit should be accompanied by a detailed list of spending categories. This section describes the major categories for inclusion or exclusion from limitations.

Program Expenditures

The class of expenditures — known technically as program expenditures — clearly must be included in the set to be limited. This category consists of all spending on public goods, such as education, health, defense, the judiciary, regional development, foreign aid,

---

35 The technical problems that cause this inefficiency are as follows. First, during a recession, when a deficit is incurred and permitted under the rainy day fund provision, spending rises more rapidly than tax revenue. Second, inflation that affects public sector output more than private sector output will produce the result that an equal percentage increase in GDP and spending reduces the real share of government in the economy. Third, an analogous result is brought about by the slower productivity growth in the public relative to the private sector. The last two problems would become important only in the long run but cumulatively could still have a significant impact on the efficiency of the mixed economy unless they are corrected by devices, the design of which should not be beyond the skill of accomplished economists and lawyers.

international representation, and social overhead for facilities such as airports and harbors. The second category for inclusion is comprised of transfers to persons under social assistance, unemployment, support for the native population, and so on. In addition, program expenditures include transfer payments to poor provinces.

Debt Service

Debt-service payments should be excluded from the limits on spending levels because their size has been predetermined by previous governments and is heavily influenced by interest rate levels over which the government has very limited control. Moreover, if debt service were included and the debt ceased to grow because of the prohibition on deficits, the payments, as a percentage of GDP, would fall with economic growth through time, which, in turn, would leave room for undesirable spending.

However, debt payments should be included in annual budgets subject to the prohibition on deficits. Otherwise, the debt payments could be financed by borrowing and, in the extreme, irresponsible governments could increase the size of the debt and interest payment obligation at the rate of interest.

Tax Expenditures

Governments usually provide benefits to special-interest groups through traditional programs of spending or subsidies. However, they can also provide benefits of equal value by granting tax concessions. The use of these so-called tax expenditures is popular with both politicians and beneficiaries because the costs do not appear in annual budgets and therefore escape the usual competition for resources within the government. To curb this half-hidden leak of government funds, tax expenditures should be limited to curtail the undesirable expansion of government influence, especially when outright spending is limited by constitutional clauses.

During the 1970s, the idea of controlling tax expenditures received much political and academic attention. However, no policies came of this work, primarily because of difficult conceptual problems encountered in defining tax expenditures. The most revealing of these appears when one asks whether basic personal exemptions in income tax are tax concessions. After all, they give a break to taxpayers at the expense of a reduction in the tax base. This example would seem to imply that the government has a right to tax rates taking away 100 percent of income, so that everything short of that represents a tax expenditure.[36]

These conceptual and practical difficulties suggest that tax expenditures would best be omitted from the design of general spending limits. In the long run, the public would be protected from the excessive use of tax expenditures by political forces: raised tax expenditures reduce the tax base and thereby force costly increases in tax rates if the government in power is to maintain total revenue. This unpopular measure would certainly exact its price at the ballot box.

Unfunded Liabilities

Politicians also court special-interest groups by providing their members with legislated social security benefits, the real costs of which only appear in future budgets. Outstanding examples of such practices are promises of generous pension benefits to government employees and higher pension or health benefits under the Canada Pension Plan. Only a very small fraction of the cost increases caused by such legislation appears in the budgets of the government passing

---

36 David Keating has pointed out to me that the indexation of Canadian income tax can be interpreted technically as a tax expenditure because it has resulted in the lowering of tax payments by Canadians. The elimination of indexation would imply a reduction in such tax expenditures. Therefore, a government operating under a grandfather clause, which would be necessary after the introduction of spending limits and the inclusion of tax expenditures in the limit, could increase income tax rates and spending without violation of the limits on total spending as a percent of GDP. The result of such a set of policies would clearly be in violation of the spirit of the proposed constitutional spending limits.

it because the bulk of payments is scheduled to take place in the future.[37]

Achievement of the intent of constitutional restrictions on spending levels requires, therefore, that any legislated changes to the present value of such unfunded, contingent liabilities be accounted for in budgets and credited to the total spending limit. This proposal forces governments to make policies that are economically efficient as well as equitable for future generations.

Seigniorage

Modern governments have a substantial and regular income as a result of their "seigniorage," or revenue arising from the issue of bills and coins and from the central bank's holding of interest-earning government securities that are matched by deposits from commercial banks, which pay no interest.[38] In practice, seigniorage enters into the general revenue of the federal government when central bank profits are transferred. These revenues should be counted explicitly in the determination of deficits and limits on total spending.

37 The value of the unfunded liabilities of the pension plan for the Public Service of Canada was $4.2 billion on December 31, 1986, though by the end of 1989 actuaries had assessed it to have been only $2.4 billion (see Canada, Office of Superintendent Financial Institutions, *Pension Plan for the Public Service of Canada, Actuarial Report* [Ottawa: Supply and Services Canada, 1991], p. 22). Before the 1990 report on the Old Age Security Program, an analogous figure for the unfunded liabilities had been published upon request of the Auditor General of Canada. However, the 1990 report merely expresses the annual payment obligations until 2100 as a percent of total earnings. Depending on assumptions about population, earnings, and inflation growth rates, the rate for 2035 varies from 6.77 percent to 3.12 percent with the "best" projection of 4.61 percent of earnings. See Canada, Office of the Superintendent of Financial Institutions, *Old Age Security Program: First Statutory Actuarial Report* (Ottawa: Supplies and Services Canada, 1990), various tables.

38 In West Germany during the 1980s, the treatment of seigniorage in the form of profits by the Bundesbank became a hot political issue when the government contemplated changing traditions. It wanted to count seigniorage like tax revenue and thus offset current expenditures. The sums involved were substantial and represented about 3 percent of total federal government outlays.

Decentralized Government Structure

As a result of the Quebec independence movement, Canada is likely to adopt a new form of confederation in which some of the traditional spending programs will become the responsibility of provincial governments. These programs cover higher education, regional development projects, health, welfare of natives, fisheries, and others. Reductions in, and possibly the elimination of, federal transfers to the provinces for these types of programs will reduce total federal and increase total provincial spending budgets. The proposed constitutional limits for the different levels of government should, of course, reflect these changes.

Protection of Provinces

One of the ways in which politicians at the federal level of government can and have courted the favors of special-interest groups has been to make provincial programs meet costly mandatory standards that can be met only by taxes raised by the provincial governments. The outstanding example of such an exercise involves health care. The federal government has prevented provinces from restricting access to the health system through such measures as user fees, while failing to maintain transfer payments at levels adequate to meet the demand generated by a universal system. Such abuse of federal government power and potential violation of spending restraint provisions must be prohibited by appropriate statutes.

Investment

Efficiency in the allocation of resources between time periods and different generations of people requires that all capital formation be financed by borrowing. The effect of such borrowing is to raise the interest rate and to signal to market participants the relative costs of present and future consumption. Similarly, government spending that leads to such real capital formation, after the depreciation of existing stocks, should also be financed by borrowing. The resultant growth in the public debt would have none of the negative effects discussed above. Future generations would face higher tax payments to service the debt, but they would also enjoy a corresponding stock of maintained roads, sewers, schools, hospitals, and other real capital owned and operated by their governments.

One of the most important insights of postwar economics has been the discovery of the quantitative and qualitative significance of social capital in the form of education, health, and knowledge. In principle, such capital formation should also be financed by borrowing so that the efficient intertemporal allocation of resources will be assured. However, I recommend that such spending on human and knowledge capital be financed from current revenue, preferably by means of a statute. In practice, it is very difficult to measure depreciation and therefore net capital formation resulting from these types of expenditures. This handicap would permit opportunities for political manipulation of the estimates of allowable exclusions from current spending limits. The efficiency costs of financing from current revenue are likely to be relatively minor relative to the potential costs of the political manipulations possible under the economically more appropriate approach.

The Rainy Day Fund

The proposition of a rainy day fund causes one to ask why it is preferable over a simple prohibition of all deficits. On the surface, the rainy day fund seems to complicate the process and open opportunities for political manipulation. There are, in fact, two main reasons for maintaining a rainy day fund.

The Difficulty of Maintaining a Continuously Balanced Budget

Budgets, by their very nature, can only be forecasts of the actual spending and revenues covering a certain length of time, typically a year. Actual spending and tax revenues are almost always different from those planned because of a host of random influences beyond the control of the government, such as the forces of nature, foreign economic forces, and business cycles.

These forecasting uncertainties ensure that maintaining a consistently balanced budget, although not impossible, would create undesirable inefficiencies. For instance, a temporary decrease in foreign demand for Canadian goods might reduce economic activity and tax revenues in a given period. The maintenance of the budget balance would require an immediate and corresponding decrease in spending on education, health, road maintenance, or similar programs, in order to make up for the assumed shortfall in tax revenues. Such spending cutbacks of essential programs are not efficient.

Another problem with attempting to balance every single budget is that budgets require the assumption of a finite time period over which the balance has to be achieved. But, in practice, tax revenues and expenditures cannot be equal every hour, day, or even week. Essentially, the proposal for the establishment of a rainy day fund selects the business cycle as the period over which a balanced budget must be achieved. The length of this period will have to be set in a statute after careful consideration of historic experience and economic theory. The period should be long enough to permit surpluses and deficits — caused by nature and other external circumstances — to offset each other and create a balance, much as they did during the long periods of time in Canadian history during which there was no net growth in the size of the debt.

Business Cycle Stabilization

The second reason why a rainy day fund is desirable is found in modern macroeconomic theory. In particular, the flexibility of a rainy day fund permits built-in stabilizers to reduce the size of business cycle fluctuations. For instance, cyclical decreases and increases in demand by consumers and investors can be offset, to some degree, by the complementary increase and decrease in government spending due to cyclically variable outlays under unemployment and other social insurance programs. Similarly, cyclical variations in tax payments will affect the after-tax income of consumers and investors and result in more stable aggregate demand.

In practice, it is difficult to assess whether surpluses and deficits are cyclical or the function of fundamental structural changes that generate a permanent change in spending levels and taxation revenues. For this reason, an initially balanced spending and taxation program could easily lead to unexpected growth or depletion of the rainy day fund during a business cycle, and governments should have the opportunity to correct minor fluctuations in their subsequent budgets.

Achieving Balance with the Rainy Day Fund

I propose that, when the depletion of the rainy day fund approaches a zero balance, the government be required to take corrective action by lowering spending, raising taxes, or both. Total depletion of the fund would trigger the dissolution of Parliament. On the other hand, excessively high funds, at something like 10 percent of total spending, should trigger adjustments to taxation and spending programs to eliminate the excess. Increased spending, of course, has to be considered in the light of the limitation on the permitted level.

It would only be a lucky coincidence if the rainy day system for cyclically balanced budgets came into operation at the beginning of a boom, thus permitting the accumulation of funds. At any other time, setting aside the funds would require immediate and economically undesirable changes in taxation and spending.

For this reason, the rainy day fund would probably have to be endowed initially with a certain sum of money. Unfortunately, this would have to be raised by the sale of government securities and an increase in the government debt. However, because the rainy day fund can use its endowment to buy government securities, the net debt in the hands of the public would remain unchanged by such a course of action.

Problems in the
Design of Restraint Provisions

Penalties

One fundamental objection to the use of constitutional limitations on spending and deficits consists of the lack of obvious mechanisms for punishing violators. Proponents of this argument claim that constitutions can make many demands that may not be met. For instance many totalitarian countries assure civil liberties and *habeas corpus* in their constitutions, yet the citizens of these countries enjoy none. Such regimes would certainly disregard a provision demanding that they call an election upon exhaustion of a rainy day fund — just as they violate the civil rights of their citizens.

But Canada is anything but a totalitarian country. Canada has a long history of democratic and responsible government acting with due process and within a universally respected legal framework. Constitutional spending limits, quite simply, would be obeyed. The judicial system could be used to establish when violations take place using the technical specifications that are outlined below. Penalties would be enforced.

Objections can also be raised concerning the severity of the proposed punishment. It may seem harsh to force an election call regardless of the particulars, especially if one considers that some violations may be due to circumstances beyond the control of the government or ruling coalition.

This argument falls flat, however, because the severity of the punishment would be taken into account when the permitted spending limits and the size of the rainy day fund are first established, such that a substantial margin of safety will exist. Studies of historic, cyclical swings in the growth rates of national income, mandatory spending, and tax revenues can provide reliable information for estimating appropriate spending limits and the size of a rainy day fund. After the initiation of the system, the threat of penalty assures that politicians will curb the growth in spending and taxation and maintain the rainy day fund as a margin of safety. Politicians who gamble with the safety margin in order to gain short-run benefits for themselves should, and will, bear the consequences of their actions.

Imposing mandatory election calls may seem an inefficient punishment because it removes from public service politicians with experience and dedication. On the other hand, the induction of new people into politics often brings substantial benefits. New ideas and ways of doing things will replace entrenched powers and symbiotic relationships between politicians and special-interest groups.

Fudging the Books

Creative accounting methods have long been used to lie with statistics and thus alter the apparent health of governments. It seems obvious that future governments will attempt to fudge their books in order to avoid the intent of the constitutional limitations. The most blatant of these methods are to shift expenditure and revenue items between accounting periods, to redefine investment and consumption expenditures, to move activities into and out of the public sector, and to use varying valuation criteria in assessing assets and liabilities.

The use of such creative accounting can be a serious matter. However, its quantitative influence can be limited by the application of a simple rule used by taxation authorities in all countries. Agents can choose among a set of accounting principles and, under certain conditions, such as the opening of a new business, can switch from one to the other. However, once a rule has been adopted, it cannot be changed.

Under such a system, initial opportunities for creative accounting will exist, especially when the constitutional restraint provisions are first made operational. However, within a short period of time these opportunities will disappear and the intent of the restraints will be achieved. The Canadian auditor general can be charged with the policing of the government's accounting system and a judiciary can be made responsible for settling disputes and determining fines and corrective measures.

The Need for Statutes

In economics and politics, nothing is ever quite as simple as it first appears. The preceding discussion shows that the implementation of constitutional limitations on government spending levels and deficits will be a rather complex process. A clear and simple outline of restraint principles in the Constitution will have to be supplemented by a substantial set of statutes for fixing levels and specifying processes through which the intent of the constitutional clause can be realized.

The need for such statutes detracts from the attractiveness of the basic restraint proposals. They will invariably open the gate for the politicization of the restraint program, providing opportunities for politicians to cater to special-interest groups and giving the judiciary the power to influence the outcome of restraint by its decisions. As well, there exists the danger that Parliament might manipulate these statutes to avoid the intent of the restraint provisions. However, this danger can be reduced by the appointment of a permanent panel of independent, quasi-judicial experts responsible for assessing the impact of these statutes and generally overseeing the implementation of the constitutional restraint provisions.[39]

Summary and Conclusions

This study proposes to enshrine in Canada's Constitution clauses designed to limit the level and deficits of the federal and provincial

---

39 The state of Delaware has created such a panel of independent experts to make economic forecasts that are discussed widely and used by the government in the design of its budgets. Details on the operation and success of this panel are found in Pierre DuPont, "Executive Summary of Delaware's Financial Controls" (Dover, Delaware: Office of the Governor, no date): "Prior to 1977 [the year in which the panel was created], the State had overestimated revenue time and again, in several years by as much as 15 percent. Successful revenue and expenditure forecasting has provided a sound basis for financial decisions. At no time have the revenue forecasts deviated more than two percent from actual collections" (ibid., p. 2).

governments. Violation of these requirements would automatically invoke the dissolution of the responsible legislature and the calling of an election.

This proposal has the potential to reduce excessive spending levels and deficits, thus protecting the economic right of Canadians to the fruits of their labor and investments and eliminating a threat to the democratic system of government. The growth in spending of recent years directly reduces the income of Canadians because it is wasteful and does nothing to raise the efficiency of the economy. This wastefulness is the result of the actions of unethical politicians who cater to special-interest groups in order to obtain their support for upcoming reelections.

Spending deficits crowd out private investment and require ever-increasing rates of taxation, both of which reduce economic growth and burden future generations. Deficit spending seems to be out of control, partly because of powerful special-interest groups and partly because of a breakdown of an historic public stricture of such policies.

Technological innovations that drastically lower the cost of organization and political lobbying have spurred on the growth of special-interest-group power. Only constitutional spending limitations can effectively curb this power by imposing on legislators a budget constraint and, thus, a need to be selective when distributing society's resources.

The demands for Quebec independence and the resulting federal government proposals for the revision of the Constitution have opened a window of opportunity for the inclusion of spending restraints. Quebec separatists have long used the existence of the federal deficit to justify independence. Yet they also oppose, as an infringement of Quebec sovereignty, the proposals of the federal government to coordinate federal and provincial fiscal policies. The adoption of constitutional spending restraints would destroy the validity of the first argument and eliminate the need for the controversial coordination. Thus, constitutional spending limits can be used to further the cause of Canadian unity.

I believe that the relatively minor problems of implementation will not eliminate the merit of the proposed constitutional restraints. The existence and successful operation of such restrictions in the United States suggests that the potential benefits will far outweigh any difficulties, costs, or risks. In all likelihood, these restraints will engender great benefits for Canadian society in the form of protection of economic rights and of the democratic system itself.

[13]

The Canadian Journal of Higher Education, Vol. XI-1, 1981
La revue canadienne d'enseignement supérieur, Vol. XI-1, 1981

Canadian Economists' Citation and Publication Records*

HERBERT G. GRUBEL†

ABSTRACT

This paper uses the Social Science Citation Index *to count the number of citations received and publications made by all economists teaching at Canadian universities in 1975.*

It is shown that the top decile of individuals received 72 per cent of all citations and 50 per cent received none. The University of British Columbia and Simon Fraser University departments of economics have the highest and second-highest average citation counts of all Canadian universities, respectively. The age-profile of citations, self-citation propensities and the journals of publication are analysed from a sub-sample of data

RESUMÉ

Cet article utilise le Social Science Citation Index *pour relever le nombre de citations reçues et de publications au crédit de tous les économistes qui enseignaient dans les universités canadiennes durant l'année 1975.*

Il est démontré que le décile supérieur d'individus a reçu 72 pour cent de toutes les citations et que 50 pour cent en ont reçu aucune. Les départments d'économique des universités de la Colombie-Britanique et Simon Fraser ont respectivement le plus grand et le deuxième plus grand nombres moyens de citations de toutes les universités canadiennes. L'aspect temporel des citations, les propensions à l'auto-citation et les revues de publication sont analisés à l'aide d'un sous-échantillon de données.

Since 1974, the publication of the *Social Science Citation Index*[1] has made it practical to use citation and publication counts for individual economists as supplementary information in decisions about hiring, promotion and tenure of professors, the allocation of resources among and to university departments and the choice of university departments for study or work, much as has been done for many years in the physical sciences. One problem in the use of these counts for individuals is the absence of any information

* The work on this paper was supported by grant S75-1194 from the Canada Council. I have received helpful comments on an earlier draft by P. Copes and J. Vanderkamp.

† Department of Economics, Simon Fraser University.

about such counts for a large number of social scientists by which individual records can be put into perspective. It is the main purpose of this paper to provide such a standard through the analysis of the distribution of publication and citation counts for all Canadian academic economists and subsets of economists in individual departments of economics. However, the data also provide some useful information about the relative research productivity of individual university departments as of the middle of the 1970's. The paper also provides basic information which can be used in the future to study trends in publication and citation records, to compare the records of Canadian economists with those of other subsets drawn from different countries or areas of specialization and to compare economists with groups of scientists from other fields.

In Part I of this paper the purpose and merit of publication and citation studies are considered in the light of similar work in the natural sciences that has been going on for over a decade. Part II discusses the nature and sources of the data underlying this study. Part III considers the characteristics of the total population. In Part IV, the records of individual Canadian university departments of economics are presented. The age and other characteristics of citations are studied in Part V. Part VI presents and analyses the list of journals in which Canadian economists publish. Individuals with the largest number of citations and publications are identified in Part VII. The paper closes with a summary and some implications of the analysis.

THE PURPOSE AND MERIT OF PUBLICATION AND CITATION COUNTS

The popularity of studying publication and citation counts of individual scientists and institutions is evidenced by the large number of publications on this subject, a selection of which is shown in the attached bibliography. However, popularity is an unreliable guide to scientific merit and the field has a number of sceptics and critics. (See Hanson and Weisbrod, (1972) and Comfort, (1970)). Anyone exposed to, or involved in, academic politics knows all the arguments about the merit of quality against quantity of publications. The journals *Science* and *Nature* contain a number of letters to the editor in which scientists point out why citation counting may be an imperfect method for assessing a scientist's productivity or the importance of his contribution to knowledge.[2]

Whatever may be the appeal of theoretical arguments about the merit of citation and publication counts, basically it is an empirical question whether they are a useful measure of scientists' contributions to knowledge and the prestige and influence derived from them. Several studies have attempted to answer this empirical question. Clark (1957) conducted a survey of psychologists and on the basis of about 1,200 replies constructed a ranking of U.S. psychologists according to their peers' informal evaluation of the merit of their work and the resultant prestige and influence. Clark then correlated this ranking with rankings based on objective measures of productivity and prestige, such as membership in professional associations, number of publications, listing in Who's Who, editorship of professional journals and citations. He found the greatest correlation of informal peer judgements with the number of citations (R = .67). In another study, Hagstrom (1971) attempted to explain the well-known Cartter (1966) ratings of U.S. graduate schools, which are based on surveys of a relatively large number of department chairmen in every field. Like Clark, the author used many other objectively measurable characteristics that can be expected to reflect or determine quality of university departments on a priori grounds. Of the about 12 such characteristics analysed, both the number of publications and citations dominate the rest, but as a result of a multiple regression result the author concludes "Citations to published work are a better predictor of department prestige than is quantity of articles published."(Hagstrom, 1971, p. 373).[3]

The Use of Citation Counts

Students and potential users of citation counts apparently have been convinced by the available evidence that the technique represents a low-cost and sufficiently reliable technique to find "major uses in decisions at the level of national science policy, as an adjunct to the peer-review process, and in evaluating the performance of individual scientists". (Wade, 1975, p. 429). The author of this quotation notes that the U.S. National Science Foundation already uses citation counts in its decisions about the allocation of research funds in chemistry, especially to aid in reducing awards to individuals who write good proposals but have a poor record of scientific achievement and increasing awards to those who are not good writers of proposals but have a superior record of citations.

SOURCES OF DATA

The study was made feasible by the availability of the annual volumes of the *Social Science Citation Index* (SSCI) for the years 1970-76. It is produced by the private Institute for Scientific Information (ISI) of Philadelphia which manipulates electronically citation information contained in hundreds of journals from the social sciences published in many countries. Two ISI publications are relevant for this study. First, an alphabetic listing of authors shows their journal publications during a given year.[4] Book reviews are identified and are excluded from the counts prepared in this study. Papers with multiple authors are identifiable for each author. They are counted as one publication for each of the multiple authors.

Second, an alphabetical listing shows for every author the citations that were made to his works, including the name and publication in which the citation appeared. Importantly, while the publication counts cover only journals, the citations from journals cover all publications by the individuals, including books, edited works, government reports, mimeographed papers and dissertations. However, unfortunately citations to papers with multiple authors are attributed only to the first listed author. This fact introduces a bias of unknown but possibly serious magnitude into the ranking of individuals. In the ranking of departments, on the other hand, there should be no serious bias introduced since the incidence of multiple authorship can reasonably be assumed to be distributed normally across departments.

The collection and processing of the data was subject to a more than normal margin of error because the clerical work in searching and transferring the information is especially tedious. Also, there are sources of error resulting from sloppy citation habits, such as the use of only one or wrong initials, and from the fact that there are some individuals that have the same names and initials. Double-checking by two different clerks of citations to individuals who in the first run showed up as having had more than 3 citations during the period was used in an attempt to minimize clerical errors.

The number of social science journals fully surveyed by the SSCI is over 1,000. Furthermore, references to social scientists found in over 2,000 natural science journals are included. The journals cover those published in the United States and Canada as well as many other countries. Indicative of the broad coverage is the fact that the 1,502 publications by Canadians appeared in 233 different journals (see Section VI below).

The population of Canadian economists was defined as consisting of individuals who were listed on the faculties of the universities shown in Table 5 according to the *Commonwealth Universities Yearbook*, 1976, giving the status as of the middle of 1975. Part-time lecturers and teaching assistants were excluded.

CHARACTERISTICS OF THE TOTAL POPULATION

Table 1 shows the frequency distribution of citations and articles for the entire population of 768 Canadian academic economists, which in turn is summarized in Table 2 by the percentages by deciles, both absolute and cumulative. As can be seen, the top decile of Canadian academic economists accounts for 72.3 and 43.7 per cent of all citations and articles, respectively, while 50 per cent have not been cited or have not published at all. These results are similar to those found by Cole and Cole (1972) for physicists, though in all studies of this type it is difficult to obtain a list of names representing the full population, since those who do not publish or are not cited do not appear in the literature.[5]

However, the frequency distributions of Canadian academic economists' citation and publication counts do not conform with Lotka's Law (Lotka, 1926), which has been found to hold in many scientific disciplines. The law says that $N = K/n^2$, where K is the number of people publishing one article, n is the number of articles published by each of the individuals numbered N. Thus, according to Lotka's Law, the fact that 114 Canadian economists have published one article (see Table 1), implies that 28.5 should have published two, 13 published three, about 8 published four, etc. In reality, as can be seen from Table 1, the distribution is much less skewed. The same conclusions hold for the frequency distribution of citations. Perhaps this result is due to the fact that the present sample consists of academics with high publication propensities while Lotka's Law applies to professionals in all types of employment. Very likely, the results simply invalidate Lotka's Law, which has no theoretical foundation at all.

Canadian and Global Performance

In an attempt to put the population of Canadian economists' records into a global perspective, a world-wide population of international trade economists was defined by obtaining 2,813 names of individuals who published at least one article that entered category 400 in the *Journal of Economic Literature* during the period 1970-76 and by comparing them with the 1,158 names of persons who identified themselves as specialists in international economics (catagory 400) in the American Economics Association *Handbook* (1974). Of those 1,158 specialists only 371, or 32 per cent showed up as having published according to the list derived from the *Journal of Economic Literature*. Since about 50 per cent of all Canadians published at least one paper, the comparison with the population of international economics specialists favors Canadian economists. However, the results of this comparison are probably biased since the number of journals surveyed by the *Journal of Economic Literature* is much smaller than that included in the *SSCI*.

For the population of international trade economists who have published at least three articles according to the *Journal of Economic Literature* (N = 455), citations were counted for the period 1970-76 and analyzed in Grubel (1980). The list is headed by P.A.

31 Canadian Economists' Citation and Publication Records

Table 1

Frequency Distribution of the Number of Citations

and Articles, 1970-76

	Absolute Numbers of		
Citations	Persons	Publications	Persons
Above 200	3	17	1
199–100	15	15	2
99–90	3	14	1
89–80	5	13	3
79–70	4	12	4
69–60	5	11	8
59–50	6	10	7
49–40	10	9	9
39–30	16	8	4
29–20	34	7	15
19	3	6	25
18	8	5	37
17	5	4	40
16	4	3	60
15	5	2	90
14	7	1	114
13	10	0	348
12	6		768
11	11		
10	12		
9	10		
8	11		
7	27		
6.	13		
5	20		
4	14		
3	30		
2	44		
1	71		
0	356		
	768		

Source: Compiled by the author from citations in annual volumes of the Social Science Citation Index, 1970-76. Names of persons from Commonwealth Universities Handbook, 1976.

Samuelson and H.G. Johnson with 2,898 and 1,498 citations, respectively. These two men are followed by five individuals with 613-682 citations. Canadian economists among the top 70 show up in 15th place, 37th, 53rd, 67th and 69th. Since Canada's population is about 10 per cent of that of the United States, random geographic distribution of a combined U.S.-Canada population with equal productivity should have produced the observed fact that about 10 per cent should be Canadian. While these results are sensitive to the field studied and the cut-off point chosen on the list (among the top 60 there are only 3 Canadians and none among the top 14), the results reported here may be interpreted tentatively as suggesting an approximate equality in the productivity of U.S. and Canadian academic economists.

32 Herbert G. Grubel

Table 2

Inequality Measures of Citations and Articles of

768 Canadian Economists 1970-76

Deciles Persons	Citations				Articles			
	Numbers		Percent		Numbers		Percent	
	N	Cumul.	Total	Cumul.	N	Cumul.	Total	Cumul.
1	4730	4730	72.3	72.3	636	636	43.9	43.9
2	989	5719	15.1	87.4	968	968	22.9	66.8
3	490	6209	8.5	94.9	1182	1182	14.8	81.6
4	228	6437	3.5	98.4	1328	1328	10.1	91.7
5	92	6529	1.4	99.8	1405	1405	5.3	97.0
6	16	6545	0.2	100.0	1448	1448	3.0	100.0
7	0		0					
8	0		0					
9	0		0					
10	0		0					

Gini Coefficient: .82   Gini Coefficient: .67

Source: Same as Table 1.

The Cause of the Skewed Distribution

Generally, the extreme skewness of the frequency distribution of publication and citation counts represents a puzzle, since presumably practically all economists in the sample have a Ph.D. and therefore the basic qualifications to be contributors to the stock of knowledge through publications. Furthermore, all studies of single, measurable human abilities and characteristics show them to be normally distributed. Allison and Stewart (1974) analyze this question theoretically and empirically. On the theoretical level, they cite work which suggests that while single skills are distributed normally, combinations of skills are required to perform complicated tasks and the combinations determine productivity multiplicatively. (See Shockley (1957) and Aitchison and Brown (1957)). Since the publication of scientific work involves a more complicated task and requires the combination of a large number of specific skills and characteristics than does study leading to a Ph.D., the observed skewness theoretically is consistent with other empirical knowledge.

In addition to the purely theoretical explanation, Allison and Stewart also postulate that the reward structure of science reinforces the skewness of the distribution through what they call a process of cumulative advantage. This process is reflected in the fact that the award of resources, the invitation to conferences, journal editorships, etc., tend to favor productive individuals, further adding to their differential productivity. An empirical analysis of the Gini coefficients of scientists from several different disciplines in certain age-cohorts determined by the time since receipt of the Ph.D. showed that the degree of inequality increases through time.[6]

33 Canadian Economists' Citation and Publication Records

ANALYSIS OF DEPARTMENT STATISTICS

Table 3 presents data on citation and publication counts averaged by university departments, according to economists' affiliation as of the middle of 1975. The first column shows the number of faculty in each department and the following columns show for each department the total, mean, variance, Gini-coefficient (for faculties with more than 21 members only) and rank by average, first for citations and then for publications. The correlation coefficient (R^2) for the citations and publications is .65

As is well known, the mean is often a misleading measure of the average of a distribution, especially if it is as skewed as the one for all economists noted above. To deal with the problems inherent in the case of the mean, Table 3 contains the variance and Gini coefficients characterizing the distribution for each department. However, the biases introduced by the use of the mean are apparent much more directly through the data contained in Table 4, the number of citations received by the median and 80th percentile member of each faculty. Because the median was zero for many departments for reasons obvious from the fact that about 50 percent of all economists have zero citations, and because both the medians and percentile measures are not suitable measures in small departments, the list in Table 3 contains data on only the top 12 departments, though the rankings in each column are based on the full population of departments.

The most notable fact apparent from Table 4 is that the top 12 universities by the mean are also the top 12 by the 80th percentile, while by the median the University of Ottawa and Dalhousie University move from the top 12 into 13-18th rank. These two universities are replaced by the Royal Military College in 9th place and Mt. St. Vincent University in 10-11th rank. The fact that the latter 2 departments have faculties of 8 and 2 members only shows one of the difficulties in using the median as a measure of the average.

By all three measures the University of British Columbia heads the list consistently, while other universities show some changes in ranking. Most notable differences in the ranks by mean and median are that the University of Toronto moved from its 6th place by the mean rank, into a tie for second place with Simon Fraser University in the median rank and that Carleton University and University of Montreal, respectively, moved up from 8th to 4th and 12th to 5th. Lowering of rank finds Queens University drop from 3rd place by the mean to 7th by the median and the University of Western Ontario from 4th to 6th. The rankings by means and 80th percentile are remarkably consistent, with a move up of 3 by the University of Ottawa and the University of Montreal and a move down of 2 by Simon Fraser University and Queens University.

The main message implicit in Table 4 seems to be that the leading departments are characterized by both the presence of "stars", giving rise to large means and of a substantial proportion of faculty with high citation counts resulting in large medians and 80th percentile values. The University of British Columbia's position of leadership is strengthened not only by its consistent top ranking by all these measures of average, but also the absolute number of citations by all three measures in relation to those of any other Canadian university.

Returning to Table 3, it is worth noting the last column which shows the difference between the university's rank on the citation and publication counts. The interpretation of these figures is that large positive numbers indicate that in the future the department's ranking by citation counts is likely to improve and large negative numbers indicate the

34 Herbert G. Grubel

Table 3

Citation and Publication Averages by Universities

Name of University	Faculty No.	Citations Total	Citations Average	Citations Variance	Citations Gini	Citations Rank Average	Publications Total	Publications Average	Publications Variance	Publications Gini	Publications Rank Average	Difference* Rank Cit.-Rank Publ.
Univ. British Columbia	35	1,114	31.83	43.63	0.60	1	130	3.71	3.26	0.45	3	-2
Simon Fraser Univ.	24	700	29.17	67.41	0.45	2	95	3.96	4.31	0.51	1	1
Queens Univ.	36	905	25.14	78.90	0.74	3	69	1.92	2.66	0.63	14	-11
Univ. Western Ontario	39	895	22.95	41.25	0.72	4	149	3.82	3.00	0.42	2	2
Univ. Ottawa	18	375	20.83	45.82	-	5	35	1.94	2.92	-	13	-8
Univ. Toronto	64	1,287	20.11	31.94	0.65	6	198	3.09	3.28	0.55	6	0
Carleton Univ.	34	579	17.03	24.25	0.65	7	110	3.24	3.95	0.58	4	3
McGill Univ.	25	312	12.48	25.55	0.76	8	37	1.48	2.20	0.63	20	-12
McMaster Univ.	29	344	11.86	24.97	0.71	9	90	3.10	3.58	0.59	5	4
Dalhousie Univ.	19	221	11.63	32.17	-	10	33	1.74	2.42	-	17-18	-7.5
Univ. Guelph	18	182	10.11	25.85	-	11	36	2.00	3.05	-	11-12	-0.5
Univ. Montreal	20	154	7.70	8.76	-	12	56	2.80	2.33	-	7	5
Memor. Univ. Newfdld.	10	69	6.90	13.40	-	13	20	2.00	3.56	-	11-12	1.5
York Univ.	24	150	6.25	17.60	0.76	14	40	1.67	1.44	0.48	19	-5
Univ. Windsor	20	112	5.60	11.02	-	15	44	2.20	2.80	-	9	6
Univ. Victoria	12	60	5.00	7.15	-	16	26	2.17	2.08	-	10	6
Univ. Alberta	27	130	4.80	11.99	0.79	17	47	1.74	2.98	0.70	17-18	-0.5
Univ. Waterloo	15	64	4.27	8.69	-	18	20	1.33	1.96	-	22	-4
Univ. Lethbridge	4	16	4.00	8.00	-	19	4	1.00	1.41	-	25-26	-6.5
Univ. Laval	20	64	3.20	6.43	-	20	48	2.40	2.44	-	8	12
Royal Milit. College	3	24	3.00	3.96	-	21	9	1.13	1.36	-	24	-3
Univ. Calgary	22	45	2.05	3.12	0.65	22	41	1.86	2.61	0.60	16	6
Mt. St. Vincent Univ.	2	4	2.00	2.83	-	23	2	1.00	0.00	-	25-26	-2.5
Univ. Manitoba	34	63	1.85	4.69	0.78	24	25	0.74	1.50	0.78	28	-4
Univ. Saskatchewan	26	44	1.69	5.26	0.85	25	14	0.54	0.95	0.71	33	-8
Univ. Sherbrooke	11	16	1.46	2.77	-	26	14	1.27	1.68	-	23	3
U. Quebec @ Montreal	19	24	1.26	4.13	-	27	26	1.37	3.08	-	21	6
Univ. New Brunswick	13	15	1.15	3.87	-	28	3	0.23	0.83	-	37	-9
Lakehead Univ.	10	9	0.90	1.85	-	29	19	1.90	2.28	-	15	14
Mt. Allison Univ.	9	8	0.89	2.32	-	30	5	0.56	0.88	-	32	-2
Concordia Univ.	29	23	0.85	1.83	0.78	31	19	0.70	1.24	0.78	30	1
Brandon Univ.	4	2	0.50	1.00	-	32	0	0.00	0.00	-	40-44	-10
St. Mary's Univ.	7	3	0.43	0.79	-	33	3	0.43	0.54	-	34	- 1
Univ. Winnipeg	8	3	0.38	1.06	-	34	6	0.75	2.12	-	27	7
St. Francis Xavier Univ.	6	2	0.33	0.82	-	35	6	0.00	0.00	-	40-44	- 7
Wilfrid Laurier Univ.	12	4	0.33	0.65	-	36	7	0.58	1.44	-	31	5
Laurentian Univ.	9	2	0.22	0.67	-	37	0	0.00	0.00	-	40-44	- 5
Bishop Univ.	5	1	0.20	0.45	-	38	0	0.00	0.00	-	40-44	- 4
Trent Univ.	7	1	0.14	0.38	-	39	5	0.71	1.11	-	29	10
Univ. of Regina	9	1	0.11	0.33	-	40	3	0.33	0.71	-	36	4
Univ. of Moncton	8	0	0.00	0.00	-	41-44	3	0.38	0.74	-	35	7.5
Acadia Univ.	5	0	0.00	0.00	-	41-44	1	0.20	0.45	-	38	4.5
Univ. Pr. Edw. Isld.	6	0	0.00	0.00	-	41-44	1	0.17	0.41	-	39	3.5
Brock Univ.	8	0	0.00	0.00	-	41-44	0	0.00	0.00	-	40-44	0.5
Sum or (average)	768	8,027	(10.45)	(30.89)	0.82		1,493	(1.94)	(2.79)	0.67		

Source: Same as Table 1.

Note: * Note on last column: In case of ties, difference is between midpoints.

opposite. This interpretation is based on the fact documented below, that publications lead to citations with a lag, so that high publication ranks may at a later time lead to high citation ranks and vice versa.

CHARACTERISTICS OF CITATIONS

A stratified sample of 1/7th of all citations to the writings of Canadian economists was analyzed to establish facts in three areas: the distribution of citations between different forms of publications, their age profiles, and the frequency of self-citations.

35 Canadian Economists' Citation and Publication Records

Table 4

Rankings of Top Departments by Alternative

Measures of Average for Citations

Department	Mean	Rank	Median	Rank	80th Percentile	Rank
Univ. British Columbia	31.9	1	11	1	75	1
Simon Fraser Univ.	29.2	2	9	2-3	34	4
Queens Univ.	25.1	3	4	7	29.5	5
Univ. West. Ontario	23.0	4	5	6	36	3
Univ. Ottawa	20.8	5	1	13-18	41	2
Univ. Toronto	20.1	6	9	2-3	23	6-7
Carleton Univ.	17.0	7	8	4	23	6-7
McGill Univ.	12.5	8	2	10-11	16.5	8
McMaster Univ.	11.9	9	3.5	8	14	10
Dalhousie Univ.	11.6	10	1	13-18	7.5	11
Guelph Univ.	10.1	11	1.5	12	7	12
Univ. Montreal	7.7	12	5.5	5	16	9

Source: Same as Table 1.

Note: Ranks are based on full population of universities.

Table 5 shows that of the 1152 citations originating in journals 826, or about 72 per cent, made reference to journal articles or mimeographed discussion papers and 326, or about 28 per cent, to books, theses, government reports or anthologies. Unfortunately, the basic distribution of total writings published in these two different categories is not known so that no inferences can be made about the relative intensity of citations to journal and other forms of publications. However, the data do suggest that the publication counts shown above for individuals and departments are incomplete because they cover only journals. If there are different propensities of individuals to publish in forms other than journal articles, therefore, the rankings are biased. No attempts were made to correct for these biases. It could be that they account for some of the pronounced differences in rankings among university departments made according to citations and publications shown in Table 3.

The age-profile of citations is also shown in Table 5, using as the basic statistic the number of years between publication of the cited work and citations to it. A lag of zero years arises in cases of simultaneous publication years and when the reference is to work "to be published". As can be seen from Table 5, journal articles tend to be cited with a somewhat greater lag after publication than books, etc. This is a surprising result which may be explained by the fact that the latter forms of publication tend to have a longer

36 Herbert G. Grubel

Table 5

Age Profile of Citations of Canadian Economists

Number of Years Between Publication and Citation	Journals Discussion Papers			Books, Theses, cvts. Reports, Anthologies		
	N	%	Cum.%	N	%	Cum.%
0	30	3.6	3.6	17	5.2	5.2
1	89	10.8	14.4	54	16.6	21.8
2	107	13.0	27.4	66	20.2	42.0
3	141	17.1	44.5	40	12.3	54.3
4	107	13.0	57.5	38	11.7	66.0
5	76	9.2	66.7	19	5.8	71.8
6	42	5.1	71.8	10	3.1	74.9
7	46	5.6	77.4	13	4.0	78.9
8	31	3.8	81.2	9	2.8	81.7
9	39	4.7	85.9	11	3.4	85.1
10	38	4.6	90.5	13	4.0	89.1
11	10	1.2	91.7	14	4.3	93.4
12	5	0.6	92.3	2	0.6	94.0
13	3	0.4	92.7	5	1.5	95.5
14	10	1.2	93.9	?	0.6	91.1
15	7	0.8	94.7	-	-	-
16	17	2.1	96.8	7	2.1	98.2
17	5	0.6	97.4	2	0.6	98.8
18	9	1.1	98.5	-	-	-
19	6	0.7	99.2	-	-	-
20	4	0.5	99.7	-	-	-
22	1	0.1	99.8	1	0.3	99.1
25	1	0.1	99.9	-	-	-
33	2	0.2	100.0	-	-	-
38				2	0.6	99.7
49				1	0.3	100.0
	826	100.0		326	100.0	

Notes and Sources: Sample of one seventh of all citations to Canadian economists 1970–76. Stratification achieved by use of list of names arranged in descending order of total citations received. For individuals ranked 1, 8, 15, 22, ... the year 1970 was used. For those ranked 2, 9, 16, 23 ... the year 1971 was used, and so on for 7 years.

lag between completion and publication, leaving more time for them to be circulated in manuscript and for their contents to be discussed informally and at meetings of specialists.

The data of Table 5 imply that scientific knowledge in economics is subject to rapid obsolescence. One half of all references are to journal articles published less than 4.0

years before and for the other forms of publication the figure is 2.6 years. Only about 10 per cent of all references are to works published more than 10 years before. Of course, the data refer to publications of only presently active Canadian economists, which sets an upper limit on the possible age of the citations in the sample. Perhaps this explains why the results differ from those found in some other studies. In a review of citation studies in different fields Broadus (1971) noted that in economics one analyst had found that 45 per cent of all citation were to works no older than 10 years while another found that 50 per cent were to works published within 6 years. Lovell (1973) found that in the year 1965, 46.5 per cent of citations in economics journals were to works published in the preceding five years.

It is possible to consider the age-profile of citations to the works of individual economists and departments and compare them with the norms presented in Table 5, though this is not done here. On the one hand one could argue that average ages of citations greater than the norm imply that an author has made contributions with a greater durability than average. This fact influences estimates of the quality of a person's life-time productivity. On the other hand, it is not certain that one can draw any particularly useful inferences about the relative productivity of two individuals with the same number of life-time citations to their work, if the average age of the citations of one is greater than that of the other. One simply may have produced more papers than the other, but by the criterion of citation counts assumed to measure influence as perceived by others, they have done equally well.

One question often raised in connection with citation counts is the frequency of self-citations. In the sample under consideration there are 221 individuals, 50 or 23 per cent of which have one or more self-citations. As can be seen from Table 6, about 18 per cent of all citations are to own work on average, with a wide dispersion around this mean. Further analysis of self-citation frequencies shows that of the eleven individuals who owed 100 per cent of citations to themselves, 8 had only one citation altogether, one each had only two, three and seven. One person owed 17 out of 18 citations to his own publications. However, there does not seem to be any correlation between total citations and the frequency of self-citations. The observed behavior seems to be determined by personal preferences.

JOURNALS OF PUBLICATION

Table 7 shows the journals in which the 1502 publications of Canadian academic economists appeared during the period 1970-76. It comes as no surprise that the *Canadian Journal of Economics* contained 177 or 11.7 per cent and the French language *Canadian L'Actualite Economique* 91 or 6.1 per cent of all publications by Canadians. Surprising is, however, the large number of journals, 233, in which Canadians have published a mean of 6.45 articles. The distribution of articles per journal is quite skewed, with 66 journals having only one publication and the top 18, or 7.7 per cent of all journals accounting for about 50 per cent of all publications.

The international nature of much of the work by Canadian economists is reflected in the fact that out of the top 29 journals only five are Canadian, two are published in Britain *(Economica, Economic Journal)*, three in Continental Europe *(Welwirtschaftliches Archiv, Kyklos and Étude Internationales)*, one in Australia *(Economic Record)* and the rest in the United States. Only three of the 29 journals have a French title, though some publish in both French and English, such as the *Canadian Journal of Economics* and

38 Herbert G. Grubel

Table 6

Self-Citation Percentages

Percentages of Self-Citations	Number of Individuals	Total Sample Self/Total Citations
1 - 9	4	
10 - 19	6	142/799 = 18 percent
20 - 29	7	
30 - 39	3	
40 - 49	3	
50 - 59	5	
60 - 69	5	
70 - 79	1	
80 - 89	1	
90 - 99	1	
100	11	

Notes and Sources: sample of one seventh of all citations to Canadian economists 1970-76. Stratification achieved by use of list of names arranged in descending order of total citations received. For individuals ranked 1, 8, 15, 22, ... the year 1970 was used. For those ranked 2, 9, 16, 23 ... the year 1971 was used, and so on for 7 years.

Kyklos. Finally, it should be noted that for unexplained reasons the journal *Canadian Public Policy/Analyse de Politiques* has not been covered by the *SSCI* since it commenced publication in Winter 1974. Since this journal has become an important publication outlet for Canadian economists, the analyses of journals as well as of citations and publications of individuals and departments above are not complete.

CITATION AND PUBLICATION COUNTS FOR INDIVIDUALS

For some purposes of analysis and policy it is useful to know the names of individuals who have received the largest number of citations and published the most journal articles. The names of Canadian economists with more than 100 citations during the period 1970-76 are shown in Table 8. Remarkable in this table is the dominance of persons from the University of British Columbia, which of course explains the institutions performance noted in Table 3.

Since there exists an often substantial lag between publications and their recognition through citations, highly productive individuals may not be found in Table 8 but could be expected to do so if a similar table were compiled in later years. Table 9 contains the names of persons who, during the period 1970-76 had at least 10 publications but fewer than 100 citations.

It should be noted that the rankings of individuals by citations is subject to the bias

39 Canadian Economists' Citation and Publication Records

Table 7

Journals in Which Canadian Economists Published

Rank		Publication	
		Number	Percent
1)	Canadian Journal of Economics	177	11.7
2)	L'Actualité Économique	91	6.1
3)	Econometrica	66	4.4
4)	American Economic Review	56	3.7
5)	Review of Economics and Statistics	51	3.4
6)	Industrial Relations Industrielle	44	2.9
7)	Journal of Political Economy	40	2.7
8)	Journal of Economic Inquiry (Western Economic Journal)	27	1.8
9)	Journal of Finance	25	1.6
10)	Economica	24	1.6
11)	Canadian Public Administration	24	1.6
12)	Southern Economic Journal	21	1.4
13)	Journal of the American Statistical Association	21	1.4
14)	Public Finance	20	1.3
15)	Land Economics	20	1.3
16)	Journal of Regional Science	18	1.2
17)	Journal of Economic History	16	1.1
18)	Economic Record	16	1.1
19)	Quarterly Journal of Economics	15	1.0
20)	Economic Journal	15	1.0
21)	Journal of International Economics	15	1.0
22)	Weltwirtschaftliches Archiv	14	0.9
23)	American Journal of Agricultural Economics	14	0.9
24)	Kyklos	14	0.9
25)	Journal of Canadian Studies	13	0.9
26)	Economic Development and Cultural Change	12	0.8
27)	Industrial Relations	11	0.7
28)	Etudes Internationales	11	0.7
29)	Public Finance Quarterly	11	0.7

Frequencies for remaining journals:	Number of Journals	Publications
	3	10
	5	9
	11	8
	3	7
	10	6
	13	5
	17	4
	22	3
	30	2
	66	1

Total number of Journals   233
Publications   1502

noted above and arising from the fact that references to publications with multiple authors are given only to the first-named author. While this bias, as well as clerical errors, tend to cancel in the calculation of university department means and medians, they may distort the rankings of persons in the last two tables. Therefore, in interpreting these tables, it may be safer to consider them to contain the names of groups of most widely cited and publishing individuals rather than a precise ranking.

40 Herbert G. Grubel

Table 8

Individuals with over 100 Citations 1970-76

Name	University	Number of	
		Citations	Publications
Lipsey, R.G.	Queens	474	6
Grubel, H.G.	SFU	334	17
Laidler, D.E.W.	U. of W. Ontario	200	10
Higgins, B.H.	Ottawa	187	6
Archibald, G.C.	UBC	172	5
Breton, A.A.	Toronto	149	6
Marfels, C.T.	Dalhousie	140	8
Helliwell, J.F.	UBC	138	11
Scott, A.D.	UBC	126	4
Dales, J.H.	Toronto	120	2
Helleiner, G.	Toronto	120	7
Cragg, J.G.	UBC	115	11
Wannacott, R.J.	U. of W. Ontario	111	2
Vandercamp, J.	Guelph	110	5
Winch, D.M.	McMaster	110	3
Melvin, J.R.	U. of W. Ontario	108	12
Diewert, W.E.	UBC	105	10
Bird, R.M.	Toronto	103	9

Source: Same as Table 1.

Table 9

Individuals With More Than Nine Publications and
Fewer Than 100 Citations 1970-76

Name	University Affiliation	Number of	
		Articles	Citation
Maule, C.J.	Carleton	15	9
Chung, J.H.	Quebec @ Montreal	12	18
Adam, J.	Calgary	11	9
Casas, F.R.	Toronto	11	13
Palmer, J.P.	U.W. Ontario	11	5
Abouchar, A.	Toronto	10	18
Belanger, G.	Montreal	10	6

Source: Same as Table 1

41 Canadian Economists' Citation and Publication Records

SUMMARY AND CONCLUSIONS

This paper has analysed the citation and publication counts of Canadian economists as a whole and grouped by individual departments, which may be useful in combination with other information about individuals in tenure and promotion decisions by departments and universities and in the allocation of resources among departments within and between universities. Of particular interest is the result that such a very large percentage of all economists appear to be concentrating their energies on teaching, synthesis and administration rather than publication. University administrators may find the information about department rankings useful in intra university resource allocation strategies. Sociologists and other specialists in organizational behavior may find the results worth attempts to explain differences in departments' productivity. Agencies and governments granting resources for research and the development of centers of excellence may add the information in this paper to their data on which they base their decisions. Undergraduate, graduate students and faculty members may wish to choose their universities of study or employment keeping in mind the results of this study. The data on journals of publication provide useful insights into the relative popularity and prestige of these publications outlets.

FOOTNOTES

1. See Part II below for a detailed description of this publication.

2. References to these letters and the papers prompting them are not shown in the bibliography appended to this paper. They can be found in the bibliography in the front of the annual volumes of the *Social Science Citation Index*.

3. Further analysis in this tradition is found in Bayer and Folger (1966); Margolis (1967); Cole and Cole (1967) and (1972); Garfield (1970) and (1979); Roche and Smith (1978); Miller and Tollison (1975); Hogan (1973); Siegfried (1972); and Dean (1976), the last four of which deal with departments of economics ranking using measures other than citations.

4. Since 1975 this list also indicates whom the author has cited in these publications. No use was made of this information, though it could serve as a base of studies of citation networks among Canadians and with foreign centers of learning.

5. Allison and Stewart, 1974 give reference to 8 studies that have found such skewness in the distribution for other scientific disciplines. They also report that in these studies citation counts are more skewed than publication counts, just as in the case of Canadian economists.

6. The result could also be due to the more rapid growth in the stock of publications by scientists who were more productive initially and did not enjoy any cumulative advantage through the reward system. This proposition is valid clearly for the life-time citations used in the study but may or may not be significant for the publication Ginis which are based on the record of the preceding 5 years.

REFERENCES

Aitchison, J. and J.A.C. Brown. *The Lognormal Distribution*. Cambridge: Cambridge University Press, 1957.

Allison, F.D. and J.A. Stewart. Productivity differences among scientists: Evidence for accumulative advantage. *American Sociological Review*, 1974, 39, *4*, 596-606.

American Economics Association, *Handbook*. Menasha, Wisc.: American Economics Association, 1974.

Bayer, A.E. and J. Folger. Some correlates of a citation measure of productivity in science. *Sociology of Education*, 1966, 39, *4*, 381-390.

Billings, B.B. and G.J. Viksnins. The relative quality of economics journals: An alternative rating system. *Western Economic Journal*, 1972, 10, *4*, 467-469.

Bordo, M.D. and D. Landau. The pattern of citations in economic theory 1945-68: Towards a quantitative history of economic thought. *Carleton Economic Papers* (mimeo), 1974-08.

42 Herbert G. Grubel

Broadus, R.N. The literature of the social sciences: A survey of citation studies. *International Social Science Journal,* 1971, 23, *2,* 236-243.

Brookes, B.C. The growth, utility and obsolescence of scientific periodical literature. *Journal of Documentation,* 1970, 26, *4,* 283-294.

Bush, W.C., P.W. Hammelman and J.R. Staff.A quality index of economics journals. *Review of Economics and Statistics,* 1974, 56, *1,* 123-125.

Cartter, A.M. *An Assessment of Quality in Graduate Education.* Washington,D.C.: American Council on Education, 1966.

Cawkell, A.E. Science perceived through the science citation index. *Endeavor,* 1977, 1, *2,* 57-62.

Clark, K.E. *America's Psychologists: A Survey of a Growing Profession.* Washington, D.C.: American Psychological Association, 1957.

Cole, J. and S. Cole The Ortega hypothesis: Citation analysis suggests that only a few scientists contribute to scientific progress. *Science,* 1972, 178, 368-374.

Cole, S. and J.R. Cole Scientific output and recognition: A study in the operation of the reward system in science. *American Sociological Review,* 1967, 32, *3,* 377-390.

Comfort, A. Pop charts for science. *Nature,* 1970, 227, *5262,* 1069.

Dean, J.E. An alternative rating system for university economics departments. *Economic Inquiry,* 1976, 14, *1,* 146-153.

De Solla Price, D.J. *Little Science, Big Science.* New York, N.Y.: Columbia University Press, 1963.

Dieks, D. and H. Chang.Differences in impact of scientific publications: Some indices derived for citation analysis. *Social Studies of Science,* 1976, 6, *2,* 247-267.

Eagly, R.V. Economics journals as a communications network. *Journal of Economic Lterature,* 1975, 13, *3,* 878-888.

Frankena, M. and K. Bhatia.Canadian contributors to economics journals 1968-72. *Canadian Journal of Economics,* 1973, 6, *1,* 121-124.

Journal articles from Canadian economics departments, 1968-71. *Western Economic Journal,* 1972, 10, *3,* 352-353.

Garfield, E. Citation analysis as a tool in journal evaluation. *Science,* 1972, 178, *4060,* 471-479.

Citation indexing for studying science. *Nature,* 1970, 227, 669-671.

Citation Indexing: Its Theory and Application in Science, Technology and the Humanities. New York, N.Y.: J. Wiley and Sons, 1979.

Grubel, H.G. Citation counts for economists specializing in international economics: A tribute to the memory of Harry G. Johnson. *Malayan Economic Review,* 1980, forthcoming.

Citation counts for leading economists. *Economic Notes,* 1979, 8, *2,* 134-145.

Hagstrom, W.O. Inputs, outputs and the prestige of American university science departments. *Sociology of Education,* 1971, 44, *4,* 375-397.

Hansen, W.L. and B.A.W. Weisbrod.Towards a general theory of awards or do economists need a hall of fame. *Journal of Political Economy,* 1972, 80, *2,* 422-431.

Hawkins, R.S., L.S. Ritter and I. Walter.What economists think of their journals. *Journal of Political Economy,* 81, *4,* 1017-1032.

Hogan, T.D. Rankings of Ph.D. programs in economics and the relative publishing performance of their Ph.D.'s: The experience of the 1960's. *Western Economic Journal,* 1973, 11, *4,* 429-450.

Institute for Scientific Information.*Social Science Citation Index,* annual volumes, available from 1970.

Kaplan, N. The norms of citation behavior: Prolegomena to the footnote. *American Documentation,* 16, 179-185.

Lotka, A.J. The frequency distribution of scientific productivity. *Journal of the Washington Academy of Sciences,* 1926, 16, *12,* 317-323.

Lovell, M.C. The production of economic literature: An interpretation.*Journal of Economic Literature,* 1973, 11, *2,* 52-75.

MacRae, D. Growth and decay curves in scientific citations. *American Sociological Review,* 1969, 34, *5,* 631-635.

43 Canadian Economists' Citation and Publication Records

Margolis, J. Citation indexing and the evaluation of scientific papers. *Science,* 1967, 155, 1213-1219.

Miller, J.C. and R.D. Tollinson. Rates of publication per faculty member in forty-five 'rated' economics departments. *Economic Inquiry,* 1975, 51, *4,* 924-931.

Oppenheim, C. and S.P. Renn. Highly cited old papers and reasons why they continue to be cited. *Journal of the American Society for Information Science,* 1978, 29, *5,* 225-231.

Quandt, R.E. Some quantitative aspects of the economics journal literature. *Journal of Political Economy,* 1976, 84, *4,* 241-255.

Roche, T. and D.L. Smith. Frequency of citations as criterion for the ranking of departments, journals, and individuals. *Sociological Enquiry,* 1978, 48, *1,* 49-57.

Siefgried, J.J. The publishing of economic papers and its impact on graduate faculty ratings, 1960-69. *Journal of Economic Literature,* 1972, 10, *1,* 31-49.

Stigler, G.J. and C. Friedland. The citation practices of doctorates in economics. *Journal of Political Economy,* 1975, 83, *3,* 477-507.

Wade, N. Citation analysis: A new tool for science administrators. *Science,* 1975, 188, 429-432.

Citation Counts for Leading Economists *

Citation counts have been employed in the natural sciences for some time as an aid in reaching decisions about promotion, tenure, the awards of research grants by foundations and government agencies and the allocation of resources within universities [1]. Citation counts for economics and other social sciences have begun to be used for the same purposes and it is very likely that these uses will spread rapidly as it becomes better known that the publication of the Social Science Citation Index (SSCI) in recent years has made such counts feasible and efficient [2].

In this paper I present and analyse the citation counts for a selected group of economists, Nobel Price winners in economics, past officers and defeated candidates of the American Economics Association (AEA), and past presidents of the Canadian Economics Association (CEA) for two purposes. First, the data present a norm by which the citation counts of others can be evaluated. Second, the data permit investigation of the correlation between individuals' citation counts and the recognition of their professional prestige by peers through awards and the election to offices in professional associations.

However, before presenting the empirical results, I review briefly the arguments over the meaning and usefulness of citation counts which have been made in the literature, largely in response to the use of these data in the natural sciences.

I. The Meaning of Citation Counts

The usefulness of citation counts in the types of personnel and resource allocation decisions noted above depends decisively on the meaning of such counts, which in turn is determined by the motives underlying those who cite the works of others. In principle and ideally, authors cite the works of others to indicate that it has influenced their own research, to convey to readers information about the general area in the knowledge frontier on which they are making a contribution and to indicate precisely

* The work on this paper has been supported by grant S25-1194 from the Canada Council. Comments are invited on this first draft of the study.

[1] For a descrition of such uses of citation counts see Wade (1975).

[2] The SSCI appears three times a year and in annual, bound volumes. The coverage of journals and other important information about the SSCI is presented in Part II below.

the foundations in which their work rests and where their own contributions begin [3]. Such ideal citation practices play a profound role in the sociology of science. As Kaplan (1965) argues, « The citation is probably among the more important institutional devices for coping with the maintenance of the imperative to communicate one's findings freely as a contribution to the common property of science while protecting individual property rights with respect to recognition and claims to property ». He argues furthermore that as a result of this role played by citations, the scientific community has developed informal systems for penalizing individuals who do not behave according to this norm and in effect are infringing on the property rights of others. Both these sanctions by the scientific community as well as self-interest in the protection of one's own property rights represent powerful incentives for individuals to provide accurate information about influences on, and the foundations for their own work.

However, this view on the motives for citation may be excessively ideal and the literature contains a list of somewhat more whimsical reasons for citing any publications [4]. Citations may not be to influential work, but to the work of one's professor who decides on the award of a degree; to the work of « stars » in the profession to show that the author's research is in the mainstream; to recent publications to show that the author is well-connected and up-to-date; to articles that are bad or only marginally important; to articles whose only merit is that they were published by the citing author; to articles written by friends or members of a citation cartel [5]; to articles that developed a widely used econometric and statistical technique; to articles that are bad and were written by a person whose reputation the citing author wishes to diminish. On the other hand, there are reasons why influential work may not be cited: It is ahead of its time; its author has a feud with the writher who should cite it or it is so well known that citation seems superfluous, as in the case in economics with respect to the influential work of J.M. Keynes and K. Marx.

It is impossible to know on a priori grounds whether the ideal or more whimsical motives for citations are more important in the real world. However, it is possible to shed light on this question through empirical research and several studies have attempted to do so.

These empirical studies have in common the use of indices alleged to reflect individual scientists', or groups of scientists', influence and prestige which were constructed by drawing on opinion surveys of peers. For example, Clark (1957) surveyed U.S. psychologists and obtained a ranking of indi-

[3] See Cole and Cole, 1967 for an elaboration on these arguments.

[4] This list was compiled from a series of letters to the editors of *Science* and *Nature*, which were published during the early sixties after citation counts were first performed in the natural sciences. References to these letters are not in the bibliography appended to this paper but can readily be found in the bibliographical section in the first annual volume of the SSCI.

[5] If citation counts become popular in the social sciences and are put to uses of the types described above, then citation behavior may well change and lead to the establishment of cartels among friends. On the other hand, the popularity and use of citation counts may also induce journal editors and referees to pay greater attention to the correctness and completeness of footnotes and bibliographies.

viduals according to their peer's perceived level of influence on the field
and resultant prestige. Clark then correlated this ranking which was based
on over 1200 survey responses with other sets of rankings based on objectively measurable indices of influence and prestige such as number of
publications, listing in Who's Who, editorship of professional journals,
professional rewards, and, for our purpose of analysis most important,
citations to published work. Clark found that the number of citations was
more strongly correlated (R = .67) with the prestige ranking produced by
the surveys than any other objective indicator.

Hagstrom (1971) used the Cartter (1966) ratings of U.S. graduate
schools as the measure of influence and prestige to be correlated with
objectively measurable determinants. As is recalled, this well-known study
by Cartter was based on opinion surveys of a large number of university
department chairmen, who produced surprisingly consistent orderings if
the own university of each ranking person was omitted from the list he
had produced. Hagstrom found that the simple correlation of the Cartter
rankings with the number of publications was marginally better than that
with the number of citations, while the correlations of both were much
greater than with any other indicators. However, in multiple regressions,
where such other characteristics of faculty as the number of full professors,
individuals with Ph.D. as the highest degree were held constant, the author
finds « Citations to published work are a better predictor of department
prestige than quantity of articles published » (Hagstrom, 1971, p. 383).

The award of Nobel prizes presumably is a reflection of the recipients'
influence and prestige. Therefore it is interesting to note that a list of the
50 most cited scientists in the single year 1967 includes 6 who had won
Nobel prizes before that year and 6 who had received them between 1967
and 1974 (Wade, 1975). R. Quandt (1976) used citation counts to economists' work, taken from a relatively small number of journals, to prepare
lists of approximately the 20 most cited economists in the years 1920, 1930,
..., 1970. The list of 23 in 1960 contained 7 Novel-prize winners, of which
P. Samuelson, J. Hicks, W. Leontief and T. Koopmans had also appeared
on the 1950 list - all well before these prizes were awarded.

In the tradition of these studies, the empirical results presented below
represent a test of the proposition that there is a high correlation between
economists' citation counts on the one hand and the propensity of their
peer to acknowledge the prestige and standing of these individuals through
the award of prizes and the election to offices in the professional association.

In conclusion of this discussion of the meaning of citation counts it
should be noted that scientists can be and often are productive in many
ways other than through publications that lead to citations. Thus, scientists
are productive through administrative work in which they use their professional skills in the evaluation of individuals and scientific projects;
through criticism of the work of students and colleagues in seminars and
personal contacts; through synthesis and popularization of scientific work
conveyed through teaching, popular writings and speeches to the general
public; through the writing of reports and direct personal contacts with

politicians and government employees. Because the productivity of scientists takes so many forms, citation counts can and should always be used only as one of many different inputs into decisions concerning hiring, salaries, promotion and tenure.

II. *Description of the Data Sources*

This study was made feasible through the publication of the Social Science Citation Index (SSCI) by the Institute of Scientific Information located in Philadelphia, Pennsylvania. This firm subscribes to the major scientific journals published in the world, amounting to «several thousand» [6]. By a simple clerical process information concerning the title of papers, their authors and citations contained in them is transferred into electronic storage. From there it is arranged by computers in different ways to serve efficiently specific needs of information retrieval and published three times a year. Relevant for the present study is only the listing of citations in alphabetical order, which was used to count the number of citations received by the individuals considered here.

The basic list of citations has a number of short comings which affect the accurancy and meaning of the information provided below. First, at the time of writing, the SSCI was available only for the years 1970-76, so that counts of life-time citations are not possible. Some attempts are made in the analysis to provide information on average counts adjusted for age to overcome possible problems with citation life-cycles. Second, citations are only to the first-named author of publications with multiple authors. As a result, individuals whose names start with a letter low in the alphabet and who have written jointly-authored publications show up with citation counts that are biased downward. However, the comparison of average counts by categories of authors should not be affected by this bias if it is correct to assume that the characteristics of names and the propensity to co-author work is distributed randomly among the groups.

Third, the citations are only those found in journals, thus leaving out dissertations, books, pamphlets and government publications. It should be noted, however, that the citations proper are to all publications of authors, regardless where they appeared.

The names of the individuals for whom the citation counts are reported were obtained from Rendig Fels for AEA officers and candidates, from *The World Almanac* for Nobel Prize winners and from various issues of the *Canadian Journal of Economics,* for past presidents of the Canadian Economics Association. The *AEA Handbook* served as the main source of information on the year of birth of the persons surveyed. Other biographical sources were consulted to obtain the date of birth for non-members of the AEA.

---

[6] A precise coverage of journals is given in each SSCI. The coverage of journals has increased gradually from 1970. Through a special process citations to social sciences found in natural science journals are selected from the latter surveys and reported in the SSCI.

The citation counts are subject to clerical errors, in large part due to sloppy citation practices and misprints. Thus, in many instances the same person's citations are attributed to two or even more apparently different persons, depending on whether the name and initials are given fully and accurately. Furthermore, difficulties can arise when there are more than two social scientists with the same name and initial or initials. Efforts were made to deal with these problems, but often undocumented judgements were made since it is impossible to know whether a given economist has published in other than strictly economics journals.

III.   *Empirical Results*

The full population of economists considered in this study is made up of 158 persons, 143 of which are past and present officers and defeated candidates for office of the AEA, 12 are winners of Nobel prizes and 14 are past and present presidents of the CEA and some of which belong to all 3 groups [7].

Table 1 contains the names of 50 persons with the largest number of citations to their work during the years 1970-76. The ages at which the individuals received their honors or were elected to office are included in the table for general information. They are not analysed further, but the age of the individuals in 1978 is used for some cross-classifications below.

As can be seen, the list is headed by three U.S. Nobel-prize winners, P. Samuelson, M. Friedman and K. Arrow. G. Myrdal is the next Nobel-prize winner on the list in 6th place. He is followed by S. Kuznets (19), W. Leontief (23), J. Tinbergen (27), T. Koopmans (37) and F. Hayek (45), with the figures in parentheses showing the rank in the full list. Not shown in Table 1 are Nobel-laureates R. Frisch (68) and L. Kontorovich (91) who had 254 and 148 citations, respectively.

The frequency distribution of the entire population is given in Table 2. It has a mean of 362 and a median of 199, with only 20 per cent of the individuals having 500 or more citations. It may be useful to put this distribution into perspective by comparison with the distributions describing two other populations I have studied and analysed in different papers (Grubel 1978a and b). The first of these populations constitutes all persons publishing in the field of international economics which was defined operationally as all those whose name appeared at least 3 times as authors or co-authors of papers in the *Journal of Economic Literature* under Category 400 during the period 1970-76. This population consits of 455 persons, some of whom, such as Samuelson and Johnson, also appear in the preceding list. For this group the mean number of citations is 57 and the median is 17. Only about 2 per cent of the individuals have more than 500 citations.

The second population constitutes all persons who were teaching economics at Canadian universities in 1975. This group consists of 768

---

[7] See Table 3 for overlaps in these categories.

TABLE 1

CITATION COUNTS FOR 1970-76 IN DESCENDING ORDER FOR THE TOP 50

Rank	Name	Number of Citations	Category	Age at			In 1978
				Highest AEA Office	Earliest AEA Candidacy	Receipt of Nobel Prize	
1	Samuelson, Paul A.	3063	1	45	34	55	63
2	Friedman, Milton	2806	1	54	43	64	66
3	Arrow, Kenneth J.	2533	1	51	40	51	57
4	Baumol, William J.	1553	4	45	41	—	56
5	Galbraith, John K.	1502	3	63	52	—	70
6	Myrdal, Gunnar	1500	2	—	—	76	80
7	Stigler, George J.	1482	3	52	43	—	67
8	Johnson, Harry G.	1460	4,7,8	53	41	—	55
9	Hicks, John R.	1348	3	—	—	—	74
10	Theil, Henri	1323	4	—	47	—	54
11	Boulding, Kenneth E.	1314	3	57	42	—	68
12	Buchanan, James M.	1224	3	52	47	—	59
13	Tobin, James	1219	3	52	40	—	60
14	Becker, Gary S.	1112	4	44	43	—	48
15	Solow, Robert M.	992	3	54	40	—	54
16	Modigliani, Franco	914	3	57	49	—	60
17	Musgrave, Richard A.	872	4	52	46	—	68
18	Jorgenson, Dale	828	6	—	42	—	45
19	Kuznets, Simon	799	2	—	—	70	77
20	Merlove, Marc	747	5	44	44	—	45
21	Klein, Lawrence R.	675	3	56	46	—	58
22	Phelps, Edmund S.	667	5	40	40	—	45
23	Leontief, Wassily	661	1	63	46	67	72
24	Houthakker, Hendrik S.	650	4	48	42	—	54
25	Debreu, Gerard	633	6	—	51	—	57
26	Schultz, Theodore W.	611	3	58	47	—	76
27	Tinbergen, Jan	552	2	—	—	66	75
28	Machlup, Fritz	541	3	63	54	—	76
29	Bowles, Samuel	533	6	N.A.	N.A.	—	N.A.
30	Kindelberger, Charles P.	525	4	56	51	—	68
31	Coase, Ronald H.	517	6	—	62	—	68
32	Lewis, W. Arthur	500	4	50	50	—	63
33	Harberger, Arnold C.	495	5	46	46	—	54
34	Hirshleifer, Jack	469	6	—	50	—	53
35	Adelman, Irma	468	5	43	43	—	48
36	Denison, Edward	459	4	63	63	—	63
37	Koopmans, Tjalling	451	1	68	56	65	68
38	Bain, Joe S.	444	4	57	50	—	66
39	Eckstein, Otto	436	5	41	41	—	51
40	Fogel, Robert W.	424	6	—	50	—	52
41	Alchian, Armen A.	422	6	—	57	—	64
42	Dorfman, Robert	414	5	54	54	—	62
43	Thurlow, Lester	414	6	—	40	—	40
44	Eisner, Robert	390	4	55	49	—	56
45	Von Hayek, F.A.	384	2	—	—	75	80
46	Marschak, Jacob	364	3	79	65	—	81
47	Weisbrod, Burton A.	360	5	44	44	—	47
48	Morgan, James N.	353	6	—	57	—	60
49	Scitovsky, Tibor	342	4	60	53	—	68
50	Easterlin, Richard A.	324	6	—	41	—	52

Source: See text.
Note: Categories are defined in the heading of Table 2. Ranking are distorted by the fact that citations are only to first-named author of publications with multiple authors.

TABLE 2

FREQUENCY DISTRIBUTION OF CITATIONS FOR FULL POPULATION

	Number of People	%
More than 3,000 . .	1	.6
2999-2000 . . .	2	1.2
1999-1500 . . .	3	1.9
1499-1000 . . .	8	5.0
999-900 . . .	2	1.2
899-800 . . .	2	1.2
799-700 . . .	2	1.2
699-600 . . .	6	3.8
599-500 . . .	6	3.8
499-400 . . .	11	6.9
399-300 . . .	13	8.2
299-200 . . .	23	14.6
199-100 . . .	33	20.9
fewer than 99 . . .	46	29.1
	158	

Mean   362
Median   199

persons and differs fundamentally from the other two just discussed in that it includes persons who were not pre-selected as having published or been elected to offices in a professional association. For this group the mean number of citations is 8.5 and the median is less than one. Only 3 persons have more than 200 citations. This population of Canadian academic economists appears to be representative of the world total since among the 70 international trade specialists with the largest number of citations (i.e. 100 or more), 7 are Canadian residents. Therefore, since Canada's population is about 10 per cent of that of the United States in this field of specialization at least. Canadians are represented as one would expect if citation patterns were distributed randomly among all North American English-speaking economists. Since the population of international economics specialists was selected from the world as a whole and one third of Canadians' mother tongue is French, Canadians in this field may well be represented more than proportionally in relation to the relevant base population.

These comparisons of citation frequencies of different populations establish clearly the point that economists who are elected to or nominated for offices in the AEA and who receive Nobel prizes are distinguished by having had their work cited much more frequently than those economists who publish regularly in one field and those employed by universities. Thus, at a very high level of aggregation and very generally, the data support the propositions that if peers select scientists for offices and prizes on the basis of their prestige and contributions to the science, then citation counts are a reasonably good proxy for this prestige and the volume of contributions.

A Further Relationship

The general propositions just discussed are examined further by the arrangement of the available data in Table 3 on the basis of categories of prestige. In descending order the categories are (1) persons who have won the Nobel prize and have been president of the AEA [8]; (2) Nobel laureates; (3) presidents of the AEA; (4) vice-presidents of the AEA; (5) members of the executive of the AEA; (6) defeated candidates of the AEA; (7) presidents of the CEA who have also been executives of the AEA; (8) presidents of the CEA and (9) editors of the AER, JEL and secretaries of the AEA. In the cases where persons belong to more than one category they are shown only in the highest, except for category (7) which includes 3 persons who also appear in the preceding classes.

The first five categories most unambiguously represent an ordering by prestige of the office and awards, while the others require some comments. Category (6) consists of candidates for office in the AEA that were defeated and have not been nominated and elected subsenquently, as has happened to a large proportion of those in categories (1), (3)-(5). These defeated candidates were included on the grounds that nomination for election to an office in the AEA by itself constitutes a form of professional recognition.

Categories (7) and (8) are included in this study in order to examine the propositions that there are peer-groups other than the AEA which give recognition to scientific contributions as reflected in citation counts, that these peer-groups are linked and that the smaller, regional associations bestow recognition to persons with lower citation counts than do larger groups [9]. Finally, for the sake of completeness, in category (9) are shown the citation counts of the remaining officers of the AEA not appearing in other groups.

The results of Table 3 clearly lend strong support to the basic hypothesis advanced above. Considering the mean citations in each full group shown in columns (2) and (3), their size is a decreasing function of the rank ordering from categories (1) through (6). In the ranking by medians the functional relationship is disturbed only by the non-U.S. Nobel laureates (category (2)), who have about 5 per cent fewer citations than past AEA presidents who have not won Nobel prizes.

This observed consistency of the results with the hypothesis comes as some surprise because of the heterogeneity of most groups by age and the expectation that both professional contributions and citations follow a life cycle pattern. To analyse the influence of age on the results, columns (4)-(7) in Table 3 were produced. Generally, they reinforce the findings for the full groups. Clearly, median citations for all age groups except that for 54-45 years are distinctly decreasing function of recognition categories (1)-(5). Only vice presidents and executive members in the 54-45 age group

---

[8] In this group is also T. Koopmans who had been vice president in 1966 and acted as president after the death of J. Marschak in 1977-78.

[9] Presumably this proposition can be tested by the analysis of U.S. regional associations' officers citation counts, but resource limitations prevented me from taking on this job.

have unexpectedly reversed median citation counts. The results for category (6), the defeated candidates, are inconsistent with the hypothesis that nomination for election and subsequent non-election represents a form of recognition by peers less strong than actual election to office: For several age-groups and categories the median citation counts for defeated candidates are higher than those for the elected officials. I cannot explain this phenomenon satisfactorily, though I suspect that it may have something to do with a customary lapse of time between a first and subsequent nominations and elections, which in turn may be related to the early recognition of promising economists by a small, well-informed nominations committee and the delayed recognition of their quality by the general peer group casting the ballots.

TABLE 3

AVERAGE CITATIONS BY CATEGORIES OF OFFICES, AWARDS AND AGE

	Total Number in Group	Number of Citations						
		Total Median	Group Mean	Median Bq Age in 1978 (N)				Median Age
Category				≥ 65	64-65	54-45	≤ 44	
1 Nobel Prize-Winners and Presidents of AEA . . .	5	2333	1863	661(3)	2668(2)	—	—	64
2 Nobel Prize Winners . .	7	552	212	552(7)	—	—	—	77
3 Presidents of AEA . . .	16	576	681	364(11)	795(4)	992(1)	—	70
4 V.P. of AEA	31	296	407	135(13)	352(12)	316(5)	134(1)	63
5 Members of Executive of AEA	26	169	240	99(8)	164(7)	398(10)	41(1)	55
6 Defeated candidates for AEA offices	58	156	214	186(12)	182(24)	256(11)	266(3)	61
7 Presidents of CEA and AEA offices	3	164	543	—	164(3)	—	—	55
8 Presidents of CEA . . .	11	33	53	—	27(3)	42(4)	—	54
9 Editors of AER, JEL and Secretaries AEA	4	49	68	34(1)	49(2)	138(1)	—	58

Source: See text for details, compiled from Social Science Citation Index.

Notes: a) Persons in more than one group appear only in higher category, except for category (7), which appear also in categories (4)-(6).
     b) Age is not available for all persons.

Returning to the total group data and categories (7) and (8) in Table 3 it is apparent that, as hypothesized, the Canadian economics profession awards the highest office of its association to persons with relatively smaller citation counts than does the AEA, while those former CEA presidents who were also officers of the AEA tend to have counts equal to those of the members of the AEA executive. This conclusion is based on the median figure since the mean for the small group of three persons seems to have been made unrepresentative by Johnson's very large count. Finally, it should be noted that the citation counts of category (9) are well below those of the other officers of the AEA, but that they are well above the averages postulated above as being representative of the full population of academic economists.

Some Implications and Qualifications of the Results

I believe that the results reported in Table 3 shed some interesting light on the international character and interdependence of the economics profession and the apparent absence of national bias in the selection of Nobel prize-recipients by the Swedish Academy. These propositions seem to follow from the fact that non-U.S. Nobel prize-winners' average citation counts dominate those of AEA presidents both for the entire group and for the relevant age groups, though there is considerable overlap between the two groups. This result is particularly interesting since it is not unreasonable to assume that most of the Nobel laureates from countries other than Britain and the United States have published some of their important scientific work in languages quite inaccessible to the majority of the world's economists and therefore these works are less likely to be cited than the work of those who have been presidents of the AEA.

The preceding analysis of course, suggests only that high citation counts are a necessary condition for peer recognition. There remains the question whether it is also a sufficient condition. To answer this question ideally one would want to have a list of economists from the entire world with the largest number of citations and compare it with the list compiled for the present study. Unfortunately, such a list does not exist and can be compiled only at great expense [10].

However, my studies of the populations of international trade specialists and Canadian economists can provide some insights into the existence of persons who have at least 324 citations, the minimum required to make the list of the top 50 given in Table 1, but who have not been members or candidates for office of the AEA. In these two studies, there were 16 names of persons with more than 324 citations. Of those, 5 appeared in Table 1, 2 are British, 1 is Australian, 2 are Canadian and 6 are Americans. The names of the 6 Americans with at least 324 citations are (with the number of citations in parentheses): B. Balassa (682), R. Vernon (633), H. Chenery (613), R. Mundell (597), J. Bhagwati (542) and R. Caves (372). If these results can be generalized for other fields of specialization they suggest that U.S. economists with the largest number of citations have about a 50 per cent probability of being selected by their peers for election as officers of the AEA. Having large numbers of citations is a necessary but not a sufficient condition for peer recognition of the sort discussed in this paper.

IV. *Summary and Conclusions*

The publication of the SSCI has made possible the efficient counting of citations to the works of individual economists. There is little doubt

---

[10] Even though the raw data are in the computer banks of the ISI, considerable difficulties exist in identifying economists and purging the data of many sources of inaccuracy. Also, passes at the full computer tapes are rather expensive since they contain very large numbers of social scientists other than economists.

that as a result of this fact, citation counts will become an important adjunct to personnel and resource allocation decisions, much as they have in the physical sciences.

The purpose of this paper is to provide some information which should aid the use of citation counts in decision making. Arguments about the practice and meaning of citations are presented and evaluated in the light of existing studies. Counts for a selected group of economists are presented and compared with those from two other populations. The empirical results of this study provide a norm for the assessment of such counts generally. Furthermore, they imply strongly that there exists a high correlation between individuals' citation counts on the one hand and the amount of recognition peers accord to them through election to the executive of the profession's association and the award of the Nobel prize on the other. However, peer-awards of this sort do not accrue to all persons with high citation counts.

Simon Fraser University

Burnaby, B.C., Canada

[15]

CITATION COUNTS FOR ECONOMISTS SPECIALIZING IN INTERNATIONAL ECONOMICS: A TRIBUTE TO THE MEMORY OF HARRY G. JOHNSON*

HERBERT G. GRUBEL

I. INTRODUCTION

Harry G. Johnson believed strongly that economic knowledge produced by economists is socially useful only if it is published and thus becomes accessible to a large number of people and influences their research, teaching and policy advice.[1] Johnson worked very hard and successfully at the task of publishing. Several studies have documented how prolific he has been both in the absolute and relative to other economists (Quandt, 1976; Stigler, 1975; Hansen and Weisbrod, 1972).

However, there is a frequently voiced opinion in the economics profession that the quantity of publications is an unreliable proxy for the magnitude of contribution to the stock of knowledge and socially useful influence in research, teaching and policy advice by other scientists. Fortunately, in recent years a new approach to the objective measurement of scientific productivity and influence has been developed. This method involves the counting of citations to scientists' work.

Citation counting has become popular in the natural sciences and the dangers and limitations inherent in this measure of productivity and influence have been discussed intensively. I will summarize the results of this discussion and present information about the uses to which citation counts have been put in the first part of this paper.

The surge of interest in citation counts had begun in the early 1960s when the private Philadelphia firm, the Institute for Scientific Information (ISI) started publication of computer-processed bibliographical information taken from natural science journals, providing for the first time the opportunity to compile citation statistics cheaply for many individuals and from large numbers of journals. Only since 1975 has the ISI extended its coverage to the social sciences. It has since produced annual volumes of the *Social Science Citation Index* (SSCI) covering the years 1970-76 and it keeps publishing current data every four months. In the present study I am drawing on this newly available set of data to produce citation counts for a world-wide popula-

---

* This work was supported by grant S75-1194 from the Canada Council. I am deeply indebted to Johnson for the tutoring, advice and encouragement he gave me while he employed me as his Research Associate and I served as an Assistant Professor at the University of Chicago 1963-66. Through his example, he set standards of excellence in research and writing which I am attempting, but cannot expect ever to attain.

1. This conviction he expressed often in conversation. He considered it especially unfortunate if persons with great intelligence and originality of thought failed to write and publish their analyses.

tion of economists specializing in international economics, using methods and definitions to be discussed in the second part of this paper.

As the data will show, the documentation of the magnitude of Johnson's scientific productivity and influence is a fitting memorial to him. However, I hope that Johnson also would have considered useful some of the other information which is contained in this paper: the names of the 70 most cited international economics specialists, the names of 46 others who have fewer than 100 citations but 10 or more journal articles during the period 1970-76 and the frequency distributions and Lorenz curves of all international economics specialists for publications as well as citations. The potential use to which such information can be put will be discussed in the concluding section of the paper. In Part IV I present a list of published works by Harry Johnson, which have received at least 4 citations during the period under study. The types, titles and time profile of these publications permit the identification of individual contributions and their contents to assess the nature of Johnson's influence.

II. THE MEANING OF CITATION COUNTS

At the outset it is important to make clear that citation counts do not measure individuals' total productivity as academics or economists. There are indeed many persons who have published little and have few or no citations but who have been enormously productive as teachers, critics or administrators. Citation counts ideally can only reflect the extent to which individuals have contributed through publications to the stock of knowledge and have influenced the work of others.

There are many scientists who doubt that citation counts can perform even this more limited task. After the first citation counts had been produced in the natural sciences during the early sixties, several letters to the editors of *Science* and *Nature* were published in which writers give reasons for distrusting citation counts as measures of scientific productivity and influence. I have omitted references to these letters in the appended bibliography. Interested readers can find them in a long bibliography concerned with citation counting analysis attached as front material to the annual volumes of the SSCI.

The points made in these letters can be summarized quite readily as follows: Citations may not be too influential work, but to the work of one's professor who decides on the award of a degree; to the work of "stars" in the profession to show that the author's research is in the mainstream; to recent publications to show that the author is well-connected and up-to-date; to articles that are bad or only marginally important; to articles whose only merit is that they were published by the citing author; to articles written by friends or members of a citation cartel;[2] to articles that developed a widely used econometric and statistical technique; to articles that are bad and were written by a person whose reputation the citing author wishes to diminish. On the other

---

2. If citation counts become popular in the social sciences and are put to uses of the type described below, then citation behaviour may well change and lead to the establishment of cartels among friends. On the other hand, the popularity and use of citation counts may also induce journal editors and referees to pay greater attention to the correctness and completeness of footnotes and bibliographies.

hand, there are reasons why influential work may not be cited: it is ahead of its time; its author has a feud with the writer who should cite it or it is so well known that citation seems superfluous, as in the case in economics with respect to the influential work of J.M. Keynes and K. Marx.

Some Arguments in Favour of Citation Counting

Defenders of the idea that citations reflect scientific productivity and influence have used two approaches. First, there are authors who attempted to establish theoretically the norms guiding citation practices of scientists which, if they are determined by sufficiently powerful motives of self-interest, could be expected at least in principle to dominate the kinds of behavior noted above. The analysis along these lines led to the following conclusions.

The most basic reasons why scientists cite others' work are that it provides an efficient method for conveying to readers information about the general area on the knowledge frontier in which the author is making a contribution; to indicate the foundations on which the contribution rests and to delineate precisely where the author's own contribution begins. (See Cole and Cole, 1967 for a statement of this general view). One of the most useful perspectives is put on this type of citation behavior by Kaplan (1965), who argues that ''The citation is probably among the more important institutional devices for coping with the maintenance of the imperative to communicate one's findings freely as a contribution to the common property of science while protecting individual property rights with respect to recognition and claims to property''. He argues furthermore that as a result of this role played by citations, the scientific community has developed informal systems for penalizing individuals who do not behave according to this norm and in effect are infringing on the property rights of others. Both these sanctions by the scientific community as well as self-interest in the protection of one's own property rights represent powerful incentives for individuals to provide accurate information about influences on, and the foundations for their own work.

Deductive reasoning of this sort, of course, is insufficient to establish whether citation practices are in fact dominated by motives which permit us to interpret them as evidence of productivity and influence on whether the other, more whimsical motives noted above, destroy their meaning. In order to resolve this question, several researchers have resorted to a second approach, the use of empirical studies.

The empirical studies have in common the use of indices alleged to reflect individual scientists', or groups of scientists', influence and prestige which were constructed by drawing on opinion surveys of peers. For example, Clark (1957) surveyed US psychologists and obtained a ranking of individuals according to their peers' perceived level of influence on the field and resultant prestige. Clark then correlated this ranking which was based on over 1,200 survey responses with other sets of rankings based on objectively measurable indices of influence and prestige such as number of publications, listing in Who's Who, editorship of professional journals, professional rewards, and, for our purposes of analysis most important, citations to published work. Clark found that the number of citations was more strongly correlated ($R = .67$) with the prestige ranking produced by the surveys than any other objective indicator.

Hagstrom (1971) used the Cartter (1966) ratings of US graduate schools as the measure of influence and prestige to be correlated with objectively measurable determinants. As is recalled, this well-known study by Cartter was based on opinion surveys of a large number of university department chairmen, who produced surprisingly consistent orderings if the own university of each ranking person was omitted from the list he had produced. Hagstrom found that the simple correlation of the Cartter rankings with the number of publications was marginally better than that with the number of citations, while the correlations of both were much greater than with any other indicators. However, in multiple regressions, where such other characteristics of faculty as the number of full professors, individuals with Ph.D. as the highest degree were held constant, the author finds "Citations to published work are a better predictor of department prestige than quantity of articles published." (Hagstrom, 1971, p. 383).

The award of Nobel prizes presumably is a reflection of the recipients' influence and prestige. Therefore it is interesting to note that a list of the 50 most cited scientists in the single year 1967 includes 6 who had won Nobel prizes before that year and 6 who had received them between 1967 and 1974. (Wade, 1975). R. Quandt (1976) used citation counts to economists' work, taken from a relatively small number of journals, to prepare lists of approximately the 20 most cited economists in the years 1920, 1930, . . ., 1970. The list of 23 in 1960 contained 7 Nobel-prize winners, of which Samuelson, Hicks, Leontief and Koopmans had also appeared on the 1950 list—all well before these prizes were awarded.

Interesting Uses of Citation Counts

The type of empirical results just discussed have been interpreted apparently as sufficiently strong evidence to justify the use of citation counts in a number of important applications. In an excellent review of the subject Wade [(1975), p. 429] concludes that citation counts will find "major uses in decisions at the level of national science policy, as an adjunct to the peer-review process, and in evaluating the performance of individual scientists." As specific evidence of such uses he notes that the National Science Foundation employs citation counts to assist in the allocation of grants to chemists, especially in sorting out those applications that are well written but whose authors have inferior records of citations while at the same time searching for grants that are poorly written and would not qualify for support on these grounds but whose authors have a superior record of achievement as measured by citations.

In another application reported by Wade, citation counts were used to counter the arguments that US science advisory boards are heavily loaded with members of Eastern US Establishment schools, leaving out many deserving scientists from other regions of the country. Citation counts showed that by these criteria few "deserving" scientists were omitted from the boards.

Another application of citation counts has been in a precedent-setting law-case, where expected life-time citations extrapolated from past citation records, were admitted as evidence in a court challenging the decision of a university in the New York State system to deny tenure to a person on the grounds of insufficient scientific productivity. The data showed that by the criterion of expected lifetime citation counts the person denied tenure had a superior record of performance than did two persons who were granted tenure at the same time.³

Finally, one of the leading contributors to the sociology of science, de Solla Prie (1963) has advanced the idea that scientific progress relies on the contributions by all scientists, even though the contribution of many may be only minor. As Cole and Cole (1972) have shown for a number of fields in the natural sciences and as this paper will show for international economics, this proposition is not substantiated by data. The greatest share of contributions to knowledge in science, including international economics, is made by a very small proportion of all scientists, with about one half of them never making any written contribution at all. A documentation and widespread acceptance of these facts might well facilitate and rationalize decisions about promotion and tenure that are often made with very incomplete knowledge about these matters in many academic institutions.

III. DATA SOURCES AND PROBLEMS

The first problem encountered in this study is to define operationally the population of economists specializing in international economics. In this study I have used two definitions. First, there is the group of 1,158 individuals who are members of the American Economics Association and who have indicated in the AEA Handbook (1974) that their primary field of interest is international economics (Category 400 according to the AEA classification code). Second, there is a group of 3,184 individuals who have published either alone or as co-authors during the period 1970-76 at least one article which was listed under Category 400 in the *Journal of Economic Literature*. Of these 3,184 published in the *JEL*, 371 also indentified themselves as international economics specialists in the AEA *Handbook*.

The availability of limited resources forced me to concentrate the counting and analysis of citations to only 455 persons whose names have appeared at least three times as single or joint authors in the *JEL* during the period 1970-76.⁴

The names of the 455 persons were then looked up in the annual volumes of the SSCI for a count of both publications and citations. The main tables giving names in the next part listing names are based on this work.

Some facts about the SSCI and operational procedures used in compiling the data of this study are important to know for an accurate assessment of the results. First, the number of journals fully indexed by the *SSCI* is "over 1,000" *(SSCI,* Preface) and more than 2,000 other journals, mostly from the natural sciences, are searched for references to social scientists. The journals

---

3. Unfortunately, Wade's (1975) article written in the form of an editorial does not contain a reference to his source of information and no indication as to the outcome of the trial in which the evidence was used.

4. I supplemented the original mechanical selection procedure by inspecting the list of names that appeared no more than twice in the *JEL*. This list contained the names of J.E. Meade and R.A. Mundell, who are well-known specialists in international economics and whose citation counts are included in Table 2.

cover both US and foreign publications. The first two columns of Table 2 below show the number of publications attributed to individuals according to the *SSCI* and *JEL* source. The data show that for 11 out of 70 persons the *JEL* gives a greater publication count than the *SSCI*. I have not been able to identify the sources of this discrepancy.

Second, the count of citations and publications in the *SSCI* is subject to a more than usual margin of clerical error because of sloppy citation practices showing wrong or incomplete sets of initials of cited persons, the existence of persons with identical names in other fields and the complexity of some coding practices used in the *SSCI*. The existence of the first two problems made it necessary for my research assistant to use some judgement, especially in identifying journals in fields other than economics. However, there is no reason to believe that any of the sources of difficulty in this clerical work should bias the overall results, especially as they affect rankings of individuals.

Third, while publications listed in the *SSCI* identify the names of co-authors and therefore made it possible to attribute a publication to each co-author, the citations are only to the first named person of co-authored work. This fact introduces a bias into the results, showing up as a potentially serious underestimate of the number of citations for persons who have done much co-authored work and whose name starts with a letter low in the alphabet. I have not corrected the results for this bias.

Fourth, book reviews are not counted as publications, even though they appear in the *SSCI*. Fifth, while the count of publications is limited to journal articles, citations refer to all of an author's past work, including text-books, monographs, edited works, unpublished dissertations and discussion papers. Finally, self-citations are not identified in this study. In a sample of Canadian economists (1978), I have found that self-citations represent 18 per cent of the total, with widely varying propensities among individuals. Without having actually attempted to verify this proposition, I believe that the elimination of self-citations would not alter significantly the rankings presented in the main tables below.

IV. EMPIRICAL RESULTS — THE MOST PRODUCTIVE INDIVIDUALS

Table 1 presents documentation related to the definition of the field of specialists in international economics, which contains also some interesting information about the number of those who have published no journal articles at all. As can be seen, of the 1,158 persons listed as primary specialists in category 400 in the AEA *Handbook,* (group B and C in Tabe 1), only 371 also were in the group of 2,813 persons who appeared under category 400 in the *JEL* 1970-76. This fact indicates that 787, or 67 per cent of the total specialists identified in the *Handbook* published no journal articles during this period. This figure for zero publications is slightly higher than that found for physicists (Cole and Cole, 1972) and Canadian academic economists (Grubel, 1978). Perhaps the results are due to the fact that the *Handbook* contains the names of many persons in occupations other than academic, which can be expected to have a lower propensity to publish than academics, who made up the population in the other two studies cited.

Table 1, part B shows the frequency distribution of articles by persons whose names have appeared in the *JEL*. As can be seen, 2,257 individuals appeared only once, 942 twice and 609 three times and so on in a rapidly declining series, resulting in a mean of 1.71 for those who appeared at least once and 1.37 for the entire group. Harry Johnson leads the field by a large margin with a count of 40. In Part C of Table 1, the cumulative frequency of this distribution is shown and reveals that the top 10 and 20 per cent of individuals published 38 and 54 per cent of the total, respectively. The overall distribution has a Gini-coefficient of .47.

Data on Citations

Table 2 may be considered to provide the most important results of this study. The table shows the names of the 71 persons who had at least 3 publications in the *JEL* during the period 1970-76 and more than 100 citations. The number of publications shown in Table 2 are the results of counts from the *SSCI* (first column) and *JEL* (second column).[5] Since the first figure refers to all and the second to publications in international economics only, the relationship between the two may be taken as an indication of the extent to which the individuals are on the list because they are genuine specialists or because they publish only occasionally in the field. However, I have made no attempt to quantify this phenomenon and have not used it to make adjustments to the citation counts and corresponding rankings. Such an exercise may be useful for a study concerned primarily with identifying contributions to international economics, but this is not the intent of my study.

The table provides clear and powerful evidence for the outstanding amount of contributions and influence on others Harry Johnson has made during this period. His citation count of about 1,500 is topped only by that of P. Samuelson with about 2,900 and is more than twice that of the next group of 6 economists who have between 600 and 700 citations.

It is tempting to divide the number of citations by the number of journal publications to derive an index of "quality" per article published. I have not provided this statistic in Table 2 for two reasons. First, for this statistic to be meaningful, it would have to cover total publications and citations of an author, since citations to published work appear with a lag and decay rapidly at rates that differ according to the "quality" of the publication. I do not have access to the complete list of Johnson's and other economists' total publications and all citations to their work. Second, and more fundamentally, this study attempts to measure the magnitude of influence and for this purpose it matters little whether it is achieved through many or few publications.

In a study of a sample of Canadian economists' citations (Grubel, 1978), I

---

5. Since the first source should provide a broader coverage of journals than the second, the count of publications from the latter should never exceed that from the former. As the table shows, however, this is not the case. I cannot explain this fact and can only speculate that it results from incomplete coverage of journals by the *SSCI* in the early years. An inspection of the *SSCI* publications shows that they are growing every year. However, unless there is some systematic bias in the omission of journals *and* publication preferences of authors, the ranking of individuals in Table 2 is not biased and only a proportional adjustment of citations would be brought about by a full coverage.

8   CITATION COUNTS IN INTERNATIONAL ECONOMICS

TABLE 1

NUMBER OF PUBLICATIONS BY SPECIALISTS IN INTERNATIONAL
ECONOMICS, 1970-76

A.	Source of Names of Individuals	Number of Individuals
I.	Published at least one article listed under category 400, in Journal of Economic Literature but did not appear under (II)	2,813
II.	Registered in AEA Handbook (1974) with first field of interest category 400, but did not appear under (I)	787
III.	Appeared in Journal of Economic Literature and registered in AEA Handbook under 400	371
	Total Population	3,971

B.		Frequency distribution of articles taken from JEL			
Number of Articles	Individuals	Total Articles	Number of Articles	Individuals	Total Articles
1	2,257	2,257	11	6	66
2	471	942	12	3	36
3	203	609	13	3	39
4	92	368	14	4	56
5	59	295	15	3	45
6	24	144	17	1	17
7	23	161	18	1	18
8	10	80	19	1	19
9	13	117	20	2	40
10	6	60	25	1	25
			40	1	40
				3,184	5,434

Mean of all publishers   Mean of total population
5,434:3,184 = 1.71   5,434:3,971 = 1.37

C.	Inequality Measure for Number of Publications Based on Part B of this Table		
	Publications		
Decile	N	%	Cumul. %
1	2,058	38	38
2	853	16	54
3	530	10	64
4	397	7	71
5	397	7	78
6	397	7	85
7	397	7	92
8	397	7	99
9	8	0	99
10	0	0	99
	5,434	100	

(N = 3,971)
Gini Coefficient = .47.

CITATION COUNTS IN INTERNATIONAL ECONOMICS   9

TABLE 2

SPECIALISTS IN INTERNATIONAL ECONOMICS WITH MORE
THAN 100 CITATIONS, 1970-76

Name		Publications		Citations
		SSCI	JEL	
1.	Samuelson, P.A.	43	6	2,898
2.	Johnson, H.G.	59	40	1,498
3.	Balassa, B.A.	23	25	682
4.	Kaldor, N.	9	3	649
5.	Houthakker, H.S.	9	4	643
6.	Vernon, R.	15	9	633
7.	Chenery, H.B.	7	3	613
8.	Mundell, R.A.	2	1	597
9.	Machlup, F.	6	7	549
10.	Bhagwati, J.N.	17	15	542
11.	Kindleberger, C.P.	8	10	520
12.	Meade, J.E.	8	1	493
13.	Caves, R.E.	7	4	372
14.	Kemp, M.C.	22	20	324
15.	Grubel, H.G.	20	11	313
16.	Bronfenbrenner, M.A.	22	5	309
17.	Vanek, J.	15	5	300
18.	Harrod, R.F.	6	3	292
19.	Corden, W.M.	8	5	266
20.	Fellner, W.J.	10	4	262
21.	Jones, R.W.	13	9	256
22.	Walters, A.A.	9	3	244
23.	Hymer, S.H.	8	3	242
24.	Cooper, R.N.	15	8	239
25.	Hansen, B.	14	3	236
26.	Haberler, G.	5	6	236
27.	McKinnon, R.I.	2	5	207
28.	Behrman, J.	7	4	204
29.	Bergsten, C.F.	19	5	202
30.	Baldwin, R.E.	11	7	192
31.	David, P.A.	10	3	190
32.	Griffin, K.B.	9	5	180
33.	Kravis, I.B.	9	4	180
34.	Bauer, P.T.	11	7	176
35.	Branson, W.H.	9	9	172
36.	Turnovsky, S.J.	21	4	165
37.	Laidler, D.E.	8	3	164
38.	Hufbauer, G.C.	10	7	160
39.	Sunkel, O	6	4	156
40.	Dunning, J.H.	2	7	151
41.	Negishi, T.	10	5	149
42.	Keesing, D.B.	5	3	149
43.	Kenen, P.B.	8	9	146

Continued overleaf

TABLE 2 (Cont'd)
SPECIALISTS IN INTERNATIONAL ECONOMICS WITH MORE
THAN 100 CITATIONS, 1970-76

Name		Publications		Citations
		SSCI	JEL	
44.	Leff, N.H.	13	7	142
45.	Bruno, M.	5	4	142
46.	Kolm, S.C.	20	3	139
47.	Mikesell, R.F.	2	3	136
48.	Brimmer, A.F.	18	5	136
49.	Streeten, P.	10	3	135
50.	Triffin, R.	4	11	135
51.	Krueger, A.O.	10	4	124
52.	Massell, B.F.	4	3	124
53.	Helliwell, J.F.	13	4	123
54.	Kreinin, M.E.	12	12	122
55.	Bardhan, P.K.	12	3	119
56.	Wallich, H.C.	17	4	118
57.	Krause, L.B.	9	5	117
58.	Lutz, F.A.	2	4	110
59.	Burns, A.F.	3	9	108
60.	Batra, R.N.	32	19	107
61.	Arndt, H.W.	12	10	106
62.	Pattanaik, P.K.	18	5	106
63.	Dornbusch, R.	8	4	106
64.	Niehans, J.	8	4	103
65.	Clark, P.B.	12	9	103
66.	Aliber, R.Z.	13	17	103
67.	Goldman, M.I.	10	3	102
68.	Helleiner, G.K.	7	6	102
69.	Kojima, K.	14	15	102
70.	Melvin, J.R.	11	11	101
71.	Papanek, G.F.	5	3	101

Sources and Notes: Population limited to those who have appeared at least 3 times in Journal of Economic Literature 1970-76 under Category 400. Number of articles and citations shown are from Institute of Scientific Information and JEL.

have found that the frequency distribution of the number of years between the publication and citation of a work is extremely skewed and indicates a rapid rate of obsolescence of knowledge in economics. One half of all references are to journal articles published less than 4.0 years before, while for other forms of publications the figure is even lower at 2.6 years. Only about 10 per cent of all references are to works published more than 10 years before. This kind of obsolescence pattern has also been found by other researchers, Broadus (1971) who cites and surveys several studies of the subject, and Lovell (1973) who deals with citations in economics. The Canadian results reported here are underestimating somewhat the life of citations because they are only to the works of currently active economists, but the lag structure implies the general principle that large numbers of publications are a necessary condition for large numbers of citations at a later time.

The existence of this principle has led me to prepare Table 3, which contains a list of names of persons who have published at least 10 journal articles but have fewer than 101 citations during the period 1970-76. Presumably, on this list is a large proportion of the names of economists who will in the future receive many more citations and thus, will be found in lists analytically equivalent to the one contained in Table 2.

V. EMPIRICAL RESULTS—SOME AGGREGATE STATISTICS

Table 4 contains the frequency distribution of citation counts of all 455 economists whose names had appeared at least 3 times in the *JEL* during the period 1970-76. This distribution further documents the relative dominance of Harry Johnson's influence by showing the heavy concentration of individuals in the categories with few citations, even though the 455 in turn are the most productive of an even larger population of economists in the field.

The skewness of the distribution has been quantified by the cumulative frequency distribution shown in the bottom part of Table 4. As can be seen, the top decile of individuals received 67 per cent and the top half received 96 per cent of all citations. The Gini-coefficient measuring the inequality is .75.

Table 5 presents the frequency distribution of journal articles of the 455 people whose citation record is contained in Table 4. As can be seen, the distribution of articles is also very skewed. Harry Johnson's record of 59 is leading the field again by a large margin. However, the cumulative frequency shown at the bottom of Table 4 indicates that publications are distributed more evenly than citations. The top 10 per cent of individuals published only 30 per cent of all articles, which is less than half the concentration of citations. Similar relationships exist for the rest of the distributions as may be seen by comparing Tables 4 and 5.

The strong skewness of frequency distributions of publication and citation counts has been noted by other researchers for other fields of science. Allison and Stewart (1974) contains a review of the evidence and an attempt to explain it theoretically. These analysts proceed from the observation that the skewness showing about 50 per cent of all scientists as publishing nothing at all is a puzzle in light of the facts that all have passed through an intensive graduate training and that all measurable, simple human characteristics and skills appear to be distributed normally. According to Shockley (1957) and Aitchison and Brown (1957), the explanation of the puzzle lies in the fact that the more complicated a task is, the greater is the number of simple characteristics and skills required to perform them.

While the simple characteristics and skills are normally distributed among the population, combinations of them determine new distributions through a multiplicative combination of the simple probability distributions. Thus, since research and publication require a greater number of characteristics and skills than does meeting the requirements of a graduate degree, the existence of a normal distribution among successful graduate students with respect to the requirements for schooling is perfectly consistent with the observed skewness of the publications frequency distribution.

Allison and Stewart argue that the sociological and reward structure of science contribute to a greater skewness of the distribution than that which

12   CITATION COUNTS IN INTERNATIONAL ECONOMICS

TABLE 3

SPECIALISTS IN INTERNATIONAL ECONOMICS WITH
MORE THAN 10 PUBLICATIONS 1970-76*

Name	Articles/(SSCI)	Citations
Cebula, R.J.	38	63
Willett, T.D.	23	62
Fishcher, S.	22	43
Razin, A.	21	8
Sethi, S.P.	19	59
Parkin, M.	18	73
Brems, H.	17	79
Lev, B.	17	77
Frenkel, J.A.	17	33
Clark, R.J.	17	13
Krauss, M.B.	16	44
Tower, E.	16	33
Adler, M.	16	28
Thirwall, A.P.	15	48
Schmitz, A.	15	33
Srinivasan, T.N.	15	30
Banks, F.E.	15	19
Holmes, J.M.	14	48
Makin, J.H.	14	45
Lloyd, P.J.	14	37
Scully, G.W.	14	33
Finger, J.M.	14	19
Mitchell, D.J.	13	24
Murray, T.	13	16
Farmer, R.N.	12	94
Williamson, J.	12	90
Horvath, J.	12	53
Ozawa, T.	12	36
Officer, L.H.	11	91
Black, S.W.	11	62
Walter, I.	11	59
Donnelly, J.H.	11	38
Richardson, J.D.	11	29
Gray, H.P.	11	29
Berglas, E.	11	27
Casas, F.R.	11	12
Maule, C.J.	11	9
Fan, L.S.	11	6
Lomax, D.F.	11	5
Gold, J.	10	68
Berry, R.A.	10	41
Floystad, G.	10	23
Bertrand, T.J.	10	21
Wilford, W.T.	10	16
Yeats, A.J.	10	6
Stokes, H.H.	10	4

* *Notes:* Excluding individuals with more than 100 citations shown in Table 2.
        Source same as Table 2.

CITATION COUNTS IN INTERNATIONAL ECONOMICS   13

TABLE 4

SPECIALISTS IN INTERNATIONAL ECONOMICS* FREQUENCY
DISTRIBUTION OF CITATIONS, 1970-76

Number of Citations	Individuals	Number of Citations	Individuals
more than 3000	1	99—90	7
2900—2000	1	89—80	7
699—600	5	79—70	6
599—500	4	69—60	8
499—400	1	59—50	13
399—300	5	49—40	17
299—200	12	39—30	27
199—150	11	29—20	46
149—100	30	19—10	77
		9—0	177
			455

Cumulative Frequency

Decile	N	Citations %	Cumul. %
1	17,435	67	67
2	3,608	14	81
3	1,901	7	88
4	1,249	5	93
5	855	3	96
6	568	2	98
7	323	1	99
8	70	0	99
9	45	0	100
10	6	0	100
	26,060		

(N = 455)
Gini Coefficient = .75

* Population limited to those who have appeared at least 3 times in Journal of Economic Literature 1970-76 under Category 400. Number of citations shown are from Institute of Scientific Information.

results from basic ability differences alone. This reward structure provides proportionately and increasingly more resources to the relatively most productive scientists, thus creating a process of "cumulative advantage". This process was documented empirically by Allison and Stewart (1974) who found that the inequality of publication counts with age-cohorts is an increasing function of age since receipt of the Ph.D.

As a final note on the results of Tables 4 and 5 it is interesting to attempt

TABLE 5

SPECIALISTS IN INTERNATIONAL ECONOMICS FREQUENCY
DISTRIBUTION OF NUMBER OF ARTICLES FROM ISI SOURCE

Number of Articles	Individuals	Articles	Individuals
59	1	13	6
43	1	12	13
38	1	11	14
32	1	10	14
23	2	9	23
22	3	8	26
21	2	7	27
20	1	6	35
19	2	5	43
18	3	4	51
17	6	3	52
16	5	2	42
15	7	1	13
14	7	0	54
			455

Cumulative Frequency

| Decile | N | Publications | |
		%	Cumul. %
1	862	30	30
2	498	18	48
3	382	13	61
4	303	11	72
5	245	9	81
6	198	7	88
7	159	6	94
8	121	4	98
9	69	2	100
10	0	0	100
	2,837		

an explanation of the much greater inequality of citation-compared with publication-counts. There are two basic forces at work that can explain the phenomenon. First, a "halo effect" appears to surround the "stars" of the field, inducing researchers to cite them even if an idea or empirical result may have been produced simultaneously by a lesser known economist. Presumably, the halo-effect of the cited star lends greater authority and prestige to the citing author's own work. Also, the star may be in a better position to reward the perceptive author recognizing the value of his contributions than is the lesser-known colleague, though there is a risk that the lesser-known author may ultimately become a star and hedging one's bet may not be a bad strategy. Second, and perhaps more important than the halo-effect, is the stock-effect. The publication count shown in Table 5 is only over the output of a 7-year period, but the citations shown in Table 4 are to the cumulated stock of all preceding publications. This stock-cumulation effect is operative in addition to the cumulative advantage due to the reward structure noted above. All three effects are responsible for the greater skewness of frequency distributions for citations as compared with publication counts.

VI. JOHNSON'S MOST FREQUENTLY CITED PUBLICATIONS

If citations do indeed reflect the importance of a publication in the sense discussed in Part I above, then the record of citations to individual pieces of work can be used to identify Harry Johnson's most important contributions. Accordingly, I have set out in Table 6 all books and journal articles which have received at least four citations in any of the seven years 1970-1976, showing the citation counts in each of the years and the total.

As can be seen, the book *International Trade and Economic Growth*, published in 1958 and containing a number of previously published essays which Harvard University accepted as meeting its dissertation requirements for the Ph.D., received 46, the largest number of citations, and showed no signs of obsolescence during the period. In fact, the eleven citations in 1976 exceeded those in any of the other years under study. His second most widely cited work is the book *Economic Policies Towards Less Developed Countries*, which was published in 1967 under the auspices of the Brookings Institution.

Thirteen of the 25 works most widely cited are books, of which 6 are anthologies of Johnson's own previously published journal articles and 5 are symposia he had edited. Journal articles in the list number 10 and there are two publications which appeared in symposia.

The titles of journal articles and books permit some insights into the topics and fields in which Johnson's contributions appear to be concentrated. Tariff theory generally, the theory of effective protection, the theory of growth and international trade, the economics of the brain drain, the effects of factor market distortions, the theory of direct foreign investment and the role of money in the domestic economy and the balance of payments. Two articles that might be considered to contain the review and synthesis of the field of monetary and macro-economics received large numbers of citations ("Monetary Theory and Policy", *AER*, 1962 and "The Keynesian Revolution and Monetarist Counter-Revolution", *AER*, 1971).

The time-period covered by the data in Table 6 is too short to reach a definitive judgement, but the overwhelming impression is that Johnson contributed a fairly even flow of work that received large numbers of citations. The largest number of publications [5] on the list appeared in 1971 while three each were published in 1965 and 1967. Also, there appears to be no significant trend in the preparation of articles, anthologies of his own work and edited symposia on the list.

I know of no other studies which permit me to put the information contained in Table 6 into perspective with records of other economists. Perhaps in

TABLE 6

WORKS BY HARRY G. JOHNSON CITED AT LEAST 4 TIMES IN ONE YEAR

Year of Publication	Book Title or Article	Year and Number of Citations							
		1970	71	72	73	74	75	76	Σ
1958	*International Trade and Economic Growth*	9	7	6	7	6	3	11	49
1960	"The Cost of Protection and the Scientific Tariff," *JPE*	3	7	3	1	6	0	4	24
1962	"Monetary Theory and Policy," *AER*	4	5	2	1	3	3	4	22
1962	*Money, Trade and Economic Growth*	5	7	5	1	3	1	2	24
1965	*Trade, Growth and the Balance of Payments*	6	6	2	4	8	3	7	36
1965	"The Economics of the Brain Drain," *Minerva*	2	5	5	2	3	2	1	19
1965	"The Theory of Tariff Structure," *Trade and Dev.*	6	7	2	2	3	2	1	23
1966	"Factor Market Distortions and the Shape of the Transformation Curve," *Econometrica*	2	9	1	3	4	8	1	28
1967	*Essays in Monetary Economics*	6	4	7	5	3	2	6	33
1967	*Economic Policies Towards Less Developed Countries*	5	8	5	5	11	3	6	43
1967	*Economic Nationalism in Old and New States*	1	4	1	1	1	1	2	11
1969	"Inside Money, Outside Money . . ." *JMCB*	5	4	5	3	3	1	4	25
1969	"Theory of Effective Protection," *Economica*	6	5	3	1	1	1	1	18
1970	"Effective of Unionization on Distribution of Income," *QJE*	—	4	2	2	5	5	4	22
1970	"Efficiency and . . . International Corporation," (Symposia)	—	5	0	6	9	6	4	31
1971	*The Current Inflation*	—	—	5	2	1	2	7	17
1971	*Two Sector Model of General Equilibrium*	—	—	6	2	1	3	5	17
1971	"Trade and Growth: A Geom. Exposition," *J. Int. Econ.*	—	—	2	3	2	5	1	13
1971	*Aspects of the Theory of Tariffs*	—	—	4	0	3	2	1	10
1971	"The Keynesian Revolution and Monetarist Counter-Revolution," *AER*	—	—	4	2	2	4	4	16
1972	*Inflation and the Monetarist Controversy*	—	—	—	3	6	6	6	21
1972	"The Monetary Approach to Bal. of Payments Theory," *J. Fin. Qn. A.*	—	—	—	—	9	4	11	24
1973	*Economics of Common Currencies*	—	—	—	—	4	1	1	6
1975	*On Economics and Society*	—	—	—	—	—	—	4	4
1975	*Technology and Economic Interdependence*	—	—	—	—	—	—	5	5

the future, if the ready availability of citation information stimulates more research in this field, it will be possible to compare Johnson's record in this detail with that of others.

In closing, I would like to suggest some interesting areas for further research which suggested themselves to me during my study of the literature. First, it would be most interesting from the point of view of the history of thought in economics and the sociology of science, to map the flow of citations between Johnson and others, to discover spheres and channels of influence. This information might be supplemented by judgements as to whether citations were favourable or unfavourable, as Stigler (1975) has done. Through such a study it might be possible to identify groups of economists belonging to certain "schools" or adhering to particular paradigms and the institutional characteristics common to them, such as being graduates or faculty of certain universities. Judgements about individual scientists' influence might be adjusted according to the universality of the sources of their citations. Analogous use can be made of information concerning the journals in which publications occurred and from which and to which citations were sent.

VII. SUMMARY AND CONCLUSIONS

In this paper I have assembled information on the publication and citation counts of Harry G. Johnson during the period 1970-76 and of a group of individuals who either through their publications or their own statements were identified as being specialists in the field of international economics. The results show that Johnson's record of overwhelming dominance in the field is not limited to the quantity of his publications but extends to general influence as measured by citations to his work.

While this paper thus is a tribute to the memory of Harry Johnson, it also represents an attempt to introduce into the economics literature information about the convenient availability of comprehensive raw data on citations, the results of studies using this kind of data in other fields of science and the conclusions reached by others about the merit and dangers of using citation counts in the evaluation of individuals' past productivity in terms of contributions to the stock of knowledge.

The rankings of individuals by the number of citations to their work presented in this paper in my judgement contains few surprises to economists working in the field. They represent a quantification of information which has been and is available as part of an informal process of evaluation of peers going on continuously. However, it is useful to have an objective and published record of performance that may have the following practical applications: as an adjunct to hiring, tenure and promotion decisions for both highly and less productive economists, where the latter group might benefit from the fact that so large a proportion of all economists publish and are cited very little; as an adjunct to decisions about the allocation of resources for research and hiring of individuals for consulting and advice; for prospective students and faculty members in choosing departments for study and work and for decisions by institutions granting honors and awards.

Simon Fraser University
Canada

REFERENCES

[1] Aitchison, J. and Brown, J.A.C., *The Lognormal Distribution,* Cambridge: Cambridge University Press, 1957.

[2] Allison, R.D. and Stewart, J.A., "Productivity Differences among Scientists: Evidence for Accumulative Advantage," *American Sociological Review,* 1974.

[3] American Economics Association, *Handbook,* (American Economics Assoc.: Menasha, Wisc.), 1974.

[4] Broadus, R.N., "The Literature of the Social Sciences: A Survey of Citation Studies," *International Social Science Journal,* 1971.

[5] Cartter, A.M., *An Assessment of Quality in Graduate Education,* Washington, D.C.: American Council on Education, 1966.

[6] Clark, K.E., *America's Psychologists: A Survey of a Growing Profession,* Washington, D.C.: American Psychological Assoc., 1957.

[7] Cole, J. and Cole, S., "The Ortega Hypothesis: Citation Analysis Suggests that only a Few Scientists Contribute to Scientific Progress," *Science,* 178: 368, 1972.

[8] Cole, S. and Cole, J.R., "Scientific Output and Recognition: A Study in the Operation of the Reward System in Science," *American Sociological Review,* 32(3), 1967.

[9] De Solla Price, D.J., *Little Science, Big Science,* New York, N.Y.: Columbia University Press, 1963.

[10] Grubel, H.G., "Canadian Economists' Publication and Citation Records 1970-76", *Simon Fraser University Discussion Paper,* (mimeo), 1978.

[11] Hagstrom, W.O., "Inputs, Outputs and the Prestige of American University Science Departments," *Sociology of Education,* 1971.

[12] Hansen, W.L. and Weisbrod, B.A.W., "Towards a General Theory of Awards or Do Economists Need a Hall of Fame," *Journal of Political Economy,* March-April, 1972.

[13] Kaplan, N., "The Norms of Citation Behavior: Prolegomena to the Footnote," *American Documentation,* July 1965.

[14] Lovell, M.C., "The Production of Economic Literature: An Interpretation," *Journal of Economic Literature,* March 1973.

[15] Quandt, R.E., "Some Quantitative Aspects of the Economics Journal Literature," *Journal of Political Economy,* August 1976.

[16] Shockley, W., "On the Statistics of Individual Variations of Productivity in Research Laboratories," *Proceedings of the Institute of Radio Engineers,* March 1957.

[17] Stigler, G.J. and Friedland, C., "The Citation Practices of Doctorates in Economics," *Journal of Political Economy,* June 1975.

[18] Wade, N., "Citation Analysis: A New Tool for Science Administrators," *Science,* 1975.

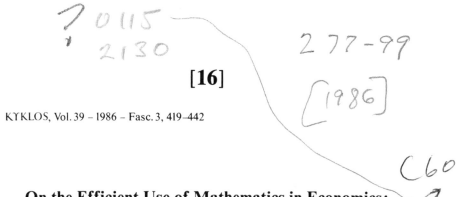

KYKLOS, Vol. 39 – 1986 – Fasc. 3, 419–442

[16]

On the Efficient Use of Mathematics in Economics: Some Theory, Facts and Results of an Opinion Survey

HERBERT G. GRUBEL and LAWRENCE A. BOLAND*

Has the use of mathematics in economics grown too much? We discuss this question by assuming that mathematics is an input into the production of human and knowledge capital in economics. As a result, the question turns on the efficiency of its use. We consider models which imply alternatively that competition generates efficiency and that interest group behaviour produces inefficiencies. Obviously, theoretical models alone cannot resolve the basic issue, which is essentially empirical, but we believe that the models are useful in focussing attention on some central issues.

The empirical question is addressed with a set of statistics that document the growth of mathematics used in professional journals during the postwar years and the extent to which mathematical and non-mathematical journal articles cite each other. The empirical question is addressed also in the analysis of a survey concerning a number of issues surrounding the use of mathematics in economics, which has been completed by about 250 economists.

* The authors are Professors of Economics at Simon Fraser University in Vancouver, B.C., Canada. The empirical part of this paper would not have been possible without the cooperation of the many economists who completed the questionnaire analyzed in the paper. It has also benefitted greatly from the B.C. government's Challenge 1985 program of financial support for students, which provided research assistance in the compilation of statistics on the incidence of use of mathematics in professional journals. A number of people, too large to name here, contributed to this paper by detailed comments on an earlier draft.

419

HERBERT G. GRUBEL AND LAWRENCE A. BOLAND

I. MATHEMATICS AS A PRODUCTIVE INPUT

We assume that economics knowledge is socially useful[1]. It is produced through the application of human capital and disseminated through the publication of journals and books. Mathematics is one of many inputs into the production of this knowledge and human capital. Therefore mathematical economics has a positive social product. More specifically, this productivity takes the following form.

First, mathematics can be a precise language. As such it can contribute to logical rigour, the cumulative nature of knowledge and innovative analytical approaches. *Second,* mathematics has permitted the development of structural and dynamic models in the form of input-output tables and linear-programming models, which have contributed substantially to the understanding of how economies work and to the application of measurement techniques.

Third, mathematics is an input into the training of economists. As such it has increased the efficiency of the education process and served as an effective screening since mathematical abilities appear to be useful in the study of economics.

The validity of the preceding statements is independent of a precise definition of 'mathematics in economics' or 'mathematical economics'. This is a great advantage of our methodical approach since it allows us to avoid having to deal with very technical and contentious issues such as the type of mathematics used, the quality of the mathematical economics and the need of different types of students to know math-

---

1. We thought that this proposition was rather uncontentious and obvious. To our surprise we found that some people do not share this view. They contend that many research fields pursued in universities have no social usefulness. They believe that some economics knowledge has this characteristic and therefore should be evaluated by the same criteria as other socially useless research. We do not pursue this line of analysis further here.

It is clear that we also rule out by assumption the possibility that the use of mathematics in economics may have a negative social product, as when it leads to excessively mechanistic thinking, what Hayek called 'scientism'. This danger of the use of mathematical economics may well exist to some degree, but it is probably not true on balance.

420

ON THE EFFICIENT USE OF MATHEMATICS IN ECONOMICS

ematics[2]. Concerning these dimensions of the problem we simply assume that the mix of types, quality and targets of mathematics input in economics are optimal and thereby focus our attention on the quantity.

Starting with these premises, the question about the growth of mathematics in economics can now be formulated technically and neutrally as follows. Is the quantity of mathematics applied to the production of knowledge and human capital efficient? Is its marginal product equal to that of other inputs, such as economic and doctrinal history, political science, sociology, statistics, the natural sciences, law, liberal arts, accounting and grammar?

Economics knowledge and human capital are sold in markets. For most economists this implies a strong presumption that both are priced correctly and produced efficiently. Any university using too little or too much mathematics teaching economists should find that its graduates are at a competitive disadvantage, its training program should shrink and finally disappear. Similarly, knowledge that contains inappropriate amounts of mathematics should lose out in the market and its production will contract or cease.

To the extent that there are externalities in the production or use of economics knowledge and human capital, governments may be presumed to use subsidies to correct these market failures. Market imperfections and lags in the transmission of information suggest that efficiency would not prevail at all times, but there would be a strong tendency for it to be achieved. The competitive model appeals to many economists[3].

An alternative model considers mathematical economists to be economists who are concerned with the mathematics of economic analysis thereby to be an interest group that attempts to generate economic rents for its members. Members of that group do so individually or collectively by lobbying with authorities which can increase the demand for their

2. In response to an earlier draft of this paper K. ARROW wrote to us that the central question is whether the mathematics used in economics is good or bad. We agree that everyone should be against bad and in favour of good mathematical economics. But, as in all research and teaching, the good and bad are not easily distinguished and always occur together. What counts is the relative quantities of the two types. In our analysis we assume that the mix of good and bad is optimal and that the key analytical question concerns the quantity and marginal productivity of the input of mathematical economics in human and knowledge capital formation.

3. GEORGE STIGLER and our colleague PAO CHENG hold this view.

HERBERT G. GRUBEL AND LAWRENCE A. BOLAND

services[4]. Targets for such efforts are: the curriculum committees of universities; library committees which influence the purchase of journals; editorial committees of professional associations which select articles for publication and set the agendas for conferences; bodies which determine the granting of prizes and prestigious lectures; government grant committees which provide support for research and others.

Non-mathematical specialists in economics have similar incentives for rent-seeking. Their efforts, however, are subject to different influences and constraints than those of mathematical economists, all of which result in relatively lower rates of return to rent-seeking and make it more difficult to defend against outsiders the gains that they have made.

First, non-mathematical economists have opportunities for employment in private industry, the media and policy oriented government agencies while mathematical economists have practically no other employment opportunities outside of universities and a very small number of specialized institutes. This leaves mathematical economists with relatively more incentives to seek rents in the academic environment that other types of economists.

Second, objective tests of competence can be administered and used as barriers to entry and in defense of rents more easily by mathematical than other types of economists since mathematics lends itself well to the design of such tests. As a result, rents are more likely to persist and expected rates of return to rent-seeking are higher whenever mathematical competence tests can be used to reduce transactions and monitoring costs.

Third, the specific activities for rent-seeking by mathematical economists noted above have the important characteristic that the output of

---

4. Interest group behaviour must not be the outcome of an explicit conspiracy. It can be pursued by individuals acting in their own interest and that of the science, as they see it. Explicit and self-selected representatives of developing but unorganized constituencies in a discipline need not be ruled out as (inchoate) interest groups, however, even though to outsiders they might on occasion be mistaken for conspiracies. Along these lines DAVID EASTON, former professor of Political Science at the University of Chicago, told us about an explicit (and successful) strategy for influencing the management of the American Political Science Association and the *American Political Science Review* during the 1960's that he and a number of colleagues had undertaken. The purpose of the exercise was to encourage a more sympathetic attitude toward the new and developing behavioral approach with its partiality to quantitative research orientations, an approach that was being resisted by much of the then current establishment in the profession, especially in the *APSR*.

ON THE EFFICIENT USE OF MATHEMATICS IN ECONOMICS

these activities is subject to few or no market tests and therefore can readily and for prolonged periods be subjected to criteria that serve the interest group. Space in journals, demand for teaching, conferences and research grants for mathematical economics can be raised in this manner. Increased publications and citations, course enrolment, grants and conference invitations can then be used as evidence of the field's growing importance and acceptance in further lobbying with agencies. The output of most non-mathematical economists, by its very nature, is much more subject to market- and user-tests and much less capable of stimulation and evaluation by its own producers. As a result, mathematical economists face higher returns to rent-seeking than their colleagues in other fields of specialization.

Fourth, rent-seeking mathematical economists have found ready and eager allies in other interest groups using mathematics, such as natural scientists, statisticians, econometricians and, of course, mathematicians. In addition, the universality of mathematics as a language permits the internationalization of the interest group, which raises its comparative membership and prestige[5]. These advantages are not available to other disciplines and are responsible for higher expected returns to rent-seeking by mathematical economists.

Fifth, a dynamic process for expansion of the scope of mathematical economics has been operating for some time. This dynamic process had its start when mathematical economists captured university committees which set curricula and grant financial assistance to graduate students during an era of great optimism about the usefulness of natural science methodology to the social sciences in the 1950s and 1960s. It also received a stimulus from the increase in government support for the training of mathematical economists in the wake of the expansion of science generally in the post-Sputnik era[6]. Such developments stimulate an increased demand for teachers of mathematical economics, more

5. These characteristics, however, also involve some costs in the form of reduced ability to limit entry. Mathematical economics appears to have a proportion of practitioners, trained originally in other disciplines and countries, much larger than that found in other fields of economics.

6. See KOOPMANS [1957] and TINTNER [1968] for the discussion of how the development of input-output analysis and linear programming were encouraged by grants from the US Navy, which was interested in these techniques for the solution of its problems of logistics.

HERBERT G. GRUBEL AND LAWRENCE A. BOLAND

research output, more journals, more citations and other signals of importance of the group's work. Through all this, current practitioners earned a rent.

One can imagine, however, that an unbridled emphasis on the mathematics of economic analysis would produce at some point an excess supply of mathematical economists and thereby threaten these rents. In response, mathematical economists can make further investments in training that qualifies them to take on teaching in applied fields, such as labour economics and finance. Once in these positions, they can mathematize the knowledge, teaching curriculum and research of these fields. Permanent new demand for mathematical economists can be created and, at least temporarily, tendancy towards excess supplies can be reduced. The dynamic process just described can conceivably repeat itself several times and lead to ever higher and ultimately inefficient levels of mathematics in education and the production of knowledge. A similar process is not likely in the application of the specialized knowledge in other fields. There is, for example, only very little room for expanding the scope of money and banking in the field of labour economics. Therefore, the dynamics of rent-seeking in the academic world yields much higher returns to mathematical than to other types of economists.

Of course, the preceding description of the interest group model should not be construed to imply that the growth of mathematical economics is without limit. Eventually, consumers and interest groups suffering from the activities of the mathematical interest group are likely to find it worthwhile to resist further losses or to fight for changes benefitting them, as BECKER'S [1983] analysis predicts they should. In fact, such a process appears to have begun recently, if the amount of attention given the subject in the popular press is any indication[7]. Our study and the extensive cooperation we received from colleagues may also be part of the process.

---

7. See *Newsweek* [1985], *The Economist* [1984] and *Christian Science Monitor* [1985]. In addition, there has been a wave of criticism of mathematical economics on grounds of methodology by LEIJONHUFVUD [1973], LEONTIEF [1971] [1982], McCLOSKEY [1983], CHRESSANTHIS [1985] and BOLAND [1982][1986a][1986b]. We have avoided discussion of methodological issues in this study because they are too complex and contentious and would have distracted from the relatively more simple arguments made.

ON THE EFFICIENT USE OF MATHEMATICS IN ECONOMICS

II. MATHEMATICS IN ECONOMICS JOURNALS

We have chosen the American Economic Review (AER) for the following analysis because it is the official publication of the main professional association of the United States, which in turn has the world's largest stock of economists. Studies have also established it as the most widely cited and the most prestigious economics journal in the world [LIEBOWITZ and PALMER 1984]. We have also replicated the AER data analysis for the Journal of Political Economy (JPE). The results for the two journals are almost identical and to save space, we do not present the JPE data here.

As can be seen from *Figure 1*, we have analyzed the contents of all pages in each issue of the AER between 1950 and 1983, assigning them to categories depending on whether they contained diagrams, charts, tables of data and equations or only text. In *Figure 1* the pages in each category are expressed as a percentage of total text pages (including bibliographies and appendices) in every year.

Figure 1 shows that the percentage of pages with one or two analytical diagrams was without a distinct trend. On the other hand, there has been a slow rise in the proportion of pages that contain a diagram together with at least one equation, though the upward trend has stopped since the middle 1970s. Tables and charts with empirical data have taken up relatively constant proportions during the entire period. The upper part of Figure 1 shows that the proportions of AER pages containing one, two and three or more equations (and no diagram, chart or table) have risen continuously and at a fast rate throughout the period. In 1951 only 2.2 percent of all pages contained at least one equation. By 1978 this proportion had risen to 44 percent.

Another way of looking at the trend of interest here involves the pages with text only. We found that in 1950 fully 86 percent of all pages contained text only. Thereafter, this proportion had fallen steadily to an historic low of 36 percent in 1981. In 1982 a sharp reversal took place and all text pages occupied again 52 percent. This reversal was at the expense of all other types of material, but especially pages containing one of more mathematical equations.

The growth of mathematics in other economics journals was quantified by a somewhat simpler procedure. We defined articles to consist of 'Pure Mathematical Models' if they contained several equations, but no

HERBERT G. GRUBEL AND LAWRENCE A. BOLAND

Figure 1

American Economic Review

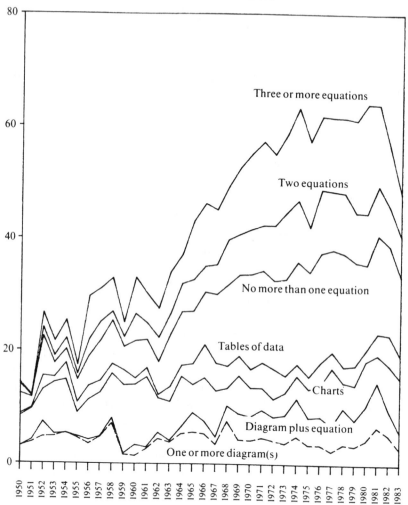

empirical results presented in tables, charts or regressions. This definition does not capture exactly the concept 'mathematics in economics'
which was the focus of our analysis in section one. We simply were
unable to find an operationally feasible measure of the extent of mathe-

ON THE EFFICIENT USE OF MATHEMATICS IN ECONOMICS

matics input generally into the production of economics knowledge published in journals. We believe, however, that there is a high degree of correlation between the concept used in section one and the empirical measure we have chosen.

We have collected data separately for articles, notes and comments. We found generally that during the first part of the period covered, notes and comments were more heavily mathematical than articles, but that this difference has since been eliminated. The data presented here have consolidated articles, notes and comments. We also analyzed mathematical as a proportion of the total number of publications. This index was highly correlated with the one based on pages and is not reported. In the category of pure mathematical models we also included articles devoted to surveys of pure mathematical topics, econometric theory and the geometric approach to pure theorizing. There were very few articles in these categories.

Mathematics has grown not only in the application to pure theory articles. It also has been increasingly used to specify models for empirical testing. To measure the growth of this phenomenon we collected data on the proportion of pages containing pure mathematical equations in articles reporting the results of empirical work. We found that there has been a clear upward trend in the use of mathematics in empirical papers in most journals surveyed. But the level of use has not been very high, even in recent years. In our sample of journals, the Review of Economics and Statistics had the highest level with about 20 percent of pages of empirical studies devoted to mathematical modeling during the 1970s. Before 1965 this level had been four percent.

We selected the 15 journals on the basis of a ranking provided by LIEBOWITZ and PALMER [1984]. This rank is based on the frequency of citations in the journals literature to the articles appearing in these publications. However, in order to obtain some variance on the age and regional distribution of journals', we used informal criteria to add some and to drop others. Thus, for example, we excluded the Yale Law Journal on the grounds that it was too specialized and we added Weltwirtschaftliches Archiv and Kyklos as representatives of European journals with a predominance of material published in English. Our selection procedure for the journals was not intended to be scientific and representative. It is designed to provide some illustration of the growth of mathematics in some widely known and used journals.

427

HERBERT G. GRUBEL AND LAWRENCE A. BOLAND

Figure 2

Mathematics in journals (low levels)

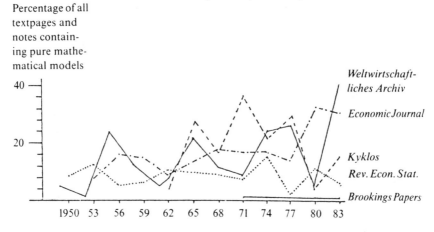

Figure 3

Mathematics in journals (medium levels)

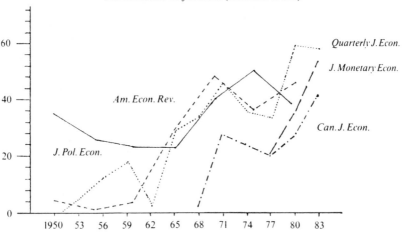

The information contained in *Figures 2, 3* and *4* suggests the following generalizations and groupings of journals. One group of journals has a low percentage of mathematical contents and only a small upward trend in this measure. Leading this group with the lowest level by far is the Brookings Papers. It is followed by the European journals Weltwirt-

428

ON THE EFFICIENT USE OF MATHEMATICS IN ECONOMICS

schaftliches Archiv, Kyklos and The Economic Journal and the empirically oriented Review of Economics and Statistics.

The second group of journals shows a strong upward trend in the publication of pure mathematics treatises which reached the level of about 50 percent in recent years. In this group we find the oldest and most influential journals in the profession, the AER, JPE, Quarterly Journal of Economics, as well as the more recently founded Journal of Monetary Economics and the Canadian Journal of Economics.

The highest proportion of total pages consisting of pure mathematical material is found in the third group of journals. It is dominated by the Journal of Economic Theory, which publishes practically only articles of the pure mathematical genre. It contains also the Bell (now the Rand) Journal of Economics, the International Economic Review and the Review of Economic Studies. These journals generally show only a slight upward trend in the proportion of space devoted to pure mathematical work during the period under study. It is worth noting that in this group only the Review of Economic Studies is relatively old. The rest of the journals were all established recently.

From these data we draw conclusions. *First,* the old, established and most prestigious two journals have increased the space devoted to mathematical models strongly and continuously during the postwar years to a point where about half of the journal space is devoted to this purpose. *Second,* there has been a further increase in the total journal space devoted to pure mathematical models since several new journals have been committed to the publication of this material from the beginning.

The last conclusion, however, has to be modified since there has been also an increase in journal space devoted to non-mathematical material. Since it was impossible to survey all journals, we do not know what happened to the proportion of space devoted to mathematics in all journals, a measure which for some purposes of analysis is more relevant than the total space in journals devoted to mathematical economics[8].

8. Partly as a reaction to dissatisfaction with the amount of mathematics in the Canadian Journal of Economics, the Canadian Economics Association has launched as an official publication the journal Canadian Public Policy. It specializes in articles that are policy oriented and that have little or no mathematics. Allegedly, a similar journal is being considered for publication by the Australian Economics Association,

HERBERT G. GRUBEL AND LAWRENCE A. BOLAND

Figure 4

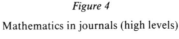

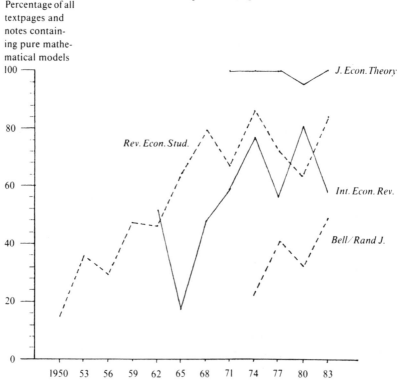

One of the criticisms often heard about the growth of mathematical economics rests on the perception that it has developed into a separate field of knowledge with very little interaction with empirical and policy-oriented work. We thought it interesting to attempt a quantification of this phenomenon[9] and for this purpose constructed *Table I*.

also in response to complaints about the amount of mathematics in its official publication, The Economic Record.

9. In this we follow DIAMOND [1985] who showed that of 88 papers citing the work of G. DEBREU only 5 involved empirical work. After a study of these 5 papers the author concluded: 'Only in one paper were the references to DEBREU important to the substance of the paper. But even there, the references were in a mathematical theory section that was only tenuously connected to the brief, marginally empirical pages at the end.'

ON THE EFFICIENT USE OF MATHEMATICS IN ECONOMICS

Table 1

Citation pattern in 1983

Citing journal Original distribution			*Articles cited* Pure mathematics		Other	
	N	%	N	%	N	%
1) *AER*						
Pure math	23	19.8	147	63.9	180	24.0
Other	93	80.2	83	36.1	569	76.0
	116	100.0	230	100.0	749	100.0
2) *Brooking Papers*						
Pure math	0	0	0	0	23	14.7
Other	13	100	0	0	133	85.3
	13	100	0	0	156	100.0
3) *J. Econ. Theory*						
Pure math	57	100	467	90.8	0	0
Other	0	0	47	9.2	0	0
	57	100	514	100.0	0	0
4) *Weltwirtschaftliches Archiv*						
Pure math	14	40	80	68.3	28	16.7
Other	21	60	37	31.6	139	83.3
	35	100	117	100.0	167	100.0

The left column of *Table 1* shows the number and proportion of pure mathematical and other articles found in the four journals surveyed. The remainder of the table shows the characteristics of the articles cited. We should note that a substantial proportion of all citations, especially in the pure mathematical articles, were to discussion papers unpublished at the time. These papers were not accessible to us and simply omitted from the count. We treated in the same way a few articles in journals not in the university library and references to articles in conference proceedings and mono-graphs. We feel that any possible bias from this procedure was probably small and worth incurring, given the cost of tracking down and evaluating these citations.

431

HERBERT G. GRUBEL AND LAWRENCE A. BOLAND

Table 1 shows that articles in the two categories on average cite work from the other with some frequency. Most notable, however is the fact that references in the Journal of Economic Theory consisted of 91 percent of mathematical articles, suggesting that the authors of pure mathematical articles in that journal deal to a very substantial degree with rather self-contained stocks and frontiers of knowledge.

Much the same can be said about the material contained in the Brookings Papers. The non-mathematical articles published there had only 15 percent of their references to mathematical articles. The distribution in the AER is more even. Mathematical articles had 36 percent of their citations to non-mathematical material, which is more than the tendency of other articles to cite mathematical works (25 percent). Finally, there is a remarkable similarity in the citation practices of the two types of publications in the AER and Weltwirtschaftliches Archiv.

III. A SURVEY OF ECONOMISTS

In the Spring of 1985 we mailed about 800 survey questionaires to three different sets of people. *First,* about 400 individuals listed in the AEA 1978 Handbook, choosing one from each page and only persons with US addresses; *second,* about 200 persons from the Canadian Economics Association 1983 Membership Directory shown to be living in Canada[10] and *third,* 200 names from BLAUG and STURGES [1983], supplemented by the names of all living Nobel-prize winners and past presidents of the American Economics Association. Each questionnaire was accompanied by the first draft of a paper making essentially the same points as the present study, including the working definition of pure mathematical work and giving percentages of articles in pure mathematical economics in the AER, JPE and EJ[11].

---

10. Canadian economists loom relatively large in the sample because we have some special interest in conditions in our home country. We hope that at some point it will be possible to make explicit comparisons of attitudes towards mathematics in economics held in different countries and we invite interested persons to collaborate with us on such a project.

11. We wish to acknowledge the receipt of valuable comments on the first draft of the questionnaire from K. ARROW, A. BLINDER, P. CHENG, P. DAVIDSON, B. VON HOHENBALKEN, R. SOLOW, G. STIGLER and J. TOBIN.

ON THE EFFICIENT USE OF MATHEMATICS IN ECONOMICS

The response rate was about one third, though not all respondents completed all questions[12]. We requested some biographical information from respondents. The demographic characteristics of the sample will become obvious from some of the cross-tabulations presented below.

Table 2 presents the questions and the distribution of answers from the entire sample. In *Table 3* we list a few responses stratified according to certain population characteristics. It is obvious that we had to limit these to just a few, the selection of which is certain to have been influenced by our own biases. A number of people returned the completed survey with the comment that its outcome was predictable and some criticized us for letting an anti-math bias show through the design of the questions. We tried to word the questions neutrally, but obviously have not succeeded.

We did not know what answers most people had expected from the survey, nor were we sure of our own expectations. In such a situation it seems best to let the questions and answers speak for themselves. Therefore, we limit our comments to the following few, which are most interesting to us in the light of our introductory discussion.

First, at least 50 percent of all respondents consider adequate the amount of government support for mathematical economics. Well over 50 percent think appropriate also the amount of mathematics in education, though more respondents see a need for increased mathematics in undergraduate rather than graduate education. At the same time it is noteworthy that about a quarter think that there is too much mathematics in graduate education. Least dispersion in the answers in the entire survey concerns the level of mathematics in journals, with 64 percent saying that it is too high and 34 that it is adequate. In the light of the hypothesis that the market of economics output is determined competitively and therefore is efficient, these last results raise a very uncomfortable question as to how the profession got into this position of having so many of its consumers find the product inappropriate for their use.

Second, 45 percent of respondents believe that mathematical economists act like rent-seekers and 30 percent are uncertain about it. However, only 21 percent think that this rent-seeking is successful while 40 per-

12. The following information may be of interest to some readers. First, because of financial constraints we were unable to attach stamps to self-addressed return envelopes mailed with the questionnaire. This omission has probably affected the return rate and may have biased it. Second, nearly one hundred envelopes were returned

HERBERT G. GRUBEL AND LAWRENCE A. BOLAND

Table 2

Responses to survey questionnaire on mathematical modeling

Questions	Answers percent			Total
	too little	ade- quate	too much	
I. The appropriate role and level of mathematical economics				
1. The amount of resources devoted to teaching mathematical economics to undergraduates is	37	51	11	(248)
2. The amount of resources devoted to teaching mathematical economics to graduate students is	17	54	28	(245)
3. The proportion of journal space devoted to mathematical economics articles is	1	34	64	(251)
4. The degree of mathematical sophistication used in the formulation of most models designed for testing and measurement is	11	48	40	(245)
5. The quantity of resources devoted by government and research foundation to the development of mathematical economics is	14	52	33	(225)

Questions	Answers percent			Total
	yes	un- certain	no	
II. The appropriate use of mathematical modeling in economics				
6. Is the development of the mathematical modeling skills of research economist, in our opinion, the main reason for the progress and growing public prestige of the economics profession since 1950?	31	50	17	(244)
7. In your opinion, does emphasis on the development of pure mathematical modeling skills leave young economists poorly prepared for work in government or industry?	61	29	9	(253)
8. Do you believe that attempts are made by the economics profession to use the level of mathematical modeling skills as a device to limit entry into the profession?	26	59	14	(253)
9. In your opinion, is the demonstration of mathematical modeling skills a reliable screening device to limit entry into the profession?	25	64	10	(250)

434

ON THE EFFICIENT USE OF MATHEMATICS IN ECONOMICS

Table 2 (continued)

Questions	Answers percent			Total
	yes	un- certain	no	
10. In your opinion, do mathematical modeling specialists have less trouble finding jobs in universities than do others?	57	19	23	(253)
11. Would you think that most economists who specialized in mathematical modeling when they were young, turn to less mathematically oriented work later in life?	63	14	21	(252)
12. In your opinion, does mathematical modeling work lead to publications more quickly and easily than other economics research?	70	15	14	(254)
13. In your opinion, is there strong evidence that past investments in the development of mathematical modeling have yielded a high payoff in terms of better and clearer understanding of how the economy works?	33	48	18	(252)
14. Do you think that mathematical economists behave like a rent-seeking interest group?	45	25	29	(251)
15. Do you believe that mathematical economists' interest-group behaviour can lead to greater economic rents than those of others?	23	36	40	(243)

16. What do you think is the criterion of successful mathematical modeling today? Elegance 31%; practical usefulness 22%; professional advancement 17%; original twist on otherwise popular model 12%; other 16%.

17. Please list one or two major achievements in economics knowledge during the last 30 years and indicate whether or not mathematics has contributed to them: Most often mentioned were: Input-Output analysis, linear programming; rational expectations; finance theory; econometric measurement; general equlibrium analysis.

because the addressee was unknown. We believe that these letters were addressed to people who were graduate students and who had changed their residences. Third, four questionnaires were returned from retired economists in their eighties who felt that they were unable to answer the questions because of their age. Fourth, the following sent us lengthy and very helpful comments on mathematical economics and methodology: E. F. BEACH, T. DICK, L. KEYSERLING, W. LEONTIEF, D. MCCLOSKEY, A. MCKEE, A. MELTZER and G. TULLOCK. Fifth, most of the unpublished manuscripts in the bibliography were sent to us after their authors learned about our study.

Table 3

Answers by some subsets of respondents (percentages)

	UG resources are				GRD resources are				Journal space is				Sophistication is				Govt support is			
	TL	A	TM	No.	TL	A	TM	No.	TL	A	TM	No.	TL	A	TM	No.	TL	A	TM	No.
Under 35	48	48	2	37	21	70	8	37	5	48	45	37	19	44	36	36	11	70	17	34
35–49	43	49	6	119	20	52	26	119	0	38	61	121	9	54	35	121	17	56	25	106
Over 50	24	54	21	90	11	49	39	87	1	21	76	91	9	40	50	86	9	38	51	83
Distinguished	26	58	14	63	17	51	31	64	0	29	70	64	12	44	42	63	15	41	46	60
Others	41	48	10	185	17	55	27	181	1	35	62	187	10	50	39	182	15	55	29	165
Academic	36	52	10	212	17	54	28	210	1	36	62	213	10	50	39	208	14	52	33	190
Non-academic	41	44	13	36	14	57	28	35	0	23	76	38	13	40	45	37	14	51	34	35
Published math	42	52	5	92	21	60	17	91	2	41	56	96	18	47	34	94	16	52	30	84
Others	34	50	14	156	14	51	34	154	0	29	69	155	6	49	44	151	12	51	35	141
Top US grad.	34	52	12	104	21	50	27	102	1	37	60	107	15	47	36	103	18	45	36	94
Others	39	50	10	144	13	57	28	143	0	31	67	144	7	49	42	142	11	56	32	131
Top US dept.	45	54	0	35	25	61	13	36	2	45	51	37	13	55	30	36	17	55	26	34
Others	36	50	13	213	15	53	30	209	0	32	66	214	10	47	42	209	13	51	35	191

	Gave prestige?				Poorly prepared?				Limits entry?				Screening device?				Get job easier?			
	Y	N	U	No.	Y	N	U	No.	Y	N	U	No.	Y	N	U	No.	Y	N	U	No.
Under 35	29	48	21	37	48	40	10	37	27	64	8	37	35	59	5	37	59	21	18	37
35–49	38	45	15	120	61	32	5	123	29	55	15	123	26	62	11	122	55	21	22	123
Over 50	22	60	17	85	67	20	12	91	23	61	15	91	19	70	10	89	59	15	25	91
Distinguished	33	53	12	63	56	31	12	64	20	65	14	64	25	62	12	64	62	18	18	64
Others	30	49	19	181	62	29	7	189	28	57	14	189	25	65	9	186	55	19	24	189
Academic	34	48	17	208	57	32	10	215	25	62	12	215	26	64	9	214	59	20	19	216
Non-academic	16	66	16	36	81	15	2	38	34	39	26	38	19	69	11	36	43	13	43	37

Table 3 (continued)

	Gave prestige?				Poorly prepared?				Limits entry?				Screening device?				Get job easier?			
	Y	N	U	No.	Y	N	U	No.	Y	N	U	No.	Y	N	U	No.	Y	N	U	No.
Published math	34	47	17	92	48	40	11	95	22	71	6	95	37	52	9	93	60	24	15	95
Others	29	52	17	152	68	23	7	158	29	51	18	158	17	71	10	157	55	16	27	158
Top US grad.	32	50	16	102	57	32	9	107	18	73	7	107	23	63	12	105	62	19	17	107
Others	30	50	18	142	63	27	8	146	32	48	19	146	26	65	8	145	53	19	27	146
Top US dept.	37	40	21	37	57	31	10	38	10	84	5	38	29	56	13	37	59	21	18	37
Others	30	52	16	207	61	29	8	215	29	54	15	215	24	66	9	213	56	18	24	216

	Less math later?				Quick publication?				Higher payoff?				Rent seekers?				Successful?			
	Y	N	U	No.	Y	N	U	No.	Y	N	U	No.	Y	N	U	No.	Y	N	U	No.
Under 35	45	24	29	37	54	24	21	37	54	27	18	37	43	32	24	37	13	50	36	36
35–49	62	17	20	123	65	19	14	123	32	49	17	123	47	20	32	121	20	38	41	121
Over 50	73	6	20	90	82	6	10	92	25	55	18	90	46	26	27	84	32	28	39	84
Distinguished	71	12	15	64	79	9	10	64	31	46	21	64	44	33	22	63	30	37	32	59
Others	60	15	23	188	66	17	15	190	34	48	17	188	46	21	31	188	21	36	42	184
Academic	64	14	21	214	71	16	11	216	35	44	20	214	44	25	29	213	24	38	37	207
Non-academic	60	18	21	38	60	10	28	38	23	71	5	38	52	18	28	38	19	27	52	36
Published math	70	11	17	95	68	20	10	96	45	33	21	95	40	34	25	96	24	43	31	91
Others	59	16	24	157	70	12	16	158	26	57	16	157	49	18	32	155	23	32	44	152
Top US grad.	67	12	20	107	70	17	12	108	32	51	15	108	43	28	27	107	21	39	38	103
Others	60	16	22	145	69	14	15	146	34	45	20	144	47	21	31	144	25	34	40	140
Top US dept.	81	5	13	38	76	15	7	38	36	36	26	38	36	50	13	38	21	56	21	37
Others	60	16	23	214	68	15	15	216	32	50	16	214	47	20	32	213	23	33	43	206

HERBERT G. GRUBEL AND LAWRENCE A. BOLAND

cent are uncertain about this outcome. These answers give fairly strong support to the interest group hypothesis in our introductory analysis.

Third, a strong majority of respondents (around 60 percent) believes that mathematics leaves students poorly prepared for non-academic work; serves as a device for screening entrants and limiting entry into the profession; permits quick and easy publication and leads many to turn to other work later in life. We believe that these perceptions, if they are correct, lend support to the interest group hypothesis in obvious ways.

The demographic categories in *Table 3* are self-explanatory except for the following two. *First,* we asked respondents about their publication record, specifically whether they have ever published pure mathematical works. As can be seen, 95 of the respondents said that they had done so and 155 said they had not. *Second,* we requested information about the academic institution at which the respondents were teaching and at which they received their highest degree. We classed the following institutions into what we consider to be the leaders: Harvard, Yale, Princeton, Columbia, Stanford, Universities of Chicago, Michigan, Wisconsin, California at Berkeley and Los Angeles, and the Massachusetts Institute of Technology. Of the respondents, 81 had earned their degrees and 26 are teaching at these institutions.

We find the following to be the most interesting generalization about the data in *Table 3*. The dissatisfaction with the present level of mathematics in human and knowledge capital formation is an increasing function of age. This fact may be explained as having its origin in the lack of mathematical training and sophistication of the older. It may also stem from their maturity and experience and the accompanying increased awareness of the limitations of mathematics in economics. We have not been able to devise a method for choosing among the two competing explanations. Probably, there is some truth to both. However, there is one bit of information in the survey results with some bearing on the issue.

It can be seen that the group of distinguished economists, i.e. Nobel laureates, AEA executive officers and Who is Who in Economics biographies, are considerably more negative on the use of mathematics than the rest of the respondents. It is note worthy that while these individuals are also older than the average, most of them have made contributions to and are very familiar with mathematical economics. It may not be unreasonable to suggest that for these economists a genuine awareness

438

ON THE EFFICIENT USE OF MATHEMATICS IN ECONOMICS

of the limitations of mathematical economics is the dominant motive for their answers.

Another noteworthy result concerns the view that there is too much mathematics in the journals. As can be seen, those who had published mathematical works and had education or employment relationships with one of the leading universities were less inclined than the rest to consider journals to carry too much mathematics. Furthermore, there is an interesting difference between those who have and those who have not published mathematical articles. More of the latter than the former believe that mathematics training leaves economists poorly prepared for work in government and the private sector. In the case of all these responses, for us the surprise came not so much in the fact that the answers differed, but in the large margin of the differences.

Finally we may note that those teaching or educated at the leading universities tend to hold different views than the rest of the respondents on such matters as the propensity of mathematically oriented econ-omists turning to other work later in life, the use of mathematics as a screening and entry limiting device, the usefulness of mathematics in understanding how the economy works and the operation of interest group activities. To the extent that these people are leaders of the profession, they are also leading opinion about the merit of mathemat-ical economics and its natural dominance over other tools of analysis.

IV. SUMMARY AND CONCLUSIONS

Our study has one rather clear-cut conclusion: The editors of economics journals should reduce the space devoted to mathematically oriented material. In addition, the results of the survey suggest that the use of mathematical economics should be reduced or at least not increased any further in both human and knowledge capital formation, though the results are not overwhelmingly strong in support of this conclusion.

We do not believe it to be desirable that any collective action be taken to reduce the power and influence of mathematical economists who act independently or in groups to further the interests of their professional specialty. We see, instead, the signs of increased awareness of the results of these activities. The signs are the popular press attention given to the subject, the number of critical papers written, the answers provided to

HERBERT G. GRUBEL AND LAWRENCE A. BOLAND

our survey and the very response we have received to our research efforts from average economists as well as some distinguished leaders. There has also been the sharp rise in pure text pages in the AER that took place during the period when ROBERT CLOWER was editor. It is not clear whether this has been a temporary change due to the editor's preferences or whether his very selection and style had the covert support of the leadership of the American Economics Association.

In the context of special interest group dynamics, such developments may be interpreted as signals that the victims have become aware of the costs that have been imposed upon them. The next step following such awareness would then be deliberate resistance to and ultimate reduction of the interest group influences and costs. After completion of this process, it may well appear in retrospect that the growth of mathematical economics in the postwar years has raised the productivity of human and knowledge capital in the science. At the same time, the developments and opinions noted in this study might then be interpreted merely as a temporary episode of overshooting and inefficiency.

REFERENCES

BECKER, GARY S.: 'Competition Among Pressure Groups for Political Influence', *Quarterly Journal of Economics,* Vol. 98 (1983), pp. 371–400.

BLAUG, M. and STURGES, P.: *Who's Who in Economics: A Bibliographic Dictionary of Major Economists 1700–1981,* Cambridge: MIT Press, 1983.

BOLAND, LAWRENCE: 'Economic Methodology: Theory and Practice', in M. AUDET and J.-L. MALOUIN (eds.): *The Generation of Scientific Administrative Knowledge,* Laval University Press, 1986(a).

BOLAND, LAWRENCE: *Methodology for a New Microeconomics,* Boston: Allen & Unwin, 1986(b).

BOLAND, LAWRENCE: *Foundations of Economic Method,* London: Geo. Allen & Unwin, 1982.

CHRESSANTHIS, G.: 'Mathematical Economic Thought and Language: Creation of the New Reality', Discussion Paper, Texas Tech University (January 1985).

Christian Science Monitor: 'Are Math Formulas Washing Common Sense out of Economic Theory?' (April 2, 1985), p. 35 (by DAVID R. FRANCIS).

DIAMOND, ARTHUR M., Jr.: 'DEBREU's Impact on Empirical Work: An Empirical Test', Ohio State University, mimeo, June 1985.

The Economist: 'School Briefs' (December 15, 1984), pp. 72–73.

ON THE EFFICIENT USE OF MATHEMATICS IN ECONOMICS

KOOPMANS, TJALLING: *Three Essays on the State of Economic Science*, New York: McGraw-Hill, 1957.

LEIJONHUFVUD, AXEL: 'Life Among the Econ', *Western Economic Journal* (1973), pp. 327–337.

LEONTIEF, WASSILY: 'Theoretical Assumptions and Nonobserved Facts', *American Economic Review* (1971), pp. 1–7.

LEONTIEF, WASSILY: Letter to the Editor of *Science*, Vol. 217 (July 9, 1982), n. 4555.

LIEBOWITZ, S.J. and PALMER, J.P.: 'Assessing the Relative Impacts of Economics Journals', *Journal of Economic Literature* (March, 1984), pp. 77–88.

McCLOSKEY, DONALD N.: 'The Rhetoric of Economics', *Journal of Economic Literature* (June, 1983), pp. 481–517.

Newsweek: 'What Good are Economists?' (February 4, 1985), pp. 60–63.

ROTWEIN, EUGENE: 'Mathematical Economics: The Empirical View and an Appeal for Pluralism', in SHERMAN RAY KRUPP (ed.): 'The Structure of Economic Science', *Essays in Methodology*, Englewood Cliffs: Prentice Hall, 1966, pp. 102–113.

TINTNER, GERHARD: 'Methodology of Mathematical Economics and Econometrics', *International Encyclopedia of Unified Science*, Chicago: University of Chicago Press, 1968.

WELLINGTON, DONALD: 'Publication Games', unpublished manuscript, Vergennes, Vermont.

SUMMARY

We consider mathematics to be an input into the production of human and knowledge capital in economics. The competitive and the interest group models are analyzed as to their predictions about the efficient use of this input. Many stylized facts are found to be consistent with the interest group model and the implication of an excess use of mathematics. Mathematics in journal articles is shown to have grown significantly during the postwar years. In a survey, 250 economists express the view that there is too much mathematics in professional journals. Only a minority of respondents rejects the view that interest group behaviour is taking place.

The Canadian Journal of Higher Education, Vol. XXI–3, 1991
La revue canadienne d'enseignement supérieur, Vol. XXI–3, 1991

[17]

The Making of Canadian Economists - Results of a Survey of Graduate Students

HERBERT G. GRUBEL*

Abstract

The responses to questions by 155 students revealed the following, most important facts. The students predominantly came from families with high incomes. They have leftist political leanings, though through their training, more have turned right than left.

The students share most strongly the views on fundamental propositions in economics held by U.S. graduate students and less those held by Canadian and U.S. professionals. Students from different Canadian universities hold very similar views on price-theoretic propositions but rather widely differing views on some important issues of macro-economics and income distribution.

The most important finding is that, like their U.S. colleagues, Canadian graduate students believe that for professional success it is more important to learn technical skills rather than about institutions, history and policy. As a result they end up poorly prepared for work on economic policy issues and their research tends to lack real world relevance, even though real world and policy problems attracted them to the graduate programs.

* Professor of Economics, Simon Fraser University

"Departments of economics are graduating a generation of idiots savants, brilliant at esoteric mathematics yet innocent of actual economic life." This quote from Kuttner (1985) was presented by Colander and Klamer (1987) in a review of 212 survey responses by U.S. graduate students in economics. These authors had designed the survey in order to gain insights about the validity of the Kuttner observation and, more generally, the sociological characteristics of graduate students, their views on methodology and the importance and acceptance of certain ideas.

This study reports the results of a similar survey of Canadian graduate students in economics. Many of the questions of the Colander and Klamer study were used in order to shed some light on the similarity of Canadian and US graduate programs. Some of the questions are also the same as those given to professional economists in Europe and the United States, as reported by Frey et al. (1984) and in Canada as reported by Block and Walker (1988). In addition some questions have been included concerning the optimum use of mathematics raised in a survey of academic economists by Grubel and Boland (1986).

The first section discusses briefly the design for the survey and presents a demographic profile of the students who returned completed questionnaires.

I Survey Design and Student Profile

In the Spring of 1987 questionnaires were distributed to professors of economics at 23 Canadian universities; and these recipients were asked to make the survey available to graduate students, to designate a mail–box for their return and to mail the completed surveys to the author. Anonymity of responses was assured since the questionnaire did not contain names. The author's thanks go to those colleagues who by this mechanism generated the return of 158 completed questionnaires.[1]

Data were received from 17 universities. The number of responses in the aggregate represents 24 percent of the graduate students who received the survey.[2] The response rate from universities in Quebec which have French as the language of instruction was limited to four from the University of Laval. This may be due in part to the fact that the questionnaire was in English. For this reason and because of the biases which creep into all survey answers, it is wise to retain a healthy skepticism about the validity of any generalizations for the population as a whole.

Demographics

The surveys were completed by 128 males and 27 females[3], with average ages of 27.5 and 29.9 respectively. The foreign born were 42 percent of the number of students who responded. Those with visitors' visas and non–Canadian citizenship represented 35 percent of the total. Among the foreign born, the largest number were from China (10), USA (7), UK (6), Hong Kong (4), India (4), South Africa, Ghana, Greece and Pakistan (3 each), other Asia (7), other Europe (5), Middle East (1), other Africa (5), Latin America (3) and Australia (1). Fifty-eight percent of the students had a long–term relationship and 22 percent had children.

The parental background of the students is summarized in Table 1, showing separate data for Canadian and foreign nationals. Half of the Canadian students have parents with an annual family income between $30,000 and $80,000 while about half of the parents of foreign students have annual incomes below $30,000. However, it is interesting to note that in the income class of $80,000 and over Canadians and foreigners are represented by nearly the same percentage of 17 and 15, respectively.

Table 1 also shows that large proportions of the Canadian students have parents who are either professionals (such as doctors, lawyers, engineers, dentists and managers) or academics and teachers, and have high levels of educational attainment. Perhaps the findings are best summarized by the fact that 30 percent of the fathers are either professionals, academics or teachers and 48 percent have a B.A., professional, M.A. or Ph.D. degree. A separate compilation shows that 7 percent of the students come from families where both the father and mother are professionals, academics or teachers.

Of the Canadian and foreign students, 16 and 26 percent, respectively, graduated from a private high school. Economics was a major or minor for 119 of all of the students during their undergraduate studies. Other majors and minors noted were Natural Sciences and Engineering (11), Business Administration (7), Mathematics (6), Political Science (4) and Psychology (2), as well as one each in Computer Science, Urban Planning, History, Sociology, International Affairs, Statistics and Philosophy. Over one half of all students (53 percent) had full–time work experience before entering graduate school.

4   Herbert G. Grubel

Table 1
Background of Parents

	Nationality	
	Canadian	Foreign
	(Percent of All Students in Category)	
A. Annual Family Income ($ thousand)		
Less than 30	34	48
Between 30 and 80	49	37
More than 80	17	15
B. Mother's Occupation		
Retired, deceased or not available	10	24
Professional	11	3
Academic or teacher	5	13
Other	74	60
C. Father's Occupation		
Retired, deceased or not available	12	22
Professional	23	12
Academic or teacher	7	13
Other	58	53
D. Mother's Educational Attainment		
High School or less	61	63
BA or equivalent	33	27
Professional, MA or PhD	6	10
E. Father's Educational Attainment		
High School or less	52	50
BA or equivalent	23	24
Professional, MA or PhD	25	26

Current Educational Interests

Among the respondents, one-half expected to graduate with an M.A. and one-half with a Ph.D., respectively. Fifty–two percent were in their first year, 21 percent in the second, 10 percent each in the third and fourth and 7 percent in the fifth and later years of graduate study. Of those in a Ph.D. program, 39 percent had completed all of their coursework. Fifty–eight percent were working on an MA or Ph.D. thesis. Table 2 shows the fields in which the thesis is written. International Economics dominates by a wide margin.

Table 2
Fields of M.A. or Ph.D. Thesis

Total Replies: 95		Number in Field
International Economics		19
Public Finance, Taxation		13
Money, Banking, Finance		12
Natural Resource Economics		9
Economic Development		9
Micro–Economics		6
Macro–Economics		6
Econometrics		4
Labour Economics		4
Industrial Organization		4
Dynamic or Linear Programming		3
Regional Economics		2
Law and Economics, Health Economics, Demography, Game Theory	each	1

In response to the question, "In 15 years from now you hope to be where?", 27 percent answered 'teaching at a major university'; 6 percent 'teaching at a good liberal arts college'; 11 percent 'working at a major research institution'; 15 percent 'doing research in a policy oriented think tank'; 29 percent 'working in the private sector'; and 12 percent 'working in government'.[4]

Financing

Before starting graduate work, 55 percent of the students had the assurance of a scholarship, 76 percent of a teaching assistantship. Only 5 percent have taken out a private sector loan and 28 percent receive financial help from parents. For 80 percent of the students scholarships and teaching assistance provide the most important source of finance. For about 20 percent private income from their own work or that of spouses is the most important source of finance.

Influences on Study and Thesis

The question "How important were the following in your decision to do graduate work in economics?" was answered by students marking the choice 3: very important, 2: somewhat important or 1: unimportant. A simple summary index of the responses was constructed by calculating the mean of the numerical values given by the students.[5] The ranking of the answers is determined by the value of the index of importance.

a. Economics seemed the most relevant field given my intellectual interest – 2.40

b. Enjoyed undergraduate classes in economics – 2.38

c. Desire to engage in policy formulation – 2.31

d.Good grades in economics classes – 2.21

e. Advice of undergraduate teachers – 1.71

f. Wanted a job in academia and economics seemed the best possibility – 1. 65

g. Political reasons – 1.32

The question "What has been the major factor in your choice of a thesis topic?" produced the following indices of importance, constructed in the manner discussed above.

a. Finding answers to pressing current economic problems – 2.30

b. The desire to understand some economic phenomenon – 2.12

c. The feasibility of a topic and to get it done quickly – 2.03

d. The suggestions of a teacher 1.82

e. The application of some econometric technique – 1.67

f. The application of a mathematical technique – 1.52

Importance of Learning Vehicles and Sources of Stress

In response to the statement "The different learning vehicles have been for me: 3: very important; 2: moderately important; and 1: least important", the responses produced the following values and ranking for the summary index:

a. Classroom lectures – 2.48

b. Assigned readings – 2.38

c. Discussions with other student s– 2.10

d. Unassigned readings – 2.02

e. Seminars 1.94

f. Classroom discussions – 1.86

g. Teaching classes – 1.84

The question "How stressful have different aspects of graduate student life been for you?" was answered on a scale from 4 (very stressful) to 1 (not stressful). The responses are as follows:

a. Coursework – 2.94

b.Maintaining a meaningful life outside of grad. school – 2.39

c. Financial situation – 2.27

d. Conflict between course contents and your interest – 2.25

e. Doing mathematics – 2.22

f. Finding a dissertation topic – 2.13

g. Relations with faculty – 1.72

h. Relations with students – 1.40

Most Respected Economists

The request to write in the names of the three most respected economists, dead or alive, resulted in the following list of names with the number indicating the frequency with which the name was given:

Keynes 58, Marx 21, Samuelson 20, Smith 17, Friedman 17, Lucas 13, Galbraith 11, Marshall 8, Stiglitz 6, Schumpeter 6, Ricardo 6, Solow 4, Baumol 4, Stigler 4, Steven Cheung 4, Coase 4; 3 each: A. K. Sen, Hicks, Tobin, Arrow, Demsetz, Pigou, Buchanan, Gerald Helleiner, Hayek, Joan Robinson, Debreu, Myrdal; 2 each: Dornbusch, Sargent, Okun, Barro, Patinkin, Lionel Mackenzie, W.W. Rostow, Walras, Alchian, Becker, Boulding, Heilbronner.[6]

Political Leanings and Changes

The request to indicate political leanings was not met by 15 percent of the students. They tended to accompany their act with such comments as 'do not understand the labels'[7], 'depends on the issue' and 'don't know any more'. One student ticked the entry 'communist'. Three students indicated that they were leaning towards the politics of the 'Green Party and similar organizations concerned with the environment'. Most of the responses went to the following categories where the percentages add to 100 by the inclusion of the entries noted in the preceding paragraphs:

Socialist 13, Social Democrat 18, Liberal 22

Neo–Conservative 12, Conservative 13, Libertarian 8.

A summary representation of these findings indicates that 63 percent were liberal or to the left and 33 percent were to the right of liberal.

A separate question concerned students' movement on political leanings since entering graduate school. There has been movement to the left for 12 percent, to the right for 21 percent and no change for 67 percent. This result confirms Stigler's (1982) suggestion that graduate studies in economics tend to make people more conservative.

Satisfaction with Studies

The question "Knowing what you know now, would you start graduate school again?" elicited 'Yes, definitely' from 52 percent; 'Probably yes" from 35

8   Herbert G. Grubel

percent; 'Probably No' from 8 percent; 'Definitely No' from 3 percent; and 'No, but ask me again tomorrow' from 3 percent.

Evaluation

Whether or not one finds the demographic information interesting and worthy of comment depends on one's priors. The author found no particular surprise in the age, sex and foreign student composition of the sample and the proportion of students with long–term relationships, children and work–experience. Noteworthy, however, is the relative importance of students from China and other Asian countries, who make up about two–thirds of the foreign students who responded to the survey.

The data on the students' family backgrounds add evidence in support of the view that higher education accrues predominantly to families with high incomes and high levels of education. This is especially so given the fact that 80 percent of the students have their studies financed predominantly through scholarships and research and teaching assistantships. Very surprising is the almost identical educational attainment of the fathers of Canadian and foreign students, where the latter include a large number from China.

The distribution of students according to their intended terminal degree reflects roughly that found at Simon Fraser University and possibly at other graduate departments. There appears to be somewhat of a bias in favour of responses by students during the first two years of their studies. This is unfortunate and should be kept in mind in the interpretation of some of the views discussed below. Given the nature of graduate studies in economics it should not come as a surprise that only about 29 percent of the respondents expect to use their degrees in private sector employment, even in the light of the fact that about half of these degrees are expected to be M.A.'s.

The decision to undertake graduate study in economics was influenced most heavily by personal preferences and abilities. The desire to become involved in policy formation ranked highly, though political considerations and distinct career objectives in academia carried relatively little weight. The choice of thesis topics was influenced most heavily by factors that may be described as idealistic rather than practical, as is evidenced by the relatively low weight given to the suggestions of teachers and the application of mathematical and econometric techniques. Somewhat surprising was the relatively small importance which students attached to teaching classes, classroom discussions and seminars as vehicles of learning.

It is interesting to have a record of the political leanings of Canadian graduate students in economics. Some readers may be surprised by the relative size of the group with strong preferences for the ideology of the left, especially since these students have developed their attitudes during the period when conservative economic policies were adopted in many countries, including the Soviet Union and China. It is not clear whether these political leanings reflect simply the students' age and the normal idealism accompanying it or whether they have been and are influenced by their teachers and readings. The former interpretation is supported by the finding that 21 percent of the students have moved to the right and only 12 percent to the left since they entered graduate school.

On the other hand, the ranking of Keynes, Marx and Galbraith (and perhaps even Samuelson) as the most respected economists relative to the ranking of conservatives like Friedman, Lucas and Schumpeter, indicates the influence which these leftist economists have had on the thinking of the students. Presumably, these preferences were influenced heavily by the readings and lectures of their teachers at the undergraduate and graduate levels. Many of those, especially in social sciences other than economics, have been staunch defenders of the leftist ideologies during the years when electorates and politicians in many countries have shifted their alliances.

Given the stresses associated with graduate school, it should please those responsible for the design and management of the graduate programs in Canada that only 11 percent of the students would not again choose their program of study.

The demographic characteristics and views on schooling of the individuals studied here are very similar to those surveyed by Colander and Klamer. The major difference lies in the proportion of M.A. and Ph.D. students. In the sample analyzed by Colander and Klamer were only students at the major U.S. universities: Chicago, M.I.T., Harvard, Stanford, Columbia and Yale. The graduate programs at these institutions are almost exclusively aimed at the graduation of Ph.D.'s. Furthermore, these universities have considerably higher admissions standards than most other U.S. and Canadian universities with graduate programs in economics. This fact should be remembered in the analysis of differences in views on economic propositions and methodology presented in the next section.

II   The Socialization of Students

In their study of the economics profession, Grubel and Boland (1986) and Kuttner (1985) discovered a widespread concern with the growth of mathematics in the curriculum of graduate students and the production of knowledge. At the risk of oversimplification, it might be suggested that this concern arises from the perception of two undesirable developments which accompany these trends towards mathematics and rigour. First, it will make economics increasingly irrelevant to the understanding of real world problems. Second, access to the profession will become increasingly more difficult and success in it a function of conformity to its sociological norms rather than the production of economic knowledge relevant to the real world.

The following questions were designed to discover the extent to which the views of graduate students reflect the drift to mathematics and the elitism of the profession. Table 3 presents answers to the question: "How important to your development as an economist would you, if you had the time and option, consider readings in or discussions about topics in the following fields?" Answers were 4: very important; 3: important; 2 moderately important; 1 unimportant. The responses of U.S. graduate students to the same questions as reported by Colander and Klamer are given also.

Table 3
The Importance of Reading in Other Fields

Field	Canadian Students	U.S. Students
Mathematics	3.08	3.08
Political Science	2.77	2.65
Humanities	2.65	N.A.
Computer Science	2.55	2.12
History	2.55	2.94
Philosophy	2.47	2.50
Sociology	2.23	2.40
Psychology	2.11	2.11
Languages	2.05	N.A.
Physics	1.47	1.45

Table 4 presents answers to the question "How important do you consider the following characteristics for students and academics who wish to get ahead quickly in the economics profession?" The scale of answers was the same as in the preceding question except for 1: 'don't know'. In the calculation of the index the 'don't know' answers were omitted.

Table 4
Perceptions of Success

Question	Can.	U.S.
	Students	
Being smart in the sense of being good at problem solving..	3.53	3.63
Excellence in mathematics and model building.....	3.42	3.55
Being interested in, and good at, empirical work..	3.19	2.98
Being very knowledgeable in one particular field..	3.14	3.18
Ability to make connections with prominent Professors...	3.02	3.14
A broad knowledge of the economics literature....	3.00	2.62
Thorough knowledge of the economy and its history...	2.73	2.30

Evaluation

The perceived importance of readings in other fields reflects the role played by mathematics and computer science in the profession. On the other hand, the importance attached to readings in other social sciences and humanities suggests that most students are aware of the extent to which knowledge in these fields is necessary to be a good economist. It is worth mentioning here that Colander and Klamer in personal interviews of students discovered that few had the time to read anything in other fields, in spite of their expressions of the desirability to do so. Presumably, the same is true for Canadian students and the data should be interpreted in the light of this possibility. The comparison of the responses of Canadian and U.S. students shows a surprising correspondence in the ratings for mathematics, physics and most of the social sciences. Canadians attached more importance to readings in political and computer science than did their U.S. colleagues. The opposite was true for history.

The data in Table 4 are most relevant to the assessment of the extent to which graduate student attitudes reflect the trend towards mathematization and model-building in the profession. Students believe that advancement is aided much more by skills in these fields than it is by broad, historic knowledge of the economy. Even the benefits from specialization and skills in empirical work are considered much less important than the skills of problem-solving, mathematics and model-building. A comparison of Canadian and U.S. students shows that the latter consider empirical and broad knowledge to be even less important than do the former.

III Opinions on Key Propositions in Economics

Frey and his colleagues (1984) surveyed U.S. economists on a set of key economic propositions.[8] The results were considered to be of sufficient scientific interest that the paper was acceptable to the editors of the American Economic Review. It also stimulated others to ask the same questions of different populations of economists, Colander and Klamer (1987) and Block and Walker (1988), who surveyed U.S. graduate students and Canadian professional economists, respectively. In Table 5 the results of the survey of Canadian graduate students is shown along with those from the other populations. In all surveys there were minor differences in the wording of some questions. Answers were given in the classes: 4 agree; 3 agree with some reservations; 2 disagree; 1 no view. The index in this and all of the following tables was calculated by multiplying the number of responses in each category by the values of 4 to 2, respectively and division by the total number of responses in these classes.[9]

Canadian graduate students are strongly convinced that protection reduces general economic welfare, that fiscal policy is an effective stabilization tool and that inflation is primarily a monetary phenomenon. They are somewhat less convinced that minimum wages cause unemployment and that central banks should behave in a monetarist fashion. They disagree quite strongly with the ideas that wage and price controls should be used to control inflation and that the capitalist system is crisis prone.

Kendall's rank correlation coefficients for the first six propositions and concerning the 4 groups were as follows. For Canadian graduate students and Canadian professionals, the coefficient is .67, which is about the same as that between U.S. graduate students and professionals. The correlation in the rankings is highest between the graduate students of the two countries and lowest between Canadian students and U.S. professionals. At a less formal level, the following matrix provides some useful insights about agreement among the four groups.

Proposition	Rank for Groups			
	A	B	C	D
1	2	3	2	2
2	5	5	5	5
3	4	2	3	1
4	1	1	1	3
5	3	4	4	4
6	6	6	6	6

Table 5
Views on Key Propositions

Question	Canadian		U.S.	
	Students (A)	Profess. (B)	Students (C)	Profess. (D)
1. Fiscal Policy can be an effective tool in stabilization policy	3.09	3.33	3.25	3.57
2. Central banks should maintain a constant rate of growth in the money supply	2.85	2.58	2.59	2.53
3. Minimum wages cause unemployment among the young and unskilled	2.95	3.53	3.17	3.58
4. Tariffs and quotas reduce general economic welfare	3.32	3.67	3.28	2.98
5. Inflation is primarily a monetary phenomenon	3.05	3.19	2.98	2.84
6. Wage and price controls should be used to control inflation	2.44	2.30	2.21	2.34
7. Worker democracy increases productivity	3.05	N.A.	2.84	N.A.
8. The market system tends to discriminate against women	2.84	N.A.	2.83	N.A.
9. The capitalist system has an inherent tendency towards crisis	2.64	N.A.	2.51	N.A.

All four groups are unanimous in their answers to propositions 2 (monetarism for central banks) and 6 (the merit of controls). Canadian students are on the side of the majority of groups with respect to proposition 1 (the merit of fiscal policies) and 4 (the cost of protection). They are in the distinct minority on question 5 (the monetary explanation of inflation).

Views by Universities of Enrolment
One interesting aspect of differences in views on some key economic propositions concerns the influence of schools of thought and academic

traditions. In the study of U.S. students the views on propositions were broken down by the universities at which they were enrolled. Large differences emerged between Chicago, M.I.T.,Harvard, Stanford and Columbia, especially with respect to the merits of fiscal policy and monetarist propositions. In Table 6 the views of Canadian students on these questions are shown for 10 universities from which at least 6 completed surveys had been received.[10]

It can be seen that there are substantial differences in the levels of the index across the universities listed. Dalhousie, Calgary and Queen's students believe most strongly in the efficacy of fiscal policies. Students at the other end of the spectrum on this question are at Saskatchewan, Toronto, Carleton and Simon Fraser University. Monetarism as evidenced by the indices on questions 2 and 5 has its greatest following at Simon Fraser University and somewhat less so at Toronto and Saskatchewan. There appears to be some correlation between the strength of belief in fiscal policy and the lack of belief in the monetarist propositions.

Simon Fraser University students again have the highest degree of conviction that minimum wages raise unemployment while Dalhousie and Queen's students least believe in the validity of this proposition. The highest index of agreement and consensus among students in all universities is found on the harmful effects of protection. The efficacy of wage and price controls and the leftist proposition about the capitalist crisis receive universally low support. A wide dispersion of views is found on the market's discrimination against women, with Dalhousie, University of British Columbia and Victoria students supporting the assertion the most and those at Toronto, Carleton and Simon Fraser University the least.

Evaluation
The data in Table 5 suggest that the views of Canadian graduate students on some basic propositions in economics are very similar to those of professionals in Canada and the two U.S. groups. Consensus among the groups as measured by rankings extends over both some price–theoretic and Keynesian–Monetarist propositions in macro–economics. This is in contrast with the findings by Block and Walker that consensus among economists is highest on matters concerning micro–economic phenomena, less so on macro–economic issues and least on policy problems that involve income redistribution.[11] Most puzzling is the fact that the correlation of the rankings is highest among the students of the two countries. One possible explanation of this phenomenon is that the students reflect the views of their teachers, almost all of whom have a Ph.D. and pass on

Table 6
Comparison Among Canadian Universities

University:	Dalhousie	Carleton	Toronto	Queen's	U.B.C.
Numb. Observ.	16	9	6	19	9
Question					
1 Fiscal Policy	3.50	2.89	2.83	3.17	3.00
2 Money Supply	2.91	2.78	2.50	3.00	2.44
3 Min. Wages	2.53	3.11	3.00	2.56	3.00
4 Protection	3.00	3.56	3.60	3.22	3.22
5 Inflation	2.69	3.00	3.33	2.72	2.89
6 Controls	2.43	2.00	2.33	2.28	2.00
7 Worker Demo	3.23	3.00	3.17	2.92	3.00
8 Women Discr	3.22	2.43	2.33	2.78	3.14
9 Capit. Crisis	2.50	2.38	2.33	2.60	2.43

University:	S.F.U	Victoria	WestOnt.	Calgary	Sask.
Numb. Observ.	26	20	10	8	8
Question					
1 Fiscal Policy	2.92	3.05	3.00	3.25	2.57
2 Money Supply	3.09	2.71	2.63	2.63	3.00
3 Min. Wages	3.15	3.14	3.00	2.88	3.00
4 Protection	3.38	3.23	3.44	3.25	3.25
5 Inflation	3.48	3.20	2.80	2.50	3.29
6 Controls	2.17	2.35	2.45	2.13	2.63
7 Worker Demo	3.00	3.13	3.00	2.50	2.86
8 Women Discr	2.68	3.12	2.71	3.00	2.88
9 Capit. Crisis	2.63	2.68	2.67	2.88	2.71

the latest knowledge in both countries.[12] The broader populations of economists contain many with qualifications lower than the Ph.D. and possibly holding views acquired many years ago.

The main conclusion emerging from a study of Table 6 is that there is relatively great consensus among Canadian graduate students at different universities with respect to propositions that involve price–theoretic principles, such as the effects of protection and wage and price controls. At the other extreme, there is a wide dispersion of views on propositions from macro and monetary economics. Undoubtedly, schools of thought have developed and the views of students are influenced heavily by the culture and work of professors in their respective institutions. In this respect, Canadian and U.S. universities are very similar.It can be seen from Table 6 on the issues of macro–economics, the opinions of Simon Fraser University students are the most distinctly different from those held by students at other Canadian universities. In comparison with the results reported by Colander and Klamer, the Simon Fraser University students' views resemble most those of Chicago students .

IV Issues of Methodology

Differences in the views of economists in the longer run are influenced partly by the theoretical, empirical and institutional knowledge they acquired in graduate school. However, more important may well be the methodological principles that they have learned. These tend to influence their approach to the study and interpretation of the constantly changing environment and new knowledge for at least some time after completion of their studies. For this reason, Colander and Klamer and the survey of Canadian students have asked for views on some fundamental issues of methodology. Because Colander and Klamer found large differences in students' answers from different universities, the summary index of those and of students from Canadian universities are presented in Table 7.[13]

The first proposition, which concerns the relevance of neoclassical economics, most differentiates the attitudes of students at Chicago and the other U.S. universities, but especially M.I.T. and Harvard. An interesting approach to the analysis of Canadian views is to see into which of the three U.S. camps they fall. Canadian students on average clearly believe much less in the validity of the proposition than do the U.S. students on average. In fact, the overall index for Canada is about the same as that for Harvard, which is the second lowest of the U.S. universities. Toronto students have the second highest index on the list, following Chicago's. Simon Fraser University is second in Canada but is lower than that of Stanford and Yale and equal to that of Columbia. The students at Carleton, Dalhousie, Western Ontario, Queen's and University of British Columbia share a skepticism that resembles that held by students at M.I.T. and Harvard. The proposition concerning the scientific nature of economics also shows a great variance among universities in both countries and shows Chicago students with the strongest confidence in the validity of the proposition. The Canadian universities Victoria, Calgary and Saskatchewan are closest to Chicago. Simon Fraser University students, after those from Dalhousie, have the least confidence in the scientific nature of economics.

A look at the range of values for all Canadian and U.S. respondents shows an interesting difference. The range of values is only .54 for the Canadian and 1.23 for the U.S. responses. This may be interpreted as indicating that U.S. students

The Making of Canadian Economists – Results of a Survey of Graduate Students   17

tend to have stronger and more "extreme" views on the issues surveyed or that there is a wider range of scholarly–ideological traditions.

Table 7
Views on Methodology

Universities	Questions (For formulation see at bottom)			
	1	2	3	4
Dalhousie	2.79	2.33	2.47	2.56
Carleton	2.63	2.75	2.71	2.89
Toronto	3.40	2.00	2.80	2.80
Queen's	2.89	2.53	2.60	2.82
University of British Columbia	2.89	2.43	2.00	2.63
Simon Fraser University	3.17	2.63	2.68	2.71
Victoria	3.00	2.59	2.31	3.35
Western Ontario	2.88	2.56	2.33	2.71
Calgary	3.13	2.05	2.38	3.33
Saskatchewan	3.14	3.14	2.00	3.29
All Canadian	2.97	2.47	2.43	2.90
Chicago	3.66	2.56	2.87	3.45
M.I.T.	2.39	2.39	2.31	3.03
Harvard	2.98	2.30	2.20	2.74
Stanford	3.28	2.57	2.51	3.05
Columbia	3.16	2.58	2.38	3.09
Yale	3.28	2.63	2.47	2.73
All U.S.	3.23	2.00	2.43	3.10

Questions:
1.   The study of neoclassical economics is relevant for the
     economic problems of today
2.   Economists agree on fundamental issues
3.   There is a sharp line between positive and normative economics
4.   Economics is the most scientific social science

Scoring Categories — 4: strongly agree; 3: agree somewhat; 2: disagree; 1: no opinion.
The index is the weighted average of responses in the first three categories.
Note: The index for all Canadian universities includes those in the table and all those for which the number of responses was too small to warrant calculation of a separate index. The U.S. index is based on the sample of universities shown only.

Views on Mathematics

Mathematical skills are acquired at the expense of skills in other fields. The extent to which students are willing to sacrifice the learning of one at the expense of the other depends on the views they hold about their usefulness. These views are probed with the questions reviewed in Table 8. Differences among universities and schools of thought are of some interest and therefore are shown in Table 8.

One of the outstanding characteristics of the natural sciences is that knowledge is cumulative. In all Canadian universities surveyed students believed strongly that economics in this sense is a science. It appears that this view is held widely among economists, though the rise and fall of economic doctrines, such as the quantity theory of money, Keynesianism and purchasing power parity has led some to question its validity.

Some methodologists argue that mathematical models are sophisticated tautologies since all conclusions follow strictly from the assumptions made. Since assumptions can be chosen from a very large set and since all must of necessity involve a drastic simplification of the real world, such models can be designed to prove almost anything and their usefulness for the guidance of policy is strictly limited.[14] Students at Canadian universities on average are split on their acceptance of these propositions. Those at Carleton, Victoria, Calgary and British Columbia showed the strongest faith in the usefulness of mathematical models for policy, those at Toronto and Simon Fraser University the least.

The proposition that mathematical modelling is useful for the understanding of economics is accepted more strongly than that about the use of the methodology for the guidance of policy. The views on this matter differ widely among universities. The validity is accepted most strongly at Victoria and Queen's and least at Simon Fraser and Dalhousie.

The question concerning the realism of assumptions is closely related to the issue of mathematical model-building. Friedman argues that the usefulness of all models is determined by the empirical support that can be found for them, especially their ability to predict relationships between variables. On average, Canadian graduate students disagree with the validity of this methodological proposition. Students at the University of British Columbia are the most consistent in the strength with which they support the usefulness of mathematical models and insist on the realism of assumptions. It would seem that the economics profession is split on the validity of the proposition that econometrics can be used to support any desired hypothesis. On the one hand, it is widely recognized that with the low cost of computing services and an abundance of data, there is a lot of data–mining and simultaneous model building. On the other hand, there is much econometric work which draws on sound models and classical testing and measurement. The problem for the reader of econometric studies is to know reliably which methodology was used by the author. Graduate students at Canadian universities reflect this problem and the division in the profession at large. At Toronto and Saskatchewan they are the most cynical about the use of econometrics, they are least so at Queen's, by a large margin over the rest.

Table 8
Mathematics, Econometrics, History and Institutions

Universities	Questions (For formulation see at bottom)							
	1	2	3	4	5	6	7	8
Dalhousie	3.7	2.6	2.7	2.3	3.6	3.6	2.1	2.9
Carleton	3.7	3.0	2.8	2.4	2.8	3.3	2.4	3.0
Toronto	2.8	2.2	3.0	2.6	4.0	4.0	2.0	3.0
Queen's	3.2	2.7	2.4	2.4	2.7	3.3	2.4	3.3
U.B.C.	3.3	2.9	2.6	2.1	3.3	3.4	2.0	3.0
S.F.U.	3.4	2.6	2.8	2.8	3.5	3.5	2.3	2.8
Victoria	3.5	3.0	2.7	2.4	3.0	3.1	2.2	3.5
Western Ontario	3.3	2.7	2.8	2.3	3.5	3.3	2.2	2.8
Calgary	3.1	3.0	2.8	3.0	3.0	3.1	2.8	3.1
Saskatchewan	3.8	2.8	3.0	2.9	2.7	3.5	2.0	3.1
All Universities	3.4	2.7	2.8	2.4	3.2	3.4	2.2	3.0

Questions:
1.   Economics knowledge is cumulative
2.   Mathematical models reflect the real world and therefore can help guide policy
3.   Econometrics can be used to support any desired hypothesis
4.   The realism of assumptions is irrelevant for the value of models
5.   The study of economic history and institutions is necessary to become an effective economist
6.   There is no such thing as a value–free model in economics
7.   The history of thought is irrelevant for today's students of economics
8.   Mathematical modelling is essential for understanding economics
Answers:
4: strongly agree; 3: agree with reservations; 2: disagree; 1: no views.
The index omits answers in category 'no views'.

Canadian graduate students are quite strongly in support of the view that the study of history, institutions and economic doctrines are important for economists. This is consistent with a belief in the usefulness of rigorous mathematical modelling since, presumably, such broader historic and institutional studies encourage the choice of appropriate assumptions. There is a problem associated with these views, as has been pointed out elsewhere (Grubel and Boland (1986)). The study of mathematics and modelling competes for time with the study of history, doctrine and other less rigorous fields. During the postwar years the former have won out over the latter to a degree which is disturbing to some; the situation has elicited such extreme statements as the one about the graduation of idiots savants quoted above. In a sense it is reassuring to know that students value the historic, institutional and doctrinal studies and that the problem may lie with supply rather than demand.

V Summary and Conclusions

The survey of Canadian graduate students in 1988 provides some interesting demographic data concerning their age, sex, nationality, parental background, professional aspirations and financing, which may well serve as an historic benchmark for the assessment of trends in the future. Perhaps most interesting is the parental background, which supports the view that graduate studies in economics attracts the children of highly educated families with high incomes. On the other hand, the results also show that through the availability of scholarships and work as teaching assistants, the system permits the enrolment of many from families with low income and educational attainment.

The political leanings of graduate students are distinctly to the left. However, in the course of their studies, more have turned right than left.

The survey of views on fundamental propositions in economics showed a widespread agreement with the views held by Canadian and U.S. professionals and U.S. graduate students. Perhaps most interesting is the finding that the views of Canadian graduate students correlate most strongly with those of U.S. graduate students. Another interesting result of the study of views on basic propositions concerns responses classified by universities of enrolment. There is widespread agreement on price–theoretic propositions. The dispersion of views is widest on issues of macro–economic policies and income distribution.

Students in Canadian graduate schools believe strongly in the importance of technical and particularly mathematical skills for getting ahead in the profession. Empirical and historical knowledge are the least important in this sense. At the same time, they strongly support the view that such empirical and historical knowledge is important for becoming an effective economist. Interest in getting involved in policy formulation has been an important influence on their entry into graduate studies in economics.

Perhaps this conflict between technical and other knowledge is the most important finding of this survey. It agrees roughly with that done by Colander and Klamer (1988) and the analysis of Grubel and Boland (1986). The need to get established in an increasingly technical discipline has forced students to accept its norms. This acceptance has taken place in spite of the students' conviction about the importance of less technical knowledge and the risk that the discipline is becoming irrelevant for policy and current problems.

Footnotes

[1] Twenty-six responses were received from students at Simon Fraser University, where 75 in residence received the questionnaire. The number of responses, size of the student population who received the questionnaire, names of universities and professors who handled the chores are as follows: 20/26 responses from the University of Victoria; 19/103 from Queen's University, Douglas Purvis; 16/35 from Dalhousie University, Paul Huber; 10/60 from the University of Western Ontario, John Palmer; 9/35 from Carleton University, Steven Ferris; 8/72 from the University of British Columbia, Sam Ho; 8/37 from the University of Calgary, Malcolm Brown; 8/35 from the University of Saskatchewan, Isabel Anderson; 6/50 from the University of Toronto, Edward Safarian; 5/? from Concordia University, Philippe Callier; 5/12 from the University of Waterloo, Wayne Thirsk; 4/? from McGill University, John McCallum; 4/12 from Laval University, Roger Dehem; 4/35 from McMaster University, William Scarth; 4/22 from the University of Guelph, John Vandercamp. Paul Booth at the University of Alberta, Rodrigue Tremblay at the University of Montreal, Michel Bergeron at the University of Quebec at Montreal, Norman Cameron at the University of Manitoba, Don McCharles at the University of New Brunswick, and Ronald Bodkin at the University of Ottawa were mailed questionnaires but for a variety of reasons did not generate any responses. Many thanks to those colleagues who cooperated in this venture and to the students who took the time to complete the questionnaire.

[2] It can be seen from the preceding footnote that in the case of two universities the size of the student population could not be ascertained. These were omitted from the calculation of the response rate. It may also be worth noting how the students were approached. In the case of the University of Calgary, University of British Columbia and Carleton University, the survey went to all registered students. In all other cases the survey was distributed to students on campus through mail–boxes in the department.

[3] Three otherwise useful questionnaires did not have demographic information. In the remainder of this paper the number or percentage of incomplete answers is not noted, except where this information is important.

4 Many students indicated preferences for several of the categories. Each of the preference was recorded without any weight given to rankings. Two students expressed an interest in working for international organizations.

5 Some information is lost by not providing the reader with a complete distribution of answers in each category. However, the saving of space and reduced risk of informational overload influenced the decision to use only the summary index. As it turns out, the ranking of answers by the index and the number of answers in 'very important' is almost perfectly correlated. For these reasons, all of the results below are presented also in the form of a summary index.

It should be noted that the index used here does not give an indication of the dispersion of answers or degree of consensus. For example, the index has the same value of 2 under two vastly different conditions. Under the first, all answers are in the category 'somewhat important'. Under the second, half of the answers each are in the categories 'very important' and 'unimportant'. The degree of consensus in this sense can be measured by an index of entropy used by Block and Walker (1988). Such an index is not presented here since the degree of consensus is not of any particular analytical interest. Furthermore, a casual inspection of the responses suggests the almost total absence of bimodality in the answers.

6 First names were omitted except in cases where it was felt identification was facilitated. The names of individuals mentioned only once are Akerloff, Arnott, Baron, Bator, Bauer, Bhagwati, Blaug, Blinder, Carnoy, Fidel Castro, Diamond, Dockner, H. Scott Gordon, Heckscher, Hotelling, Jevon, Ron Jones, Alfred Kahn, Knight, Elisabeth Landes, Leontieff, Arthur Lewis, Richard Lipsey, Little, Malinvaud, Gerald Meier, Richard Merton, von Mises, J.S. Mill, Mundell, R.R. Nelson, T.W.Schultz, Schumacher, Shackle, Herbert Simon, Lawrence Summer, Thurow, Von Neuman, O. Williamson, J.R. Winter. Not listed are 4 individuals (including the author) who were obviously current or recent teachers of the students who completed the survey. Two of the three references to Helleiner came from students at the University of Toronto.

7 This may have been a difficulty for some others, especially with respect to the term 'libertarian'. Two students who identified themselves as libertarians at the same time noted in a subsequent response that they 'moved to the right' since they entered graduate school.

8 They also surveyed economists from European nations. To keep the analysis manageable, these findings are not discussed here.

9 The indices for the survey results of other authors were calculated in the same manner from the data published in the original sources.

10 It should also be noted that in the calculation of the index, responses of 'No view' were excluded. In the case of some questions with already small number of observations, the index is therefore based on very few observations.

[11] It should be noted that the Block–Walker conclusions are based on a larger set of questions and the use of an index of entropy. This index reflects the degree of dispersion of answers in the classes of response.

[12] Block and Walker found significantly different answers on a large number of issues given by Canadian economists with and without a Ph.D.

[13] Canadian students were also asked to indicate their views on these methodological issues before they entered graduate school and currently. The data in Table 7 are current views. The following are the indices for the four issues held currently and before, respectively. 1: 2.97 from 2.94; 2: 2.47 from 2.59; 3: 2.43 from 2.67; 4: 2.90 from 2.99. On each question, about half of the respondents did not change their views.

[14] These views on methodology are not anti–theoretical. To the contrary, methodologists from this tradition typically argue that theory is needed to guide empirical work. The main point at issue is that mathematical models without empirical support are not reliable guides for policy.

References

Block, Walter, & Walker, Michael. (1988). Entropy in the Canadian economics profession: Sampling consensus on the major issues. *Canadian Public Policy, 14* (2), June.

Colander, David, & Klamer, Arjo. (1987). The making of an economist. *Economic Perspectives, 1* (2), Fall.

Frey, Bruno S., Pommerehne, Werner W., Schneider, Friedrich, & Gilbert, Guy. (1984). Consensus and dissension among economists: An empirical inquiry. *American Economic Review, 74* (5), December.

Grubel, Herbert & Boland, Lawrence. (1986). On the efficient use of mathematics in economics: Some theory, facts and results of an opinion survey. *Kyklos, 3*.

Kuttner, Robert. (1985). The poverty of economics. *The Atlantic Monthly,* February.

McCloskey, Donald. (1986). *The Rhetoric of Economics.* Madison: University of Wisconsin Press.

Stigler, George. (1982). *The Economist as Preacher.* Chicago: Chicago University Press.

Ward, Benjamin. (1972). *What's Wrong with Economics.* New York: Basic Books.

Aitchison, J. 236, 269
Alchian, A.A. 306
Allison, F.D. 236, 269, 271
Anderson, T. 181
Arrow, K.J. 1, 4–5, 172, 252, 306

Balassa, B. 257
Barro, R. 306
Baumol, William J. 306
Becker, Gary S. 282, 306
Bentham, Jeremy 63
Bhagwati, J. 257
Birch, David C. 169
Blaug, M. 290
Block, Walter 301, 311, 313
Boland, Lawrence 301, 308, 319–20
Boulding, K.E. 306
Broadus, R.N. 241, 268
Brown, J.A.C. 236, 269
Buchanan, James 210–11, 306
Butler, Stuart M. 122

Cairns, Robert D. 130
Carter, Billy 181
Cartter, A.M. 232, 250, 262
Caves, R. 257
Chenery, H. 257
Cheng, H.-S. 120
Cheung, Steven 306
Clark, K.E. 232, 249–50, 261
Clower, Robert 298
Coase, R.H. 306
Colander, David 301, 308–11, 315, 320
Cole, J. 234, 261, 263–4
Cole, S. 234, 261, 263–4
Comfort, A. 232

de Solla Price, D.J. 263
Debreu, Gerard 306
Decaminada, Joseph P. 121
Demsetz 306
Diamond, Walter H. 118
Dickens, Charles 61
Dornbusch, R. 306

Ely, Bert 95

Feige, Edgar L. 129

Fortin, P. 54, 189
Frey, Bruno S. 301, 311
Friedman, Milton 140, 181, 252, 306, 308, 317
Frisch, R. 252

Galbraith, John K. 155, 306, 308
George, Henry 100–101, 112
Giersch, Herbert 169
Gilder, G. 69
Gordon, R.J. 183
Grubel, H.G. 60, 74, 97, 131, 173, 184, 234, 252, 264–5, 301, 308, 319–20

Hagstrom, W.O. 232–3, 250, 262
Hansen, W.L. 232, 259
Hayek, F.A. von 252, 306
Heilbronner, R.L. 306
Helleiner, Gerald 306
Hicks, J. 250, 262, 306
Hill, P.J. 181
Hitler, A. 208
Hiylrt, A. 208
Hobbes, Thomas 61
Holen, A. 32
Horowitz, S. 32

Johnson, H.G. 235, 252, 256, 259–60, 265, 269, 273–5
Johnston, J. 22

Kahn, L. 52
Kalymon, B.C. 133
Kane, Edward J. 87, 89–90, 95–6
Kaplan, N. 249, 261
Kendall, M.G. 311
Keynes, John M. 178, 249, 261, 306, 308
Khan, Genghis 81
Klamer, Arjo 301, 308–11, 315, 320
Knight, Frank H. 1, 7–8, 88, 167–8
Kontorovich, L. 252
Koopmans, T. 250, 252, 262
Kuttner, Robert 301, 308
Kuznets, S. 252

Lee, Sheng-Yi 146
Lee (Tsao) Yuan 149, 153
Leontief, W. 250, 252, 262

Lesieur, F.G. 164
Leibowitz, S.J. 283, 285
Lind, Robert 172
Lindbeck, A. 77, 173, 206
Lotka, A.J. 234
Lovell, M.C. 241, 268
Lucas, R. 306, 308

Mackenzie, Lionel 306
Maki, D. 74
Marsden, Keith 207
Marshall, Alfred 101, 103, 306
Marx, Karl 249, 261, 306, 308
Mincer, Jacob 51–2
Mirus, Rolf 79, 129
Mitchell, D.J.B. 164
Moriume, K. 52
Mulroney, B. 213
Mundell, Robert 138, 144–6, 148, 257
Myrdal, G. 252, 306

Nightingale, D.V. 164

Okun, Arthur M. 44, 48–9, 306
Olson, Mancur 207

Palmer, J.P. 283, 285
Patinkin 306
Pauly, M.V. 1, 4
Phaneuf, L. 54
Phelps, E. 10
Pigou, A.C. 306

Quandt, R.E. 250, 259, 262

Rabushka, Alvin 207
Rajaratnam, S. 149
Reynolds, Alan 207
Ricardo, D. 306

Robinson, Joan 306
Rostow, W.W. 306

Samuelson, P.A. 235, 250, 252, 262, 265, 306, 308
Sargent, J. 306
Schumpeter, J.A. 164, 169–70, 173, 306, 308
Schwartz, Anna 140
Schwindt, R. 184
Seah, Linda 153
Sen, A.K. 306
Shockley, W. 236, 269
Smith, Adam 306
Smith, Roger S. 79, 129
Snower, Dennis J. 173
Solow, R. 306
Spindler, Zane 173
Stewart, J.A. 236, 269, 271
Stigler, G.J. 259, 275, 306
Stiglitz, J. 306
Sturges, P. 290

Thatcher, Margaret 206
Tinbergen, J. 252
Tobin, J. 306

Vasil, K. Raj. 149
Vernon, R. 257

Wade, N. 233, 250, 262
Wagner, Richard 210–11
Walker, M. 184
Walker, Michael 301, 311, 313
Walrus, L. 306
Weisbrod, B.A.W. 232, 259
Weitzman, Martin L. 164, 167, 170, 174
Wilson, Harold 5
Wolf, Charles Jr 130

Economists of the Twentieth Century

Monetarism and Macroeconomic Policy
Thomas Mayer

Studies in Fiscal Federalism
Wallace E. Oates

The World Economy in Perspective
Essays in International Trade and European Integration
Herbert Giersch

Towards a New Economics
Critical Essays on Ecology, Distribution and Other Themes
Kenneth E. Boulding

Studies in Positive and Normative Economics
Martin J. Bailey

The Collected Essays of Richard E. Quandt (2 volumes)
Richard E. Quandt

International Trade Theory and Policy
Selected Essays of W. Max Corden
W. Max Corden

Organization and Technology in Capitalist Development
William Lazonick

Studies in Human Capital
Collected Essays of Jacob Mincer, Volume 1
Jacob Mincer

Studies in Labor Supply
Collected Essays of Jacob Mincer, Volume 2
Jacob Mincer

Macroeconomics and Economic Policy
The Selected Essays of Assar Lindbeck, Volume I
Assar Lindbeck

The Welfare State
The Selected Essays of Assar Lindbeck, Volume II
Assar Lindbeck

Classical Economics, Public Expenditure and Growth
Walter Eltis

Money, Interest Rates and Inflation
Frederic S. Mishkin

The Public Choice Approach to Politics
Dennis C. Mueller

The Liberal Economic Order (2 volumes)
Gottfried Haberler
Edited by Anthony Y.C. Koo

Economic Growth and Business Cycles
Prices and the Process of Cyclical Development
Paolo Sylos Labini

International Adjustment, Money and Trade
Theory and Measurement for Economic Policy, Volume I
Herbert G. Grubel

International Capital and Service Flows
Theory and Measurement for Economic Policy, Volume II
Herbert G. Grubel

Unintended Effects of Government Policies
Theory and Measurement for Economic Policy, Volume III
Herbert G. Grubel

The Economics of Competitive Enterprise
Selected Essays of P.W.S. Andrews
Edited by Frederic S. Lee and Peter E. Earl